# *Hume's*
## *Philosophy of Common Life*

# Hume's
## Philosophy of Common Life

Donald W. Livingston

The University of Chicago Press · Chicago and London

Donald W. Livingston is associate professor of
philosophy at Emory University.

The University of Chicago Press, Chicago 60637
The University of Chicago Press, Ltd., London
© 1984 by The University of Chicago
All rights reserved. Published 1984
Printed in the United States of America
93 92 91 90 89 88 87 86 85 84   54321

*Library of Congress Cataloging in Publication Data*

Livingston, Donald W.
  Hume's philosophy of common life.

  Bibliography: p.
  Includes index.
  1. Hume, David, 1711–1776.   I. Title.
B1498.L58   1984     192        83-18227
ISBN 0-226-48714-8

For Jenny and Mary Margaret

# Contents

# *Preface*

In this book I present a comprehensive interpretation of Hume's philosophy based on all of his writings, historical as well as philosophical. But even a general study must be selective and projected from a certain point of view. This study differs from others in that it views Hume's philosophical and historical work as mirrors to each other. What we find of significance in the work of a philosopher very much depends on the questions we ask. The questions usually put to Hume's work are epistemological ones which typically suppose natural science to be the paradigm of knowledge. This has been a fruitful approach to understanding Hume but it is not the only one that can be taken.

Hume, like Vico, was working towards a reform in philosophy that takes history, not natural science, as the paradigm of knowledge. As Hume observes in the Introduction to the *Treatise of Human Nature*, the ultimate science is the science of man, for even "Mathematics, Natural Philosophy, and Natural Religion, are in some measure dependent on the science of Man; since they lie under the cognizance of men, and are judged of by their powers and faculties" (xv). Although it does, and must have, certain affinities with natural science, Hume's science of man is primarily a historical science.

Consequently, the questions I have put to Hume's work in order to understand the significance of his philosophical achievement are projected not from the philosophy of science but from the philosophy of history. How does Hume think about the reality of time? What, on Hume's theory of concept formation, is the meaning of statements purportedly about the past? What is the nature and limit of historical knowledge, and what is the status of the objects of historical knowledge? What is the nature of narration, and what role does narrative thinking play in historical understanding? Do the natural and the historical sciences have the same form of explanation, or is there a special form of understanding that is unique to the historical sciences? Is a speculative philosophy of history possible? And finally, what is the relation between philosophy and history: is philosophy independent of history, or is historical thinking somehow internal to philosophical thinking?

Some of these questions Hume himself raised explicitly; others are in his work only in embryonic form. Around the answers to these questions I have tried to build a general interpretation of Hume's philosophy which enables us to view his philosophical and historical works as of a piece and Hume as the philosophical man of letters he considered himself to be.

In presenting this study, I am conscious of a great many debts I owe to friends and colleagues from whom I have learned and who have encouraged and criticized my work over the years. I want first to express my appreciation to Richard A. Watson, whose spirited teaching first interested me in the history of modern philosophy and in the study of Hume. I should like to acknowledge also a debt to Richard H. Popkin, whose labors have enriched our understanding of modern philosophy not only in detail but in concept and have served to emancipate us somewhat from that lack of historical self-knowledge to which philosophers especially seem prone. The influence of his work runs throughout this study.

My reflections on Hume have been significantly shaped by the work of Páll Árdal, Antony Flew, Terence Penelhum, Peter Jones, Fred Wilson, and George Davie. Special thanks are due to David Norton, whose research on the relation between Hume's philosophical and historical work encouraged me to begin this study and to Nicholas Capaldi, with whom I have had many fruitful discussions about Hume's philosophy. Both read the entire manuscript, and it has been much improved by their criticism.

The philosophy of history presupposed in this study, particularly the idea of narrative thinking, leans heavily on the work of Arthur Danto. I have also learned much about the philosophy of history from Alan Donagan and W. H. Walsh. I am especially grateful to the encouragement Professor Walsh gave during the early stages of this study.

I wish to express my thanks also to Marion Hanny, a true educator, who introduced me to the world of letters, and to another friend, Michael Gelven, with whom I have had unrestrained and invaluable philosophical discussions over the years. Finally, I own an immeasurable debt to Mary Livingston, who has been a source of inspiration and encouragement, making this book and much else possible.

The leisure for the first draft of this study was provided by a sabbatical leave from Northern Illinois University and a National Endowment for the Humanities Independent Study Fellowship. I am grateful to

PREFACE

both of these institutions. Earlier versions of some of the ideas developed in chapters 4, 8, and 10 first appeared, respectively, in *Hume, A Re-Evaluation, The New Scholasticism*, and in *McGill Hume Studies*. I wish to thank the editors of Fordham University Press, Austin Hill Press, and *The New Scholasticism* for permission to include this material. The articles are: "Hume's Historical Theory of Meaning," in *Hume: A Re-Evaluation*, edited by D. W. Livingston and James King (New York: Fordham University Press, 1976); "Time and Value in Hume's Social and Political Philosophy," in *McGill Hume Studies*, edited by D. F. Norton, N. Capaldi, and W. Robison (San Diego: Austin Hill Press, 1979); "Hume on the Problem of Historical and Scientific Explanation," *The New Scholasticism* 37 (1973).

# Abbreviations for Hume's Works

T        *A Treatise of Human Nature*, ed. L. A. Selby-Bigge. 2d edition with text revised and variant readings by P. H. Nidditch. Oxford: Clarendon Press, 1978.

A        *An Abstract of A Treatise of Human Nature*, ed. J. M. Keynes and P. Sraffa. Hamden: Archon Books, 1965.

EU      *David Hume's Enquiries Concerning Human Understanding* [EU] *and*
EM     *Concerning the Principles of Morals* [EM], ed. L. A. Selby-Bigge. 3d ed. revised P. H. Nidditch. Oxford: Clarendon Press, 1975.

EUH    All editions of the *Enquiry* on understanding except the last contain a discussion of narrative thinking in section iii, "Of the Association of Ideas." The discussion is omitted from the Selby-Bigge edition but is included in Charles W. Hendel's edition, *An Inquiry Concerning Human Understanding*. Indianapolis: Bobbs-Merrill, 1955.

E        *Essays, Moral, Political, and Literary*. Oxford: Clarendon Press, 1966.

DP      *A Dissertation on the Passions*, in *Essays Moral, Political and Literary*, ed. T. H. Green and T. H. Grose. London: Longmans Green, 1898.

NHR    *The Natural History of Religion*, ed. H. E. Root. London: Adam and Charles Black, 1956.

D        *Dialogues Concerning Natural Religion*, ed. Norman Kemp Smith. Indianapolis: Bobbs-Merrill, 1947.

LG      *A Letter from a Gentleman to His Friend in Edinburgh*, ed. Ernest C. Mossner and John V. Price. Edinburgh: University of Edinburgh Press, 1967.

H        *The History of England, From the Invasion of Julius Caesar to the Abdication of James the Second, 1688*, with the author's last corrections and improvements. 6 vols. Boston: Phillips Sampson, 1854. Since there is no critical edition of the *History*, references are to chapters as well as to pages.

HEM    "Hume's Early Memoranda, 1729–40: The Complete Text," *Journal of the History of Ideas* (1948): 492–518.

RH     "Review of Robert Henry's *History of Great Britain*," printed in *David Hume: Philosophical Historian*, ed. David Norton and Richard Popkin. New York: Bobbs-Merrill, pp. 377–88.

MOL    *My Own Life*, in *An Inquiry Concerning Human Understanding*, ed. Charles W. Hendel. Indianapolis: Bobbs-Merrill, 1955.

L    *The Letters of David Hume*, ed. J. Y. T. Greig. 2 vols. (Oxford: Clarendon Press, 1969.

NHL    *New Letters of David Hume*, ed. R. Klibansky and E. C. Mossner. Oxford: Clarendon Press, 1954.

# Introduction

Those who study Hume's philosophy with care inevitably come away impressed by the tension between the surface of his smoothly flowing style and the complex philosophical structures that move beneath. This tension between style and content makes it possible for some to think they understand Hume quite clearly and for others to think that they do not understand him well at all. There are those who find profundity beneath the surface: Nicholas Capaldi thinks "the *Treatise* is on a par with Immanuel Kant's *Critique of Pure Reason*."[1] Others think the *Treatise* is not really worth reading. Prichard wrote: "there is a great deal of cleverness in it, but the cleverness is only that of extreme ingenuity or perversity, and the ingenuity is only exceeded by the perversity."[2] Such antinomic interpretations do not exist for other modern philosophers. Nearly a century ago L. A. Selby-Bigge warned that "Hume's philosophic writings are to be read with great caution" and that failure to do so "makes it easy to find all philosophies in Hume, or, by setting up one statement against another, none at all."[3] More than any other modern philosopher, Hume has appeared as the construct of the conceptual frameworks that interpreters have imposed upon him.

One reason for this out-of-focus picture of Hume's achievement is due, in part, to the fact that not all of his works have been studied with equal care and in relation to each other. Because of their own preoccupations with the problems of knowledge, most of Hume's early interpreters knew him only as the author of book I of the *Treatise* and of the *Enquiry* on understanding, that is, as a philosopher concerned with epistemological problems of meaning and belief. But Hume saw himself as a moral philosopher, a student of human action in its broadest sense, comprehending aesthetics, ethics, politics, economics, literature, law, religion, and history. Epistemology served primarily the purpose of convincing the public that a conceptual framework could be established in which a nonarbitrary inquiry into these fields could be carried

1

out. Over half of what he wrote was in history proper and most of the rest was in the fields just mentioned. In the last ten years or so there has been a growing tendency to view Hume's philosophical works as of a piece and to interpret him as the pioneer in moral philosophy that he set out to be. But there is as yet no systematic study of the relation between Hume's philosophical and historical work.[4] The guiding theme of this study is that the two sets of works are mutually illuminating. It is not just that there are traces of Hume's philosophical theories (moral, political, epistemological, etc.) scattered throughout *The History of England*. It is rather that some of Hume's deepest philosophical doctrines of knowledge and existence are structured by historical, narrative categories. Viewed against the background of these categories, Hume's entire philosophical enterprise takes on a different character. Historical thinking is now seen to be an internal part of his philosophical thought. And, as we shall see later, Hume's historical work may be viewed, in part, as the fulfillment of a demand imposed by his conception of philosophy.

Collingwood once described his work as an attempt to bring about a rapprochement between philosophy and history. The same thing might be said of the work of Hegel and Marx. It could also be said of Hume. I do not mean to suggest that Hume had Collingwood's self-awareness of the problem. Perhaps Hegel was the first really to frame the problem. I do wish to suggest, however, that Hume thought about philosophical issues in such a way as to create a problem of a rapprochement between philosophy and history and that he had some awareness of the problem. If so, then, Hume should be viewed along with Vico as one of the early philosophers of history.

Hume's conception of philosophy is examined in chapter 1 and is based primarily on his *Treatise*, book I, part IV, sections ii–iv, where he works through the paradigmatic philosophical problem: our knowledge of the external world. Three theories of experience are examined: the vulgar (the world is what we immediately experience), phenomenalism (what we immediately experience is in the mind), and the doctrine of double existence (what we immediately experience is in the mind but represents a world specifically different from our experience). The three theories are arranged hierarchically and Hume's analysis of them is dialectical: difficulties in this position lead to the doctrine of double existence which, in turn, is seen to be inadequate. Hume thinks the three theories exhaust all possibilities. His own position is neither of the three. What he offers is not another theory of experience, but, in effect, a dialectical theory of the nature and limits of theories of experience. Hume calls this transcendental perspective "true philosophy." It is a perspective available only to those who have acquired "new degrees

2

of reason and knowledge" by working through the dialectic of the three theories (T, 222).

What we learn from the perspective of "true philosophy" is this. Philosophy first appears governed by what I call the *autonomy principle;* according to this principle, philosophy has an authority to command belief and judgment independent of the unreflectively received beliefs, customs, and prejudices of common life: "Reason first appears in possession of the throne, prescribing laws, and imposing maxims, with an absolute sway and authority" (T, 186). The autonomy principle is compelling, for otherwise, it would appear, philosophy could become the mere handmaiden of theology, science, politics, or whatever, and so would lose its integrity as a self-critical activity. But what Hume discovered is that such a conception of philosophy, if carried out consistently, leads to total skepticism. Philosophers seldom end in total skepticism because they do not consistently adhere to the autonomy principle; unknowingly, they rely on some philosophically uncertified prejudice or custom of common life which alone can give content to what is an entirely vacuous way of thinking. If philosophical activity is to continue at all, it must reform itself, abandoning the autonomy principle in its pure form, and recognize common life not as an object of critical reflection but as a category internal to its own critical activity. True philosophy, then, presupposes the authority of common life as a whole. A reformed version of the autonomy principle survives: philosophy may form abstract principles and ideals to criticize any judgment in common life; what it cannot do, on pain of total skepticism, is throw into question the whole order.

The relation between philosophy and common life, for Hume, is a dialectical one: the philosopher exists both within and without the world of common life. He exists within insofar as he presupposes the order as a whole. He exists without insofar as his thought is aimed at understanding ultimate reality. No custom or belief of common life however "methodized and corrected" can satisfy this demand of thought to know the real, and yet it is only *through* these customs and prejudices that we can think about the real. Skepticism, then, is internal to true philosophy. The true philosopher recognizes his cognitive alienation from ultimate reality but continues to inquire, though he has nothing but the "leaky weather-beaten vessel" of common life through which to think (T, 263).

True philosophy has a positive task and a negative, therapeutic task. The positive task is to explore the structure of common life through empirical and a-priori analysis and to speculate about the real within the confines of common life. The negative task is that of purging common life of the alienating effects of false philosophy. The false philosopher, though necessarily a participant in common life, is totally alienated from its authority by virtue of the autonomy principle. As an affair of the closet, false philosophy is merely ridiculous, but when it informs moral, political, and religious thinking, it becomes a threat to the peace and well-being of society.

This study may be viewed as a discussion of both tasks. Chapters 1 through 9 explore the positive, analytical, and speculative task. Chapters 10 through 12 explore the negative, therapeutic task. I shall briefly discuss the chapters along this division.

Chapter 1, as we have seen, examines Hume's conception of the nature of true and false philosophy. In chapter 2, I discuss the relation between the rhetoric and the philosophy of the *Treatise* with the end in view of removing some of the stylistic barriers to appreciating its philosophic worth. To get the most out of the *Treatise* we must give due regard to Hume's narrative mode of exposition and to his dialectical conception of philosophy. In the last section of the chapter, with this perspective in mind, I suggest that Hume's "perceptions of the mind" might be fruitfully thought of phenomenologically rather than phenomenalistically.

In chapters 3 and 4, I examine Hume's first principle: that ideas are derived from past impressions, which they resemble. In chapter 3, I argue that the first principle does not commit Hume to the view that the meanings of words are private mental images and that much of the heavy criticism of it is misplaced. The transcendental perspective of true philosophy justified in the *Treatise*, book I, part IV, presupposes the world of common life with its public and private dimensions. Language is an essential part of this world and is explained by Hume as a convention. The concept of convention is, perhaps, the most important in Hume's philosophy. A Humean convention is not the result of conscious agreement but is arrived at over time as the unintended result of man's involvement with the world and with his fellows. The concepts that it is the task of true philosophy to bring to light (language, justice, religion, causality) are housed in the rules and principles that are implicit in a historically developed convention. Hume's first principle should be viewed as a critical principle abstracted from the convention of language and should be evaluated for the light it throws on the nature of the convention and on what modifications need to be made. I argue that the principle captures an important fact about experiential concepts (which, as a moral philosopher, Hume is primarily concerned to explicate) but obscures our understanding of concepts in theoretical science.

In chapter 4, I show that the theory of concept formation presupposed by the first principle makes use of the *past* and has a narrative structure that distinguishes Hume's historical empiricism from other empiricisms such as phenomenalism, pragmatism, and logical empiricism. Whatever difficulties it might have, Hume's first principle allows an important class of concepts which make essential reference to the past as a condition for their application in the present. Though unimportant for theoretical science, these past-entailing concepts are essential to history and to an understanding of the world of common life generally. They are logically excluded from the theories of concept formation in phenomenalism, pragmatism, logical empiricism, and most forms of idealism.

In chapter 5, I examine Hume's concept of time. As discussed in book I of the *Treatise* time is an order of succession, and it is this notion of time that we apply to the physical world. In book II Hume discusses the influence of this idea of time on the imagination; the result is an order of temporal passions which yield a narrative concept of time. I argue that, for Hume, the judgments of the imagination and understanding have an irreducibly tensed and narrative structure. Timeless principles are abstractions from ideas associated narratively. But, most important, the moral world (the world of human action) is the product of ideas associated narratively, and so has, ontologically, a narrative structure. Historical understanding, then, is internal to any understanding of the existences that populate the moral world.

This is as true of philosophy (traditionally conceived as universal and timeless) as of any other human activity. So the philosophical explication of a concept such as causality requires a historical understanding of the convention of making causal judgments. In chapters 6 and 7 I examine Hume's conception of causality against the background of his views on the historically developed convention of causal judgment. Hume merely sketches out the history of this convention as it developed from primitive religion to the metaphysical speculation of sophisticated theism to modern science. Most of what has been written on Hume's conception of causality has been concerned with the question of whether he provides an adequate analysis of the concept of causality in science. For this project it would be difficult to improve on the discussion of Beauchamp and Rosenberg.[5] What I have tried to do in chapters 6 and 7 is view Hume's understanding of causality as the understanding of an idea that has developed over time from man's involvement with the world and with his conventions for understanding it. From this broader perspective the idea of causality is internal to religious, metaphysical, scientific, and historical thinking. Looked at this way, Hume's thought on causality is more complicated, wider in scope, and less consistent than is generally supposed. For one thing, the metaphysical and even some of the religious connotations survive in Hume's conception, though considerably modified and corrected.

In chapter 7 I discuss the concept of causality as applied to human action. Hume is committed to but rejects the unity of science thesis which states that causal explanation has the same form whether in the natural or the moral sciences. He holds that moral philosophy has a special form of explanation not available to natural philosophers. This form of explanation is presided over by Hume's principle of sympathy, and is a prototype of the later doctrine of *verstehen*.

Hume's conception of the historical is explored in chapter 8. The defining characteristic of specifically historical thought for Hume is not *verstehen* (as it is for Collingwood and other historicists) but *narration*. The charge made by Collingwood, Meinecke, and others that Hume's conception of history is "antihistorical" presupposes that *verstehen* is the mark of the historical. I argue that the narrative conception is superior. If so, then, Hume's conception is not antihistorical. *Verstehen*, nevertheless, plays an important role in Hume's historical work. The narrative perspective presents us with an external view of actions (the narrative significance of the action); the perspective of *verstehen* presents us with an internal view of actions (the significance they had for the agent). The tension created by these two perspectives easily leads to errors in making narrative judgments. In chapter 9 and the last section of chapter 11, I discuss the principles implied in Hume's attempt to correct false narrative judgments in his philosophical works and in *The History of England*.

The last three chapters deal with the therapeutic task of true philosophy: the task of purging common life of the alienating illusions of false philosophy generated by an unrestrained use of the autonomy principle. False philosophy has many forms ranging from religious superstition to metaphysics, but they are all cases of seeking, by way of the autonomy principle, some Archimedean point outside the prejudices and customs of common life from which the order as a whole can be judged. As long as it is confined to the closet, false philosophy is merely ridiculous and, perhaps, even entertaining, but when it becomes the governing principle of moral and political life, it is dangerous. False philosophy in politics leads to a frame of mind that we may call metaphysical rebellion: the conceptual destruction of the authority of the prejudices and customs that constitute the order of common life. The order as a whole is viewed as illegitimate and the Archimedean principles which lead to this judgment are logically of a type that make it impossible to discern the goods and evils that exist within common life, and so make it impossible to reform the order. The result is either a melancholy alienation from a world that one is forced to inhabit or an attempt at total moral, social, and political revolution.

In chapters 10 and 11, I examine two forms of false philosophy in politics. Social and political order is constituted by standards and, leaning on the discussion of narrative time in chapter 5, I show that, for Hume, social and political standards have a temporal structure conceived as a narrative relation between present and past existences. Narrative time is a value internal to the authority of social and political standards. In this, Hume's theory differs fundamentally from two types of political theory. The first sort of theory and Hume's criticism of it are examined in chapter 10. This theory is the application of what I call Cartesianism in politics and is exemplified in the natural-right, original-contract, and natural-law theories common in Hume's time. True political order is viewed as an order of nature: a timeless object of autonomous reason existing independently of the historical process. Since the narrative standards that constitute the existing political order are traditional, temporal, and contingent, they cannot be the objects of autonomous reason. The conceptual effect of Cartesianism in politics, then, is to deny *original* authority and, hence, reality for any established political order. If so, rational reform of an existing order is impossible because it is impossible to perceive narratively structured goods and evils within an existing order without affirming the original authority of some narratively structured principle internal to the order. The result of Cartesianism in politics is either total alienation from the politics of common life or a demand for total revolution.

In chapter 12, I examine Hume's relation to the conservative political tradition. The conservative tradition that originated after the French Revolution and of which Burke is often taken as the paradigm, is not merely a reaction to progressive events or a disposition to avoid change. It is most fruitfully viewed as an intellectual tradition which attempts to purge false philosophy from the politics of common life. In this view, Hume, not Burke, emerges as the first to have worked out a conservative theory of politics. I show that Hume's analysis of the Puritan Revolution in *The History of England* closely parallels Burke's analysis of the French Revolution in *Reflections on the Revolution in France*. Both events were seen as cases of the violent intrusion of misplaced philosophy into politics, and both were seen as being peculiarly *modern* events.

It is easy not to see the parallel because the Puritan Revolution was religious, whereas the French Revolution was secular and was carried out in the name of rational principles. However, Hume considered modern theistic religion to be a species of philosophy. Throughout his writings true religion is a form of true philosophy and false religion a form of false philosophy. False religion, Hume thought, permeated and infected every aspect of modern life. In this he was at one with the *philosophes*, but his criticism of modern religion was fundamentally different. For Hume, the evil of modern religion is due to its philosophical errors, not to its religious errors. Hence, the therapy for false religion is true philosophy. The error of misplaced philosophy in politics is the same whether the metaphysical principles informing it are theistic or secular.

It is for this reason that Hume was able to perceive a new threat to the politics of common life: the emergence of political parties informed not by interest or affection but by metaphysical principle. These parties were purely secular and based on rational principles. Hume considered them to be peculiarly modern and to manifest even more clearly (because of their pretended rational character) the philosophical errors that had informed the Puritan metaphysical rebellion.

Hume embraced the emerging order of commercial republican empires and saw in it the possibilities of unlimited development in the arts and sciences. But he saw, as few at the time did, that philosophy under modern conditions can no longer remain in the closet but, for good or ill, has become a form of thought internal to social and political life and on an increasingly popular level. False philosophy as bound up with modern religion, but also in its new secular form in metaphysical political parties, is a threat to civil society. This moral mission to explain the nature and limits of philosophy and the threat it poses to social utility is a theme running through all of Hume's work from book I, part IV of the *Treatise*, where it is first broached, to the history of the Stuart kings.

By exploring the unity that exists between Hume's historical and philosophical thought, I hope to provide a more cosmopolitan conception of just what his philosophical achievement is. The emphasis throughout is on a sympathetic reading. I have concentrated on those aspects that seem philosophically valuable and have been more concerned to explain the way in which this or that doctrine is insightful than to dwell on the inconsistencies and extravagances that inevitably attend a really determined attempt to open up a new philosophical perspective.

# 1
# Post-Pyrrhonian Philosophy

The manner of study in ancient times is distinct from that of modern times, in that the former consisted in the veritable training and perfecting of the natural consciousness. Trying its powers at each part of its life severally, and philosophizing about everything it came across, the natural consciousness transformed itself into a universality of abstract understanding that was active in every matter and in every respect. In modern times, however, the individual finds the abstract form ready made.

G. W. F. Hegel

## PHENOMENALISM AND THE PUBLIC WORLD

From its first appearance, Hume's philosophy has been interpreted as a form of phenomenalism. Thomas Reid, in the *Inquiry into the Human Mind* (1764), interpreted Hume as holding the central thesis of phenomenalism: "that nothing is perceived but what is in the mind which perceives it." The same sort of reading was continued by the Absolute Idealists in Britian who after Reid were the most important commentators on Hume. T. H. Green republished Hume's philosophical works in 1874-75, attaching a long introductory essay which was then and remained, until Kemp Smith's *The Philosophy of David Hume* (1941), the most influential study of Hume's philosophy. Green's essay so established the phenomenalistic interpretation that well into the twentieth century the logical positivists, many of whom were phenomenalists, could readily find their own views in Hume. A. J. Ayer records how the Vienna Circle in its manifesto of 1929 officially included Hume as a precursor of the movement: "those who stand closest to the Vienna Circle in their general outlook are Hume and Mach. It is remarkable how much of the doctrine that is now thought to be especially characteristic of logical positivism was already stated, or at least foreshadowed by Hume."[1] Although the phenomenalist interpretation has not been without challenge, it is still the most popular reading. It is also the greatest barrier to appreciating Hume's philosophy and the more so because it appears to be a plausible interpretation. Certainly there are many passages in Hume which can be seen as supporting it. But in the end, it is fundamentally mistaken, as I shall try to show in this and the next chapter.

Phenomenalism can be characterized as the belief that in some way a satisfactory account can be given of the public world of physical objects and of other minds by reference only to sets of logically private experiences. That Hume appears to be guided by this belief seems clear from passages such as the following: "no beings are ever present to the mind but perceptions" (T, 212). If this is so, and if we are to have a satisfactory account of the public world or, indeed, of any being whatsoever, it must be in terms of perceptions. But what exactly does Hume mean by the term "perception"? The traditional answer from Reid on is that Hume meant by it, roughly, what Locke would have meant. Writing around a century ago, William Knight explains Hume's doctrine of perceptions not by a searching examination of Hume's own remarks but by way of "Locke's Phenomenalism." In "explaining Locke, we virtually explain the doctrine of Hume."[2] And more recently Antony Flew can remark that "Hume is in effect restating in his own way what were at the time the commonplaces of Locke's new way of ideas, supplementing these with one or two precisifying amendments of his own."[3]

It is true that Hume inherited Locke's "new way of ideas" but, for that matter, so have we. The conceptual framework of modern philosophy is still very much alive, whether we are working critically to develop it or to free ourselves from it. We have, however, modified the way of ideas considerably, and so has Hume. His doctrine of perceptions is not simply a more fine-tuned version of Locke. In his hands the term "perception" leaves the Lockean way and moves into a radically different and distinctively Humean conceptual framework. But this framework is not easy to discern, and not only because commentators have approached the *Treatise* with phenomenalistic preconceptions. It is not presented at the outset of the *Treatise* but is virtually buried some 200 pages later in what are notoriously the most diffcult sections (book I, sections ii-iv, vii). It is in these sections, and not at the beginning of the *Treatise*, that Hume's views on the status of perceptions and their relation to the public world is most thoroughly worked out.

But he also does much more. In section ii, Hume examines the famous problem of what it is to perceive a material world, raising in the process the question of what inferences, if any, justify belief in material objects and the question of how we come to believe there are material objects. What is not recognized is that these questions are examined in the light of an analysis of the nature and limits of philosophical inquiry. The analysis continues in sections iii and iv, "Of the Ancient Philosophy" and "Of the Modern Philosophy," and ends in section vii, the "Conclusion of this book." Together these sections constitute Hume's prolegomena to any future metaphysics.

Questions about perceptions are questions about the world. Questions about the nature of philosophy are transcendental questions about ultimate frameworks for interpreting the world. Hume does not separate the first kind of question from the second. Indeed, we shall find that it is from an analysis of what philosophy is and what it can and cannot do that he frames a doctrine of perceptions, and not the other way around. That is, he does not begin, as is usually thought, by presenting some content of the mind called a perception and from that generate a doctrine of what philosophy can do. That would be Locke's "way of ideas." Hume's way is transcendental and points more in the direction of Kant's critical philosophy than back to Locke's and Berkeley's method of beginning with the "contents of the mind," an approach grounded in the very substance-modification ontology which Hume is well known for having rejected. The problem of the external world examined in these later sections of book I is treated by Hume as the paradigmatic *philosophical* problem. An analysis of that problem yields a doctrine of the limits of philosophical inquiry which in turn yields a doctrine of perceptions. It is this doctrine, developed in the last sections of book I, that we are to read into the early pages of book I and not the alien phenomenalistic conception that is usually brought to them. The remainder of this chapter is an attempt to provide support for these claims and to develop them more fully.

## THREE THEORIES OF EXPERIENCE

The problem of the relation of perception to the public world is first raised in part IV, section ii. At the very beginning of the section Hume puts forth a thesis that appears to fall outside the egocentric "way of ideas" approach to philosophical problems: "We may well ask, *What causes induce us to believe in the existence of body?* but 'tis in vain to ask, *Whether there be body or not?* That is a point, which we must take for granted in all out reasonings" (T, 187). How are we to interpret the modal expression "must take for granted in all our reasonings"? Does Hume mean a psychological necessity, a natural belief we cannot avoid? Or does he mean some sort of formal necessity connecting the belief to the nature of "our reasonings"—what we might call a transcendental necessity. We shall see that he has in mind both sorts of necessity.

There are good reasons for thinking that Hume has in mind only a psychological necessity, for he suggests at the beginning of section ii that his task is simply that of giving a causal account of belief in bodies. But the causal account he gives is so bound up with epistemological issues that at the end of the section and in sections iii and iv he is able to frame a number of skeptical theses about belief in the external world. These theses would be inexplicable on a purely causal account. In the remainder of this section, I shall bypass Hume's causal account and concentrate on what I take to be the central epistemological issue raised in sections ii-iv, namely, the status of what Hume calls the "vulgar" or "popular system" in our understanding of the world.

The idea of the physical world common to us all is this popular system, the view that our perceptions are our "only objects" and that "the very being, which is intimately present to the mind, is the real body or material existence" (T, 206). Moreover, "this very perception or object is suppos'd to have a continu'd uninterrupted being, and neither to be annihilated by our absence, nor to be brought into existence by our presence" (T, 207). And the popular conception of the world is consistent: "The supposition of the continu'd existence of sensible objects or perceptions involves no contradiction" (T, 208). But if the popular system is consistent, then the phenomenalist conception of perceptions is false, for a phenomenalist would have to define perceptions as logically private mental existences. A perception, then, existing independently of the mind would be not merely a false supposition but contradictory as well. Hume, however, is careful to exclude this meaning from the term "perception": "as every perception is distinguishable from another, and may be consider'd as separately existent; it evidently follows, that there is no absurdity in separating any particular perception from the mind" (T, 207). Likewise, "objects" considered as mind-independent existences can be directly present to the mind: "If the name of *perception* renders not this separation from a mind absurd and contradictory, the name of *object*, standing for the very same thing, can never render their conjunction impossible" (T, 207).

In the popular system, then, some perceptions, "what any common man means by a hat, or shoe, or stone, or any other impression convey'd to him by his senses" (T, 202), are thought of as continuous and independent objects; whereas other perceptions, such as pains, are thought of as "fleeting and perishing" private mental existences.

Hume presents the popular system as the way everyone thinks about the world. Even philosophers think this way, except in those rare moments in their closets when, by a special sort of reflection, they are able to emancipate themselves from the system. (The nature and worth of this peculiar sort of reflection are discussed in the last two sections of this chapter.) Though philosophically unreflective, the popular system is not entirely unreflective. Within the system, critical judgments are made through the use of causal and demonstrative principles.

But if we ask whether the popular system is itself true, we are no longer thinking within that system. To ask this question, for Hume, is to ask whether there are any bodies at all, a question he has said " 'tis in vain to ask." How does it come about, then, that anyone asks this question? According to Hume we achieve transcendence from the popular system by a natural extension of causal arguments already operative within the system. In explaining the causes of those perceptions which are originally thought to be mind-dependent, we find that the other perceptions originally thought of as objects are also mind-dependent: "When we press one eye with a finger, we immediately perceive all the objects to become double. . . . But as we do not attribute a continu'd existence to both these perceptions, and as they are both of the same nature, we clearly perceive, that all our perceptions are dependent on our organs and the disposition of our nerves and animal spirits" (T, 210–11). This and "an infinite number of other experiments of the same kind" convince us that "our perceptions have no more a continu'd than an independent existence" (T, 211).

With this conclusion we have completely transcended the popular system and have spawned a new system which we may call phenomenalism, the view that "our perceptions are broken, and interrupted" and exist only as long as it takes to perceive them (T, 212-13). What does Hume think of phenomenalism? He does not ask whether it is true, or even whether it is a reasonable theory of experience. He presents phenomenalism, rather, as the first stage of consciousness as it emerges from the cocoon of the popular system into the brave new world of philosophical reflection (T, 211, 214). And what he finds remarkable is that, except for "a few extravagant sceptics," philosophers do not take phenomenalism seriously at all, and even the skeptics "maintain'd that opinion in words only, and were never able to bring themselves sincerely to believe it" (T, 214). Hume has in mind here Berkeley, whose arguments for phenomenalism are also referred to in the *Enquiry* and are said to be "merely sceptical" in *"that they admit of no answer and produce no conviction. Their only effect is to cause that momentary amazement and irresolution and confusion, which is the result of scepticism"* (EU, 155n).

Under the popular system perceptions are conceived as objects (continuous, independent existences). Phenomenalism turns the popular system inside out, yielding the thesis that objects are merely perceptions (now conceived as private mental existences). Phenomenalism is rejected because the mind cannot accept the elimination in experience of a world of public objects. But the idea that what we perceive are public objects is not a philosophical idea but a popular one, so philosophy is not fully emancipated from the popular system. The philosopher's consciousness contains within itself a "struggle and opposition" between the belief that we perceive public objects and the belief that we perceive only private mental images (T, 215). Relief from this dialectical tension is sought in a third theory which Hume calls the doctrine of "double existence" (T, 215). In this theory perceptions are distinguished from objects, the former being conceived as private mental existences (which satisfies the demands of phenomenalism), the latter as public existences (which satisfies the demands of the popular system).

The doctrine of double existence is further removed from the popular system in that it conceives of perceptions as mere appearances and objects as realities. Moreover, the properties of objects are quarantined as far as possible from the properties of perceptions, so that objects are thought of as radically different from perceptions. With the doctrine of double existence philosophical reflection appears virtually free of popular thinking. All that remains of the popular system is the bare formal idea of a public world emptied of all perceptual content.

But even this slight infection of popular thinking is enough to eventually throw the doctrine of double existence into logical convulsions. For Hume observes that we cannot really conceive of objects devoid of perceptual content: "we may well suppose in general, but 'tis impossible for us distinctly to conceive, objects to be in their nature any thing but exactly the same with perceptions" (T, 218). If so, then the attempt to be free of the popular system by positing a world of objects devoid of perceptual content is in fact just the position of "a new set of perceptions" (T, 218). The doctrine of double existence, then, must have all the difficulties of the popular system "and is over-and-above loaded with this absurdity, that it at once denies and establishes the vulgar supposition" (T, 218).

With these three systems, Hume thinks he has "given an account of *all* the systems both popular and philosophical, with regard to external existences" (T, 217, emphasis mine). And he concludes that it is "impossible upon *any* system" to give a coherent account of what it is to perceive a physical object (T, 218, emphasis mine). If so, what, may we ask, is Hume's conception of the relation between perceptions and physical objects? The answer is complicated.[4] But one thing can be said right away. Hume's conception of perceptions is not worked out *within* either the popular system, the phenomenalistic system, or the system of double existence. Although Humean perceptions have been interpreted in all of these ways, Hume makes it clear that none of the systems are coherent.

The fact is that Hume is not, in section ii, working out a theory of how perceptions are related to the mind and to the external world. Rather he is examining claims about perceptions locked into contrary metaphysical systems of experience. His main concern is to exhibit the rationale of these systems and their dialectical relation to each other. To do this is not at all to provide a theory of perceptions. It is rather to provide a critical analysis of *theories* of perceptions, not with the end in view of determining what perceptions in themselves really are but of determining how we must think about them if our thought is to be coherent. The conclusion of the analysis is skeptical. Metaphysical thinking about the ultimate nature of perceptions is antinomic: there is and can be no coherent account of the nature of perceptions and their relation to the world. We solve the metaphysical problem by not asking the question: "Carelessness and in-attention alone can afford us any remedy" (T, 218). Having followed this remedy and bracketed out all three systems, Hume now presents a framework for interpreting experience. He observes that "whatever may be the reader's opinion at this present moment, [caught as he may be in the grip of one of the three systems] that an hour hence he will be persuaded there is both an external and internal world" (T, 218). This dark saying is the conclusion of section ii and is the point at which the entire section is aimed. How are we to interpret it?

## The Transcendental Status of the Popular System

The first thing to appreciate is that the conclusion is not about perceptions but about a "world" having internal and external dimensions; more precisely, it is about an ultimate conceptual framework for interpreting perceptions. Further, Hume's claim about "an external and internal world" is not a thesis developed *within* any of the three systems concerning the relation of perceptions and objects. Nor is it a further system of the same type, since Hume thinks the three systems are exhaustive (T, 217). It is in fact a transcendental thesis external to the three systems. Its authority consists not in being a true account of the nature of perceptions and objects or even in being a justified account (Hume is clear that there are no justified accounts of that type [T, 218]). Its authority consists in being the framework for interpreting experience that is internal to the nature of "our reasonings" (T, 187).

We are to appreciate the *necessity* of the framework as an insight achieved by a painful working through of the dialectical analysis of the three systems. What we learn is this. Philosophical thinking may be viewed as thought attempting critically to emancipate itself from the confines of popular thinking, but in this it can only partially succeed. The popular view that perceptions are objects is a constituent of our thinking about experience. Philosophical reflection in the form of phenomenalism can question this view and can even provide plausible grounds for rejecting it, but it cannot establish an alternative thesis in thought or experience: "That opinion has taken such deep root in the imagination, that 'tis impossible ever to eradicate it, nor will any strain'd metaphysical conviction of the dependence of our perceptions be sufficient for that purpose" (T, 214). Philosophical reflection in the form of the doctrine of double existence, the natural critical outgrowth of phenomenalism, presupposes the very popular conception of objects that it attempts to replace. Now since Hume thinks the three systems are exhaustive, he may conclude that the popular conception of objects is a necessary structure of how we understand experience. Without the popular system we would not have the idea of a public world.

But philosophical reflection is not without authority (T, 215). The solid achievement of phenomenalism and the system of double existence is the idea of an *interior* world of perceptions, an idea that was not part of the essentially unreflective and outward-looking popular system.

Occupying a transcendental point outside the three systems, Hume is able to discern a categorical framework internal to our popular and philosophical thinking about what we experience, namely, perceptions. Some perceptions such as trees are to be thought of as public objects, others such as pains are to be thought of as internal and private. Whether this or that perception has a public or a private dimension, or both, is an empirical matter, but that there is a public world and a private world is not an empirical matter.

In the Introduction to the *Treatise*, Hume observes that "we can give no reason for our most general and most refined principles, beside our experience of their reality" (T, xviii). To talk of experiencing "principles" is to use the term "experience" in a radically different sense from the way it is usually employed in the empirical tradition. Hume is quite clear that the principle that perceptions are housed in a public and private world can be denied without contradiction and that there is and can be no empirical support for it. We "experience" the reality of this principle as a structure internal to our thinking about experience and within which empirical inquiry goes on. The principle is accepted not because we are empirically justified in thinking it *corresponds* to the world; rather we recognize it to *constitute* the world of our experience,

16

and accept it because of its "suitableness and conformity to the mind" (T, 214, cf. 272). The world-making character of the principles of the imagination is strikingly brought out in the *Abstract*, where those principles are pictured as nothing less than "the cement of the universe" (A, 32). Hume often refers to this world that has internal and external dimensions as the world of "common life" (EU, 162), and that is the expression I shall use henceforth. As we shall see, Hume means more by "common life" than the bare privacy and publicity of the world of experience, but he means at least that.

We are in a position now to answer the question posed at the beginning of this section. When Hume says in the first paragraph of section ii that belief in external objects "is a point we must take for granted in all our reasonings," he has in mind that belief in an external world under the popular conception of it which is exhibited in the dialectical analysis of the three systems as a necessary constituent of our thinking about experience (perceptions). He does not mean merely that belief in body is a natural belief which we cannot psychologically avoid except for brief periods of reflection exemplified by phenomenalism and the doctrine of double existence.

Yet that is how the section is usually read, yielding the view that Hume's conception of body is entirely psychologistic. It is also commonly held that Hume thought phenomenalism to be true and the popular system false. The popular belief in body, therefore, must be thoroughly irrational since we should then be compelled by our nature to believe what we know to be false and to reject what we know to be true. I shall examine these points in turn.

Did Hume think phenomenalism is true? Phenomenalism is one of the three theories of experience which we have examined and is presented by Hume as the first move of philosophical reflection away from the unreflective popular system. Moreover, it has some empirical support in causal accounts of perceptions (double images and the like) which suggest that they are private mental existences. But phenomenalism is a theory of experience. Theories of experience may be suggested by experiences, but they cannot be conclusively confirmed or disconfirmed by them. Hume is aware of this and describes phenomenalism as a "strain'd metaphysical conviction of the dependence of our perceptions" (T, 214), indicating that an empirical thesis is being given an ultimate metaphysical meaning which it cannot bear.

Phenomenalism is also presented as an especially absurd form of skepticism, "peculiar to a few extravagant sceptics" (T, 214). It is unlikely that Hume could think phenomenalism is true and that it is also a case of extravagant skepticism. He could, of course, mean that anyone who tries to resist natural belief in the popular system is a skeptic. But that would be a strained use of the term. "Skepticism" is not a psychological concept but an epistemological one which applies to beliefs only on condition that certain semantic conditions are satisfied or thought to be satisfied. There is no reason to think Hume is using the term in a nonepistemological way. As a case of extravagant skepticism, phenomenalism is somehow cognitively defective.

But how? In section iv Hume discusses the modern distinction between primary and secondary qualities, a version of the doctrine of double existence examined in section ii. He rejects the theory, using Berkeleyan arguments to show that if we are to think of the secondary qualities as perceptions in the mind and not real qualities of public objects, the same must be true of the primary qualities. So the distinction collapses into the phenomenalism of section ii, which is believed by only "a few extravagant sceptics." But phenomenalism in section iv is presented as a reduction to absurdity of the modern primary-secondary quality-distinction. And the reason Hume gives for its absurdity is not that we are psychologically incapable of believing it; rather, he observes that although "many objections might be made" to the distinction, he will confine himself to one "which is in my opinion very decisive. I assert, that instead of explaining the operations of external objects by its means, we utterly annihilate all these objects, and reduce ourselves to the opinions of the most extravagant scepticism concerning them" (T, 227-28). The primary-secondary quality-distinction is absurd *because* it collapses into phenomenalism, which Hume takes to be the denial that the objects we experience are to be thought of as public objects at all. And, of course, if we do not experience public objects, there can be no empirical explanations of "the operations of external objects" (T, 228). If we are to have empirical explanations of bodies at all, we must think of them as having the secondary qualities: "after the exclusion of colours, sounds, heat and cold from the rank of external existences, there remains nothing, which can afford us a just and consistent idea of body" (T, 229). It is body under the popular conception of it that provides us with "a just and consistent idea" and enables us to explain "the operations of external objects" (T, 228).

We may conclude, then, that Hume did not think that phenomenalism is true. It is a case of "extravagant scepticism" and a "strain'd metaphysical conviction." Phenomenalism is what is wrong with the primary-secondary quality-distinction. Nor is it these things merely because it is psychologically difficult to believe. Phenomenalism is incompatible with the way we understand our experience and that understanding conceptually requires the popular system of objects having the primary and secondary qualities.

Hume's analysis of the popular and philosophical conceptions of body presents us with an antinomy. Causal reason if left to itself, without any restriction, totally subverts the imagination (which constitutes the popular and philosophical conception of body). But the subversion of the imagination entails the elimination in experience of all public objects and so the total subversion of causal reasoning. Without the idea of objects, causal reasoning would be impossible, because causal connections as specified in Hume's two definitions of cause presented in part III are universal conjunctions of like *objects* (T, 170). There is, Hume says, "a direct and total opposition betwixt . . . those conclusions we form from cause and effect, and those that persuade us of the continu'd and independent existence of body" (T, 231). How is this antinomy resolved? It can be resolved only by stepping out of the three systems to the transcendental perspective of "true philosophy" which recognizes the categorical role of the popular system in our understanding of experience, and, in the light of this, places limits on the activity of causal argument. Henceforth, causal reason must operate within the popular system, transcendentally conceived, on pain of not being able to understand the world of experience at all.

But how can one reconcile these remarks in section iv that the popular conception of body is the only "just," or "satisfactory," or "consistent" one with the many remarks in section ii that the popular system is false, illusory, contrary to the plainest experience (T, 209, 210, 213)? The answer is that the popular system has an entirely different logical status in section iv from what it has in section ii (with the exception of the last page of section ii where the popular system emerges as the external side of that world having internal and external dimensions which Hume presents as the ontological framework for interpreting perceptions). In section ii, the popular system is introduced as a thesis about the world vulnerable to empirical test. The problem with the popular system is that in identifying perceptions with objects it completely ignores the internal world of consciousness. This internal world is forced on our attention by causal reasoning that shows our perceptions to be dependent on the mind and the state of our sense organs. This is the kernel of truth in phenomenalism. Insofar as the popular system ignores these obvious facts it is false. But such facts cannot show that the basic idea of the popular system is false, namely, that what we perceive is a public world of objects having the sensory properties we observe them to have. And it is just this idea that by the end of section ii and in section iv has been transformed from an empirical thesis about objects in experience to a transcendental thesis about the *constitution* of the world of experience. Such a thesis could not be empirically true or false. It is enough that it be "satifactory to the mind" and that it be in fact the canon of intelligibility internal to our thinking about experience that Hume thinks it is.

## TRUE AND FALSE PHILOSOPHY

Throughout his writings Hume makes a distinction between "true metaphysics" and "the false and adulterated" and, what comes to the same thing, between "true philosophy" and "false philosophy." The required distinction is not one that can be made on the basis of logical or empirical criteria designed to pick out true propositions about the world from those that are false. Metaphysical propositions do not admit of empirical test, and false metaphysics might well be consistent. Rather the distinction must be made by grasping the standard of coherence internal to philosophical thinking. So "true philosophy" is philosophy that is true to its idea in the sense of being "genuine" or "authentic." The search for true philosophy is best carried out dialectically by working through the levels of incoherence revealed in an actual piece of philosophical thinking until we begin to understand why our thinking is incoherent and, consequently, what the standard of coherence is that is driving it.

To bring the standard of coherent philosophical thinking to light Hume contrived the dialectic between the popular system, phenomenalism, and the doctrine of double existence, in part IV, sections ii–iv, and the dramatic questioning of philosophy itself, in section vii. The problem of the external world is presented by Hume as the paradigmatic philosophical problem. The dialectical analysis of the three systems functions as a kind of natural history of the philosophical consciousness. Thought moves hierarchically from the philosophically unreflective state of the popular system (perceptions are objects) to the discovery of inner consciousness in phenomenalism (objects are perceptions) to the attempt at reconciliation in the doctrine of double existence (perceptions and objects are different sorts of things). Each stage is a form of philosophical error, but the erroneous character of the whole is not recognized until we see that phenomenalism and the doctrine of double existence presuppose the very popular system they attempt to replace. It is through a confrontation with this incoherence in thought that philosophical reflection is driven to the transcendental perspective of true philosophy; in this perspective we recognize that the idea of the world of common life is internal to our popular and philosophical thinking, and that genuine philosophical thinking must go on within that framework.

But we cannot fully grasp the meaning of true philosophy unless we work through the errors of the false. It is to this end that Hume wrote sections iii and iv, entitled respectively "Of the Ancient Philosophy" and "Of the Modern Philosophy." These sections are rarely mentioned in discussions of section ii. But the three form a unity, as, indeed, do all the sections of part IV. Failure to read them as such, along with the tendency to read Hume as a phenomenalist, has made section ii seem extraordinarily difficult and even bizarre. Much of the difficulty vanishes when the three sections are read as a piece.

When this is done, it becomes clearer that section ii is primarily about the nature and limits of philosophical thinking. At the end of the section, having introduced the conceptual framework of the world of common life, through which we are to understand perceptions, Hume says that he will use "that supposition . . . to examine some general systems both ancient and modern, which have been propos'd of both [the internal and external world], before I proceed to a more particular enquiry concerning our impressions" (T, 218). The "more particular inquiry concerning our impressions" occurs in book II, "Of the Passions," and in book III, "Of Morals." The remaining sections of book I are devoted primarily to discussing examples of philosophical errors, the rationale of the errors, and "the means by which we endeavour to conceal them" (T, 219). Section iii, "Of the Ancient Philosophy," and section iv, "Of the Modern Philosophy," explore the philosophical errors that generate the ancient and modern conceptions of the external world. Section v, "Of the Immateriality of the Soul," and section vi, "Of Personal Identity," explore the philosophical errors that generate ancient and modern conceptions of the internal world.

Sections iii and iv are especially important because in them Hume uses the natural history of philosophical consciousness worked out in section ii as a model for reading the history of ancient and modern philosophy as the story of error, thereby distinguishing his own philosophy from the entire philosophical tradition. What is the difference? Hume takes the doctrine of double existence presented in section ii to be not simply a quirk of modern thought but a permanent tendency of the philosophical imagination whereby perceptions are treated as mere *appearances*, and objects, specifically different from perceptions, are treated as *realities*. The contents of the distinction have varied. Objects, for instance, have been conceived as Platonic forms, Aristotelian substances, Cartesian substances, and so on, but the distinction has remained invariant. Hume shows in these sections how the history of ancient and modern philosophy may be seen as almost neurotic compulsive behavior whereby men reenact over and over again some traumatic primordial experience. Reality is again and again invested in "objects" as philosophers, ancient and modern, flee in vain from the conceptual authority of the popular system and the trauma of being emancipated from it. Hume uses the myth of "*Sisyphus* and *Tantalus*" to illuminate the history of ancient and modern philosophy, and he recommends the model of those moralists who say we should study our

21

dreams framed in the unconscious as clues to understanding our conscious behavior (T, 219, 223). Similarly, the various systems of double existence contrived throughout the history of philosophy are treated by Hume as so many dreams, the understanding of which may serve to raise philosophers to a higher degree of self-conscious, critical activity.

What do we learn from this metaphysical dream called the doctrine of double existence? There are two lessons. One is that all forms of the doctrine are incoherent because they all attempt to replace totally the popular system while at the same time presupposing it. The second thing we learn from Hume's use of the doctrine in interpreting the history of philosophy is the nature of what he calls *true philosophy:* "In considering this subject we may observe a gradation of three opinions, that rise above each other, according as the persons, who form them, acquire new degrees of reason and knowledge. These opinions are that of the vulgar, that of a false philosophy, and that of the true; where we shall find upon enquiry, that the true philosophy approaches nearer to the sentiments of the vulgar, than to those of a mistaken knowledge" (T, 222). False philosophy would include phenomenalism as well as all forms of the doctrine of double existence, and, for Hume, this would include virtually all systems in the history of philosophy. What then is true philosophy? It cannot be the vulgar way of thinking, that is, the popular system, for that system is defined as philosophically unreflective. Yet Hume says that "true philosophy approaches nearer to the sentiments of the vulgar."

What can this mean? The true philosopher understands and avoids the errors of false philosophy. The false philosopher believes himself to be completely emancipated from the popular system, which he thinks of as a tangle of error, obscurity, and illusion. He attempts to replace totally this system with an alternative one which alone bears the mark of reason and reality. But such systems are absurd because they presuppose, yet deny, the popular system (T, 218). Like Tantalus, the false philosopher searches for what is forever just out of reach and despises the popular system which makes even this mindless search possible and without which the whole project, if consistently carried out, would collapse into total skepticism. The false philosopher lacks self-knowledge about his own inquiry, the true philosopher does not.

The true philosopher, having worked through the errors of false philosophy, recognizes the authority of the popular system in his own thought. In this way the popular system is transformed by reflection from a thesis about the world vulnerable to empirical test into an a-priori framework for interpreting experience.

We must now examine the principles that drive thinking through the three stages of critical reflection: vulgar thought, false philosophy, and true philosophy. Two principles are internal to this process. I shall call these the *ultimacy principle* and the *autonomy principle*. We shall have many occasions throughout this study to refer to them. Let us begin with the ultimacy principle. Philosophical questions are pitched against the background of the whole of reality, and nothing but "the original and ultimate principle" of whatever the object of thought might be can satisfy us: "This is our aim in all our studies and reflections" (T, 266-67; EU, 15; E, 161). Philosophical inquiry is also supposed to be autonomous: it is philosophically irrational to accept any standard, principle, custom, or tradition of common life unless it has withstood the fires of critical philosophical reflection (EU, 149; T, 186). It is, of course, just this principle that informs Descartes' method of universal doubt.

But philosophy conceived as an autonomous and ultimate inquiry leads to absurdity. On the autonomy principle, philosophical under-standing is consituted by standards totally different from those employed in common life. We are necessarily carried "into speculations without the sphere of common life" (T, 271). Thinking of this sort "opens a world of its own, and presents us with scenes, and beings, and objects, which are altogether new" (T, 271). The world of metaphysical reflection contains not only the demons and angels of superstition but also the "substantial forms," "horror of a vacuum," and other occult qualities of the ancient philosophers (T, 219-25). Nor is the matter improved among modern philosophers. An object of common life such as a table is transformed by the "monstrous" modern doctrine of "double existence" into two sets of entities, one a set of sensory entities existing in the mind of the perceiver but connected in some way to another set of entities having no sensory qualities (T, 215). Likewise, the legitimacy of an act by a magistrate is not judged by a historically established constitution which informs a certain political order but by an "original" contract framed in a philosophical state of nature, and so on.

The ultimacy principle requires that philosphers consider this alternative world as reality and the corresponding world of common life as an illusion. The table we see is not the real table but merely a set of perceptions in the mind; the act of the magistrate which is in accord with the historically established constitution is not really legitimate, because it violates the original contract. Philosophy, then, governed by the autonomy principle and the principle of ultimacy, leads, logically, to a total alienation from common life. Alienated in this way, the philosopher falls prey to "philosophical melancholy and delirium," a "forelorn solitude," and is a threat to civic order itself (T, 269, 223; E, 54-62).

But this alienated state of mind brought on by the ultimacy and autonomy principles is just the consciousness of the false philosopher. To free the philosopher from this state and to move thought to a more coherent perspective Hume abandons the autonomy principle: "the understanding, when it acts alone, and according to its most general principles, entirely subverts itself, and leaves not the lowest degree of evidence in any proposition, either in philosophy or common life" (T, 264, 267-68). As we have seen, in Hume's analysis of our belief in the external world, the popular system is presupposed by any philosophical system that attempts to replace it. So philosophical reflection can continue only on the condition that the authority of the popular system is recognized. Philosophy is in need of the "gross earthy mixture" of common life (T, 272). But to say that philosophy is parasitic upon common life is not to say that it must submit to every principle, custom, or prejudice of common life. This or that principle can be criticized, but what cannot be done is to pursue a conception of philosophy such as Descartes', which requires, as a matter of method, that prima facie we view the order of common life to be illusory as a whole. In Hume's conception, philosophy must begin *within* the frame-work of common life, for in the end "we can give no reason for our most general and most refined principles, beside our experience of their reality; which is the reason of the mere vulgar, and what it required no study at first to have discovered" (T, xviii). The principles and maxims of common life are internal to our thinking and cannot be abandoned without abandoning thought itself. What we can do is become self-conscious of the practices of common life, codify these, discover their rationale, order them into systems, and correct them by reference to their coherence with other practices: "philosophical decisions are nothing but the reflections of common life, methodized and corrected" (EU, 162).

Although Hume purged true philosophy of the autonomy principle, the ultimacy principle remained intact. Philosophical questions are still set against the background of the whole of reality. Once we have achieved the level of self-consciousness that constitutes a philosophical question, there is no nonarbitrary way to limit or to eliminate the question. Perhaps the most natural attempt to restrict philosophical questions is through pragmatic considerations. Certainly it has been a favorite twentieth-century move. And some commentators have interpreted Hume's conception of philosophy as essentially pragmatic in outlook. But Hume lived before the pragmatic age. His thought is still rooted in the ancient and medieval contemplative tradition of philosophy, and in this view philosophical questions cannot, in any way, be settled by practical considerations: "My practice, you say, refutes my doubts. But you mistake the purport of my question. As an agent, I am quite satisfied in the point; but as a philosopher who has some share of curiosity, I will not say scepticism, I want to learn the foundation of this inference" (EU, 38). To abandon the ultimacy principle would be to abandon philosophy itself.

Moreover, it is the ultimacy principle that makes Hume's skepticism possible. If ultimate questions about existences are possible, then answers to them are possible. But the only nonarbitary answers we can give to these, or to any other question of fact and existence, are based on experience and so are contingent. But contingent answers, by the very principle of ultimacy, are inadequate: "Who will assert that he can give the ultimate reason why milk or bread is proper nourishment for a man, not for a lion or a tiger?" (EU, 28). If we philosophize, then, we are bound to raise ultimate questions the answers to which are radically unsatisfying: "The most perfect philosophy of the natural kind only staves off our ignorance a little longer, as perhaps the most perfect philosophy of the moral or metaphysical kind serves only to discover larger portions of it. Thus the observation of human blindness and weakness is the result of all philosophy, and meets us, at every turn, in spite of our endeavors to elude or avoid it" (EU,31).

True philosophy, then, is distinguished from false in that it abandons the autonomy principle, recognizing the a-priori structure of common life as a structure internal to its own activity.[5] The true philosopher methodizes and corrects judgments made within the order of common life. But the activity of true philosophy still presupposes the ultimacy principle and is carried on against the background of the idea of ultimate reality and an awareness of our cognitive alienation from it. Skepticism, then, is not overcome by true philosophy but is a constituent of it. We must now examine more closely the relation of skepticism to true philosophy.

## THE PYRRHONIAN ILLUMINATION

Until well into the twentieth century, Hume's philosophical writings were viewed as skeptical in an especially vicious way. In a letter to Andrew Miller, William Warburton wrote of Hume's thought that "there are vices of the *mind* as well as the body: and I think a wickeder mind, and more obstinately bent on public mischief, I never knew."[6] James Beattie set out to refute Hume in *The Nature and Immutability of Truth in Opposition to Sophistry and Scepticism* (1770), which was extremely popular, going through eleven editions in the first decade after its publication. Beattie agreed that "scepticism, where it tends to make men well-bred, and good natured, and to rid them of pedantry and petulance . . . is an excellent thing. And some sorts of scepticism there

 **CHAPTER ONE**

are, that really have this tendency." But Hume's skepticism is not of this sort: "Mr. Hume, more subtle, or less reserved, than any of his predecessors, hath gone to still greater lengths in the demolition of common sense."[7] John Stuart Mill conveys a similar picture: "Hume possessed powers of a very high order; but regard for truth formed no part of his character. He reasoned with surprising acuteness; but the object of his reasoning was, not to obtain truth, but to show that it is unattainable. His mind, too, was completely enslaved by a taste for literature . . . that literature which without regard for truth or utility, seeks only to excite emotion."[8] The same reading has continued into the twentieth century. John H. Randall wrote of Hume's philosophy that it is "extremely acute, and malicious throughout,"[9] and Prichard said of the *Treatise:* "of course there is a great deal of cleverness in it, but the cleverness is only that of extreme ingenuity or perversity, and the ingenuity is only exceeded by the perversity."[10] Recently, D. C. Stove has defended the interpretation of Hume as a subversive skeptic: "The overall impression made by Hume's philosophy on its readers has always been remarkably uniform; and it has been the kind which they have tried to express by calling it 'sceptical,' or 'negative,' or 'critical,' or 'destructive.' Hume has appeared to his readers as pre-eminently a *subverter* of natural or common-sense beliefs . . . and no one, I think, before the present century, ever saw any reason to dissent from that verdict. There is, indeed, room and need for a precise account of what his characteristic scepticism consists in. But as to the broad fact, opinion has been uniform and emphatic."[11]

The scholars in "the present century" who reject this picture of Hume as a subversive skeptic are those who, following Kemp Smith, interpret Hume as a naturalist. On this view, Hume is not a skeptic at all. The presence of skeptical arguments in his works is designed to show that belief is determined not by rational insight or inference but by instinct, habit, and feeling. Hume's theory is a positive, not a subversive, one because he offers a causal theory of how these natural features of the mind determine belief. It is an essential part of Kemp Smith's reading that reason, for Hume, is entirely governed by instincts and feelings.[12]

Working within the broad outlines of this Kemp Smith interpretation, Richard Popkin has argued that Hume should be interpreted as a modern Pyrrhonian skeptic. Pyrrhonian skepticism as presented in the works of Sextus Empiricus is a way of life designed to overcome that peculiar melancholy to which those of a philosophic nature are given. Philosophers, who take thought seriously, may achieve peace of mind either through possession of ultimate truth or by acquiring a disposition to suspend judgment on questions of ultimate reality and to govern their lives not by philosophic truth but by natural feeling, custom, and tradition. The Pyrrhonian first sought the truth but found to his dismay that the contradictory of any proposition he thought was true was equally well supported. This first produced anxiety but, after long experience of suspending judgment, the Pyrrhonian discovered to his surprise that the peace of mind he had sought in possessing ultimate truth had come about accidentally in the disposition to suspend judgment. Popkin shows that Hume deployed Pyrrhonian arguments to show that there is no justification for belief in natural objects, the causal principle, demonstrative reasoning, and probabilistic reasoning. But unlike the ancient Pyrrhonians, Hume did not think that we could suspend judgment on these matters. Like Kemp Smith, he argues that nature compels us to have beliefs of all sorts including beliefs about ultimate reality which, given the Pyrrhonian arguments, we know are not justified.[13] And this is a psychological state conducive not to peace of mind but to anxiety, and perhaps even to madness.[14]

This Kemp Smith and Popkin interpretation is, I think, correct as far as it goes. But in setting up, as it does, a sharp dichotomy between reason and natural belief, it leaves little room for the refinements in the concept of reason that must be made if we are to have an adequate appreciation of the role Pyrrhonism plays in Hume's philosophy. For one thing the dichotomy of reason and natural belief has left in the minds of many the belief that, for Hume, reason is Pyrrhonian and that natural belief runs free, uncontrolled and unshaped by anything that could be called rational criticism. This enables us to trade the image of Hume as a subversive skeptic for a picture of him as an irrationalist for whom all thought is determined by feeling.[15]

Such an interpretation emerges from an overemphasis on Hume's causal theory of belief. Causal theories of belief are often used to reduce what was thought to be conscious critical reflection to whatever the favorite causal mechanisms happen to be. Certain forms of Marxism and Freudianism come readily to mind. But Hume begins by taking rational reflection (the autonomy principle) as primitive and underived. Reason is presented as having independent authority to command belief (T, 215, 268). And the relation between reason and natural belief is a complicated, dialectical one. If so, then, it is not causal analysis but a rational analysis of the dialectic of reason and natural belief that will reveal the normative nature of each. And that is precisely what Hume undertakes in what I have called the natural history of philosophical consciousness in section ii and its application to ancient and modern philosophical errors in sections iii and iv. Viewed in this way the Pyrrhonian arguments are a necessary stage in the natural history of philosophical reflection from vulgar thought through false philosophy to philosophy that is true. The point of the Pyrrhonian arguments is not to show, as Popkin has suggested, that, for Hume, a person is forced to believe "whatever nature leads him to believe, no more and no less."[16] Their function is, rather, to illuminate the nature of true philosophy. We may speak, then, in Hume of a "Pyrrhonian illumination" which reveals something of the nature and limits of philosophical inquiry. The main points of this insight are as follows.

1. Pyrrhonism is implicit in the idea of philosophical reflection. The very idea of philosophy requires both the autonomy principle and the ultimacy principle. Philosophy that does not seek to know what is ultimately the case must be arbitrarily limited to a particular point of view. Likewise, to abandon the autonomy principle is to make philosophy the handmaiden of theology, science, politics, or whatever. Yet Hume discovered that, contrary to appearances, philosophy informed by these principles ends in the total doubt of Pyrrhonism, and Pyrrhonism is the end of philosophy. Philosophy, then, is incoherent with itself.

2. Hume likens this Pyrrhonian state of mind to a philosophical "dream" from which the philosopher is awakened by the "first and most trivial event in life." And the dream has an interpretation: "When he awakes from his dream, he will be the first to join in the laugh against himself, and to confess that all his objections are mere amusement, and can have no other tendency than to show the whimsical condition of mankind, who must act and reason and believe, though they are not able, by their most diligent inquiry, to satisfy themselves concerning the foundation of these operations or to remove the objections which may be raised against them" (EU, 160). The Pyrrhonian suspension of belief breaks the grip of all philosophical propositions, and the sheer primordial and inarticulate insistence of common life breaks the grip of the Pyrrhonian doubt.

3. From the perspective of Pyrrhonian doubt, the philosopher can see for the *first* time the magnificent, philosophically unreflective order of common life in opposition to whatever order is constituted by autonomous philosophical reflection and with an authority all its own to command belief and judgment. We recognize that we are determined to make judgments and have beliefs about reality within this order no matter what the dictates of philosophical reflection might be. And yet recognition of the peculiar authority of common life is dependent upon a philosophical process of working through philosophical incoherence to the point where we are "thoroughly convinced of the force of the Pyrrhonian doubt" (EU, 162). This is an important point and needs elaboration. Philosophy governed by the autonomy and ultimacy principles fancies itself to be self-justifying and entirely emancipated from

philosophically unreflective common life, which is viewed as a tangle of prejudice, custom, and tradition.

This conception is incoherent because all philosophy, true and false, presupposes the original authority of common life. The false philosopher is prevented from seeing this by the autonomy principle: "Reason first appears in possession of the throne, prescribing laws, and imposing maxims, with an absolute sway and authority" (T, 186). To recognize the original authority of common life is to abandon the autonomy principle, and this must appear to the false philosopher as an act of bad faith whereby he forfeits his integrity as a thinker. Once caught in the coils of false philosophy, one finds it difficult to escape through *arguments*. The autonomy principle and the self-justifying character of philosophy which appears to follow from it make rational criticism seem impossible and even perverse.

Yet what Hume discovered is that, applied consistently, the autonomy principle leads not to self-justification but to the self-destruction of philosophy in the form of total Pyrrhonian doubt. The false philosopher is astonished to find "that he cannot defend his reason by reason" (T, 187). Numbed by total doubt, the false philosopher is finally transported to the transcendental perspective of "true philosophy" where he can "see through" the illusion of the autonomy principle and recognize for the first time the original authority that philosophically unreflective common life has and always did have in his thinking. It is important to see that this insight is not the conclusion of a philosophical argument. Assertion and denial are propositional states of mind; Pyrrhonian suspension of judgment on *all* propositions is not a propositional state of mind. The insight is gained dialectically by working up to and *having* the Pyrrhonian doubt (EU,162). Through this process the vacuity of the autonomy principle and the unspeakable primordial authority of common life are "shown" in a way roughly analogous to Wittgenstein's position in the *Tractatus* where he argues that "the logical form of reality" expressed in propositions cannot be represented by them, but "propositions *show* the logical form of reality. They exhibit it." Similarly, the reality of the public world of common life is not known *through* philosophical arguments. Rather philosophical arguments (Pyrrhonian arguments) are used to clear the landscape of *all* philosophical argument, thereby uncovering the common world unspotted by philosophical reflection. What is revealed has rational authority insofar as the Pyrrhonian arguments that bracket out all philosophical arguments have rational authority, as Hume thinks they do.

The false philosopher never enjoys the Pyrrhonian illumination which leads to the perspective of true philosophy because he is never "thoroughly convinced of the force of the Pyrrhonian doubt." He is protected from total doubt only because he secretly and unknowingly borrows some favorite prejudice, custom, or tradition from common life to give content to the otherwise empty autonomy principle.

4. The idea of common life and its special authority is not an idea available to the vulgar, who are sunk in its unreflective order. Hume is not defending philistinism, nor does he claim to find in the order of common life a new foundation of true propositions on which philosophy could be built, as Thomas Reid and the Scottish school of common sense claimed to have found. Common life, as Hume understands it, is an object of thought only for a philosophical consciousness that has passed through the exacting route of philosophic self-doubt. The philosopher cannot abandon philosophy for common life; he cannot go home again. The very idea of rejecting philosophy is contradictory: "you expressly contradict yourself; since this maxim must be built on the preceding reasoning, which will be allow'd to be sufficiently refin'd and metaphysical" (T, 268, 271). Nor can he continue with a conception of philosophy that leads to total doubt. There is a Hegelian thesis-antithesis conflict in the philosopher's own mind between the authority of philosophical reflection, conceived as an autonomous and ultimate inquiry, and the authority of the unreflective order of common life. And, in Hegelian fashion, the conflict is resolved by moving to a synthesis which transcends but still contains the conflicting elements. The move is governed by the philosopher's determination to make his own philosophical thinking coherent. But coherent with what?

Through the shock of Pyrrhonian doubt, philosophy is seen to be incoherent with itself, for the reason that it is incoherent with common life as a whole, which is presupposed by Philosophy. The philosopher now realizes that he exists both within and without the world of common life; to make philosophy coherent is to reconstruct it in conformity to the peculiar necessities of that fact. And that means abandoning the autonomy principle: "the understanding, when it acts alone, and according to its most general principles, entirely subverts itself, and leaves not the lowest degree of evidence in any proposition, either in philosophy or common life" (T, 267-68). Philosophical reflection, then, must work, paradoxically, both within and without the world of common life. It works within insofar as the authority of common life as a whole is internal to philosophical thinking. It works without insofar as the philosopher can frame abstract ideals and principles which can be used to correct any particular belief or maxim of common life in the light of other beliefs and maxims considered at the time to be unproblematic. In this way a reformed version of the autonomy principle survives. Philosophy is still autonomous in that it can question *any* belief or practice of common life. What it cannot do is question the whole order.

5. Hume's Pyrrhonism does not bring peace of mind, as ancient Pyrrhonism was supposed to do. Suspension of judgment is, for Hume, merely a moment in the natural history of philosophical consciousness which brings to light an incoherent conception of philosophy and enables thought to move on to a more coherent conception. But the old conception is not entirely abandoned. The ultimacy principle survives and with it the distinction between appearance and reality. The philosopher still must make judgments about what really is the case, and so his judgments are made against the background of what is thought to be ultimate reality. But these judgments are not only contingent; they may be incoherent to some degree with other judgments equally established. For instance it is a judgment of common life and of post-Pyrrhonian philosophy that we perceive physical objects, that is, entities with sensory properties existing independently of our perception of them. But, as we have seen, that judgment is not entirely coherent with other equally important judgments. The Humean philosopher still believes himself to be alienated from ultimate reality. Hence he proposes that "mitigated scepticism" made possible by the Pyrrhonian illumination which makes a "merit of our ignorance" and which Hume hopes will inspire philosophers with "more modesty and reserve, and diminish their fond opinion of themselves and their prejudice against antagonists" (EU, 161). It must be stressed that Hume's mitigated skepticism is not a form of positivism. The rationale of positivism is to shut off completely any inquiry into the nature of ultimate reality. Common life is not made up of positive facts over which the empirical scientist can generalize and with which he can be content. Common life for Hume is an order of passion, prejudice, custom, and tradition. It is in this world that the philosopher has his being. He is, however, never entirely at home in it. But unlike Descartes Hume does not, methodologically, view the customs and prejudices of common life as barriers to understanding. Rather he views them as the only instruments through which we can understand the real, however darkly and obscurely. In this Hume is in agreement with the Scottish common-sense school and with the Descartes of the Sixth Meditation. But he differs in rejecting the providential naturalism which they had taken to guarantee the validity of the prejudices of common life.[17] The Pyrrhonian illumination shows that there is no Archimedean point outside common life as a whole from which it can be either certified or criticized. We have no alternative, then, but to *use* the prejudices and customs of common life as a framework for understanding the real, with no guarantee that we shall understand things as they really are: "Methinks I am like a man, who

31

having struck on many shoals, and having narrowly escap'd ship-wreck in passing a small frith, has yet the temerity to put out to sea in the same leaky weather beaten vessel, and even carries his ambition so far as to think of compassing the globe under these disadvantageous circumstances" (T, 263–64). The true philosopher would have preferred another vessel, but he knows this is the one he must use and has the "temerity" to explore reality with it.

As the final stage of the natural history of philosophical consciousness, true philosophy has two tasks to perform, a positive one and a negative one. The positive task is that of investigating the structure of common life through empirical and a-priori analysis. This task is carried out in the theory of the mind worked out in the *Treatise* and in the "mental geography" of the first *Enquiry* where Hume discusses the task of clarifying, psychologically and logically, distinctions between mental concepts such as thinking and feeling, intellect and will, passion and reason, virtue and vice (EU, 13-14). Hume applies the result of this work in his other writings to a more concrete study of the whole range of common life: morals, politics, economics, history, art, and religion.

The negative task of true philosophy is that of clearing away its own pre-Pyrrhonian errors as manifest in the abstract web of superstition and false philosophy that is woven throughout the fabric of common life. False philosophy, as we have seen, absurdly alienates the philosopher from the world of common life in which he must live and move and have his being and *through* which he must think about the real. This therapeutic task is first laid out in book I part IV of the *Treatise*. But the *Treatise* as a whole is devoted to the positive task of constructing a theory of the mind. In the first *Enquiry*, however, the negative task of purging common life of the destructive and alienating influences of false philosophy is primary and is militantly pursued; the same task is followed throughout most of Hume's later philosophical and historical writings. Hume's philosophy is a meditation on the relation of philosophy to common life, and one form of that relation particularly interested him, that of philosophy to politics. As his career developed (especially his historical work on the British constitution), he began to think that modern politics was self-consciously philosophical and that the success and well-being of the emerging modern political order depended upon whether it would be governed by false philosophy or by the true.

In the remaining chapters I shall touch on both tasks, but the emphasis will be on the negative and therapeutic one because it has not received adequate discussion and because it is the most important for understanding the nature of Hume's philosophy. We must keep in mind that the relation of philosophy to common life for Hume is a dialectical one. False philosophy is both alienated from common life and presupposes it. This incoherence is over-come by the perspective of true philosophy through the Pyrrhonian illumination which reveals common life as having an authority underived from philosophy. Common life, then, is a transcendental concept logically located in the last stage of the natural history of philosophical consciousness. It is a concept available only to the true philosopher, and it is intelligible only against the background of philosophical error. Moreover, philosophical error is intelligible only against the background of common life. To understand the one we must explore the other. If the concept of philosophical error were somehow removed, the idea of common life would logically vanish, as would the positive task of investigating the structure of common life.

# 2
# *Hume As Dialectical Thinker*

I cannot but consider myself as a Kind of Resident or
Ambassador from the dominions of learning to those of
Conversation; and shall think it my constant Duty to
promote a good Correspondence betwixt these two States,
which have so great a Dependence on each other.
Hume, "Of Essay Writing"

## HUME'S ALLEGED LOOSENESS AND INCONSISTENCY

The conclusion of book I, IV, ii is that we are to think of our experiences (perceptions) as located in the world of common life with its internal-external dimensions. We are free, then, to think of perceptions as private or public existences, depending on the contingent relations they exhibit. This conclusion of true philosophy entitles Hume to be metaphysically diffident as to whether we describe the mind with physical or mental predicates: "Bodily pains and pleasures . . . arise originally in the soul, or in the body, whichever you please to call it" (T, 276). It allows him to place ideas in the brain (T, 60-61). It also entitles him to describe "the perceptions of the mind" physicalistically, referring to them indifferently as "perceptions" or "objects" and relying on a common-sense construction of the context to make his meaning clear. To give an instance: early in book I, when Hume is introducing the principle of the priority of impressions to ideas, he writes: "To give a child an idea of scarlet or orange . . . I present the objects, or in other words, convey to him these impressions" (T, 5). The *Treatise* abounds with passages of this kind where impressions are treated as public objects.

Such passages are usually viewed as the result of careless thinking and writing. Kemp Smith finds much of the wording of "these opening sections to be loose" and laments Hume's "unfortunate" mode of exposition. Passmore finds them due to "that insensitivity to consistency which Hume shares with Locke."[1] And Flew interprets them as the inevitable lapse of a phenomenalist into the pysicalistic language that makes phenomenalism appear plausible and hides its error: "It is only by a systematic failure to launch and to press home a really determined attempt to state the position consistently that its fundamental impossibility is concealed."[2] It is hard to know what to make of these comments, for it should be clear that Hume intends to develop his philosophy within the transcendental perspective of true philosophy which presupposes the original authority of common life.

The view that one must make allowances for Hume's unusually loose and inconsistent manner of expressing himself is common. Thus Robinson can talk of "local lucidity and global abscurity" in Hume's writings, and Passmore can discern a pattern of looseness and inconsistency which at times reaches "epic proportions."[3] These remarks are curious, for one cannot view all of Hume's writings in this way. *The History of England*, the *Dialogues*, the two *Enquiries*, and the *Essays* cannot be thought of, and are not, as especially loose and inconsistent. It is typically the *Treatise* and especially book I that is treated in this way. There are stylistic infelicities in the *Treatise* as there would be in any work of comparable scope and ambition, and there are peculiarities in Hume's style which require special attention. But the view that has developed about Hume's carelessness and inconsistency is due not merely to the peculiarities of his style but also to certain preconceptions about his philosophy. Since Hume's manner of writing has proved such a stumbling block to an appreciation of his philosophy, it might be worthwhile to examine briefly the rhetoric of the *Treatise* with the aim of removing at least some of the barriers. No attempt is made to be comprehensive, and I shall touch only those aspects of Hume's style and rhetoric that serve to illuminate his conception of philosophy. We shall find that the peculiarities of Hume's rhetoric are not due to carelessness but more or less reflect the peculiarities of the way he does philosophy.

## "OUR MISCELLANEOUS WAY OF REASONING"

There are philosophers for whom philosophy is primarily a matter of discerning and organizing true propositions about the world into a system, and there are those for whom philosophy is primarily dialectical. Aristotle, Spinoza, and Russell may be taken as examples of the first type. For philosophers of this kind, philosophy begins and ends with true propositions, and the literary form of exposition is always that of presenting true propositions as clearly as possible, typically by some device for introducing self-evident truths, by definitions, or by deductive inferences. Philosophers of the second sort, although they certainly use propositions, are more concerned to arrange them in dialectical relations to yield insights that may or may not be propositional. Plato's *Dialogues* are of this sort. It is the dialectical journey through the inquiry, from darkness to light, that is important, and the insight reached may not, in any obvious way, be propositional; it may end in the images of a myth, as in *The Republic*, or in a recognition of our own ignorance, as in the *Meno*. The *Dialogues* typically begin with a question, but equally important as answering the question is exploring its rationale. And the answers given at the beginning of the inquiry are not clear and distinct ideas but vague intuitions, modified, along with the question, as the inquiry proceeds. To understand Hegel's *Phenomenology of Mind*, one must pass through the dialectic of spirit on its way to self-consciousness; propositions acquired on the way have only a *degree* of truth, truth being a grasp of the whole in the light of the journey. Similarly, the point of Wittgenstein's *Tractatus* is not to *say* anything propositionally but artfully to "show" something about the relation of propositions to the world: "My propositions serve as elucidations . . . anyone who understands me eventually recognizes them as nonsensical, when he has used them—as steps—to climb up beyond them. (He must, so to speak, throw away the ladder after he has climbed up it.) He must transcend these propositions, and then he will see the world aright."[4] Parallel remarks apply to the *Philosophical Investigations*. Though wildly different in many respects, all of these thinkers have in common a dialectical method of doing philosophy: philosophical insight is gained by working through the contrarieties of thought which structure a drama of inquiry.

Hume is a thinker of just this sort. In most of his philosophical works his thought is put into some sort of dialectical and dramatic form where there is an attempt to come to terms with "principles, which are contrary to each other, which are both at once embrac'd by the mind, and which are unable mutually to destroy each other" (T, 215). The same pattern of understanding through opposition is to be found in his historical works and in many of his essays. The dialectic of liberty and authority is a guiding theme of the *History of England*, as is the way new forms of political order emerge, as the unintended consequences, ironically, of political as well as nonpolitical activity. The dialectic of polytheism and monotheism governs *The Natural History of Religion*, which ends not with scientific conclusions but with a philosophically edifying confession of mystery: "The whole is a riddle, an aenigma, an inexplicable mystery" through which we see the necessity of making our escape into "the calm, though obscure, regions of philosophy" (NHR, 98). Understanding comes in recognizing the contrarieties of thought and in the struggle for some sort of reconciliation or order which is achieved, in part, through the inquiry itself. Hume goes out of his way in the *Treatise* to affirm this Socratic conception of philosophy: "there cannot be two passions more nearly resembling each other, than those of hunting and philosophy, whatever disproportion may at first sight appear betwixt them" (T, 451). As there are values to the chase independent of its goal, so there are values to the spirit of inquiry independent of achieving its goal of absolute truth.

The rhetorical style of the *Treatise*, especially of book I, is at the service of Hume's dialectical conception of philosophical understanding. It is contrived to make the reader inquire as well as to present him with a system of truth. Indeed, Hume makes clear that truth is not necessarily the object of his inquiry at all. What he hopes for is "to establish a system or set of opinions, which if not true (for that, perhaps, is too much to be hop'd for) might at least be satisfactory to the human mind" (T, 272). The governing metaphor of the *Treatise* is that of a "voyage" the outcome of which is unknown to the author (T, 263). From the first pages of the *Treatise* Hume charts with rhetorical surprise his own discoveries: "This circumstance seems to me remarkable, and engages my attention for a moment" (T, 3). "Having discover'd this relation . . . I am curious to find some other . . . qualities" (T, 4). And again: "But leaving this new discovery of an impression, that secretly attends every idea . . ." (T, 375). The author is forced to abandon earlier positions: "I find I have been carried away too far by the first appearance . . ." (T, 3). "I begun this subject with premising . . . . But to be ingenuous, I feel myself *at present* of a quite contrary sentiment" (T, 217). "This opinion I can scarce forbear retracting" (T, 268). And "we here find ourselves at a loss how to reconcile such opposite opinions" (T, 205). Again: "This leads us backward upon our footsteps to perceive our error" (T, 210). Finally there is the famous Appendix, unprecedented in philosophical literature, where central doctrines of the *Treatise* are challenged on no other ground than a counterintuitive feeling of the uneasiness which they occasion. Here the inquiry seems to spill outside the book itself, and the reader is forced to view the main body of the *Treatise* with some diffidence and to continue the inquiry himself.

Insights are presented throughout the *Treatise* using the literary device of internally conflicting conceptual dramas with the author usually standing at comic distance. The conflicts are often described as "contradictions." But Hume does not usually think of these as propositions that are formally inconsistent. "Contradiction," for him, refers most often to a state of mind; it is a feature of judgments not of formal structures.[5] That Hume is aware of using the term in a special way is indicated by the following passage: "we find ourselves somewhat at a loss, and are involv'd in a *kind of contradiction*" (T, 199, emphasis added). The conflicts generated by these "contradictions" are between contrary principles both of which are embraced by the mind but "which are unable mutually to destroy each other" (T, 215). Similar conflicts hold between entire "systems which tho' directly contrary, are connected together" (T, 213).

Since "the heart of man is made to reconcile contradictions" (E, 70), one of Hume's main tasks is to explore the history of the state of mind that various contrarieties yield. Often the "contradiction betwixt these opinions we elude by a new fiction" (T, 215). Such fictions and other reconciling devices in some cases yield beneficent consequences so that an "infirmity of human nature becomes a remedy to itself" (T, 536). In some cases the skeptics may "have the pleasure of observing a new and signal contradiction in our reason, and of seeing all philosophy ready to be subverted by a principle of human nature, and again saved by a new direction of the very same principle" (T, 150). In other cases, reconciliation is merely cosmetic and therefore hopeless. The "direct and total opposition betwixt our reason and our senses" is a "malady, which can never be radically cur'd" (T, 231, 218). And again: "This contradiction wou'd be more excusable, were it compensated by any degree of solidity and satisfaction in the other parts of our reasoning. But the case is quite contrary" (T, 266). There is the dialectic of the ancient and the modern philosophy with both ending "in a very lamentable condition and such as the poets have given us but a faint notion in their descriptions of the punishment "of *Sisyphus* and *Tantalus*" (T, 223). Finally, there is the grand dialectic between philosophy and common life, the exploration of which is Hume's own special contribution to philosophy, and which, in Hegelian fashion, passes through "three opinions, that rise above each other, according as the persons, who form them, acquire new degrees of reason and knowledge . . . that of the vulgar, that of a false philosophy, and that of the true (T, 222). Here the reconciling device is not simply a fiction but a third perspective containing the original conflicting positions and, at the same time, generating a new activity, that of "true philosophy."

Hume considered the passions to be internal to reason and to philosophical understanding in particular.[6] The philosophical passions which, as we have seen, Hume compares to the passion of the chase, are sounded and explored throughout the *Treatise* but especially in the Conclusion of book I where, before launching into book II, Hume pauses "to ponder that voyage, which I have undertaken" (T, 263). He then, in Augustinian fashion, launches into a ten-page philosphic confession in which conflicts in the philosophical passions are laid bare.

This remarkable piece of analysis appears to be the first attempt of a philosopher to inquire not merely into the conceptual possibility but also into the *integrity* of his own philosophical activity.

The literary devices that the young Hume used to unfold the drama of philosophical inquiry in the *Treatise* occur in later works and reached their most polished form in the *Dialogues Concerning Natural Religion*. Indeed, we may say that in the *Dialogues* Hume's dialectical intelligence finds its true literary form, a form the analogues of which are discernible in some shape or other in most of his works from the *Treatise* on. Hume had given much thought to the relation of philosophical inquiry to literary form. Early in the *Dialogues* he has Pamphilus explain why the dialogue form is best suited to philosophical inquiry. Philosophical questions about which "human reason can reach no fixed determination . . . lead us naturally into the style of dialogue and conversation. Reasonable men may be allowed to differ, where no one can reasonably be positive: Opposite sentiments, even without any decision, afford an agreeable amusement: And if the subject be curious and interesting, the book carries us, in a manner, into company; and unites the two greatest and purest pleasures of human life, study and society" (D, 128).

It is perhaps worth noting that, prior to writing the *Treatise*, Hume was living through in his own thought those very dialectical struggles concerning religion which he later so elegantly unfolds in the *Dialogues*. His description of his own state of mind at that time is not without interest. In 1751, when he was beginning to compose the *Dialogues*, Hume wrote a friend asking for considerations that might strengthen the argument from design. The skeptical arguments, he acknowledged, needed no additional support, and he adds "Any Propensity you imagine I have to the other Side [the skeptical], crept in upon me against my Will: And tis not long ago that I burn'd an old Manuscript Book, wrote before I was twenty; which contain'd, Page after Page, the gradual Progress of my Thoughts on that head. It begun with an anxious Search after Arguments, to confirm the common Opinion: Doubts stole in, dissipated, return'd, were again dissipated, return'd again; and it was a perpetual Struggle of a restless Imagination against Inclination, perhaps against Reason" (L, 1:154).

It is characteristic of dialectical thinking to be cast into some sort of narrative form, where earlier events take on additional significance as the story unfolds. The *Treatise*, like the Dialogues, has something of a narrative structure. This fact has been observed by Páll Árdal: "In coming to the end of a good detective story one understands some of the strange happenings at the beginning of it. Things fall into place. I believe this to be true of Hume's *Treatise*."[7] In particular, Árdal has shown how the theory of the virtues in book III can help us to understand Hume's conception of reason and the theory of meaning in book I in the *Treatise*.

Hume experimented with the narrative and more particularly with the dialogue form in the philosophical works that fill the distance between the *Treatise* and the *Dialogues*. Section XI of the first *Enquiry* is cast into dialogue form, as is the last and crucial section of the second *Enquiry*. An especially interesting literary experiment is the collection of essays "The Epicurean," "The Platonist," "The Stoic," and "The Sceptic." These appear to be independent essays, each developing a theory of what constitutes human happiness. But they in fact form a narrative unity because they are so contrived that the reader experiences the seeds of each position in himself and, as he passes through them, views the earlier positions which seemed acceptable at the time in a different and critical light. The last essay, "The Sceptic," emerges as the true position which reconciles the earlier conflicting positions into a new perspective without entirely destroying them. The solution is a dialectical one and is achieved narratively. The pattern is similar in form to the "Sceptical Solution" to doubts regarding the understanding in the first *Enquiry* (Sections IV-V), which in turn is a recasting of the dialectical struggle between the popular system and the philosophical systems in the *Treatise*, book I, part IV. The pattern is similar also to the way in which Philo's "philosophical theism" emerges in the *Dialogues* as the outcome of the mind's having critically passed through the various positions of natural theology defended by Cleanthes and Demea.

In the *Dialogues*, Pamphilus rejects the idea of presenting a system such as the Newtonian one in dialogue form: "To deliver a System in conversation scarcely appears natural . . . the dialogue-writer desires, by departing from the direct style of composition, to give a freer air to his performance, and avoid the appearance of *author* and *reader*" (D, 127). This piece of literary-philosophical criticism by the mature Hume applies perfectly to the *Treatise*, where he officially presents a system but does so with literary devices that embody many of the structural elements of dialogue and conversation. The author of the *Treatise* does not merely explain and prove things to the reader, he is also a character in the work whose imaginary dialogue with himself and the reader is a vehicle that allows the inquiry to unfold. As we have seen, the author makes surprising new discoveries, dramatically changes his mind, reaches an unexpected dead end, expresses his own doubts and hesitations, is shaken to the core by them, but always has the courage to overcome misology and to continue the inquiry. The "appearance of author and reader" which Pamphilus thinks should be avoided in philosophical literature is to some extent avoided in the *Treatise* (mainly in book I), and here and there the inquiry appears to unfold in its own right, eventually spilling out of the body of the *Treatise* into the Appendix and left as a problem for the reader. But the price Hume paid is that the author becomes the main character of the dialogue, and this sort of exhibitionism was extremely mortifying to the later and more modest Hume.

Another way in which the *Treatise* has something of the character of a dialogue is the way in which faculties such as reason, the imagination, the senses, and the passions are treated as characters holding conflicting philosophical positions. And this suggests a Hegelian picture of the mind as essentially philosophic and in conflict with itself. The dialectical struggle in book I, part IV is presented as a struggle between the senses, reason, and the imagination, with each holding a contrary philosophical position. The imagination, for instance, is pictured as working through a philosophical position: "The imagination naturally runs on in this train of thinking. Our perceptions are our only objects: Resembling perceptions are the same . . .[and so on, until a full metaphysical theory of our perception of the external world is developed]" (T, 213). The passions in book II are treated in a similar manner when Hume sets up an opposition between certain philosophical theories and "*the philosophy* of our passions" (T, 311, Hume's emphasis).

But, of course, the *Treatise* is not a dialogue. It is officially presented as a system, and so there are two patterns of thought at work which are often at odds. One is the dialectical pattern we have discussed, most clearly seen in the dialectic of the three theories of perceptions in book I, part IV. The other is a theoretical pattern, guided by Hume's attempt to be the Newton of the moral sciences. It is at work in the theory of association of ideas and the theory of belief in book I, and in the theory of the passions in book II and its application to the moral world in book III. For theoretical projects of this sort, Hume has Pamphilus recommend a "direct and simple method of composition." "Accurate and regular argument, indeed, such as is now expected of philosophical enquirers [Hume has in mind here what we would call empirical scientists], naturally throws a man into the methodical and didactic manner; where he can immediately, without preparation, explain the point at which he aims; and thence proceed, without interruption, to deduce the proofs, on which it is established" (D, 127). The "methodical and didactic manner" of composition rightly dominates in the sciences which, Hume mildly complains, have largely become the model for philosophical writing. For this reason, "The form of Dialogue," used extensively by the ancients, "has been little practised in later ages, and has seldom succeeded in the hands of those who have attempted it . . . . There are some subjects, however, to which dialogue writing is peculiarly adapted, and where it is still preferable to the direct and simple method of composition" (ibid.). Philosophy, with its perennial questions, is just such a subject. In the *Treatise*, something like "the form of Dialogue," determined by Hume's dialectical or philosophical interests is inharmoniously combined with the "methodical and didactic manner," determined by his Newtonian or scientific interests. Neither form prevails nor are they coherently united. It is this stylistic infelicity brought on by two conflicting methods of thinking that explains much of the notorious "looseness" of expression and "insensitivity" to consistency that has been found in the *Treatise*.

But what we should see in the *Treatise* is an irrepressibly dialectical intelligence constrained by the confines of systematic presentation. Whenever Hume's dialectical interests dominate, "order, brevity, and precision . . . are sacrificed" for the values that dialogue can afford (D, 127). As in Plato's *Dialogues* and in Wittgenstein's *Philosophical Investigations*, the inquiry meanders along. Hume describes it as "our miscellaneous way of reasoning" and as "this careless manner" of doing philosophy (T, 263, 273). The main character in the dialogue of the first *Enquiry*, who expresses many of Hume's views, is described "as a friend who loves sceptical paradoxes" (EU, 132). Likewise, Palamedes, the central character of the dialogue in the second *Enquiry*, is "as great a rambler in his principles as in his person" (EM, 324). And in the *Dialogues* "the accurate philosophical turn of Cleanthes," which is systematic, is contrasted with "the careless scepticism of Philo," which is dialectical (D, 128). "Carelessness" here and in the *Treatise* refers not to misological irresponsibility but to the insatiable spirit of inquiry determined by the ultimacy principle. The *Enquiry* on morals may serve as another case of the difficulty Hume has in containing his thought within the limits of the systematic form. The *Enquiry* contains a systematic part in which the theory of morals is presented and ends very formally with section IX, entitled "Conclusion." But Hume cannot keep the inquiry within this limit; as in the *Treatise* it spills out, not into just one Appendix but into *four* and these are followed by a "Dialogue." Together they constitute the "dialectical" part of the work. Even within the systematic part of the *Enquiry*, which Hume presents as virtually a set of analytic truths ("The very nature of language guides us almost infallibly in forming a judgment of this nature" [EM, 174]), there is no protection from his sifting humor. Having shown in the Conclusion, with what he considers absolute certainty, that personal merit consists entirely in qualities useful or agreeable to ourselves or others, Hume points out that "though the bulk and figure of the earth have been measured, . . . the order and economy of the heavenly bodies subjected to their proper laws, and Infinite itself reduced to calculation; yet men still dispute concerning the foundation of their moral duties." He confesses that "When I reflect on this, I say, I fall back into diffidence and scepticism, and suspect that an hypothesis, so obvious, had it been a true one, would, long ere now, have been received by the unanimous suffrage and consent of mankind" (EM, 278). This disturbing reflection opens up a new path of inquiry which threatens to overturn Hume's moral theory; he does not pursue it, however, neither in the remaining parts of the Conclusion nor in the Appendices and Dialogue that follow. The result is that the reader is left with some diffidence about the whole and must view every conclusion in the light of this fundamental and unanswered question.

Hume was and saw himself to be primarily a man of letters. He considered literary form and content to be internally connected so that the cultivation of the art of literature is at the same time the cultivation of normative thought. From the *Treatise* on, as Hume sought to perfect his philosophical ideas, he experimented with various literary devices for expressing those ideas, including a set of light, Addisonian-type essays which were eventually abandoned because of their style.[8] And looking back, Hume judged the *Treatise* to be a failure because of its style. From a literary point of view, Hume's philosophical works present a rich variety of styles and experiments, something for which there is no parallel among major philosophers.

In the *Dialogues*, after much experimentation, Hume finally found a form adequate to the "sifting humour" of his dialectical mind. There the inquiry is cut free of all systematic constraints and allowed to proceed on its own. The distinctions between *"author and reader," "pedagogue and pupil"* are eliminated (D, 127). But most important, the Hume who was a troublesome character for himself in the *Treatise* and in the strident parts of the first *Enquiry* vanishes. This was an important achievement, for Hume considered it necessary that the philosopher achieve distance from his own philosophical opinions: one must be "diffident of his philosophical doubts, as well as of his philosophical conviction" (T, 273). It was for this reason that he gave special attention to the temporal character of philosophical inquiry and stressed that philosophical theses cannot be stated absolutely but only in a certain context and from a certain point of view. Hume goes out of his way to enforce the point: we are permitted "to be positive and certain in *particular points,* according to the light, in which we survey them in any *particular instant*" (T, 273, Hume's emphasis). Conclusions are relative to "the present view of the object" (T, 274). And: "I cannot, *at present,* be more assured of any truth, which I learn from reasoning and argument" (EM 278, Hume's emphasis). In the *Dialogues,* Hume solved the problem of stumbling over himself by eliminating himself as a character in the inquiry in favor of other characters. No character may be taken to represent entirely Hume's views. The result is, perhaps, the purest expression of philosophical inquiry in literature. Nothing remains for the reader but the experience of philosophical inquiry and the problem that poses for him.

## Perceptions in a Narrative Context

Let us now apply this interpretation of Hume as a dialectical thinker to the problem of how to read the allegedly loose and inconsistent opening pages of the *Treatise*.

Hume's introduction of "perception" is disarmingly informal. Perceptions are divided into "two distinct kinds . . . impressions and ideas," which differ only in "the degrees of force and liveliness" with which they "make their way into our thought or consciousness" (T, 1). Impressions are more forceful, ideas less so. Examples of impressions are "sensations, passions, and emotions." Examples of ideas are the thoughts excited by reading the *Treatise*. And then Hume adds the astonishing statement that "it will not be very necessary to employ many words in explaining this distinction. Everyone of himself will readily perceive the difference betwixt feeling and thinking" (T, 1–2).

The opening pages of the *Treatise* tell us very little about perceptions and nothing that requires us to view them as sense data or private mental images. There are a few examples and a technical expression "force and liveliness" which is primitive, and which we are to understand from the examples and our common understanding of the difference between feeling and thinking. It has been easy to miss the vague and nearly vacuous character of Hume's introduction of perceptions because of the strong presumption brought to the *Treatise* that Hume is a phenomenalist, a presumption itself deeply rooted in the idea of modern philosophy as the story of the rise of the ego-centric "way of ideas" approach to philosophy and its collapse in Hume's thought. This is a story we received when cutting our philosophical teeth, and although it has been challenged by a number of recent commentators and seems on the way to fundamental revision, it is difficult to shake off entirely.[9] Once we read phenomenalistic connotations into the first page of the *Treatise*, we will, of course, be able to find supporting passages. Hume's occasional use of the word "image," his talk of ideas copying impressions, and other remarks that can be interpreted phenomenalistically will reinforce the first error and make a phenomenalistic reading seem obvious.

But then the *Treatise* becomes a strange and unreal book, for much of it does not square with such a reading. One then hears talk of Hume abandoning his first principles, or of employing principles to which he is not entitled by his "official" view, or as being especially loose and inconsistent. I do not mean to suggest that Hume does not make mistakes. The *Treatise* was, after all, an ambitious project and especially so for a largely self-taught young man in his twenties, and one would expect Hume not to have full command of his ideas. What we cannot do is think that Hume has introduced the elements of a phenomenalistic system in the first pages of the *Treatise* and that the remainder of the work develops that system. To get the most out of the *Treatise*, we must have a due regard for its literary style. We have observed that book I inharmoniously combines systematic and dialectical modes of writing and thinking. This tension appears on the very first page. Having given a virtually vacuous definition of "perceptions," Hume disarms questions the reader may have by pointing out that by "impression," "idea," "force and livliness," he means what we all in common life mean by the difference between feeling and thinking. This, of course does not tell us much about perceptions and indeed may appear to be a retreat from explication, but it tells us quite a bit about how Hume thinks we should go about understanding them and what he thinks about the sort of inquiry he is carrying out. Two main points need to be made.

Hume is bringing to the discussion of the *Treatise*, on the very first page, the vulgar consciousness of things as having an original authority to monitor and discipline philosophical explications of concepts. Here Hume is making good his promise in the Introduction that the *Treatise* would be guided by "experience," where experience is conceived not as something arrived at introspectively as in the egocentric tradition but publicly "as they appear in the common course of the world, by men's behaviour in company, in affairs, and in their pleasures" (T, xix). This public notion of experience is the same as that mentioned in "Of Essay Writing," where Hume condemns those philosophers "who never consulted experience in any of their reasonings, or who never searched for that experience, *where alone it is to be found, in common life and conversation*" (E, 569, emphasis mine). The phenomenalistic outlook in philosophy begins not with the public but with the radically private, and so fails to satisfy Hume's conditions for the sort of experience that alone can have authority in philosophical reasoning: "common life and conversation."

Berkeley, whose thought was entirely sunk in the autonomy principle, taught that philosophers must talk with the vulgar but think with the learned. For Berkeley this meant a total transformation of the entire vulgar idiom; by contrast, Hume argues that the true philosopher recognizes that he must not only talk with the vulgar but *think* with them, as well as with the learned. We have then at the very beginning of the

*Treatise* Hume performing his own self-professed philosophical role of "ambassador" between the "learned" and the "conversable" worlds with both viewed as having equal authority and interests (E, 568-70). This dialogue continues throughout the *Treatise* and Hume's other writings, as we shall have many occasions to point out in this study.

To this some may still object that, although Hume does refer to a public world, he is not entitled to by his phenomenalistic principles. But what we have just argued is that there are no phenomenalistic principles at the outset of the *Treatise*, and further, as we saw in the last chapter, Hume explicitly rejects the phenomenalistic way of doing philosophy. Whatever "impression," "ideas," and "force and liveliness" are (and Hume has purposely at the outset given us only a minimal interpretation of them), he is clear that they are to be understood within the framework of a public and social world. Should Hume fall into phenomenalistic modes of talk later in the *Treatise*, the presumption should be that these are slips inconsistent with his explicitly stated intentions (due perhaps to a philosophical tradition from which he is not entirely emancipated) rather than as corroborating the thesis that some sort of phenomenalism is Hume's "official" starting point. And this observation brings to mind another difference between the phenomenalistic way of doing philosophy and Hume's way. The main preoccupation of phenomenalistic philosophies, whether proposed by Berkeley, Ayer, Carnap, or Goodman, is the translation of troublesome theoretical expressions which refer to objects unobservable in principle into the favored idiom. Phenomenalism is programmatic, and everything depends on stating clearly at the beginning what the principles of the program are so that one can evaluate whether or not the reduction has gone through. There are superficial resemblances between such a program and certain passages in the *Treatise*. Hume uses, for instance, the principle of the priority of impressions to ideas (discussed in the next chapter) as a norm for evaluating descriptive expressions such as "substance," "causal connection," and "external existence." These passages seem to support the view that Hume is a precursor of logical empiricism.[10] And there is no doubt that logical empiricists could and did find philosophical inspiration in these passages. But such similarities should not obscure the profound differences.

The spirit of Hume's *Treatise* is entirely different from programmatic phenomenalism. Hume begins with a presystematic understanding of "impressions" and "ideas" that is grounded in the authority of common awareness. The reader is invited to inquire into the nature of his own awareness of "the difference betwixt feeling and thinking," and the inquiry is developed roughly in a narrative way. As the inquiry unfolds, new questions are asked and new discoveries made, and so the concept of a perception is enriched. The same strategy is used at the beginning of book II, where Hume makes a distinction between the "calm and violent" passions. He acknowledges that the "division" is far from being exact, that there appear to be counterexamples and the like, but he resolves, nonetheless, that "The subject of the human mind being so copious and various, I shall here take advantage of this vulgar and specious divison, that I may proceed with the greater order" (T, 276; cf. 277). The same methodological move is made at the beginning of book I: "Having by these divisions [impressions and ideas] given an order and arrangement to our objects, we may now apply ourselves to consider with the more accuracy their qualities and relations" (T, 2). Shortly afterwards Hume makes clear that inquiry into perceptions is just beginning: "Let us consider how they stand with regard to their existence. . . . The *full* examination of this question is the subject of the present treatise" (T, 4, Hume's emphasis). Indeed, as we have observed, the inquiry continues beyond the body of the *Treatise* into the Appendix and is left as a problem for the reader. The ontological status of perceptions, then, is not decided at the beginning of the *Treatise*. The question arises only some two hundred pages later where, in the context of the dialectic between the popular and philosophical theories of perceptions, Hume asks "what we mean by this *seeing*, and *feeling*, and *perceiving*" (T, 207).

We are perhaps now in a position to appreciate another reason why Hume in the beginning of the *Treatise* invests perceptions with vague philosophical and popular connotations and why he can, at the very first, describe perceptions as having physical or mental properties and depend on common understanding to make his meaning clear. Given the categories Hume had to work with, anything more explicit would have required a definition of perceptions by reference either to mind-dependent existences or to external existences, understood in the way modern philosophers usually understood them, namely within a substance-modification ontology. But for Hume these categories are not adequate; as the inquiry of book I unfolds, it is clear that, for him, the substance-modification concepts of mind and of external existence are equally problematic. Only by working through the painful dialectic of the popular and philosphical systems in part IV can we begin to appreciate the difficulties that lurk in the use of terms like "mind," "body," and "perception" and so appreciate the sort of limit which must be placed on their use. Prior to this dialectically achieved insight no systematically acceptable explication of perceptual concepts was possible. Hume, of course, might have presented the tortured dialectic of the popular and philosophical systems at the outset, drawn his conclusions on behalf of the transcendental perspective of true philosophy, defined his terms, and delivered his philosophy of human nature. He did not do this because he was seeking to free himself of strictures imposed by the intuitively plausible categories of modern philosophy without entirely abandoning them. An effort of that sort requires a searching examination of one's own reflective and prereflective conceptual framework. Such an inquiry would necessarily be carried out dialectically, and it would be natural and pedagogically wise to use a dialectical and narrative form of exposition as a device to engage what must be a reluctant public in the same examination.

Perceptions, then, are not introduced as ontological givens in the manner of phenomenalism. Their ontological status is comprehended in the fashion of later idealism, by reference to systems of thought. The term "perception" is meaningless outside of a system, and, as it turns out in book I, part IV, three systems are required which are in conflict (the popular system, phenomenalism, and the doctrine of double existence). The tension is resolved only from the transcendental perspective of "true philosophy" which legislates that we are to think of perceptions as having internal and external dimensions. If so, then the term "perception" must contain this tension within itself not because of Hume's carelessness or looseness of expression but because of the way our thinking goes.

Perhaps enough has been said to show that the Locke-Berkeley-Hume story obscures rather than illuminates Hume's concept of "perceptions." Freeing ourselves from it, and approaching the *Treatise* as a piece of literature, we find that the concept of "perception" is internal to a narrative order of exposition. The subject of a narration becomes more intelligible as the story unfolds, and the reader is required to view earlier episodes in the light of later episodes. Perceptions are purposely obscure at the outset, and our understanding of them is almost entirely by reference to prephilosophic common life.

Since Hume's concept of a perception is presented narratively, our grasp of what he means by perceptions at the beginning of the *Treatise* depends almost entirely on what discoveries are made later on by what Hume calls "the full examination" of the subject (T, 4). I should now like to work through a few of the most important of these discoveries. No attempt is made at a thorough account of perceptions; my purpose is simply to provide additional support for the thesis that Hume presents his concept of perceptions narratively and not in the systematic, reductionist mode of phenomenalists, and to reveal something of the complexity and suggestiveness of Hume's inquiry into the nature of perceptions.

The first point to appreciate is that Hume thinks his inquiry is novel. He does not think that he is simply restating in his own terms "the way of ideas" of Locke and Berkeley. He makes clear that he is restoring "the word, idea, to its original sense, from which Mr. *Locke* had perverted it" (T, 2n). And by "impression" Hume says he means something "for which there is no particular name either in the *English* or any other language, that I know of" (T, 2n). And what he means is "the perceptions themselves" independent of all causal understanding of them. Hume has left entirely open the question of whether perceptions are produced passively in the mind, whether they are produced by the mind, or whether they are independent of the mind. Any of these possibilities could have been easily expressed in the philosophical vocabulary of his time. Hume says we are to ignore this vocabulary. But, of course, he cannot entirely ignore it. The result is that many of the original insights Hume has about perceptions (a better term would have been "experiences") must be forced into language that is not suited to the novelty of the inquiry. The meaning of Hume's language must be determined not by reading traditional connotations into it, as Hume himself warns, but by careful attention to its use.

If we are not to understand the nature of "the perceptions themselves" through causal analysis, how are we to understand them? Hume provides two ways, one contained in the doctrine of *relations of ideas* and the other in the doctrine of *distinctions of reason*. Each doctrine frames a conception of necessity which enables us to make judgments that are neither analytic nor synthetic about the a-priori structure of perceptions.

Hume divides relations into two classes: "such as depend entirely on the ideas, which we compare together, and such as may be chang'd without any change in the ideas" (T, 69). Relations of the first sort are internally connected to the relata: "*resemblance, contrariety, degrees in quality, and proportions in quantity or number*" (T, 70). These are "the only infallible relations" (T, 79). They are the sole "objects of knowledge and certainty" (T, 70) and constitute "the foundation of science" (T, 73). Propositions about these relations are necessarily true or false. Relations of the second sort are externally connected to the relata: "*identity, the situations in time and place, and causation*" (T, 73). These are contingent, and propositions describing them are vulnerable to empirical test.

It has been common since Kant to view the difference between these necessary and contingent relations as roughly the difference between analytic and synthetic propositions. Indeed, Kant thought that Hume was close to discovering the principle of his own critical philosophy and would have done so had he recognized that mathematical propositions are synthetic a-priori propositions and not, as he took Hume to think, analytic ones. Adolf Reinach, one of Edmund Husserl's students, appears to have been the first to recognize that Kant's interpretation was wrong.[11] Mathematical propositions express one of the four necessary internal relations (proportions in quantity and number). The necessity of these relations is not constituted by the formal principle of non-contradiction. Humean necessary relations hold not between "terms" or "propositions" which are formal structures but between perceptions. Nor are they expressable in synthetic a-priori propositions in Kant's sense, for they are not thought of by Hume as being imposed by the mind on appearances. Rather they are discovered as a-priori features of perceptions.[12] They immediately "strike the eye, or rather the mind" and "fall more properly under the province of intuition than demonstration" (T, 70).

The text provides such ample and obvious support for Reinach's interpretation that is is difficult to understand how the interpretation that Humean necessary relations are analytic ever became so widespread. In both the *Enquiry* on understanding and in the *Treatise*, Hume contrasts mathematical propositions with propositions plausibly interpreted as analytic: "*That the square of the hypotenuse is equal to the squares of the other two sides* cannot be known, let the terms be ever so exactly defined, without a train of reasoning and inquiry. But to convince us of this proposition, *that where there is no property, there can be no injustice*, it is only necessary to define the terms, and explain injustice to be a violation of property. This proposition is, indeed, nothing but a more imperfect definition" (EU, 163). And in the *Treatise:* "mathematicians pretend they give an exact definition of a right line, when they say, *it is the shortest way betwixt two points.* But in the first place I observe, that this is more properly the discovery of one of the properties of a right line, than a just definition of it" (T, 49-50). Here Hume is expressing the ancient conviction that mathematical propositions, in some way, give us information about the world. They are the results of "discovery" and "cannot be known . . . without a chain of reasoning and inquiry." To treat them as analytic would be to render them vacuous and their application to the world unintelligible: "In common life 'tis establish'd as a maxim, that the streightest way is always the shortest; which wou'd be as absurd as to say, the shortest way is always the shortest, if our idea of a right line was not different from that of the shortest way betwixt two points" (T, 50).

An analytic proposition such as the one above, asserting a necessary connection between property and justice, is taken by Hume to be the paradigm of propositions that are true by virtue of their logical relations alone. Such a proposition is "nothing but a more imperfect definition." And he immediately adds," It is the same case with all those pretended syllogistical reasonings which may be found in every other branch of learning, except the sciences of quantity and number; and these may safety, I think, be pronounced the only proper objects of knowledge and demonstration" (EU, 163). Demonstrations, for Hume, are not merely sound arguments, but sound arguments with necessarily true premises. The premises are necessarily true not in the logical sense that their denials are formally self-contradictory but in a special synthetic sense that Hume, oddly enough, given the importance of the idea of necessity for his philosophy, does not fully explore.

That mathematical propositions have empirical content is clearly stated by Hume and is, for him, one reason for the special clarity and precision that mathematical concepts possess: "The greatest advantage of the mathematical sciences above the moral consists in this, that the ideas of the former, being sensible, are always clear and determinate . . . If any term be defined in geometry, the mind readily, of itself, substitutes on all occasions the definition for the term defined"; that is, we can construct in the imagination the relations framed in the definition. And "when no definition is employed, the object itself may be presented to the senses and by that means be steadily and clearly apprehended" (EU, 60). The ideas of quantity in arithmetic and algebra also have a sensory constitution: "all the ideas of quantity, upon which mathematicians reason, are nothing but particular, and such as are suggested by the senses and imagination" (EU, 158n). Because mathematical ideas have an origin in experience, they are informative and can be applied to the world of experience. Hume explicitly rejects the view that there is such a thing as "pure mathematics," in the sense of an inquiry the objects of which logically make no reference to the world of experience; the doctrine, for instance, "that the objects of geometry, those surfaces, lines and points, whose proportions and positions it examines, are mere ideas in the mind; and not only never did, but never can exist in nature" (T, 42).

Although Hume considered mathematical propositions to contain information about the world, he did not think of them as synthetic in the way that Mill did. They are not natural laws testable by experience. If they were, their denials would be "conceivable and intelligible," which Hume denies: "The case is different with the sciences, properly so called. Every proposition which is not true is there confused and unintelligible. That the cube root of 64 is equal to the half of 10, is a false proposition, and can never be distinctly conceived" (EU, 164). Although "suggested by the senses and imagination" and applicable to the world, mathematical propositions are known through "the mere operation of thought" and are not dependent for their certainty on what is anywhere existent in the universe: "Though there never were a circle or triangle in nature, the truths demonstrated by Euclid would forever retain their certainty and evidence" (EU, 25).

What holds for mathematical relations of proportions in quantity and number holds also for relations of resemblance, degrees of a quality, and contrariety. Hume, strangely, gives few examples of these non-mathematical necessary relations, but his brief remarks make it clear that all of them exhibit a-priori structures of perceptions while at the same time containing contingent empirical content. Hume gives the following as an example of the relation of resemblance: "*Blue* and *green* are different simple ideas, but are more resembling than *blue* and *scarlet*" (T, 637). Resemblance is presented here not as a mere formal relation between the terms "blue" and "green" but as a relation internal to the perceptions themselves, discovered immediately by the mind and not, in Kantian fashion, imposed by it. The same holds for degrees of a quality, examples of which are degrees of "colour, taste, heat, cold" (T, 70). The relation of contrariety poses a special problem, for Hume holds "that properly speaking, no objects are contrary to each other, but existence and non-existence" (T, 173), and that there is no simple or complex idea of existence. It would seem, then, that contrariety is not a relation between ideas at all, much less a necessary one. Hume's views on contrariety can best be appreciated after working through the second way of uncovering the a-priori structures of perceptions, namely through making "distinctions of reason."

Distinctions of reason enable us to form abstract ideas and to talk about aspects of experiences which in reality are inseparable. The figure and color of a globe of white marble are inseparable. But by comparing the object with a globe of black marble and a cube of white marble, we observe "two separate resemblances, in what formerly seem'd, and really is, perfectly inseparable" (T, 25). The white globe resembles the black globe in a certain respect, and to this we apply the word "figure." Similarly, the white globe resembles the white cube in a certain respect, and to this we apply the word "color." Figure and color are "aspects" of a perception which are in reality inseparable from it.

Three points about Humean distinctions of reason must be kept in mind. First, the distinction "implies neither a difference nor separation" (T, 25). The figure is in reality "the same and indistinguishable" from the color; it is merely an aspect due to an attentive *act of the mind.* Second, distinctions of reason require "practice" (T, 25). What aspects of perceptions can be uncovered depends upon the skill of the inquirer in making contrasting comparisons with other perceptions and the range of his experience. There is no limit to the number of aspects that can be discovered in a *simple* perception. "Even in this simplicity," he

observes, we suppose "there might be contain'd many different resemblances and relations" (T, 25). Third, further evidence for the thesis that the *Treatise* must be read narratively is that the idea of a
distinction of reason, though introduced around page 25, is put to use
in the second paragraph of the *Treatise* where Hume defines the crucial
concept of a simple perception: "Simple perceptions or impressions and
ideas are such as admit of no distinction nor separation" (T, 2). A simple perception is not a phenomenal atom, something stripped of virtually all qualities, such as a minimum visible, and out of which the
rich, complex world of experience is constructed. A simple perception
may be as rich as one likes and, indeed, may have an infinite number of
parts or aspects uncoverable by distinctions of reason; it is just that
none of these parts are separable from each other. We should also note,
in passing, that Hume's concept of a simple perception requires essential reference to attentive acts of the mind and is further evidence that
the Humean mind is not the passive *tabula rasa* it is often taken to be.

Hume's two ways of investigating the a-priori structure of ideas (relations of ideas and distinctions of reason) have been inadequately appreciated by most commentators in the analytic tradition. That tradition,
which begins with Kant, takes theoretical language as the paradigm for
understanding experience. Humean relations of ideas are conceived as
analytic propositions and Humean distinctions of reason are usually not
mentioned at all. But it has been quite otherwise in the phenomenological tradition. The founder of the tradition, Edmund Husserl, was a
close and lifelong student of the *Treatise*. He returned to it throughout
his career for philosophical insights and as a focal point for understanding the place of his own phenomenological method in the history of
modern philosophy. He found in Hume's two ways of investigating the
a-priori structure of perceptions a path for understanding experience
which avoided the psychologism of Mill on the one hand, and the for-
malism of Kantian critical philosophy and absolute idealism on the
other. In this and much else Husserl found in the *Treatise* the rudiments
of the idea of phenomenological philosophy.[13]

In 1929 Husserl published, in the *Jahrbuch*, C. V. Salmon's dissertation, *The Central Problem of David Hume's Philosophy, An Essay towards a
Phenomenological Interpretation of the First Book of the Treatise of Human
Nature*. Salmon argues against the received view that Hume's method
of analysis is that of breaking experience down into phenomenal atoms.
Rather, Hume's distinctions-of-reason approach is a method for bringing into awareness a-priori structures of experience that were hidden
from consciousness. The method is similar to Husserl's and opens up a
field of phenomenological investigation which, according to Salmon,
Hume failed to exploit fully because his a-priori method of analysis is

entangled throughout with associational psychology. There has been much discussion of how Hume failed to explicate adequately the distinction between physical objects and causal connections as they are in reality and as they exist in consciousness, and the distinction between the perceptions of the mind and the continuing self which has them. Salmon's discussions of these alleged failures, however, is especially interesting because, viewing them against the background of Husserl's phenomenological method, we are able to see aspects of Hume's thought which would otherwise be hidden from view. For one thing, we see the fundamental importance in Hume's thought of the distinctions-of-reason method of examining the contents of consciousness. Until the appearance of R. J. Butler's important article in 1974, no one seems to have appreciated the importance this method has in Hume's analysis of experience. [14]

Salmon's essay was published in the *Jahrbuch* with the hope of interesting English-speaking philosophers in phenomenology and of exposing the roots of phenomenology in their own philosophical tradition. [15] In this the essay failed, and even now there is a gap in communication between English-speaking philosophy dominated by the analytic tradition and continental phenomenology, so that a phenomenological reading of Hume may sound strange and even perverse. The fact is, however, that many in the phenomenological tradition, at least that part of it which stems from Husserl, view their own history as a continuity passing from Hume through Meinong, Brentano, Avenarius, and James to Husserl. [16]

The gulf separating Anglo-American analytic philosophy from Continental phenomenology is not as great as it used to be. And a phenomenological rethinking of Hume by analytic philosophers, who often view him as an important part of their own tradition, may serve to create further lines of communication. Whether such a reading is possible depends on what we take phenomenology to be and what, in the light of it, we can find in Hume. Neither task can be taken up here. I wish to observe only that early in the twentieth century Husserl and his circle (as represented by Salmon and Reinach) had a deeper understanding of Hume's conception of the a priori than was displayed by most of their English-speaking contemporaries.

Let us return now to the thesis that Hume's conception of a perception is developed narratively and that it is only in the light of later developments in the *Treatise* that we can understand, at the beginning, what perceptions are. We have observed that the later concept of a distinction of reason is already implied in Hume's definition of a simple perception presented in the second paragraph of the *Treatise*. The same doctrine, as Professor Butler has shown, and as I shall develop below, is implied in the distinction Hume makes within perceptions between impressions and ideas.[17] Hume is clear that the only discernible difference between impressions and ideas is in the degree of force and vivacity, impressions being stronger in this regard than ideas. We are to think, then, of impressions and ideas as existing at different ends of a continuum. But now Hume says *"That all our simple ideas in their first appearance are deriv'd from simple impressions, which are correspondent to them, and which they exactly represent"* (T, 4). But this seems impossible, for a greater degree of force and vivacity cannot exactly represent a lesser degree, and there seems to be nothing else in respect to which an idea could represent an impression. The solution requires making distinctions of reason within the continuum of a perception to uncover by contrasting comparisons the different aspects internal to the perception. But how are we to do this? Hume has told us precious little about the meaning of "impression" and "idea." We know they are the same, differing only in force and vivacity, that the difference is roughly that between feeling and thinking, and that ideas represent impressions. But these expressions are just so many variables in search of values. The crucial mistake that is often made is to read a meaning into these expressions from a source external to the text. One approaches the *Treatise* with a phenomenalistic framework in mind. The term "impression" is immediately interpreted to refer to sense data presented to a passive mind, and ideas, accordingly, are interpreted as faint sense data. But there is no support in the text for substituting phenomenalistic values for the variables and, further, no support for taking impressions as the paradigm for understanding ideas. Hume's method is just the opposite: we are to understand impressions by reference to ideas. Impressions are causally prior to ideas but are not prior in the order of intelligibility.

The examination of sense impressions, he says, "belongs more to anatomists and natural philosophers than to moral" (T, 8). And since the *Treatise* is mainly a study of the passions, which presuppose ideas, "'twill be necessary to reverse that method, which at first sight seems most natural; and in order to explain the nature and principles of the human mind, give a particular account of ideas, before we proceed to impressions" (T, 8). The investigation of simple impressions of sense does not occur until some 200 pages later in part IV, book I, where they are discussed in the context of the dialectic of the popular and philosophical theories of experience. The point is an important one. Ideas are not the ghosts of simple impressions conceived as sense data. We cannot understand simple impressions without first understanding the a-priori structure of ideas, and this is done by making distinctions of reason which by contrasting comparisons can uncover characteristics internal to the nature of the ideas themselves. I shall mention only some of the most important of these characteristics.

First, ideas are intentional: "to form the idea of an object, and to form an idea simply is the same thing; the reference of the idea to an object being an extraneous denomination, of which in itself it bears no mark or character" (T, 20). The difference between an idea and its intentional object is merely a distinction of reason, the latter being internal to the former. Second, ideas are existential: "To relect on any thing simply, and to reflect on it as existent, are nothing different from each other. That idea, when conjoin'd with the idea of any object, makes no addition to it. Whatever we conceive, we conceive to be existent" (T, 66-67). Third, all ideas are propositional. Hume rejects the view "universally received by all logicians" which distinguishes conception from judgment where conception is thought of as "the simple survey of one or more ideas" and judgment as "the separating or uniting of different ideas" (T, 96n). The received view is false because simple ideas *are* judgments: "in that proposition, *God is*, or indeed any other, which regards existence, the idea of existence is no distinct idea, which we unite with that of the object, and which is capable of forming a compound idea by the union" (T, 96n, cf. 456). But as we have just seen it is an a-priori feature of *all* simple ideas that they are existential. So all simple ideas are propositional. This is not to say, of course, that the idea of God entails that God exists. The idea of God, though existential, may, nonetheless, fail to have an exemplification in reality and so be false: "But let us consider, that no two ideas are in themselves contrary, except those of existence and non-existence, which are plainly resembling, as implying both of them an idea of the object; tho' the latter excludes the object from all times and places, in which it is supposed not to exist" (T, 15).

We are now in a position to appreciate the necessary relation that Hume calls contrariety, which we put off in discussing the other necessary relations of resemblance, degrees of a quality, and proportions of quantity and number. When Hume says the only ideas contrary in themselves are existence and nonexistence, the word "existence" picks out an abstract idea the content of which is an aspect of a perception uncovered by a distinction of reason. We see then that distinctions of reason are presupposed in discerning the necessary relation of contrariety. Indeed, they are presupposed in the other necessary relations as well, for they are all grasped through acts of comparing ideas, and what is compared are aspects of ideas: figure, color, quantity, etc.

Having examined Hume's remarks on the a-priori structure of simple ideas, we may turn to simple impressions. There is no difference between a simple idea and a simple impression other than degree of force and vivacity. But, as we have seen, simple ideas are propositional, intentional, and existential. To say a simple idea exactly represents a simple impression is to say that both have the same propositional and intentional content. When Hume says that the difference between impressions and ideas is that between feeling and thinking, we are to interpret this *propositionally* as the difference between thinking that X is Y and feeling that X is Y. A simple impression of blue, then, is to be thought of as seeing *that* something is blue.

The force and vivacity of a perception is internal to it and can be discerned only through a distinction of reason. One and the same propositional and intentional content can be experienced either as an impression or as an idea, depending upon the degree of force and vivacity it exhibits. Force and vivacity is also used to distinguish an idea that is merely conceived from one that is believed, and to distinguish an idea of memory from an idea of imagination. But what exactly does Hume mean by force and vivacity? Hume has evident difficulty expressing what he means both because of the difficulty in making the relevant distinctions of reason within consciousness and because of the novelty of the idea. As before, it will be helpful to begin with ideas rather than with impressions. And here the crucial notion is *belief*, the analysis of which Hume considered to be one of his most original contributions. Hume is clear that the difference between conceiving something and believing it is merely a difference in force and vivacity which, in turn, is an *act of the mind*. Belief is, he says, simply "a particular manner of forming an idea" (T, 97). In the Appendix Hume goes out of his way to clear up difficulties he acknowledges attend his use of the expression "force and vivacity." And he makes explicit that we are to understand the expression as referring to an act of the mind: "An idea assented to *feels* different from a fictitious idea, that the fancy alone presents to us: And this different feeling I endeavour to explain by calling it a superior *force*, or *vivacity*, or *solidity*, or *firmness*, or *steadiness*. This variety of terms, which may seem so unphilosophical, is intended only to express that *act of the mind*, which renders realities more present to us than fictions, causes them to weigh more in the thought, and gives them a superior influence on the passions and imagination" (T, 629, last emphasis mine).

Since force and vivacity is an act of the mind and since some degree of force and vivacity is internal to every perception, it follows that all perceptions are internal to acts of the mind. We may explicate a perception then as (1) a propositional and intentional content inseparably connected in experience to (2) an act of the mind (felt as force and vivacity) where (1) and (2) can be differentiated only through a distinction of reason. That is, the act of the mind that is the force and vivacity of a perception is connected to its propositional and intentional content in the same way in which figure and color are connected in the perception of a blue circle. The whole perception, of course, is an act of the mind. The force and vivacity of a perception is simply that aspect, uncovered by a distinction of reason, that is "*felt* rather than conceiv'd" (the propositional and intentional content is the part conceived [T, 627]). The force and vivacity of any perception is our awareness of what its propositional and intentional content *means* to us. The *Treatise* is filled with a rich variety of terms which Hume uses to capture the various meanings which are the force and vivacity that perceptions have for us: "greater importance," "a firmer hold," "more present to us," the feeling of "something real and solid," one "enters deeper" into the object of the perception, and so on (T, 629, 624, 627, 98).

Hume apologizes for the great "variety of terms" which he thinks his readers may find "so unphilosophical" (T, 629), but we may see in this "variety" what Husserl saw: a pioneering attempt at phenomenological description.

Enough has been said, perhaps, to show that perceptions are not the phenomenal atoms of programmatic phenomenalism and that the idea of a perception is developed narratively. As the inquiry into the a-priori structure of perceptions unfolds, new discoveries are constantly being made as new aspects of perceptions are uncovered. I have stressed the a-priori side of the inquiry as distinct from the empirical because of the overemphasis that has been given to Hume's associational psychology. We cannot pursue here the intricate and, at times, perplexing ways in which a-priori and empirical modes of analysis are connected in Hume's inquiry into the perceptions of the mind. We are interested in perceptions only insofar as they throw light on his conception of philosophy.

As we saw in the last chapter, Hume's conception of philosophy is dialectical and has a positive and a negative task. The negative task is that of purging common life of false philosophy. The positive task is that of exploring the nature of common life through empirical and a-priori analysis. The *Treatise* may be viewed as an attempt to provide a kind of psychological-phenomenological account of the world of common life as constituted by acts of consciousness. Hume's analysis is full of tension and obscurity but also is rich and suggestive, which is why later philosophical movements as different as logical empiricism and phenomenology can see themselves reflected in the *Treatise*. But the fate of Hume's theory of the mind is of little interest to an overall interpretation of his philosophical achievement. The dialectic of philosophy and common life can be known independently of any particular theory of how acts of consciousness constitute the meanings that structure the world of common life. Except for some sketchy remarks in the first *Enquiry*, the theory of perceptions drops out of Hume's later work, but the dialectic of philosophy and common life first presented in *Treatise*, book I, part IV, remains.

The positive task of exploring common life through a-priori and empirical analysis is carried out in a more popular way by the "mental geography" of the first *Enquiry* and in the form of history, essays, and dialogues. The "ambassador" between the "learned" and "conversable" worlds is now more concerned to communicate with the conversable. And here the negative task of true philosophy takes on an importance it did not have in the *Treatise*. False philosophy alienates the individual and society from common life. Though conceived in the closet, the errors of false philosophy infect the conversable world, and the therapy of true philosophy must, in the nature of the case, be applied not to theory but to conversation in common life. For this project philosophy must be united with rhetoric, hence the necessity to experiment, as Hume did throughout the rest of his career, with various literary and rhetorical devices.[18]

The negative task of purging false philosophy from common life first appears fully and militantly in the first *Enquiry*, where certain books of school metaphysics and divinity are cast into the flames. The true philosopher now emerges as the guardian of the *mind* of common life against the alienating influences of false philosophy: "Chaced from the open country, these robbers fly into the forest, and lie in wait to break in upon every unguarded avenue of the mind" (EU, 11). This therapeutic task, in one form or another, is a unifying theme that runs throughout Hume's later philosophical and historical work. To appreciate it fully, we should begin by examining the main critical tool of the *Treatise* and the *Enquiry:* the principle that ideas are derived from past impressions. We shall find, in the next two chapters, that an understanding of this principle and its implications is crucial for appreciating not only the negative task but also the positive task of true philosophy.

# 3
# Hume's First Principle

These questions may seem trivial or impertinent to one
who does not know that it is a tribunal of inquisition
erected by certain modern philosophers, before which
everything in nature must answer . . . if it appear that the
prisoner is neither an impression, nor an idea copied from
some impression, immediately, without being allowed to
offer anything in arrest of judgment, he is sentenced to
pass out of existence, and to be, in all time to come, an
empty unmeaning sound, or the ghost of a departed entity.

Thomas Reid

## THE PRIVATE-LANGUAGE INTERPRETATION

The "first principle" of Hume's philosophy of common life both in order
of exposition and in order of importance is the principle that simple ideas
are derived from simple, resembling past impressions and that complex
ideas are constructed in the imagination out of past impressions which
may or may not resemble those impressions. This principle is used as a
probe to discover whether philosophical discourse is significant and, if it
is not, to purge it from common life: "When we entertain . . . any
suspicion that a philosophical term is employed without any meaning or
idea (as is but too frequent), we need but enquire, *from what impression is
that supposed idea derived?* And if it be impossible to assign any, this will
serve to confirm our suspicion" (EU, 22). Armed with this principle,
Hume is able to reject some philosophical theories not by arguing that
they are false but by arguing that they are cognitively meaningless:
"What possibility then of answering that question, *Whether perceptions
inhere in a material or immaterial substance*, when we do not so much as
understand the meaning of the question?" (T, 234). And, more generally,
this "defiance [to produce the impression of a purported idea] we are

oblig'd frequently to make use of, as being almost the only means of proving a negative in philosophy" (T, 159).

Hume's principle, however, and the conception it presupposes of what it is to have an idea of something, have not fared well. Church writes: "It is a common place that Hume's confidence in the importance for philosophy of his first principle is indefensible."[1] And Broad: "Hume's general account of what is involved in having an idea of so-and-so is, and can be shown to be rubbish."[2] Such judgments are common and not without reason. But the interpretation of a past thinker is not simply a matter of sifting out true from false propositions. Even granting that a theory, as it stands, is false, there may still be a rationale behind the theory which is worth exploring either because it contains a philosophically interesting error or because it contains an important insight capable of further development. I think both of these things are true of Hume's first principle. In this and the next chapter, I want to examine the principle in some detail both for its philosophical value and, more important, for the light it can throw on the structure and presuppositions of Hume's philosophy of common life. To do this, it will be instructive to work through the two most important criticisms of the principle.

The first criticism is based on what I shall call the private-language interpretation. In this interpretation, Hume identified ideas with private mental images and these with the meanings of words. The principle of the priority of impressions to ideas is taken to be an empirical generalization about the origins of mental imagery, and, given the identification of imagery with meaning, a ground for a criterion of how words have meaning. However, the meanings of words are not private mental images, for if they were, communication would be impossible. Communication presupposes the availability of a public world by reference to which words can have meaning. To understand the meaning of a word, it is necessary to know only to which public objects the word can and cannot be applied. The theory of meaning, then, based on the principle of the priority of impressions to ideas, commits Hume to a theory of language (later exploded by Wittgenstein) according to which public language must somehow be constructed out of private language, the terms of which refer only to private mental images.

This sort of interpretation has been advanced by, among others, Antony Flew and Jonathan Bennett. Flew writes: "The first thing to appreciate is that in Hume's official view ideas always just are mental images. Furthermore, the meanings of words are ideas, ideas again being identified with mental images."[3] And Bennett: "his equation of meaning with ideas is hopelessly wrong."[4] The evidence for this interpretation consists of passages where Hume identifies ideas with mental images, describing them as "the faint images" of impressions "in thinking and reasoning" (T, 1), and of passages where Hume *seems* to identify meanings with ideas, as when he considers whether "a philosophical term is employed without any meaning or idea" (EU, 22). Although supportive, such passages do not show conclusively that Hume identified the meanings of words with private mental images. The trouble is that Hume simply does not work out a theory of how words have meaning; so there is no "official" doctrine that the meanings of words are private mental images. Hume certainly talks at times as if meanings are private mental images, but, as we shall see later, he also talks as if they are not. The identification of ideas (which, in any case, need not be meanings) with private mental images is more persuasive, but even here one must be careful. The perspective of true philosophy defended at the end of book I entitles him to a physicalistic use of mental concepts. So even mental images can have a physicalistic public interpretation. And Hume does in fact treat them that way, going so far in the *Treatise* as to interpret association-relations physiologically and to locate ideas in the brain (T, 60-61).

The philosophical perplexities concerning language and meaning that lie behind the private-language interpretation belong only to the twentieth century and in particular to the space between the early and later Wittgenstein. We must be very careful about reading such problems into Hume's work while at the same time leaving open the possibility that analogues to these latter-day problems of language and meaning may be found there. Still, Flew rightly observes that, unlike "his classical predecessors as Plato or Hobbes or Locke or Berkeley, Hume seems himself to have had little interest in or respect for any questions which he thought of as semantic . . . The icebergs of his own assumptions about language therefore make little show about the surface."[5] They are, however, very near the surface, and with some care, an outline can be made out.

What were Hume's main assumptions about language? To answer this question, Flew (as so many others have done when faced with a problem of interpreting Hume) turns to Locke, who devoted book 3 of the *Essay* to the topic "Of Words." "Hume is and always must be the supreme authority on Hume. Yet, precisely because Hume was not so much interested [in the problems of language], it is Locke's statement which provides the sharper picture of the assumptions Hume inherited."[6] Bennett also reads Hume in a Lockean framework: "Hume's view of meaning is essentially Locke's: to understand a word is to associate it with a kind of 'idea', and 'ideas' are quasi-sensory states."[7]

Locke certainly was committed to some version of the private-language thesis: "It is a perverting the use of words, and brings . . . obscurity and confusion into their signification, whenever we make them stand for anything but those ideas we have in our own minds," and "no one hath the power to make others have the same ideas in their minds that he has, when they use the same words that he does."[8] Once Hume is read in this way the private-language interpretation becomes irresistible.

Reading Locke's theory of meaning into Hume is simply a contemporary version of the older interpretation of Hume as a phenomenalist. This comes out clearly when Flew, for instance, reconstructs the first principle to bring it in line with contemporary logical empiricism, of which he distinguishes two kinds: a subjective form which is phenomenalist and an objective form which is physicalist. According to Flew, Hume's own considered position is more akin to the former, though he admits that there are occasional hints at something like the latter. "Subjective logical empiricism is *phenomenalist*. It insists that propositions—in this case material thing propositions—can only have meaning insofar as they are logical constructions out of, and can therefore be derived from categorical or hypothetical statements about impressions or sense data."[9] It is "an approach to language, and hence to philosophy, which is wholly inverted."[10] Instead of explicating what is logically private by reference to a world of public objects, it begins in the other and impossible way of explicating the public world by reference to logically private experiences.

But the phenomenalist reading is, as we saw in chapter 1, fundamentally mistaken. Hume explicitly rejected phenomenalism and its conceptual parent, the doctrine of double existence. Writing of the guiding principle of the former, that "colours, sounds, tastes, and smells" are "merely perceptions" in the mind, he says that "instead of explaining the operations of external objects by its means, we utterly annihilate all these objects, and reduce ourselves to the opinions of the most extravagant scepticism concerning them" (T, 227-28). Hume's own considered position is the perspective of "true philosophy": had philosophers "fallen upon the just conclusion, they wou'd have return'd back to the situation of the vulgar" (T, 223).

It is remarkable that Hume's true philosophy is much the same as the objective logical empiricism that Flew defends: "The subjective version takes *experience* to be equivalent to 'the perceptions of the mind', Locke's ideas, Hume's ideas and impressions, or even more narrowly, sense data. . . . The objective version construes *experience* in a more exoteric and popular way as a matter of seeing, doing, learning, suffering, and all the other things which might ordinarily be said to constitute a man's experience of the world. It too insists that every proposition we can understand must be explicable in terms of actual or possible experience; but in this very different, entirely untechnical, and not purely subjective reading of the word."[11] This is essentially no different from Hume's world of common life with its external and internal aspects.

Experiences are "perceptions of the mind" but Hume does not think of these as logically private. In book III, he once again observes "that nothing is ever present to the mind but its perceptions; and that all the actions of seeing, hearing, judging, loving, hating, and thinking, fall under this denomination. The mind can never exert itself in any action, which we may not comprehend under the term of *perception*" (T, 456). But in saying this, Hume is not saying that the actions are perceptions (in the sense of logically private mental images); he is saying, rather, that we are to understand perceptions to include actions conceived of in the common way. And because perceptions can be thought of in a physicalist context, the actions of one mind can be public to another. Hume is quite clear on this: "So close and intimate is the correspondence of human souls that no sooner any person approaches me, then he diffuses on me all his opinions, and draws along my judgment in a greater or lesser degree" (T, 592). Locke, by contrast, holds that the perceptions of the mind are in themselves logically private existences: "Man, though he have a great variety of thoughts, and such from which others as well as himself might receive profit and delight; yet they are all within his own breast, invisible and hidden from others, nor can of themselves be made to appear"[12] No passage comparable to this is to be found in any of Hume's writings. He makes it clear that the perceptions of the mind are public: "a rational and thinking Being like ourselves . . . communicates to us all the actions of his mind; makes us privy to his inmost sentiments and affections; and lets us see, in the very instant of their production, all the emotions, which are caus'd by any object" (T, 353). "We can form no wish, which has not a reference to society" (T, 363). And more generally, it is not possible to have a concept of ourselves that does not make reference to public objects: "Ourself, independent of the perception of every other object, is in reality nothing: For which reason we must turn our view to external objects" (T, 340). So far removed from Locke is Hume's approach.

The inverted approach to philosophy which takes the private experience of one man as the standard of intelligibility and knowledge is a feature not only of phenomenalism but also of the modern tradition of philosophy going back to Descartes. Between Descartes' introspective, egocentric method for investigating the passions and Hume's historical, public method, a conceptual revolution in philosophy has occurred, In *The Passions of the Soul*, Descartes points out that the study of the passions has a certain advantage over other subjects "inasmuch as since everyone has experience of the passions within himself, there is no necessity to borrow one's observations from elsewhere in order to discover their nature."[13] Hume, by contrast, finds a special difficulty in an introspective study of the passions and recommends that they be investigated as they appear in the public world: "Moral philosophy has, indeed, this peculiar disadvantage, which is not found in natural. . . . When I am at a loss to know the effects of one body upon another in any situation, I need only put them in that situation, and observe what results from it. But should I endeavor to clear up . . . any doubt in moral philosophy, by placing myself in the same case with that which I consider, 'tis evident this reflection . . . would so disturb the operation of my natural principles, as must render it impossible to form any just conclusion from the phenomenon. We must therefore glean up our experiments in this science from a cautious observation of human life, and take them as they appear in the common course of the world, by men's behaviour in company, in affairs, and in their pleasures" (T, xviii–xix).

With the collapse of the phenomenalist reading, the private-language interpretation loses all its force. That interpretation, we recall, consists of two theses: (1) that ideas are nothing but logically private mental images and (2) that the meanings of words are ideas. We have seen that (1) is false: ideas are internal to the public world of common life, and, therefore, admit of different sorts of physical interpretation including the extreme possibility that identifies them with motions in the brain. The second thesis is so far undetermined because Hume did not develop a theory of how words have meaning. If the phenomenalist reading were correct, then Hume's conceptual framework would, indeed, be mainly a modification of Locke's and it would then be reasonable to assume that something very like Locke's theory of language is a background assumption of the first principle. But if the phenomenalist reading is wrong, as I have argued it is, then we really have no reason at all to read a Lockean theory of language into Hume and so no reason to accept the private-language interpretation.

Although Hume did not present a theory of how words have meaning, there are scattered throughout his writings many remarks on the nature of language and its role in philosophical discourse. Moreover, these remarks are not idle comments but occur at crucial places where important theses of Hume's philosophy are being developed. From these passages we can gain some idea of what Hume's views on language are. This in turn will enable us to understand some of the presuppositions about language that underly the rationale of the first principle. We shall then be in a position to give a final assessment of the private-language interpretation.

## THE NATURAL HISTORY OF LANGUAGE

Hume's most important remarks on the nature of language occur where we might expect, in book III and in the *Enquiry* on morals where he discusses men as united in society and dependent on one another. In both works he puts forth the thesis that "speech and words and language are fixed by human convention and agreement" (EM, 306). As often understood, the concept of "convention" entails a mutual promise, and in this view language could not have arisen from a convention since conventions would presuppose language. But Hume means something different by "convention"; it is, for him, a technical term and one of the most important in his philosophy. It can best be introduced by considering its role in his account of the origin of justice.

The sense of "justice and injustice is not derived from nature, but arises artifically, tho' necessarily from education, and human conventions" (T, 483). His account runs roughly as follows. Given a scarcity of goods and limited human benevolence, men, through painful experience, soon discover the advantages of society and, with this, rules for governing the transference of goods. Hume thinks there are three such rules: the stability of possession, its transference by consent, and the performance of promises. These rules are not the result of conscious reflection or of a promise; they are not "adopted" by a kind of constitutional convention of property. They arise gradually over time as people insensibly discover the disadvantages of deviating from them. They become established when a general awareness develops of the utility of the rules and of mutual confidence in adhering to them. Eventually the rules themselves become objects of reflection; we recognize their social utility and celebrate adherence to them as virtue and deviatian from them as vice. Speaking of the rules of justice, Hume writes: "This convention is not of the nature of a *promise:* For even promises themselves . . . arise from human conventions. It is only a general sense of common interest; which sense all the members of the society express to one another, and which induces them to regulate their conduct by certain rules. . . . When this common sense of interest is mutually express'd, and is known to both, it produces a suitable resolution and behaviour. And this may properly enough be call'd a convention or agreement betwixt us, tho' without the interposition of a promise; since the actions of each of us have a reference to those of the other, and are perform'd upon the supposition, that something is to be perform'd on the other part. . . . And 'tis only on the expectation of this, that our moderation and abstinence are founded. In like manner are languages gradually establish'd by human conventions without any promise. In like manner do gold and silver become the common measures of exchange" (T, 490).

Human conventions, then, in Hume's sense are natural processes whereby social rules are hammered out unreflectively over time, yielding "a sense of common interest; which sense each man feels in his own breast, which he marks in his fellows, and which carries him, in concurrence with others, into a general plan or system of actions, which tend to public utility" (EM, 306).

Hume rejected the state-of-nature outlook on man. Born into some sort of tacit convention between the sexes, "his very first state and situation may justly be esteem'd social" (T, 493). The convention of language developed to satisfy the human need to communicate about our nonlinguistic involvement with the world. But it is not a uniquely human convention: "Several expressions of our passions contain a universal language: All brute animals have a natural speech, which, however limited, is very intelligible to their own species" (D, 153). The convention of language presupposes at least (1) that we (and other animals to a limited degree) can recognize intentional behavior in ourselves and others and (2) that there is a public world by reference to which linguistic utterances are meaningful. Without a standpoint shared with others, communication about the world is impossible: " 'twere impossible we cou'd ever make use of language, or communicate our sentiments to one another, did we not correct the momentary appearances of things, and overlook our present situation" (T, 582). Here language is specified by rules framed in human conventions which constitute an objective order of discourse. The egocentric approach to language is explicitly rejected and, of course, by implication the view that the meanings of words are private mental images. If, for instance, we are to make judgments about what is just and unjust, we must learn those conditions under which it is proper to say "I have a right to X" as opposed to "I want X." The former is an objective judgment, the latter a subjective one. We learn the difference by being participants in the convention of justice: " 'tis impossible we cou'd ever converse together on any reasonable terms, were each of us to consider characters and persons, only as they appear from his peculiar point of view. In order, therefore, to prevent those continual *contradictions*, and arrive at a more *stable* judgment of things, we fix on some *steady* and *general* points of view. . . . these variations we regard not in our general decisions, but still apply the terms expressive of our liking or dislike, in the same manner, as if we remain'd in one point of view. Experience soon teaches us this method of correcting our sentiments, or at least, of correcting our language, where the sentiments are more stubborn and inalterable" (T, 581-582). And again, "The intercourse of sentiments, therefore, in society and conversation, makes us form some general inalterable standards, by which we may approve or disapprove of characters and manners. And tho' the *heart* does not always take part with those general notions, or regulate its love and hatred by them, yet are they sufficient for discourse, and serve all our purposes in company, in the pulpit, in the theatre, and in the schools" (T, 603).

Should we say that we have a right to X when it is obvious that we merely want X, a conflict in communication will occur. Those party to the convention of justice will say either that we do not know how to apply the predicates "right" and "want" or, what is more likely, that we are disingenuous. It is not only virtuous to abstain from the property of others, it is also virtuous to use moral language properly. The convention of justice depends on it.[14]

The convention of justice and the language of justice are not separable; they are internally connected parts of the order of justice and neither can exist without the other. Our private sentiments and interests give the convention life, but it is the "inalterable standard" framed in moral language that disciplines these sentiments and shapes them into an objective order of justice: "When a man denominates another his *enemy*, his *rival*, his *antagonist*, his *adversary*, he is understood to speak the language of self-love. . . . But when he bestows on any man the epithets of *vicious* or *odious* or *depraved*, he then speaks another language, and expresses sentiments, in which he expects all his audience are to concur with him. He must here, therefore, depart from his private situation . . . and must choose a point of view, common to him with others" (EM, 272). Although the convention of justice would not exist without sentiments of approval and disapproval, the convention is best known not by trying to investigate, as Locke would have it, private sentiments within a man's "own breast, invisible and hidden from others," but by an analysis of moral language. The distinction between sentiments of self-love and public regard "being so great and evident, language must soon be moulded upon it, and must invent a peculiar set of terms, in order to express those universal sentiments of censure or approbation, which arise from humanity, or from views of general usefulness and its contrary. Virtue and Vice *become then known;* morals are recognized; certain general ideas are framed of human conduct and behaviour. . . . And by such universal principles are the particular sentiments of self-love frequently controlled and limited" (EM, 274, emphasis added; cf., 229).

Moral language is not used merely to express our self-consciousness about the convention of morality, it is rather that self-consciousness about the convention of morality is achieved through the use of moral language. When Hume comes to analyze "that complication of mental qualities, which form what, in common life, we call Personal Merit," into those that are virtues and those that are vices, his objects are not psychological entities but mental concepts determined by the use of words: "The very nature of language guides us almost infallibly in forming a judgment of this nature; and as every tongue possesses one set of words which are taken in a good sense, and another in the opposite, the least acquaintance with the idiom suffices, without any reasoning, to direct us in collecting and arranging the estimable or blameable qualities of men" (EM, 174).

One is not a participant in the convention of morality unless one has learned the public conditions for applying moral terms, that is, what Hume calls the "common point of view" (EM, 272). All who are party to the convention, then, must in understanding moral language necessarily understand the norms internal to the common point of view that makes such language possible. It is for this reason that there is and must be, Hume thinks, virtually unanimous agreement about general moral precepts. He observes that for those who found morality on reason this "great unanimity is usually ascribed to the influence of plain reason, which, in all these cases, maintains similar sentiments in all men" (E, 232). Hume grants that where unanimity extends to particular cases, many do and must have a rational grasp of the convention as "a general plan or system of actions, which tends to public utility" (EM, 306). But the wide agreement in morals is limited to general moral prinicples, not to particular cases, and is due not to reason but to "the very nature of language. The word *virtue*, with its equivalent in every tongue, implies praise, as that of *vice* does blame; and no one, without the most obvious and grossest impropriety, could affix reproach to a term, which in general acceptation is understood in a good sense: or bestow applause where the idiom requires disapprobation" (E, 232-33). Hume holds, then, that moral principles are true by virtue of the rules for applying the terms that constitute them; they are, as we would say, analytic: "The merit of delivering true general precepts in ethics is indeed very small. Whoever recommends any moral virtues, really does no more than is implied in the terms themselves" (ibid. 233-34). The true force of moral norms is to be found in the rules for applying moral language, which in turn expresses and makes possible the historically developing convention of morality: "people who invented the word *charity*, and used it in a good sense, inculcated more clearly, and much more efficaciously, the precept, *Be charitable*, than any pretended legislator or prophet, who should insert such a *maxim* in his writings" (E, 234).

Language and morality are not the only conventions Hume discusses. There is a convention of aesthetic judgment. And there is even a convention of judgment about external objects: Hume buttresses his account of moral standards as conventions by arguing that "The case is here the same as in our judgments concerning external bodies" (T, pp. 603, 582). And we may note again the incompatibility of Hume's thought with phenomenalism. An external object (like a moral object, e.g., and unjust act) is not a set of sense experiences directly presented and organized by the mind. Rather, the public convention of external objects is internal to our sense experience. The convention is not the result of something done with our sense experience; rather, our sense experience is what it is because of the convention. One important discovery arrived at in the dialectical struggle between the popular and philosophical system and a corner-stone of post-Pyrrhonian philosophy is that the faculty of sense can no longer be considered independently of the imagination: "I begun this subject with premising, that we ought to have an implicit faith in our senses," but Hume is now "inclin'd to repose no faith at all in my senses, or rather imagination" (T, 217). Throughout the *Treatise*, Hume stresses the importance that the general rules which constitute the conventions of common life have in structuring our experience of the world: "our adherence to *general rules* . . . has such a mighty influence on the actions and understanding, and is able to impose on the very senses" (T, 374). With these remarks, we already have the beginning of what Kant was later to call the Copernican revolution in philosophy.

The whole moral world is viewed by Hume as a system of historically developed conventions, unconsciously contrived to satisfy various human needs. More specifically, the conventions arise out of a need to reconcile conflicting sentiments and judgments and are established when there is mutual recognition of a settled point of view whereby conflicts can be reconciled: "'tis impossible men cou'd ever agree in their sentiments and judgments, unless they chose some common point of view, from which they might survey their object, and which might cause it to appear the same to all of them" (T, 591). Each convention, then, presupposes a settled point of view which constitutes an order of objectivity within which there is an attempt to satisfy some human need in society. There is the moral point of view, the aesthetic point of view, the natural point of view (the internal and external world of common life, the objects of which are causally connected), the historical point of view whereby we are able to view past events in "their true colours, without any of those disguises which, during their lifetime, so much perplexed the judgment of the beholders" (E, 560). There is a religious point of view in which we try to reach settled beliefs and attitudes towards the ultimate origin of things, and there is finally a philosophical point of view, a convention that has developed from critically reflecting on all conventions.

The value of all conventions is social utility, which is the reason why they exist in the first place. The convention of religion, though contrived to satisfy social needs, is usually socially destructive. Similarly, the convention of philosophy, governed by the principles of autonomy and ultimacy, is not only socially destructive but self-destructive as well. And we have seen that the main point of post-Pyrrhonian philosophy is to reform the unsettled and unsettling convention of philosophy by purging it of these self-destructive and socially dangerous effects. The task of reformed philosophy is not to constitute new conventions, as it were, from a position of autonomy but to empirically and analytically uncover those standards or points of view that inform the actual conventions that make up the whole of common life, to methodize them and to bring them into some sort of mutually coherent order (EU, 162).

All the conventions of common life participate in the convention of language, understood in a broad sense to include animal speech as well as verbal behavior. Every convention is constituted by a language, and the rules for applying the language express the essential norms of the convention. One fertile source of philosophical error is due to the autonomy principle, which pretends to place the philosopher, logically, outside all conventions. But philosophical discourse outside of all conventions would be totally uninteresting and arbitrary. What philosophers typically do is to use a term from an established convention in contexts which do not satisfy the commonly received conditions of application. The result is conceptual confusion and always at the expense of the convention. Religious language affords a case of such confusion. Theologians will apply a term such as "just," which has application in the human convention of justice, to a super-natural being whose nature is such that those conditions cannot be satisfied. The result in such cases is that our ideas are "confounded by prejudice and the fallacious use of language" (T, 517). The doctrine of double existence is another instance of the same error. An ordinary term like "table" is used in a philosophical context, yielding the paradoxical ontological conclusion that real tables have no sensory properties. Addressing just such errors, Hume remarks in a passage reminiscent of the later Wittgenstein that "Nothing is more usual than for philosophers to encroach upon the province of grammarians, and to engage in disputes of words, while they imagine that they are handling controversies of the deepest importance and concern" (EM, 312). The doctrine of double existence is not a profound ontological thesis but a conceptual confusion brought on, in part, by a misapplication of language. The same is true of the rationalist's conception of necessary connection; the expression "causal connection" is taken out of its ordinary linguistic convention and *wrong apply'd* to a special philosophical context where only confusion can result (T, 162, Hume's emphasis).

In common life, verbal disputes rarely occur since "whenever any Expression or Action becomes customary it can deceive no body" (L, I, 20). It is philosophy guided by the autonomy principle and conceiving itself as an activity outside of established linguistic conventions that uses common words in a "different sense." But what Hume discovered is that philosophy is in fact parasitic upon the established linguistic conventions of common life; so if confusion occurs it is the philosopher who must explain and justify the special way in which he is using words. In this way, what appears as a profound dispute may often degenerate into a matter of rescuing the conventional use of language from an arbitrary and bemusing philosophical context. In one way, disputes brought on by misplaced philosophy are "frivolous," in another way they are morally serious. The conventions that constitute the objective orders of common life (for us the world) are held together by the rules of language. To break these rules or to not show proper repsect for them is to undermine, to some degree, the objectivity of the world and, as a consequence, the possibility of communication and society. As Páll Árdall has especially pointed out, for Hume, "The concept of a responsible language-user is strictly analogous to the concept of a just man. He will neither make irresponsible promises nor say things about the world that will arouse false expectations and therefore disappoint."[15]

## THE RATIONALE OF THE FIRST PRINCIPLE

Hume's first principle—that ideas are derived from past impressions—is not a theory of how words have meaning. Hume does, however, intend for it to be employed as a norm for bringing cognitive order into our use of language. Certain assumptions, therefore, about the nature of language and meaning are presupposed by the principle. The assumptions in question are generated not by Locke's theory of language but by Hume's own ideas as developed especially in book III of the *Treatise* and in the *Enquiry* on morals. These assumptions are not brought out in book I, in part, because of the dialectical, narrative structure of the *Treatise* which requires that we view earlier sections of the work in the light of later sections, but also because book I is mainly concerned with very broad epistemological questions about our knowledge of the physical world, and these problems can and have, traditionally, been discussed in abstraction from the historical and social conditions which make language and knowledge possible. The view of book III that language is a convention, a historically developed set of rules (not necessarily formulated) which enable participants in the convention to communicate and to achieve common goals is presupposed in book I. In book III and in the *Enquiry* on morals, language is not only treated as a convention but as one which makes possible all the conventions that constitute the moral world. And this view is reflected in Hume's method of doing philosophy. The language that informs a convention is taken to be not only the effect of the psychological and logical structures that constitute it but also the intelligible surface of the convention through which these structures can be understood. In book I, the association relations are viewed as part of the causal conditions of language; they are "the cause why, among other things, languages so nearly correspond to each other; nature in a manner pointing out to every one those simple ideas, which are most proper to be united into a complex one" (T, 10-11). Although Hume does not, in book I, investigate the association-relations through the medium of language, as he investigates moral and aesthetic sentiments and judgments in book III and in the *Enquiry* on morals, such an examination is carried out in the *Enquiry* on understanding. There the theoretical science of man is abandoned for the more modest project of "mental geography" (a descriptive and normative analysis of the ideas employed in our understanding of the world), and the association relations are introduced not as introspective entities but through their effects in historical narration and in epic poetry (EUH, 31-39).

Taken together, Hume's own remarks on language do not at all suggest that he considered the meanings of words to be private mental images. What they do suggest is that we are essentially social beings. The moral world we inhabit is to be viewed as a system of historically developed conventions; our interiors, along with whatever images we may have, become intelligible to us by being ordered in a historical convention which is necessarily public and structured by language. The meanings of words are given by the rules of their use or application in the convention: "in a living language the continual Application of the Words and Phrazes teaches at the same time the Sense of the Words and their Reference to each other" (L, II, 157). Hume was concerned to "follow the common Use of Language" (L, I, 33) in his explication of concepts not only for the sake of intelligibility but also because it is the common use of words that gives order to the ideas that structure the convention: "The very nature of language guides us almost infallibly in forming a judgment of this nature [making moral conceptual distinctions]" (EM, 174).

Hume's challenge to produce the impression from which a purported idea is derived is directed towards terms that are used referentially or descriptively. But many important terms in language (those called syncategorematic such as "is," "of," "not," and the like) do not have a referential meaning. Hume's first principle is not applicable to such terms, nor does he show any interest in analyzing them, but their meaning can be accounted for by reference to Hume's general theory of language whereby the meaning of an expression is determined by the rules for its application in a linguistic convention. Hume's explication of what he considers to be the nonreferential concept of *promising* is a brilliant example of the ends to which his general theory of language can be put. He first observes that the expression "I promise" cannot be taken to refer to any act of the mind, and since there is nothing else it could refer to, there is no impression from which the purported idea of the term could be derived. But Hume does not conclude from this that the term is meaningless, as he would have to if he thought that the meanings of words are ideas. Rather, he tries to uncover its meaning by examining its use in the convention of promise-keeping, taking care to avoid what is merely "a conclusion of philosophy" and keeping close "to our common ways of thinking and of expressing ourselves" (T, 517). The convention of promise-keeping arises from the same principles of human nature that give rise to the convention of justice. There would be no need for promises if there were unlimited goods or unlimited human benevolence. But in a world of conflicting interests and limited benevolence, it is to everyone's interest to have a convenient and reliable form for transferring goods and services. For this reason the words "I promise" developed whereby we bind ourselves to the performance of some future action. "This form of words constitutes what we call a *promise*, which is the sanction of the interested commerce of mankind. When a man says *he promises any thing*, he in effect expresses a *resolution* of performing it; and along with that, by making use of this *form of words*, subjects himself to the penalty of never being trusted again in case of failure" (T, 522). A promise is constituted by nothing other than the proper use of the words "I promise." Hume was one of the first to recognize the "performative" use of language as opposed to its descriptive use. He is aware of the radical and novel character of his analysis: "we cannot readily conceive how the making use of a certain form of words shou'd be able to cause any material difference" (T, 523). That the bonds of moral order should be tied together by a use of words must seem incredible to the rationalistic moral philosopher or even to the empiricist whose model of meaning is typically referential and who, consequently, must try to find some set of experiences or acts of mind to which the expression "I promise" refers. That a use of words can make a promise is "one of the most mysterious and incomprehensible operations that can possibly be imagin'd, and may even be compar'd to *transubstantiation*, or *holy orders*, where a certain form of words, along with a certain intention, changes entirely the nature of an external object, and even of a human creature" (T, 524). Hume then goes on to buttress his case by examining the performative use of language in religion and contrasting its rationale with that of the performative use of language in morality (T, 524-25).

The analysis of the language of promising is additional evidence that Hume did not think that the meanings of words are private mental images; nor is this analysis an isolated insight, incompatible with what might be taken as his "official" Lockean view of how words have meaning. The analysis of the linguistic convention of promising occurs in the context where Hume is stating his own ideas on language. It is because Hume holds the theory of language he does that the highly original analysis of promising is possible. Moreover, the analysis is made in full view of the first principle and is explicitly presented as a case which restricts its applicability. But Hume considers "I promise" to be a non-referential expression. What of referential expressions? Here there is no doubt that Hume considered imagery to be involved in some way in the meanings of such expressions. The question we must now ask is how is imagery involved and why does Hume think it necessary for understanding the meanings of referential expressions?

Let us begin with the analysis of the origins of abstract general terms such as "red," "x causes y," and the like. After a resemblance among several objects, we "apply the same name to all of them . . . whatever differences may appear among them" (T, 20). A custom is set up of associating the term with the set of resembling objects, so that upon hearing the word, the imagination brings up an image of one of the objects "along with a certain custom" which can produce if necessary the images of the other objects of the set to which the term applies (T, 20-21). In any given use of the term, only one image is present. The images of the remaining objects to which the term applies exist in the mind in the form of a disposition, habit, or power: "They are not really and in fact present to the mind, but only in *power*" (T, 20, emphasis added). So the meaning of the term is not identical to the image that is called up in any particular application of the term. The meaning of the term is the *custom* framed in some linguistic convention of applying the term to resembling objects along with the capacity to form mental imagery of the appropriate sort on the occasion of using the term. The meaning of a term does not change by having different images annexed to it as long as those images are of the resembling set. Moreover, the same image may be attached without confusion to words having different meanings: "Thus the idea of an equilateral triangle of an inch perpendicular may serve us in talking of a figure, of a rectilineal figure, of a regular figure, of a triangle, and of an equilateral triangle" (T, 21).

Hume also grants that in "talking of *government, church, negotiation, conquest,*" we seldom form adequate images. "'Tis however observable, that notwithstanding this imperfection we may avoid talking nonsense on these subjects, and may perceive any repugnance among the ideas, as well as if we had a full comprehension of them" (T, 23). This can be done by knowing how to apply the rules of the linguistic convention.

CHAPTER THREE

"Thus if instead of saying, *that in war the weaker have always recourse to negotiation*, we shou'd say, *that they have always recourse to conquest*, the custom, which we have acquir'd of attributing certain relations to ideas, still follows the words, and makes us immediately perceive the absurdity of that proposition" (ibid.) Here the burden of meaning is carried by the rules that govern the use of words—images or the capacity to form images being completely irrelevant. Similarly, "when we mention any great number, such as a thousand, the mind has generally *no adequate idea* of it, but only a *power* of producing such an idea by its adequate idea of the decimals, under which the number is comprehended" (T, 22-23, emphasis added). Hume does not explain what could be meant by an "adequate idea of the decimals," but the general point of the passage seems to be that we have the ability to count and that to understand the meaning of numerical expressions is to be able to understand and follow the rules for counting that are the conditions for applying the numerical expression in question. If so, then, the meaning of a numerical expression is not necessarily a mental image or even the capacity to form a mental image but rather the capacity to perform an operation laid down by the linguistic convention of mathematics. It is true that this operation presupposes an imaginary grasp of small numbers but the fact remains that large numbers have no corresponding images, complex or otherwise. A similar account holds for the idea of God "as meaning an infinitely intelligent, wise, and good being"; such an idea "arises from reflecting on the operations of our own mind, and augmenting, without limit, those qualities of goodness or wisdom" (EU,19).

The above passages show that the theory of language in book III is presupposed in book I. Language is a convention developed to satisfy the social need to communicate our sentiments, beliefs, and intentions. Language makes possible the many social conventions that constitute the moral world. To be a party to a convention is to know how to apply correctly the rules of the language which inform it, and the criteria for applying these rules are and must be public: what Hume calls "some *steady* and *general* points of view" (T, 581-82). The possibility of such a public world, so important for books II and III, is contained in Hume's justification of the world of common life presented in book I.

But along with this public and institutional way of viewing language and the meanings of words, Hume still insists on the presence of imagery or the capacity to form imagery as an important condition for understanding referential expressions. In a passage quoted above he grants that "we may avoid talking nonsense" when using expressions for which we have no adequate image, by following the public rules for the correct application of the words, but he does not consider the ability to apply a term correctly in a public language to be identical with understanding the meaning of the term. He describes such understand-ing as an "imperfection" and so as adequate only to a certain degree. Likewise, Hume's "operational" account of the meaning of numerical expressions is due to the fact that "when we mention any great number, such as a thousand, the mind has generally no adequate idea of it" (T, 23). This suggests that the operational account is a second-best affair, not yielding the sort of understanding we would really like to have. But then Hume adds significantly: "This imperfection, however, in our ideas, is never felt in our reasonings" (ibid.). In short, our reasonings in mathematics can go on whatever the state of perfection of the mental imagery we would like to associate with them.

But if Hume is prepared to go this far, why should he insist that having mental imagery has anything at all to do with possessing a con-cept or idea of something? To answer this question let us begin with the sense in which we may be said to have a concept of something without having any mental imagery. We may be said to have the concept of "red" if we can understand the meaning of the word "red," and we understand the meaning of the word if we can satisfy the public criteria for applying it to objects. For this, it is not necessary to have or to be able to form mental imagery. Thus a man born blind and presumably without mental imagery or the capacity to form it can learn, perhaps with the aid of instruments, to apply the word "red" correctly, and so can be said to have the concept of "red." Now there is no reason at all to think that Hume would want to deny this account as far as it goes. Indeed, his own explicit view of language as an insensibly contrived convention contains just such an account of how words have meaning. Moreover, Hume does hold that mastering the public criteria for apply-ing a term is a *necessary condition* for meaningful discourse (as discussed above, it is in this way that "we may avoid talking nonsense" even when there is not adequate imagery). But this is, he thinks, only *part* of what it is to have an idea of something. Consider the following passage: "We cannot form to ourselves a *just idea* of the taste of a pine-apple, without having actually tasted it" (T, 5, emphasis added). When Hume is applying his first principle, it is never simply an either/or question of whether we do or do not have an idea of something, but of whether we have a "just idea," or "adequate idea," or "perfect idea" as opposed to an inadequate or imperfect idea. Hume uses the word "idea" in two senses. In one sense an idea is an image, in which case we may be said to either have an idea or not (it is in this sense that Hume can say, for instance, that we have no idea at all of necessary connection). But in another sense having an idea is being able to follow a rule in a linguistic convention, as when Hume says that we have no "adequate idea" or "full comprehension" of large numbers (T, 23). It is not that we have no idea at all; we have *some* idea of large numbers (the idea given in the

77

ability to perform a mathematical operation), but it is not an adequate conception because it lacks appropriate imagery.

By looking again at the pineapple example we can begin to understand why Hume thinks imagery is required. Suppose one can correctly apply the expression "taste of pineapple" in all contexts but has never actually tasted the fruit. Such a person would, in a very important sense, be said to understand the meaning of the expression and to have a concept of the taste. But in another, equally important sense, he could not be said to have an adequate conception of the taste of pineapple, for although he has learned to apply the expression to others, he has not learned what it means to apply the expression to himself. He does not know himself what it is to taste pineapple and so does not have what can be called an interior understanding of the concept. Having tasted the fruit, he will come to have for the first time an interior grasp of the concept. He will now know what others have experienced and will be able to view all his past ascriptions of the expression to others as cases of a merely external understanding of the concept. It is some such view as this that Hume has in mind when he insists that no one has a "just idea" of the taste of pineapple unless he has tasted it. It is not enough to be able to apply the expression "taste of pineapple" to others. We must also achieve an internal mastery of the expression by learning how to apply it to ourselves, and for this we need an experience of the taste. Hume calls such an experience an impression, and the reflection on it, in recollection and thinking, an idea or image.

Hume's view on what it is to have an idea of something can now be stated. Ideas exist only in the context of some social convention: abstract ideas (or rather *terms*), Hume says, were contrived to "serve the purposes of life" (T, 20). To have an idea of X we must be able to apply correctly the term "X" to objects that satisfy the public criteria for being cases of X. But this is not enough. In order to have a "full," "adequate," or "perfect," concept of X, we must, in addition, understand what it means to apply "X" to our own experience. We must achieve both an external and an internal understanding of X. It is because he thinks an interior understanding of concepts is essential that Hume stresses the importance of imagery. But this does not mean that his method is phenomenalistic and that he has an inverted approach to language and philosophy, hopelessly trying to build a public world out of private mental images or public language out of private language. As we have seen, the persepctive of true philosophy with its "internal and external world," along with the physicalistic interpretation of the internal and the theory of the origin of language as an historically developed social convention, are the frameworks within which we must appreciate any Humean theory of an interior understanding of concepts.

The distinction between an external and an internal understanding of concepts is not one that Hume consciously made and defended. Indeed, he could not have done so, for the distinction is a response to certain problems in the philosophy of language peculiar to the twentieth century, problems Hume could not have had. Still, the distinction is one that occurs in Hume's work in a systematic way. With it we are able to link the first principle with (1) Hume's remarks on the nature of language and (2) his explication of the internal and external world of common life, thus achieving a relatively coherent whole. And this, in turn, enables us to view the three Books of the *Treatise* as a unity. By contrast, the phenomenalistic and private-language interpretations of the first principle render it incompatible with (1) and (2). It is this sort of reading that has led to the practice of viewing book I as a form of "radical empiricism," ending in total skepticism (and so the philosophically most interesting part of the *Treatise*) but mysteriously disconnected from the less popular and more commonsensical books II and III.

The external understanding of a concept (the ability to apply correctly expressions to objects in a public language) is a necessary condition for the internal understanding. Hume's attention, however, is largely absorbed with the latter. And it is this fact, I think, that, in large part, explains why Hume has been read so often as a phenomenalist and why the private-language interpretation of the first principle could appear reasonable. Was Hume justified in giving the importance he did to the internal understanding of concepts?

Many concepts admit of an interior grasp, concepts such as pain, love, humility. All experiential concepts are of this sort as are all concepts that apply to our experience of physical objects such as "red," "loud," and "hot." In general, any concept that applies to an object of direct experience admits of an internal understanding. But not all concepts are of this sort. Theoretical concepts such as "meson," "gravitational field," "unconscious mental process," and the like purport to refer to entities which are not thought of as having experiential properties. Since we cannot directly experience the objects which these concepts are about, an internal understanding of them is impossible. The value of Hume's first principle is that it calls to attention the fact that many concepts *do* require an internal understanding for their full comprehension. But just for this reason it can throw little light on how to understand theoretical concepts. And Hume himself makes no real attempt to understand them. He does discuss the concept of "causal power," and he concludes that we have no "idea" of it, that is, we have no internal understanding. But he does not conclude from this that causal expressions are meaningless as he would have to if he thought that the meanings of words are private mental images. Rather, " 'tis more probable, that these expressions do here lose their true meaning by being *wrong apply'd* than that they never have any meaning" (T, 162). Hume then goes on to seek the "true meaning" of causal expressions by a critical analysis of the procedures used in making causal ascriptions in common life. (Hume's explication of causal connection is discussed in some detail in chapter 6.)

There is, in the meantime, only one passage and that a footnote where Hume attempts to explain how theoretical expressions used in the science of his time can be meaningful. We have no "idea" or "image" of gravity or of the *vis inertiae* "so much talked of in the new philosophy" (EU, 73n), but that does not mean that talk about such structures is nonsense. On the contrary, there are empirically established procedures for applying the expressions in question: "We find by experience, that a body at rest or in motion continues forever in its present state, till put from it by some new cause; and that a body impelled takes as much motion from the impelling body as it acquires itself. These are facts. When we call this a *vis inertiae*, we only mark these facts, without pretending to have any idea of the inert power; in the same manner as, when we talk of gravity, we mean certain effects, without comprehending that active power" (ibid.). What is remarkable about this passage is that Hume is more interested in showing that we *do not* have an internal understanding of gravity and the *vis inertaie* than he is in explaining the external understanding he admits we do have. And what he does say by way of explanation cannot support a phenomenalistic analysis of theoretical concepts. To explain inertial power by reference to "a body impelled" is to explicate one power in terms of another power, hardly a phenomenalistic move. The most we have are two claims: (1) there is no imaginary or internal grasp of the concepts picked out by such expressions as "gravity" and "inertia," but (2) such terms are not nonsense since their application to the world can be cognitively disciplined by public empirical criteria ("These are facts."). But as to precisely how this discipline works, Hume simply does not inquire (whereas, by contrast, Berkeley did).[16]

There are hints, however, as to how Hume would account for the meaningfulness of theoretical expressions. The doctrine of relative ideas occurs as an obvious candidate. A relative idea as understood by Locke, Berkeley, and Hume picks out an unperceivable entity on the basis of the relations it bears to perceived entities. Locke held that we have no empirical idea of substance but only "an obscure and relative idea of Substance in general." Likewise, Hume held that although we cannot form an idea of external objects specifically different from perceptions, we can form a relative idea: "The farthest we can go towards a conception of external objects, when suppos'd *specifically* different from our perceptions, is to form a relative idea of them, without pretending to comprehend the related objects" (T, 68; cf. 241). Hume also held that we have a relative idea of causal power as an unperceivable entity constantly conjoined with perceived effects (EU, 77n).

To have cognitive value, a Humean relative idea must satisfy at least one condition: the relations holding between the empirical idea and the unperceivable relata must be one of the seven philosophical relations (T, 13-15). We can have relative ideas of physical objects in terms of the relations of resemblance and causation holding between a perception and the object. We can also have a relative idea of causal power as a relation of constant conjunction between a perception and the causal power. But we cannot have a relative idea of substance because the relation of "inhesion" of qualities in a substance cannot be explicated in terms of the seven philosophical relations (T, 234).

Donald Flage has explored Hume's brief and undeveloped remarks on relative ideas and has argued that the distinction between ideas as copies of impressions and relative ideas is analogous to Russell's distinction between knowledge by acquaintance and knowledge by description. Moreover, a prototype of the theory of descriptions is to be found in the widely read logical writings of Antoine Arnaud and Isaac Watts with which Hume was presumably familiar. If we may interpret relative ideas as doing the work of the theory of descriptions, then Hume could claim to have knowledge by description of theoretical entities specifically different from perceptions.

The concept of relative ideas can also throw light on why Hume found the missing shade of blue unproblematic and how he could hold that we have an idea of the thousandth part of a grain of sand even though the image of it is not inferior to the image formed of the grain of sand itself (T, 27). The idea of the thousandth part of the grain of sand is a relative idea composed of the image of the grain of sand related by the philosophical relation of proportions of quantity and number to its thousandth part.

Curiously, although Hume had the concept of relative ideas and can be interpreted as having employed it in his work, he does not develop it, nor does he display it as an important part of his system: It seems to operate in the background as something everyone understands but which Hume has no interest in discussing.

Hume's sheer lack of interest in the conceptual problems of theoretical science and of theoretical physics in particular (despite all of his ritualistic Newtonianism), and his thoroughgoing preoccupation with an interior understanding of concepts, is due, I think, to the fact that he is essentially a moral philosopher, a historian, and a man of letters. [17] The moral world presupposes that "internal and external" world of common life. But the moral philosopher is interested in the physical only as a structure that makes the internal world possible. The moral philosopher is a student of interiors. Hume makes this clear in the very first pages of the *Treatise*. He is not primarily concerned to examine our sense perception of the world. That objects are perceived is important to him only because of what perceiving them (or thinking one perceives them) can *mean* to someone. For this reason the main object of investigation in the *Treatise* is, as Hume goes out of his way to say, not our sense impressions but what these mean to us, that is, our "impressions of reflexion, viz. passions, desires, and emotions," and these "arise mostly from ideas" (T, 8).

For Hume, the paradigm of concept formation is derived from moral philosophy which, as a study of interiors, requires an internal understanding of concepts. Hume, however, extends the paradigm beyond moral philosophy to theoretical physics and mathematics, with the result that the concepts distinctively employed there are viewed as "inadequate," "not just," and "imperfect." In moral philosophy, however, we not only have an external understanding of concepts provided by the public rules for applying experiential predicates in the linguistic conventions of common life, we can also have an internal understanding of such predicates and so a "just idea" of them. For example, instead of following the rationalistic method of giving a definition of the passions of pride and humility, Hume contents himself with the more vulgar method of giving "a description of them, by an enumeration of such circumstances, as attend them" (T, 277). Such a procedure is justified in terms of both external and internal criteria: since "these words, *pride* and *humility*, are of *general use*, and the impressions they represent the most common of any, every one, of himself, will be able to form a just idea of them, without any danger of mistake" (T, 277, 399, emphasis mine).

Hume's introduction of a paradigm of concept formation, proper to moral philosophy, but misplaced in theoretical physics and mathematics, not only has the effect of making the concepts of the latter sciences appear inadequate but leads him into explications of concepts which are idle. Take the famous analysis of "A causes B" into (1) A and B are constantly conjoined and (2) the mind upon the appearance of A is psychologically determined to expect B. Statement (1) does pick out an objective condition for applying the concept of cause, and so helps us understand the concept. Statement (2), however, is contrived simply to bring causal language into conformity with the paradigm: it shows how we can have an internal understanding of such expressions as "If A occurs, B *must* follow." It is no doubt a satisfying analysis to one whose main concern is to explain what it is to have such concepts as pride and humility, but it throws little light on the concept of causal necessity as used in theoretical science. Hume could have pursued more deeply the external understanding of the concept as it appears in the linguistic conventions of theoretical science. Nelson Goodman's analysis of "law-likeness" and his development of the "new riddle of induction" are excellent examples of the sort of Humean inquiry that could have been carried out. But as a moral philosopher Hume had little inclination to go further; having shown that an internal understanding of causal necessity is possible, he was satisfied. By contrast, when faced with the class of "performative" concepts for which an internal grasp is not possible but which are crucial for moral philosophy, Hume rises to the occasion and provides us with an external understanding of the concepts by carefully working through the linguistic conventions of promise-keeping and justice.

Although the paradigm of concept formation locked into Hume's first principle is a barrier to an adequate understanding of concepts in theoretical physics and mathematics, it does illuminate the concepts employed in moral philosophy. This fact can be easily overlooked by commentators who tend to view Hume's first principle as supporting a "private language" view of meaning. Consider Flew's criticism of one of Hume's applications of his principle that "To give a child an idea of scarlet or orange, of sweet or bitter, I present the objects, or, in other words, convey to him these impressions" (T, 5). The notion of having an impression is redundant. "For to understand such words as scarlet or orange, sweet or bitter, and to apply them correctly . . . it is essential only to know to which things they can and to which things they cannot properly be applied. To be able to do this and to know this it is not theoretically necessary to possess the particular senses of sight and taste. In theory it is enough to have instruments" [18] This is just what we have called an external understanding of a concept and is granted by Hume as part of what is involved in possessing a concept. But Hume also requires that we have an interior understanding of the objects to which the concept applies. Flew considers this to be logically irrelevant: "To possess or to have possessed the particular sense which corresponds is theoretically indispensable merely in the practically trivial and derivative case of the application of the word to one's own mental imagery." [19]

But is this sort of case which Hume considers so important really trivial? In Flew's account, it is logically possible that an individual could have mastered all the public criteria for applying experiential predicates to others without ever having experienced what it is to have those predicates apply to himself. Such an individual could tell that others are tasting something sweet, that they are angry, are seeing red things, are in love, and so on for all experiential concepts without himself ever having tasted anything, seen anything, been angry, or in love. Such an individual would be like everybody else except that he would not have an interior; he would, in fact, be like a living robot. But if one individual, logically, could be this way, everybody could. We would then have a world without interiors but in which everything could go on just as it does now. We would have people who had never had the experience of sight, painting pictures and critically discussing them (with, perhaps, the aid of instruments); passionate novels about love, infidelity, revenge, and regret would be written and read by people who had never had any such experiences; and so on. But this would not be the moral world as we understand it. It is not just that these beings would be unfortunate in being blind, deaf, unable to taste, to feel anger, regret, or love; they would not *understand* the concept of an interior either as applied to themselves or to others. We cannot invest others with interiors until we have one ourselves, and we gain interiors in roughly the way Hume says we do, by having experiences and reflecting upon them. Of course, these experiences presuppose a public world and a public language in which we can talk about them, but, as we have seen, Hume's philosophy allows for both.

The moral world is made up of interiors and exteriors, To understand that world, we must be able to use experiential concepts, and these require an internal and an external understanding. Hume tends to take experiential concepts as a paradigm for analyzing all concepts, and this places an undue restriction on his account of theoretical and mathematical concepts. But the account of concept formation that appears to lie behind the private-language interpretation of the first principle makes the opposite mistake. It appears to take as its paradigm the concepts of theoretical physics and mathematics which require only an external understanding, and in so doing the interior of the moral world becomes unintelligible. But it is just this structure that Hume sets out to examine. In the end, Hume's most important philosophical contribution is not his famous analysis of causation but his doctrine of sympathy. As Kemp Smith first pointed out, it is the central doctrine of the *Treatise* and the governing idea behind Hume's favorite work, the *Enquiry* on morals. The doctrine of sympathy is that the idea of the passion of another can cause in us the same passion. It is not so much a doctrine of how we get empathetic feelings as it is a doctrine of communication of interiors, but such communication is impossible unless we have interiors. Hume's first principle is an articulation of this important conceptual fact.[20]

## THE STATUS OF THE FIRST PRINCIPLE

We come now to the question of the logical status of the first principle. It is usually interpreted as an empirical proposition open to falsifying instances, and Hume himself seems to present it as such: "Those who would assert that this position is not universally true . . . have only one, and that an easy method of refuting it; by producing that idea which, in their opinion, is not derived from this source" (EU, 19). But then almost immediately he brings forth "one contradictory phenomenon, which may prove that it is not absolutely impossible for ideas to arise, independent of their correspondent impressions" (EU, 20). The counterinstance is the famous missing shade of blue where Hume supposes that we could be familiar with all shades of color excepting a particular shade of blue. He grants that, given a color wheel with that shade missing, one could recognize the gap and from the imagination "raise up . . . the idea of that particular shade, though it had never been conveyed to him by his senses" (EU, 20-21). But he does not take this to be a falsifying counterexample, and sees no reason why "for it alone we should alter our general maxim" (EU, 21). Hume does not treat the exception seriously, I think, because it borrows heavily from the very point he wants to make. The exception assumes that we have already achieved both an external and an internal mastery of color words in the way Hume's principle requires. Moreover, the idea in question is described as the sort of idea for which an internal mastery could be achieved in the usual way and, in any case, is in fact achieved by the conditions of the hypothetical example. So whatever account we give of the exception, it is stated in such a way as to be parasitic upon the very sort of internal understanding the first principle is supposed to capture. Hume, then, can be confident that for this sort of "exception" whatever modifications are necessary will be minor, need not be explored at the outset, and so should not affect the basic utility of the principle.[21]

The really interesting candidates for counterexamples would be purported ideas referring to objects such as theoretical entities which are defined as not having experiential properties and so for which an internal understanding is impossible. But Hume does not allow any such counterexample. And this gives some justification to Flew's remark that Hume's formulations of the principles are "ambiguous: most of the time they are taken to express a contingent generalization; but at some moments of crisis he apparently construes them as embodying a necessary proposition."[22] But this interpretation does not really illuminate Hume's use of the principle. Empirical propositions, as Wittgenstein once said, "do not all have the same status since one can lay down such a proposition and turn it from an empirical proposition into a norm of description."[23] Even so, not every empirical proposition can be transformed into a norm; only those that occupy an important logical place in a theoretical framework and have lawlike status can be treated as normative. If we treat the first principle as an isolated empirical generalization, then Hume's out-of-hand rejection of counterexamples must, as Flew says, appear as a case of protecting an empirical proposition from criticism by treating it as an analytic truth.

But there are important background considerations which make the first principle something more than an isolated empirical generalization. The principle is to be understood against the background of the true philosophy developed dialectically in book I and the theory of language developed in book III. Given the narrative form in which the *Treatise* is cast, Hume could not appeal to these at the outset. Rather, he begins with our presystematic notions of what it is to have an idea of something, assuming that on such matters our common understanding cannot be far off. He then fixes on a paradigm of concept formation exemplified in such cases as where we see, for instance, that no one has an adequate idea of what it is to taste pineapple unless he has tasted it. Now it must be admitted, I think, that such cases are compelling and that they do throw some light on what it is to have an idea of something. To grasp what Hume is about, we must try to find out what is compelling about the cases he mentions and why he was able to find in them a paradigm of concept formation.

I have argued that no one fully understands experiential concepts unless he has achieved both an external and an internal mastery of them and that, as a moral philosopher, Hume could easily find to be paradigmatic this notion of what it is to have a concept. The first principle is the tool Hume fashions for implementing the paradigm. Purported ideas which are in conflict with the paradigm can and must be rejected as not yielding the sort of understanding framed in the paradigm. This, of course, is circular, but the circularity is not vicious as long as the paradigm has systematic strength: as it does for moral philosophy, for without something like Hume's first principle we would not have a theory of the concepts of the interiors that bind together the moral world. Hume's mistake was to extend the paradigm into areas such as theoretical science and mathematics where it is not only logically idle but confusing as well.

Although the first principle is not merely an isolated empirical generalization, it does have empirical content, for whatever an idea may turn out to be, it is a contingent matter that having an internal understanding of the taste of pineapple depends on having tasted it. Basson has argued, however, that although the principle is presented as an empirical one, Hume treats it as an analytic truth: "No matter how he purports to prove his principle, the use he makes of it shows that for him an idea is *by definition* a copy of an impression."[24] But Hume, in fact, does not treat the principle as an analytic proposition. Rather, it is employed as a rule for implementing a paradigm of what it is to have a concept of something. The paradigm has authority because it illuminates the structure of a very large class of concepts, namely, experiential concepts. If the first principle is to be viewed as a rule, then it must be assessed in terms of its utility in clarifying our ideas. And this is, in fact, both how Hume talks about it and how he uses it. He describes the principle as a "general maxim," as an "invention," and as "a new microscope or species of optics" for examining ideas (EU, 62). The pragmatic character of the rule is stated clearly: "Here, therefore, is a proposition, which not only seems, in itself, simple and intelligible; but, if a proper use were made of it, might render every dispute equally intelligible, and banish all that jargon, which has so long taken possession of metaphysical reasonings, and drawn disgrace upon them" (EU, 21). Hume uses his rule not to eliminate certain expressions as meaningless but to clarify them by reference to the paradigm. When he discovers that we have no idea of causal power, he does not declare talk about such power meaningless; rather he concludes that the expressions in question are "being *wrong apply'd*" (T, 162), and he then sets out (1) to examine the linguistic conventions of causal language and (2) to bring these in line with the paradigm. The result is the well-known analysis of cause as: (a) a constant conjunction of like events along with (b) a felt compulsion to expect the one on the occurrence of the other; (a) satisfies the conditions for an external grasp of the concept and (b) satisfies the conditions for an internal mastery of the concept. But some concepts, like promising, do not function referentially. To such concepts the first principle does not even apply. In this case the concept of promising is explicated by analyzing the linguistic rules that constitute the convention of promise-keeping. The first principle does apply to theoretical concepts such as "gravity" and "inertia" and Hume concludes, characteristically, that we have no adequate idea of the entities to which they refer, but he does not conclude that they do not refer at all. The meaning of such expressions must be specified by the rules for their application in the language of theoretical science.

As a moral philosopher, Hume does not try to uncover such rules. The only passage where he makes any attempt to talk about how empirical content is conveyed to theoretical expressions is disappointing (EU, 73n). As we have seen, he is content to insist again that we have no imaginary conception of the theoretical expressions "gravity" and "inertia" and to suggest that whatever the conditions for applying such terms, they can be construed as public and empirical. These external conditions for applying a theoretical expression must determine in some way the *whole* of the concept, for Hume makes no attempt to bring particular theoretical expressions into line with the paradigm as he does for the general expression "necessary connection"; that is, there is no attempt to show that we can have some sort of internal mastery of the concepts of gravity and inertia in terms of habits, sentiments, or what not. This suggests, perhaps, an advance of the first *Enquiry* over the *Treatise*, for there, at times, Hume became hopelessly bogged down in trying to bring theoretical concepts into line with the paradigm as, for instance, in his attempt to achieve an internal mastery of the concept of "vacuum" (T, 55-56). In any case, Hume did recognize that theoretical expressions could have meaning independent of the paradigm as long as there are public and empirical conditions governing their application in the linguistic conventions of theoretical science. But the deep question of just how empirical meanings can be read into theoretical expressions which has dominated so much twentieth-century empiricism and philosophy of science is not, in any interesting way, taken up by Hume at all.

Another important feature of Hume's first principle considered as a rule is that it is designed to apply specifically to philosophical discourse: "When we entertain, therefore, any suspicion that a philosophical term is employed without any meaning or idea (as is but too frequent), we need but inquire, *from what impression is that supposed idea derived?* And if it be impossible to assign any, this will serve to confirm our suspicion" (EU, 22). Here Hume supposes a presystematic distinction between the language of common life and philosophical language, and this distinction is another source of confidence in the authority of the paradigm. Expressions such as "infinity," "gravity," "ethereal spirit," "subtle electric spirit," and the like are metaphysically problematic in a way in which expressions such as "red," "sweet," "promises," and "proud" are not. The distinction between philosophical language and the language of common life along with the problematic character of the former is presystematically known. Hume's rule is an attempt to give a more explicit shape to that distinction and to provide a standard for disciplining philosophical language. Its value is that the paradigm behind it does capture the large and important class of experiential concepts that govern common life.

The intuitive distinction between discourse in common life and discourse in philosophy is given more systematic shape later on by the dialectical analysis of the relation between philosophy and common life in the last part of book I, and in book III by the theory that language is a historical convention and that common life is a system of linguistic conventions. So the experiential concepts that are required by the principle are understood to be already shaped by language and to be firmly rooted in the linguistic conventions that have been insensibly hammered out in the historical process of social life. And it is just these linguistic conventions that constitute the "steady and general points of view" that make possible the objective orders of the moral world. Hume remarks that "There are certain terms in every language which import blame, and others praise; and all men who use the same tongue must agree in their application of them" (E, 231). As participants in the conventions of aesthetics and moral judgment, we all necessarily have the same general ideas of praise and blame, that is, we all have the same external understanding of the ideas because the public criteria for applying the appropriate terms to the world are the same. But we do not all have the same internal mastery of the ideas in question: "the *heart* does not always take part with those general notions" (T, 603). And there is, in the convention of aesthetic judgment, the problem of how to detect the "pretender," the pseudo-critic who has mastered the public criteria for applying aesthetic terms but has no internal understanding of what he is talking about (E, 247-49).

Because experiential concepts are housed in the deep linguistic conventions that order common life, they have a stability that philosophical concepts do not have, and stability, for Hume, is always a prima facie mark of reality. Philosophical concepts come and go in a way that the experiential concepts of common life do not. It is for this reason, Hume argues, that there is virtually no disagreement on broad conceptual issues in morals and aesthetics; the language constituting these conventions has made it logically impossible to say that virtue is bad or elegance is in bad taste (E, 231-34). But "In all matters of opinion and science, the case is opposite; the difference among men is there oftener found to lie in generals than in particulars, and to be less in reality than in appearance" (E, 232). Philosophers cannot agree on what time is and may even be led to deny the reality of time, but they can all tell what time it is in common life. Philosophy as an autonomous inquiry pretends to be free of the unreflectively established conventions of common life; its rules for applying terms are not commonly established, are often manifestly arbitrary, and at times are even destructive of deeply established linguistic and conceptual conventions. When misplaced philosophy appears on the scene, it "bends every branch of knowledge to its own purpose, without much regard to the phenomena of nature, or to the unbiased sentiments of the mind, hence reasoning, and even language, have been warped from their natural course" (EM, 322). There is then a hard-core language of common life which we necessarily all understand and by reference to which philosophical expressions may appear odd and suspicious.

Given this presystematically known distinction between philosophical language and the language of common life, Hume does not apply his first principle in an even-handed manner, assuming, as it were, that all referential expressions are guilty until proven otherwise. Certain philosophical expressions are known to be suspect prior to the application of the principle. This helps to explain what, to many commentators, appears to be an arrogant and question-begging attitude in his handling of purported counterexamples. Speaking of Hume's rejection of such purported ideas as "necessary connection," "eventless time," and the like, Bennett asks "Why can't his opponents say that these are precisely the classes of 'ideas' for which the theory is false?"[25] But if the above distinction is granted, such terms are suspect independently of the first principle. Afer applying the principle unsuccessfully to such expressions, Hume, typically, concludes not that they have no meaning but that "this will serve to confirm our suspicion" (EU, 22). Given the bad semantical reputation of philosophical terms and the fact that Hume's first principle (if understood in the context of the whole *Treatise*) is, at the very least, a plausible start at understanding the referential expressions of common life, anyone who wishes to use a term rejected by the principle has the burden of explaining the conditions of its meaning. And, as Hume himself recognized, this can sometimes be done. If the expression is an important one clearly embedded in established conventions of common life such as "to promise," its meaning or "idea" can be determined by examining the rules for the linguistic convention of promise-keeping. The same allowance is made for especially important referential expressions such as "space" and "extension." These occupy a deep place in the linguistic conventions of common life. For terms so established Hume does not take on the inquisitorial manner; indeed, he treats them with great semantical respect, even granting out of hand that they express ideas merely on the ground that they satisfy the external conditions for determining an idea: " 'tis certain we have an idea of extension; for otherwise why do we talk and reason concerning it?" (T, 32).

The introduction of the ideas of space and time in book I of the *Treatise* is instructive for an appreciation of how Hume understands the first principle. He begins (part II, sections I and II) not by deriving these ideas from impressions but by attempting to answer the high formalistic question of whether our ideas of space and time are the ideas of structures that are infinitely divisible. In the process of answering this question, Hume develops what I have called an external understanding of the concepts of space and time along with appropriate ontological conclusions about the reality of space and time. It is only after these fundamental conceptual and ontological points are established that Hume turns, in section III, to the task of applying the first principle. He describes the task this way: "Let us apply this principle, in order *to discover farther* the nature of our ideas of space and time" (T, 33, emphasis mine). Here it is clear that Hume is not using the principle to determine whether we really have the ideas of space and time at all. Rather, it is a question of getting a deeper understanding of the ideas that we admittedly have and which Hume has just explored in sections I and II. What he shows in section III is that the ideas of space and time can be brought into conformity with the paradigm and that we have not only an external understanding of these concepts but an internal understanding as well.

# 4
# History and the Language of Common Life

> For no fact, truth, or reality is, or can be, past. . . . The world under the category of the past is the world seen imperfectly . . . the world of history is abstract and defective from end to end; and only by abandoning it altogether shall we find ourselves once more on the way to a world of experience satisfactory in itself.
>
> Michael Oakeshott

## PAST IMPRESSIONS

The private-language interpretation is a fairly recent criticism of Hume's first principle. We have now to examine two objections to the principle which are much older and more firmly established. Both are objections to the past-referring character of the principle which is, we may recall, the thesis that simple ideas are derived from simple past impressions which they resemble and that complex ideas are derived from complex past impressions which they may or may not resemble. To most commentators it has seemed that reference to the past is not necessary and, indeed, is a positive barrier to explicating what it is to have an idea of something. The concept of the past, however, occupies a very important place in Hume's philosophy of common life. Indeed, as we shall see, it is the special use Hume makes of that concept that distinguishes his empiricism from other forms of empiricism. To bring these facts, out, it will be helpful to work through both objections with the end in view of evaluating their philosophical worth and of determining how far they are adequate interpretations of Hume.

Perhaps the most obvious objection to the first principle, certainly the oldest, is that ideas cannot be derived from past impressions because past impressions cannot be recalled for comparison with present ideas. I shall call this the standard objection; it lies behind Russell's question: "How, then, are we to find any way of comparing the present image and the past sensation? The problem is just as acute if we say that images differ from their prototypes as if we say that they resemble them; it is the very possibility of comparison that is hard to understand."[1] Church writes: "For as no prototype of any memory may be revived so no original of any primary idea may be recalled. In no case, then, can an idea be known to be a copy."[2] Laird offers a similar criticism: "Yet the mere fact (if it were) that ideas are derived from impressions surely does not prove, or even suggest, that every idea is so very wise as to know its own father, or even as to know that it has a pedigree of any kind."[3] Price makes the same criticism along with a recommendation for improving the principle: "The idea is present to the mind now; the impressions from which it is supposed to have been derived are past and gone. If he can no longer inspect the past impressions, how is he to tell whether the present idea was or was not derived from them? What can even lead him to suspect that it was derived from anything at all? He ought to have made memory a third species of acquaintance, alongside of sensation and introspection."[4] These objections presuppose that Hume, in some way, is committed to the principle that resemblance comparisons are impossible unless the objects compared are available for inspection in the present. But why must Hume be committed to this principle?

It must be stressed that the standard objection is not about any difficulties Hume might have in accounting for what our reasons could be for thinking that a past impression had occurred, for even if Hume had good reasons for thinking an impression had occurred, that would not make it available for inspection in the present. The objection is simply that Hume's first principle is inadequate because past impressions, being "past and gone," cannot be recalled for inspection. But if we cannot compare a past impression with a present idea merely because the impression is past, then, presumably, we cannot compare any past existent with any present existent. And this is surely wrong. The most drastic sort of historical skepticism would follow. If we could ever know anything about an object in the past, we could then compare that object with a present existence. However, if such comparisons are impossible, historical knowledge is also impossible. But, of course, we can compare a toothache of today with one of yesterday and modern political institutions with medieval ones without having them available for inspection in the present. The question may arise of how we can know that a past existent has occurred, of how historical knowledge is possible, but that deep philosophical problem is not at issue here. The question now is simply how to interpret Hume, and in particular whether the first principle should be read so as to presuppose the counterintuitive proposition that resemblance comparisons hold only for present existences.

Hume does not explicitly affirm the proposition nor is it implied in any of his doctrines. In fact he almost explicitly denies it. After asserting that ideas resemble past impressions, he goes out of his way to say that it is "impossible to recall the past impressions, in order to compare them with our present ideas" (T, 85). Hume evidently thought that there is no inconsistency in holding both that past impressions cannot be recalled for inspection in the present and that resemblance comparisons between past and present perceptions are possible. This passage, then, provides good reason to think that Hume is not committed to the thesis that resemblance comparisons are possible only for present existences. As a consequence, the standard objection that Hume has no way to recall impressions for comparison in the present collapses for want of an object. Yet so strong is the tendency to read Hume phenomenalistically and, consequently, to place the first principle under the standard objection, that the only commentators to have noticed the passage treat it not as a significant challenge for the view but as a kind of indirect confirmation of it. Thus Zabeeh says of it that "Hume realizes that no correspondence theory of truth could be stated in this system"[5] Traditionally, the correspondence theory is a theory of the nature of truth (what it means to say that a proposition is true) and not a theory of the test of truth (how we know a proposition is true). Although the test of truth for Hume is coherence (T, 84), he explicitly holds that, regarding matters of fact, correspondence is the nature of truth: "Truth is of two kinds, consisting either in the discovery of the proportions of ideas, consider'd as such, or in the conformity of our ideas of objects to their real existence" (T, 448, 458; E, 166). The passage, then, is not an admission on Hume's part that the impossibility of recalling a past impression for inspection in the present is a barrier to forming (in the correspondence sense) a true proposition about it.

Similarly, Passmore takes the passage to be a disastrous inconsistency of which Hume was cheerfully unaware. Hume, he writes: "never realizes the full implications of this admission. Taken seriously, it would destroy his positivist method. There is now no way of discovering whether a supposed idea in fact derives from an impression."[6] It is, however, highly unlikely that Hume would state a theory that ideas are derived from past impressions (requiring that past impressions be retrievable in some way for inspection in the present) and then one page later say that past impressions cannot be recalled in the present for inspection. That would be an unusually brutish inconsistency. If one still wishes to press the standard objection, what must be shown is that, whether Hume thought so or not, he in fact did work out a theory of ideas which requires recalling past impressions for inspection in the present. This would necessitate reading into Hume a most drastic form of phenomenalism according to which resemblance comparisons can be made only between present existences. How this could be done, I cannot imagine, for those who present the standard objection give no reason why Hume's first principle should be read in that way. That it should, is simply a background assumption derived from a long tradition of reading Hume as a phenomenalist.

## HISTORICAL NIHILISM

The standard objection, then, fails. But it has an interest for us quite apart from its adequacy as an interpretation of Hume. For behind it lies the conviction that what is fundamentally wrong with Hume's first principle is that it requires reference to *past* existences. Those who deploy the standard objection seem, for whatever reason, to require of Hume that he treat past existences as being other than what they are, namely, past; that he is somehow committed to turning them, as it were, into present existences. This is why the standard objection seems, upon reflection, so odd, and why Hume's first principle read in terms of it seems so hopeless and without any value whatsoever. The conviction behind the standard objection that the past is a strange sort of reality which must be somehow conceptually transformed into something other than what it is, is very deep in modern philosophy and bears some examination not only because the conviction is a curious one but because of the light it can throw on our understanding of Hume's first principle. Hume's theory of concept formation is the only one in the empirical tradition that ties meaning to *past* existences; the other main empirical theories positively hold that sentences purportedly about the past are *meaningless* unless they can be transformed into some nonpast-tense idiom. Three forms of empiricism have dominated: phenomenalism, pragmatism, and logical empiricism. Each has had proponents who have found in Hume's philosophy a conceptual parent of their own view. But, in fact, Hume framed a quite different sort of empiricism, one that might properly be called *historical*. In what follows, I shall try to quarantine Hume's empiricism as far as possible from these later forms. We shall then be in a position to appreciate, on the deepest conceptual level, what is unique and philosophically interesting about the special sort of empiricism Hume worked out.

Most forms of phenomenalism explicate descriptive meaning by reference to actual or possible present experiences. Consequently, expressions referring to the past are fundamentally problematic. A. J. Ayer once tried to solve the difficulty this way: "propositions referring to the past . . . can be taken as implying that certain observations would have occurred if certain conditions had been fulfilled."[7] Expressions purportedly about the past, then, must be either meaningless or taken to refer to sets of actual or possible present experiences. Pragmatism on the other hand, is the view that the meaning of descriptive expressions is grounded in reference to the present and future. The view, as C. I. Lewis held it, is that "To ascribe an objective quality to a thing means implicitly the prediction that if I act in certain ways, specifiable experiences will eventuate."[8] Consequently, the "whole content of our knowledge of reality is the truth of such 'If-then' propositions."[9] If this account is right, expressions purportedly about the past would have to be either meaningless or recast somehow into expressions about the present and future. Carnap once held in a similar view that the test for the meaningfulness of any statement about the world is whether certain "perceptions or feelings or experiences . . . may be expected for the future."[10]

Phenomenalism and pragmatism may be thought of as *tensed* theories of meaning insofar as they require the use of tensed expressions. But not all forms of empiricism are tensed. Various forms of logical empiricism explicate descriptive meaning by reference to tenseless expressions with the predicate expressions referring to sense data, physical objects, or whatever the preferred object of experience might be. A. J. Ayer, who may be taken as a case of either phenomenalism or logical empiricism, depending on what phase of his philosophical development one fixes on, once held that "no sentence as such is about the past."[11] By this he meant that any statement in the past tense (or, indeed, any tensed statement at all) must be recast into a tenseless idiom on pain of being meaningless. Similar views have been put forth by Russell and Quine, the former of whom once reflected that: "There is some sense, easier to feel than to state, in which time is an unimportant and superficial characteristic of reality. Past and future must be acknowledged to be as real as the present, and a certain emancipation from slavery to time is essential to philosophic thought."[12]

It is perhaps worthwhile to observe that logical empiricism and absolute idealism, though different in many respects, share a deep common ground in the view that reality can be understood only through tenseless language and that, consequently, statements purportedly about the past are philosophically defective. Absolute idealists have been especially vigorous in rejecting the possibility of history conceived as an investigation of the past. Thus, according to Bosanquet, history is "a hybrid form of experience, incapable of any considerable degree of 'being or trueness.'"[13] And Oakeshott writes of history that "its form contradicts the nature of its content. . . . The world of historical fact, truth, and reality appears to lie in the past; historical reality is a past reality, and the notion of the past cannot be dismissed from history without dismissing history itself. But to suppose this world of history actually to lie in the past, to accept it (that is) in the form in which it is satisfactory in historical experience, involves us in a radical contradiction. It obliges us to suppose a world which is not a world of ideas, to suppose facts which are not in experience, truths which are not true, reality which is not real."[14] More recently, Jack Meiland has defended a version of the idealist view of statements about the past which he calls the "construction" theory of history. In this theory, historians should not be thought of as trying to make statements about the past, because there is no past reality for such statements to be *about*. Rather, history should be thought of as a study of the present understood in a tenseless way. The task of history is "to give a coherent account of the present world as a whole."[15]

Perhaps the first thing to point out about these quite varied but uniformly negative analyses of past-tense language is that they are not forms of skepticism about the past. They do not purport to show that we cannot know whether any statement about the past is true. They rather all make, in various ways, the more radical claim that we cannot *say* anything intelligible about the past, that any attempt to talk about the past must either turn out to be a way of talking about some nonpast-tense idiom or about nothing at all. Such a view is more properly characterized as *historical nihilism* than as historical skepticism, for if it is correct, false as well as true statements about the past are impossible, and so doubt as well as knowledge of the past is unintelligible. Phenomenalism, pragmatism, logical empiricism, absolute idealism, and kindred philosophical positions constitute a large and important portion of contemporary philosophy. Because of their influence, historical nihilism of some sort is well entrenched in the contemporary philosophical attitude. It is perhaps for this reason that many Hume commentators have had conceptual difficulties appreciating a theory of concepts based on a relation between present and past existences, a theory, moreover, which innocently betrays no suggestion that references to the past might be fundamentally problematic. Consider a comment by MacNabb: "The mysterious 'past reference' of an idea of memory is mentioned by Hume in the passage about the memory of a past idea (*Treatise*, Book I, Part III, Section VIII); but no attempt at clarification is made."[16] MacNabb gives no reason why the "past reference" of ideas should be "mysterious." It is not that mental images are logically incapable of referring to the past, for although MacNabb thinks Hume has confused mental images with ideas, that is, he says, a point "in addition to the mysteriousness of past reference."[17] It appears that some form of historical nihilism is behind Mac-

Nabb's perplexity. But one could as well say that references to the present, or to the future, or to nontemporal structures are mysterious. In the end, it is perhaps something of a mystery that anything can *refer* to anything at all. So in the absence of some special argument, there is no reason to find references to the past mysterious.

Perhaps because of the influence of historical nihilism, many commentators have been able to read Hume's first principle in such a way as to force it into conformity with the phenomenalistic paradigm and thus to prompt the standard objection despite the fact that this multiplies inconsistencies in the text beyond necessity. (An example that we have already observed is Passmore's treatment of Hume's claim that past impressions cannot be recalled for inspection in the present as being inconsistent with the first principle rather than the more natural way of reading it as being compatible with it). The influence of historical nihilism explains why Russell, caught in the coils of his own phenomenalism, found the first principle not only false but, conceptually, "hard to understand."[18] Historical nihilism is behind Price's high phenomenalistic emendation of the theory: that Hume "ought to have made memory a third species of *acquaintance*, alongside of sensation and introspection" because comparison between past and present existences "requires an immediate apprehension of past impressions themselves."[19] But Hume is surely right: it is "impossible to recal the past impressions, in order to compare them with our present ideas" (T, 85). The past is dead and gone. There is no way to inspect past existences in the present, and there is no phenomenalistic acquaintance with the past. In the end, the standard objection tells us more about the philosophical presuppositions of those who have offered it than it does about the first principle.

But leaving the standard objection aside, there still might be the nagging question of how Hume *can* compare a past perception with a present perception. The question is inappropriate, however, insofar as it presupposes that the past is a conceptually strange or problematic sort of reality requiring special explanation. For Hume, the past is an internal part of the world of common life, and reference to the past is used in the first principle as a primitive concept. And why should not references to the past be taken as primitive? Whatever difficulties it might have, there is something refreshing about Hume's first principle. It, at the very least, enables us to talk about the past without requiring that our words be "warped from their natural course" (EM, 322) and transmuted into talk about the present, or future, or some tenseless structure.

Any theory of concept formation must take some concepts as primitive, in terms of which other concepts are explicated. Phenomenalists take reference to the present as primitive. Pragmatists take reference to the present and future as primitive. Logical empiricists, absolute idealists, and many others take reference to tenseless structures as primitive. So, in reply to the challenge of how Hume can account for comparisons between past and present existences, we must say that he can account for them in whatever way phenomenalists can account for the possibility of experience of the present, or in whatever way pragmatists can account for the possibility of comparisons between present and future existences, or in whatever way logical empiricists and absolute idealists can refer to tenseless structures. A theory of meaning would destroy itself if it could succeed in accounting for its own primitive concepts, roughly in the way a definitional system which defines its own primitive terms ceases to be a definitional system. Phenomenalism, pragmatism, and logical empiricism have been interesting and fruitful philosophical theories of meaning, but they would not have been theories of meaning at all had they accounted for their primitive concepts. So unless some special argument is forthcoming (and we shall consider one shortly), Hume's choice of the past as a primitive concept for explicating meaning poses no problem that does not exist for the primitive concepts of any other theory. From the point of view of a given theory of meaning, the primitives of any other theory may appear conceptually odd and perhaps even unintelligible, but that is just the sting in constructing theories of meaning.

## PAST-ENTAILING IDEAS

We have now to consider a much more serious objection to Hume's first principle, one which, in effect, grants that comparisons between past and present existences are possible but holds that reference to the past is not part of the meanings of terms. We may begin with a comment by Jonathan Bennett: "But if it really does matter now whether a given expression makes sense, then its making sense or not ought to show *now*: we ought to be able to settle the question by attending to the present and the future. Yet Hume, in trying to answer the question through his theory, implies that it is best answered by looking to the past."[20] The rationale behind this objection is that reference to the past is not logically required to understand a concept: "What someone understands now is not logically tied to what he underwent earlier: the account of 'newly born' adults in Shaw's *Back to Methuselah* is a perfectly consistent fantasy."[21] With certain restrictions, the fantasy is indeed consistent, and it will be instructive to examine just what these restrictions are. By doing so we will gain a better understanding of what is philosophically valuable about Hume's first principle and also what its limits are.

In what way is the concept of a "newly born adult" consistent? We can logically imagine that God has created before us, out of nothing, a being having all the observation and disposition properties of an adult male human being. God could also have programmed the mind of this being with some natural language and also with a set of coherent but false ideas about the past—that he was born at a certain place, lived through a certain childhood, and the like. In short, what could be true of any adult male could be true of this being except that he has no past. Could we say of such an existent that it is a human being?

This is a question of what the criteria are for applying to a present existent the predicate "is human." The question is a deep one, but it would appear that in this case all the criteria are satisfied. Our existent would have all the observation properties of a man and so would look like one. He would have these properties because observation properties such as "is red," "is round," and the like do not logically require reference to the past as a condition of their application in the present. He would also have all the disposition properties of a man (physical, biological, and psychological) and so could behave like one. Again, he could have these properties because the concept of a disposition (construed broadly to include capacities, powers, and abilities) does not logically require reference to the past as a condition for its application in the present. Our existent would also satisfy the Kantian conditions for being a person since to be capable of action governed by the categorical imperative does not require having a past. It would appear, then, that anything which satisfies the observation, disposition, and moral conditions for being human is human. It is true that our existent would be a *strange* man, for he as yet has no past. Even after living with us a while and acquiring a past, he would still be strange because he did not enter the world as we did. But then, logically, any manner of entering the world may appear strange. Failure to have certain temporal properties should not tell against the humanity of a being any more than should a lack of spatial or color properties. Indeed, the being we have just described is roughly parallel to Adam, whom the Western tradition has allowed to be a logical possibility. So the criteria for applying the predicate "is human" do not require reference to the past or, indeed, to any other tensed dimension. Concepts of this sort we may say are tenseless because they do not require tensed conditions for their application.

If God can create "newly born adults" out of nothing and without a past, he can also create rivers, mountains, houses, indeed, the entire natural order without a past. Every house we know has a past *in fact*, but there is no contradiction in conceiving of God creating, without a past, an existent having all the observation and disposition properties for applying the predicate "is a house." If that should happen, we would have before us a house. Again, it would be a strange house, without a history, but a house nonetheless: it could be sturdy, pleasant, functional, and the like. In time, it would gain a history; attempts could be made to explain its origins, and perplexing questions could arise over who owned it. In general, any statement ordinarily true of houses could be true of it, with the exception of statements which themselves entail true statements about the past. It could not, for instance, be said to be well made, nor could it arrive with broken windows or rotten beams, though after its appearance the windows could break and the beams could begin to rot.

Much of our thought is governed by tenseless concepts. These include all sensory, dispositional, logical, and mathematical concepts; all concepts structured by tenseless scientific laws and theories, and all moral, aesthetic, and religious concepts (excluding, of course, those religious concepts which operate in the framework of a historical revelation). Indeed, the class of tenseless concepts is so large and important that it is understandable how many philosophers would fix on it as the paradigm of all concepts. The move seems reasonable: how can we universalize or even reason without tenseless concepts? And if reason is possible only through tenseless concepts, then given an ancient dictum of Western philosophy that reality must be thought of as what conforms to the dictates of reason, it might seem that reality itself must be conceived as tenseless. Some such conviction is behind the tenseless forms of historical nihilism mentioned above (for example, Oakeshott's claim that "no truth, fact, or reality is or can be past."). It is also behind Russell's famous thesis that, logically, the world could have been created five minutes ago complete with what appear to be fossils, ancient manuscripts, true memories, and so on. Experience could not refute the thesis, there being no experience of the past that could justify or falsify it. And any evidence based on experience of the present could be used to support a thesis that the world is only five minutes old. The sort of mind at work behind this skeptical thesis about the past is of a piece with that behind the standard objection to Hume's first principle, and, indeed, Russell was one of those who raised just that objection. In both cases, it is assumed that knowledge is gained through direct acquaintance with an object. To know about an object in the past, we must, somehow, be acquainted with it and that is to require that the past be in some way present; but since the past is past, this is impossible, and so it is impossible to know anything about the past. Such skepticism is the natural, if not the logical, result of a determined attempt to think about reality and knowledge only in a tenseless way.

Despite its initial plausibility, the doctrine that all concepts are tenseless must be abandoned. It amounts to the thesis that all tensed expressions can be reduced to tenseless expressions without conceptual remainder. A past-tense statement such as "X died at t" is usually analyzed in some such way as follows: (1) "X dies (tenselessly) at t" and (2) "The utterance of (1) occurs (tenselessly) after t." Statements (1) and (2) convey the information that X dies *before* the time at which (1) is uttered, but they do not convey the information that X's death is *past*. Likewise, 1994 is before 1995 but niether is past. In general, the temporal order itself, considered as an order of units in succession, is tenseless. It seems, then, that any such analysis as the above of past-tense statements is likely to fail. There will always be special information conveyed in past-tense statements that is not included in what are supposed to be their tenseless equivalents. It is just this sort of tensed information that Hume has built into his first principle. The question of the nature of this information will be discussed later. In the meantime, I want to explore the question of whether, in some way or other, past-tense information is, as Hume thought, a necessary feature of what it means to have an idea of something.

Let us return now to Bennett's thesis about the possibility of "newly born adults." The point of the thesis is to show that reference to the past is not necessary to have an idea of something. The thesis is a plausible one because without tenseless concepts we cannot universalize or reason and because much of what we understand the world to be is governed by tenseless concepts. Thus our man without a past could be said to have all the observation and disposition properties that anyone else might have; he could even be described as a rational agent, a moral agent, and a person, because past-tense conditions are not among the criteria for applying these concepts. But not all concepts are tenseless. We could not say of our man without a past that he is a father, priest, friend, senator, police officer, lover, or thief. The reason is that among the conditions for applying these predicates is that certain statements about the past are true. Athena could have been born full-grown from the head of Zeus, and Adam could have been created out of the dust of the earth without a past. But it would be a logical contradiction to suppose that God could create a priest, a U. S. senator, or a nephew without also creating a past of the appropriate length. Such concepts cannot apply logically to present existences unless certain statements about the past are true. Accordingly, we may call them past-entailing concepts.[22]

I have argued that past-tense concepts cannot be reduced to tenseless concepts. If so, then, past-entailing concepts, being tensed, cannot be reduced to tenseless concepts. But past-entailing concepts are not logically independent of tenseless concepts; indeed, they presuppose them. Consider the conditions for applying the term "is a priest": if X is a priest, it follows (1) that X is a man and (2) that certain sentences about the past are true (e.g., that, among other things, X was confirmed by a bishop in the apostolic tradition). Statement (1) is a tenseless condition, whereas (2) is tensed. So although tenseless concepts do not presuppose past-entailing concepts, the latter do presuppose the former. To eliminate all past-entailing concepts would be to impoverish our understanding of the world, but the elimination of all tenseless concepts would entail the elimination of all concepts whatsoever.

But exactly what sort of cognitive impoverishment would occur if past-entailing concepts were eliminated? B. F. Skinner has the founder of Walden Two say, "We don't teach history in Walden Two. What we give our young people is knowledge about the current forces a culture must deal with. None of your heroes, myths, no destiny, simply the Now!" The maxim to focus our attention only on something called the "now," like its epistemological counterpart the "given," is an old one and one which has received widely differing philosophical formulations. In some form or other, it is common to phenomenalism, logical empiricism, absolute idealism, and various forms of religious and philosophical mysticism. What would it be like to be logically emancipated from the past? We experience the present in just this way whenever we conceive what is going on under purely tenseless concepts. We can simply see a color or feel a pain; we can think of ourselves as just men, women, persons, rational agents, and instances of tenselessly conceived psychological, biological, and physical systems. In all such cases our past, in Husserlian fashion, is bracketed out, and we conceive ourselves as located in a timeless structure. A main motive behind this move to bracket out the past is based on the consideration that the past is dead and gone; the present is where experience goes on, and the way fully to grasp experience is through tenseless concepts. Descartes once complained that "when one is too curious about things which were practised in past centuries, one is usually very ignorant about those which are practised in our own time,"[23] and he instituted a method which required the bracketing out of all beliefs about the past, leaving as the object of inquiry a timeless present.

If we, logically, set aside the past, we would eliminate all past-entailing concepts. But though these concepts refer to the past, they are not merely about the past. To describe a being before us as a priest is to make a statement about the *present* (although that statement is not true unless certain statements about the past are true). We may say of such past-entailing concepts that they are about the *present in the light of the past*. More generally, any concept is past-entailing that applies to a temporally disposed event (whether past, present, or future) on condition that certain statements in the past tense be true of some earlier set of events. Thus "is a U. S. senator" is past-entailing because it cannot apply to an individual (past, present, or future) unless certain past-tense statements are true of events occurring earlier than the event to which the concept is supposed to apply. If, as Russell once entertained, the world were created only five minutes ago complete with apparent but false memories, fossils, and the like, then the concept "U. S. senator" could not apply to any existent however temporally disposed. But tenseless concepts such as "is a man" could apply regardless of the temporal location of the existent.

If we could not use concepts like "is a father," "is guaranteed by the Bill of Rights," "is a Rembrandt," "is a friend," virtually everything that we experience in the present would be unintelligible. Without the past, the present would not be, logically, what it is. In common life, we rarely, if ever, consider our present under purely tenseless concepts. The objects we experience are viewed under past-entailing conceptions: we experience not simply roses but Tudor roses, not just men and women but sons and daughters, not simply buildings but historic cities like Florence and Edinburgh. The world of common life, or what Hume calls the moral world, has reference to the past logically built into it. In knowing the present as constituted by common life, it is *logically* necessary that we also know the past. Descartes is wrong, then, to think that the past must be bracketed out *in order* to know the present. Such bracketing would conceptually destroy the past-entailing structure of the present and with it the world of common life. We should then be left with merely tenselessly conceived individuals (men, persons, rational agents, and the like), pursuing tenseless goals, disconnected from each other and from preceding generations like, to use a memorable image of Hume's, the silkworms of a season (E, 463).

Ideas generated by the first principle have a past-entailing content. A simple impression of scarlet is unintelligible on its first appearance because we so far have no idea of it. Only after the impression is past, and we view it in the light of a later, resembling perception can we have its idea. We may analyze a simple Humean idea, then, into two time-separated and resembling perceptions, $P_1$ and $P_2$, where $P_1$ occurs earlier and is rendered intelligible only by being viewed in the light of $P_2$, and *because* of that fact $P_2$ is called an idea. But why, we may ask, should this process make $P_2$ an idea? Or to put the question another way: what is the rationale behind calling $P_2$ an idea? This is not a question that Hume considers. He is content simply to state what he thinks are the criteria for determing an idea. But, then, that is all that most philosophers do. Rarely do we find a philosopher inquiring into the deep paradigms of understanding and significance that determine the particular theory of meaning or concept formation that he is proposing. The question is especially worth pursuing in Hume's case, however, because many commentators have found the theory conceptually odd or "mysterious," or "hard to understand," indicating that disagreement is occurring at a very deep level.

I would like to suggest that the paradigm of significance and understanding framed in Hume's first principle is the sort we find in *stories*. Events in a story are arranged temporally, and as the story unfolds we are able to read a meaning and significance into earlier events that we could not have appreciated on our first acquaintance with them. The birth of Michelangelo has a significance for us that it could not have had for those who had, as it were, an impression of it. Likewise, what to those who lived through it was known as the Great War or the war to end all wars is known to us as World War I. From our privileged position at a later time, we are able to find a significance in events unavailable to those who lived through them. Similarly, a simple impression of scarlet on its first appearance is a timeless, unintelligible existent; it is only after the impression is gone, and we view it in the light of a later resembling perception that we can have its idea. Narrative significance is conveyed to the earlier perception by viewing it in the light of the later perception, which because it bestows this light is thought of as an idea. *Narrative significance*, then, is the deep paradigm that governs the past-entailing theory of meaning contained in Hume's first principle.

The central notion here is that we understand things only after they have occurred and in the light of later occurrences, an idea that was given full metaphysical shape a century later by Hegel, who conceived of philosophy as having not only a dialectical form but a narrative form as well: "When philosophy paints its gray in gray, a form of life has become old, and this gray in gray cannot rejuvenate it, only understand it. The owl of Minerva begins its flight when dusk is falling."[24] Likewise, for Hume, it is only when impressions are over with and safely in the past that we can understand them.

We can appreciate in a different way how misdirected the standard objection against Hume's first principle is. Hume is not required to recall past impressions for inspection in the present any more than Hegel is required to recall past forms of life for inspection in the present. The standard objection is based on a paradigm of understanding according to which things are not intelligible unless they can be inspected in the present (where the present may be construed as either that of immediate sense perception or the timeless framework of an absolute perspective); in either case the past must appear problematical or even unintelligible. But Hume's narrative paradigm is just the other way around: the present by itself is unintelligible and ceases to be so only when it becomes past and is viewed in the light of a later existent.

## THE LIMITS OF HUME'S FIRST PRINCIPLE

On Hume's first principle all ideas are past-entailing. I have argued that this, by itself, constitutes no objection, since there *are* past-entailing concepts, and, indeed, without such concepts the world of common life would be unintelligible. But there are also tenseless concepts. We have now to examine how Hume can account for these concepts.

Hume's model for a simple idea is the *afterimage*, which is a past-entailing and narrative notion. A simple idea of red on its first appearance is a particular backward-looking existent. Given a number of such ideas which resemble each other in respect of being red, we can form an abstract, tenseless idea of red in the standard Humean way by fixing on a particular idea, ignoring its temporal features, and using it to stand for resembling existences. We have "a full and adequate conception" of red when we have achieved an internal and external mastery of the concept. We have an external understanding of the concept when we have mastered the linguistic conventions for applying the term "red" to objects. We have an internal understanding of the concept when we have acquired the capacity to associate the term, as properly used, with an idea of the appropriate sort. The external conditions for having the idea of red are tenseless since the linguistic conventions for applying the term "red" can, in principle, be applied by anyone at any time. Some of the internal conditions are also tenseless, for the past-entailing idea that is or can be brought to mind upon the use of the term "red" is considered in abstraction from its temporal features. Moreover, the rules that govern the process of abstraction are precisely those for applying the term "red" properly. Should we attend to the temporal features of a past-entailing idea of red and, mistakenly, incorporate these into the meaning of the term, we would immediately recognize ourselves to be in violation of the linguistic convention (T, 20-21). Yet, at the same time, Hume holds that no one has a full conception of red unless he has gone through the experience of the color and its image in recollection, a process we may call having a *narrative encounter* with the color. A narrative encounter with red yields a past-entailing idea of red or what, with perhaps greater propriety, should be called *narrative imagery* of red. I have referred to simple Humean ideas as "past-entailing ideas" to emphasize their most important logical feature (nothing is a simple Humean idea unless certain statements about the past are true), but as experiences, they are perhaps best described as "narrative images" since no perception is an idea unless it is viewed in the light of past impressions.

We may conclude, then, that no one has an adequate simple idea of red unless he has satisfied the tenseless external and internal conditions and, in addition has satisfied the tensed condition of having had a narrative encounter with red things. And, of course, what holds here for the simple idea of red holds for all simple ideas. A simple Humean idea of "X," then, is tenseless in that the term "X" is used in a tenseless way, but no one has a "full comprehension" of the idea of X unless he can associate the appropriate narrative imagery with the proper use of the term "X." In this way, something of a rememberance of things past is built, however faintly, into the narrative imagery necessary for a full internal understanding of tenseless concepts. We may now recall one of Bennett's criticisms of the first principle: "What someone understands now is not logically tied to what he underwent earlier."[25] To have lived through something is not necessary to command an external understanding of the concept of that thing. It is necessary, however, to achieve an internal understanding of the concept, the sort of understanding Hume considered most significant for moral philosophy.

As I have explicated them, all simple ideas have, on the one hand, an external side which is public and tenseless and, on the other, an internal side of narrative imagery which is private and tensed. Several recent commentators have sought to reconstruct Hume's first principle on the basis of a reading which dismisses as philosophically unimportant the internal, narrative side in favor of the public, tenseless side. Basson, for instance, distinguishes two forms of the theory: (1) that ideas resemble impressions and (2) that ideas are derived from past impressions. According to Basson, Hume treats (1) as analytic and of fundamental importance; (2), however, is "of subsidiary importance only, insofar as it lends a certain additional force to the principle of correspondence between simple impressions and simple ideas. The latter is Hume's chief analytical tool."[26] This interpretation enables Basson to see in Hume's first principle a prototype of logical empiricism and to read it as a tenseless theory, thereby avoiding its troublesome narrative imagery and past-referring character. Similar reconstructions of Hume's first principle have been put forth by MacNabb, Zabeeh, Flew, and Bennett. As charitable interpretations, they are, I think, misplaced, for it is precisely the narrative imagery and past-referring character of the theory that makes it interesting. Indeed, we may, if we wish, go on to read (2) as analytic in roughly the way Basson reads (1) as analytic, for, as we have seen, Hume will not allow that we have an adequate idea of something unless we have achieved an internal mastery of it.

But however we interpret (2), whether as analytic or not, it is an essential part of Hume's theory and has a much better claim to be his "chief analytical tool" than (1). Zabeeh has observed that all "Hume cares to establish is the fact of the priority of impressions to ideas, and the derivability of the latter from the former, and not the thesis that ideas are copies of impressions."[27] This interpretation, I think, goes too far. But it is certainly a correct reading of complex ideas and especially complex *ideas of reflection* which are the special objects of Hume's philosophy (T, 8). Such ideas, though past-entailing, need not copy the impressions from which they are derived: "I observe, that many of our complex ideas never had impressions, that corresponded to them, and that many of our complex impressions never are exactly copied in ideas." Thus "is a priest" is a complex past-entailing idea which does not copy the impressions into which it can be analyzed. So even if we rejected (1) altogether, the most important part of Hume's theory would survive. Failure to appreciate this fact about the theory has led not only to misplaced charity but to misplaced criticism.

Consider Frege's remarks: "Do the concepts as we approach their supposed sources, reveal themselves in peculiar purity? Not at all; we see everything as through a fog, blurred and undifferentiated. It is as though everyone who wished to know about America were to try to put himself back in the position of Columbus, at the time when he caught the first dubious glimpse of his supposed India."[28] Now Hume is not committed to the view that a concept like "America" is to be thought of as corresponding to resembling past America-like impressions. "America" is a complex idea and, unlike simple ideas, need not correspond to any set of past impressions. Moreover, the concept of "America" is an unhappy choice for the kind of criticism Frege wants to make, for it is also a past-entailing concept. Frege considered all concepts to be tenseless, but if, somehow, all past-entailing concepts were eliminated, expressions such as "is an American," "is the American ideal of life," "is the American Anthem" would be meaningless, for certain true statements about the past are necessary conditions for their application to any existent.

It is not with theories of meaning as with empirical statements that we can assess them in terms of their truth or falsity. Theories of meaning purport to lay down the conditions for cognitively meaningful discourse, and these conditions are logically prior to the conditions that determine the distinction between truth and falsity. Only meaningful statements can be true or false. Theories of meaning in the empirical tradition have functioned more like metaphysical systems than like analyses of how words actually have meaning. They have typically been referential theories and, in drawing a line between the meaningful and the meaningless, they have necessarily also marked off a line between the real and the illusory, Indeed, their purported power to govern ontological decisions has been their most interesting and controversial feature. If, for instance, the phenomenalistic and pragmatic theories of meaning are right, then sentences purportedly about the past are cognitively meaningless unless they can be recast into specified statements about present and future experiences. In either case, statements in the past tense are no longer to be thought of as being about the past but as being about something else. There is no past *reality*. Like metaphysical systems, theories of meaning are modeled on structures of significance which are thought to be paradigmatic for an explication of the nature of thought and reality. The phenomenalist finds a paradigm in the certainty of immediate sense experience and from that generates categories of meaningful discourse, understanding, and reality. Likewise, the pragmatist finds instrumental activity paradigmatic, and the logical empiricist, absolute idealist, and many others find timeless systematic structures paradigmatic. Hume, we may say, finds the narrative structure of *historical inquiry* paradigmatic and from it generates categories of meaning and understanding.

We cannot, of course, ask whether the theories governed by these paradigms are true. We should view them rather as instruments to be evaluated by the light they can throw on the nature of cognitive discourse. To have value, it is enough that they uncover some aspect of understanding and reality which would otherwise have remained obscure. And this is the main value of Hume's first principle. It brings into focus what the other theories of meaning (all of which entail some form of historical nihilism) had obscured: the importance of past-entailing concepts, narrative thought as a form of understanding, and the past as a category of reality. I do not mean to suggest that Hume consciously thought of his theory as containing these values. The claim is simply that the values are there and that Hume put them there. Hume did not and could not have worked out his philosophy in the light of nineteenth-and twentieth-century theories of meaning, nor could he have seen himself as part of what we call the empirical tradition, much less, as some would say, the greatest philosopher of that tradition. But we, nevertheless, can and ought to read Hume in terms of later philosophical theories. It is these very theories that enable us to discern aspects of Hume's thinking the significance of which he could not have appreciated. There is, of course, always the standing danger that we may read too much of later theories into Hume and find more of ourselves there than the evidence warrants, but this should not prevent us from uncovering and developing those structures in Hume's theory which are uniquely visible to us and which we find historically and philosophically interesting. When we view Hume's theory in terms of later empirical theories of meaning, we can see how it is unique. Hume founds meaning on a narrative relation between present and past experiences. Phenomenalists found meaning on actual or possible present experiences, pragmatists on a relation between present and future experiences, and logical empiricism on experience conceived of in a tenseless way.

No small reason for pointing out these differences is that Hume is often identified with or treated as a precursor of one or the other of the main forms of empiricism. He is most often read as a phenomenalist of some sort or as one who is committed to the main doctrines of phenomenalism. But he has also been read as a presursor of pragmatism, and, more recently, as a precursor of logical empiricism. To bring out the philosophical value of Hume's work it is necessary to "reconstruct" it in accord with what appears to be the main direction of his own philosophical principles. Most reconstructions have been in line with the principles governing the above forms of empiricism. As models for reading Hume, there is some value in each of them, but none captures what is really distinctive about Hume's empiricism. Hume worked out a "historical empiricism" which makes special use of the past and of narrative order in explaining what it means to have an idea of something. The sort of intelligibility that narrative order brings is the deep paradigm behind Hume's first principle; nor is the narrative paradigm limited to the first principle. As we shall see in later chapters, it runs throughout Hume's thinking on all levels and is a focal point where we can begin to see a mutually illuminating unity between Hume's philosophical and historical works.

The world of common life is structured by past-entailing concepts and would be unintelligible without them. The main forms of empiricism are based on theories of meaning which entail historical nihilism, the view that sentences purportedly about the past are meaningless. Since past-entailing concepts require true statements about the past as a condition of their instantiation, they are impossible in the theories of meaning we have considered. In Hume's theory, however, past-entailing concepts are possible not because Hume has a better account of what it means to refer to the past, but because he takes reference to the past as primitive and not in need of explanation. What a full Humean account of such concepts would look like will be presented in the next chapter. In the meantime, it is enough to see that Hume's first principle satisfies a necessary condition for past-entailing concepts; it allows us to make statements about the past without having to treat such statements as shorthand ways of talking about entirely different things: the present, the present-future, or some tenseless order. Whatever difficulties it may have, Hume's first principle is superior to the other empirical theories of meaning in making possible an account of past-entailing concepts.

But why is Hume's theory unique in this way? One reason, I think, is that those who have propounded the other theories have tended to take some interpretation of the language of theoretical science as their model of language. Ayer's phenomenalism, Lewis's pragmatism, Carnap's logical empiricism are vintage cases of this propensity. Each of these views has some appeal as an account of the cognitive meaning framed in scientific language. Phenomenalism fixes on the importance of scientific observations in the verification process, pragmatism on the operational definitions of theoretical terms, logical empiricism on the systematic structure of theoretical language. It has not seemed and perhaps is not plausible to think of theoretical language in terms of a tensed, narrative relation between past and present existences. Hume's model, however, is not the language of theoretical science but the language of common life. That language is the result of a natural and historical process whereby linguistic conventions are gradually established to satisfy the social need for communication; and common life, for Hume, is an open-ended system of such historically developed conventions. As a consequence, the language of common life is rich in past-entailing terms: "mother," "congressman," "friend," "the First Amendment," "the Last Supper," "bankrupt," "World War II," and so on. For the correct application of these terms to present existences, statements about the past must be true. Unlike tenseless terms, such terms are backward-looking and register faithfully our narrative involvement with the world and with each other. To eliminate these terms would be to eliminate the language of common life.

If the error of the empirical tradition was not to have taken seriously the language of common life, Hume's error was not to have taken seriously the language of theoretical science. By the first principle, we do not really have an adequate concept of X until we have achieved an external and internal mastery of the concept, and to have an internal command of the concept is to have had a narrative encounter with X. I have argued that this narrative account is a plausible way of thinking about experiential concepts which have an external and an internal side and are necessary for understanding the moral world, itself a world of internal and external existences. Hume, however, illegitimately extends the narrative analysis of concept formation beyond its proper scope to include mathematical and theoretical expressions which purport to refer to entities which in principle cannot be experienced. So in the end, Hume's first principle is inadequate as a universal theory of concept formation, but the error is instructive and, in a way, refreshing. The empirical tradition is littered with theories of meaning that have taken the language of theoretical science as the model of all language and have run afoul of the past-entailing language of common life. Hume's error is just the opposite. His narrative analysis of the language of common life runs afoul of theoretical language. The former error, however, is the more prevalent. It is a fashionable dictum that all language is theory-laden (as if, in Hegelian fashion, a universal philosophic mind were behind the construction of all language). No doubt part of language is theory-laden, but what we may learn from a meditation on the first principle is that the greater part is story-laden. The concepts expressed by the past-entailing terms that populate the language of common life frame stories, however simple, of our relation to the past.

We have seen how Hume's first principle has narrative form and how simple ideas, though tenseless in their representation, nevertheless have, by virtue of their internal side, a narrative structure. But how is narrative order possible? Hume's answer to this question can be inferred from his analysis of how the imagination combines simple ideas to form *complex ideas of reflection*, which is the subject of the next chapter. These are the most important ideas for understanding Hume's philosophy of common life; indeed, it is for the explication of these ideas that the *Treatise* was written (T, 8). We shall find that all complex ideas of reflection have a narrative structure; by seeing how this is so, we shall be able to understand how Hume can account for narrative order and also how this narrative order of ideas is, ontologically, reflected in the moral world itself.

# 5

# Time and the Moral World

> But as 'tis certain, that, however every thing be produc'd in time, there is nothing real, that is produc'd by time; it follows, that property being produc'd by time, is not any thing real in the objects, but is the offspring of the sentiments, on which alone time is found to have any influence.
>
> Hume's *Treatise*

## THE TENSELESS IDEA OF TIME

The idea of the past cannot be derived from past impressions on pain of vicious circularity. But from this it does not follow that the idea of the past is unanalyzable. Granted that we have the idea, its structure may be understood by examining the relation it has to other ideas, especially the ideas of the present, the future, and of time in general. Hume's views on the concept of the past and its relations to other temporal concepts can be inferred from the discussion of time in the *Treatise* book I, part II, sections I-V, and in book II, part III, sections VII-VIII. For convenience I shall refer to these as the accounts of time in book I and book II. There is yet no commentary on the account in book II, which is by far the most important for understanding Hume's views on the nature of time. The account in book I is generally agreed to be one of the least satisfactory parts of the *Treatise*. Laird found that it "deserves some of the very hard things that have been said of it," and Kemp Smith found it "very bewildering."[1] Some of these negative comments are due, perhaps, to the fact that Hume's two discussions of time have not been read as a piece; when this is done, we shall have a full view of the Humean conception of time and, I think, one which, despite its inadequacies, is philosophically insightful and suggestive.

The discussion of time in book I is parallel to the discussion of space.

The main point of the discussion is to show, by an analysis of their ideas, that the Parts of time and space are not infinitely divisible. This ontological project is underwritten by the principle that "Wherever ideas are adequate representations of objects, the relations, contradictions and agreements of the ideas are all applicable to the objects; and this we may in general observe to be the foundation of all human knowledge" (T, 29). Since our ideas of space and time are adequate representations of their objects, "The plain consequence is, that whatever *appears* impossible and contradictory upon the comparison of these ideas, must be *really* impossible and contradictory, without any farther excuse or evasion" (T, 29). This is Hume's version of the ancient dictum that "the real is the rational," and, indeed, these first five sections of part II, book I are the most rationalistic parts of the *Treatise*. Hume does not, as we have observed, introduce the discussion of space and time by first deriving their ideas from past impressions. Instead, he grants straight out that we have the ideas in question because the language of space and time is so deeply woven into the fabric of common life: "Now, 'tis certain we have an idea of extension; for otherwise why do we talk and reason concerning it?" (T, 32). The same courtesy is not granted to theoretical ideas such as "gravity" and "a vacuum": "The frequent disputes concerning a vacuum, or extension without matter, prove not the reality of the idea, upon which the disputes turn; there being nothing more common, than to see men deceive themselves in this particular" (T, 62). The difference between the two is that the linguistic conventions by which "we talk and reason" concerning space and time are so fundamentally a part of the conventions of common life that upon their elimination common life itself would disintegrate. There is also a suggestion here, in the light of Hume's general theory of linguistic conventions, that the fundamentally established character of the language of space and time represents a long and hard-won adjustment to the world, and so the ideas framed by these conventions must somehow be adequate representations of what they purport to be about. Some such notion as this appears behind Hume's more than facetious talk about there being a "pre-established harmony" between our ideas and the world (EU, 54).[2]

In any case, Hume is certain, before any application of the first principle, that we have an idea of space and time. The only question is about the proper analysis of the idea. Hume's method proceeds in two steps. The first, both in order of exposition and in logical importance, is an analysis of the external side of the idea; the second is the more characteristic method of presenting its internal side. The first task is carried out in the context of a set of arguments designed to show, on purely formal grounds, that the ideas of space and time are not infinitely divisible (T, 26-39). The idea of time emerges as an order of objects in succession, the simple parts of which are moments that have no duration and so are not infinitely divisible. From the analysis of this idea, Hume draws important ontological consequences: "'Tis certain then, that time, *as it exists*, must be compos'd of indivisible moments" (T, 31, emphasis mine). Moreover, "these indivisible parts, being nothing in themselves, are inconceivable when not fill'd with something real and existent" (T, 39). The idea of time, then, is not the idea of a "separate or distinct" existent but merely the idea of "the manner or order, in which objects exist: Or, in other words, 'tis impossible to conceive . . . a time, when there was no succession or change in any real existence" (T, 39-40). These arguments are supposed to show us something important about the nature of time as it actually exists, and they are presented in the high rationalistic manner of demonstrations about real existence: "'Tis therefore possible for space and time to exist conformable to this idea: And if it be possible, 'tis certain they actually do exist conformable to it; since their infinite divisibility is utterly impossible and contradictory" (T, 39). And Hume is not prepared to hear any prattle from an "obstinate defender of the doctrine of infinite divisibility" about his arguments posing difficulties: "nothing can be more absurd, than this custom of calling a *difficulty* what pretends to be a *demonstration*, and endeavouring by that means to elude its force and evidence. . . . A demonstration, if just, admits of no opposite difficulty; and if not just, 'tis a mere sophism, and consequently can never be a difficulty. . . . To talk therefore of objections and replies, and ballancing of arguments in such a question as this, is to confess . . . that human reason is nothing but a play of words" (T, 31-32).

Having shown by a-priori arguments what our idea of time is and, indeed, what time itself must be, Hume goes on to put the idea into canonical form by deriving it from past impressions. But here the first principle is bound to appear logically idle. If we already know so much about the idea of time, why do we need to discover its connections with past impressions? Hume gives two reasons. The first is that "No discovery cou'd have been made more happily for deciding all controversies concerning ideas, than that above-mention'd, that impressions always take the precedency of them" (T, 33). If one is not convinced by the formal analysis of the idea, then an actual impression of time which, as reflected in its idea, is "so clear and evident" as to "admit of no controversy" should settle the matter. The application of the first principle, then, can corroborate the logical analysis of the idea of time already given. But, as Hume has made quite clear, corroboration is not really necessary since that analysis has been sealed by demonstrations. The second reason is that the principle should be applied "in order to discover farther the nature of our ideas of space and time" (T, 33). The notion here is the characteristically Humean one that we cannot have an adequate idea of time or of anything else until we have gained an interior understanding of it. Hume's use of the first principle in explicating the idea of time is further support for the thesis that he conceives of the principle mainly as a device for critically clarifying and expanding our ideas and not as a decision procedure for determining whether we have an idea or not. Whether we have an idea of time at all is determined, in effect (in section II) by a logical analysis of the way "we talk and reason concerning it" (T, 32).

The empirical example that corresponds to the formal analysis is "five notes play'd on a flute" which affords us "the impression and idea of time" (T, 36). Hume stresses the fact that "the idea of time is not deriv'd from a particular impression mix'd up with others, and plainly distinguishable from them; but arises altogether from the manner, in which impressions appear to the mind, without making one of the number" (T, 36). And the "manner" in which objects are disposed to yield the idea of time is that of succession. The idea of time, then, is the idea of objects in succession where the objects and the order of succession are internally connected such that they cannot be conceived separately nor can they exist separately. We acquire the idea of time from "the succession of our perceptions of every kind, ideas as well as impressions, and impressions of reflection as well as of sensation" (T, 34-35). Once we have experienced a number of sets of objects in succession we can, on comparing their ideas, form, in the standard Humean way, an abstract idea of time by fixing on a particular idea which resembles all the others in respect to the "aspect" of succession (T, 35). Now Hume's application of the first principle to the idea of time may appear strange insofar as the idea of *time* is being accounted for by reference to *past* impressions. But this poses no special problem for Hume's procedure. The idea of time, as that of objects in succession, is a tenseless idea. Objects so disposed are merely before and after each other and not related as past, present, and future. The idea of tenseless time does not entail the idea of tensed time. So there is no reason why Hume cannot treat the idea of tenseless time like any other tenseless idea, such as red, insisting that an internal and narrative understanding is necessary for an adequate comprehension of the idea. Of course, the requirement that we achieve an internal narrative mastery of a concept as a condition for fully understanding it may appear strange. But that is merely an oddity about Hume's conception of what it is to have an idea and not in any special way an oddity about explicating the idea of tenseless time by reference to past impressions.

It should be pointed out, however, that the idea of something being

115

past presupposes the order of tenseless time. More generally, the whole tensed order (past, present, and future) presupposes the tenseless order of succession. But if applying the first principle, which is a narrative procedure, is necessary to enable us to have an adequate conception of tenseless time, then it appears that Hume's account of time is circular. Narrative relations are tensed and, thus, logically presuppose the idea of tenseless time. The circularity, however, is not a vicious one. That tensed ideas entail the tenseless idea of time is a logical relation, and there is no vicious circularity in using a logical relation (such as consistency) in some philosophical theory which purports to give an account of what that relation is. Indeed, this sort of circularity is a central feature of Hume's conception of philosophic method, as, for instance, when he uses the causal relation in his account of what it is to understand causal relations. Such circularity follows from Hume's rejection of the autonomy principle. The path to some Archimedean point outside common life which Descartes sought and which would prevent the circularity is, in reality, the path to Pyrrhonism. The price of abandoning Pyrrhonism is that philosophical reflection will be tainted by presupposing those very maxims of common life which it seeks to understand. So although tensed time presupposes untensed time, Hume can hold without vicious circularity that no one could have an internal mastery of the idea of tenseless time without having had a narrative encounter with objects in succession. The external mastery of the concept which Hume presents in part II, sections I-II and prior to an application of the first principle does not require a narrative context, and so the question of circularity does not arise. But more important than the question of whether Hume's account of tenseless time is circular, is the question of how he understands the idea of tensed time by reference to which the idea of untensed time is to be explained. Hume nowhere explicitly sets himself the project of accounting for our idea of tensed time. Perhaps he thought the idea too fundamental to require explanation (the idea of the past and present are, after all, taken as primitive concepts under the first principle); or perhaps he did not think of the matter at all. There is, in any case, an interesting discussion of time in book II, part III, sections VII-VIII, where Hume explicitly examines the ideas of past, present, and future and their relation to tenseless time or what he calls time "abstractedly consider'd" (T, 431). From these sections we can glean, in a fairly straightforward way, what can be considered a Humean theory of the idea of tensed time.

## THE IDEA OF TENSED TIME

The problem of these sections is to explain how different temporal and spatial distances have different effects on the imagination and, hence, on the passions. Six questions are asked: "Why distance weakens the conception and passion: Why distance in time has a greater effect than that in space: And why distance in past time has still a greater effect than that in the future." And then three questions "which seem to be, in a manner, the reverse of these: Why a very great distance encreases our esteem and admiration for an object: Why such a distance in time encreases it more than that in space: And a distance in past time more than that in future" (T, 432). In the discussion that follows, I shall concentrate mainly on Hume's doctrine that past and future time are qualitatively different and because of that fact have different effects on the imagination and passions.

The first thing to appreciate about these sections is that a new conception of time is being forged. If we had only the tenseless concept of time laid out in book I, questions about the different effects of past and future time on the imagination and passions could not even arise. So in explaining why we think and feel differently about past and future, Hume is also implicitly explaining how we understand tensed concepts. The focal idea for understanding what we mean by past and future is the idea of the present. What do we mean when we say that something is happening *now*? This question cannot be answered without reference to Hume's theory of the self. He writes: "The idea of ourselves is always intimately present to us, and conveys a sensible degree of vivacity to the idea of any other object, to which we are related" (T, 354). But it is not just the idea of the self that we always have, it is also the object: "ourself, of whom we are every moment conscious" (T, 340). The self, for Hume, is not a set of private mental images; the self is essentially related to a public world, and so the idea of the self entails reference to a public world: "Ourself, independent of the perception of every other object, is in reality nothing: For which reason we must turn our view to external objects" (T, 340). And the objects we perceive are always viewed in some temporal (untensed) order: "there is a continual succession of perceptions in our mind; so that the idea of time . . .[is] for ever present with us" (T, 65). Any state of awareness for Hume, then, involves reference to a self internally related to public objects which are ordered by the untensed idea of time. But this is not all. Our awareness of temporally disposed objects is not tenseless; it is not merely the idea of objects arranged in the order of before and after. It is, rather, the idea of objects arranged in the tensed order of past, present, and future.

The first move to accommodate tensed ideas is Hume's insistence that the present is the reference point without which perception of temporally disposed objects is impossible. He never explicitly raises the question of what we mean when we say that something is happening in the present, but an answer can be inferred from what he does say about the present and our perception of it. Consider the following passages: " 'Tis obvious, that the imagination can never totally forget the points of . . . time, in which we are existent; but receives such frequent advertisements of them from the passions and senses, that however it may turn its attention to foreign and remote objects, it is *necessitated every moment to reflect on the present*" (T, 427-28, emphasis mine). And, " 'Tis also remarkable, that in the conception of those objects, which we regard as real and existent, we take them in their proper order and situation, and never leap from one object to another, which is distant from it, without running over, at least in a cursory manner, all those objects, which are interpos'd betwixt them" (T, 428). When we reflect, then, on any object temporally distant from ourselves, "we are oblig'd not only to reach it at first by passing thro' all the intermediate space betwixt ourselves and the object, but also to renew our progress every moment; *being every moment recall'd to the consideration of ourselves and our present situation*" (T, 428, emphasis mine). In these passages, the present is experienced not as an objective property of real (untensed) time but as a certain relation between real time and self-awareness. Hume seems to be saying that by the present we mean the self-awareness that what we are experiencing is occurring at the same time as our experience of it. Or as he metaphorically puts it: our position in the present is derived from the "advertisements" of our position in time given by the "passions" and "senses" and not from any perception of a present-tense structure in time itself. Given this analysis of the idea of the present, definitions of the past and future fall easily into place. To say something is past is to say that it occurs before the present, and to say something is future is to say that it occurs after the present.

In this analysis, tensed ideas require essential reference to the self. If there were no self, there would be no tensed time. By contrast, the idea of the self does not enter at all into the analysis of tenseless time given in book I. The idea of tenseless time does not logically require any reference to the self. Consequently, if there were no self, the idea of tenseless time could still be instantiated. Tensed time, then, is mind-dependent in a way that tenseless time is not. Although Hume rejected the distinction between primary and secondary qualities, he, nevertheless, thought it metaphorically useful in bringing out certain features of the relation between ideas and impressions of reflection: "Ideas may be compar'd to the extension and solidity of matter, and impressions, especially reflective ones, to colours, tastes, smells, and other sensible qualities" (T, 366). We may use the distinction here to say that Hume treats tenseless time as a primary quality of objects and tensed time as a secondary quality. Certainly he went out of his way to ontologize the tenseless notion of time in book I, giving it a primary status (T, 39). There is no attempt to do the same for tensed time. On the contrary, Hume talks freely of tensed concepts as being essentially tied to self-awareness, suggesting that they do in fact have a secondary status. But to think of tensed qualities or, indeed, of any qualities as secondary in the modern sense is not, for Hume, to think of them as unreal. It is a favorite Humean theme that the "famous doctrine, supposed to be fully proved in modern times" that sensible qualities are mind-dependent would not, even if true, take away from their reality: "Though colours were allowed to lie only in the eye, would dyers or painters ever be less regarded or esteemd?" (E, 168n). Similarly, the properties of beauty and moral worth are not properties of objects independent of the mind: "beauty and worth are merely of a relative nature, and consist in an agreeable sentiment, produced by an object in a particular mind, according to the peculiar structure and constitution of that mind" (E, 166). But this doctrine "takes off no more from the reality of the latter qualities, than from that of the former; nor need it give any umbrage either to critics or moralists. . . . There is a sufficient uniformity in the senses and feelings of mankind, to make all these qualities the objects of art and reasoning, and to have the greatest influence on life and manners" (E, 168n).

So tensed qualities would still be real even if thought of as secondary qualities and placed alongside sensory, aesthetic, and moral qualities. There is still, however, an important difference between these qualities. As we have seen, Hume holds that it is logically possible for perceptions to exist independently of any mind (T, 207). This thesis occurs in the context of examining the status of our belief in the external world, and the perceptions Hume has mainly in mind are those sensory perceptions we take to be properties of physical objects. It is also a thesis fundamental to his criticism of the modern primary-secondary-quality distinction. Indeed, it is largely because Hume holds that there is no contradiction in saying that a color perception such as red can exist independently of any mind, that he can find the primary-secondary-quality distinction arbitrary. And in Hume's own reformed popular system, what were formerly thought of as primary and secondary qualities are brought together and placed on the same footing as qualities of objects conceived to exist independently of the mind. These include all the properties that constitute the perceivable spatiotemporal order of nature. And it is one of Hume's main purposes in book I to lay these properties out and to explain their status. In book II, however, we confront an entirely different set of properties. Book II is a study of the self through an examination of its passions. And it is the order of these passions that constitutes the moral world. Properties of the moral world such as pride, hatred, beauty, virtue, and the properties of tensed time require essential reference to the self and so are logically mind-dependent. Hume makes clear that it would not be contradictory to say that something is red, or round, or exists tenselessly before or after something else independently of there being any minds. But it would be contradictory to say that something is just, or beautiful, or past, if there were no minds relative to which things are just, beautiful, or past.

We have then a reconstitution in the moral world of the old modern distinction between primary and secondary qualities. The new set of secondary qualities are those that are logically mind-dependent; they are the qualities that characterize the order of passion and are the objects of book II and book III. The new set of primary qualities are all the perceivable qualities of the spatiotemporal world and are the objects of book I. In this new conception, secondary qualities are real and objective even though mind-dependent. Indeed, they constitute just that special reality which Hume calls "the moral world." But one might wonder whether tensed properties should be placed in the same category with moral and aesthetic properties. The latter properties pick out an order of sentiment, whereas tensed properties appear to hold independently of any sentiment. In a world with no sentiments, there could be no moral or aesthetic properties, but, presumably, there could still be tensed properties. This sharp distinction, however, between tensed properties and sentiment does not yield an adequate picture of Hume's conception of tensed time. It is a distinction that holds only at a certain level of abstraction. As we shall see, the richer notion of tensed time, the one usually at work in common life, has sentiment built into it.

## TEMPORAL PASSIONS

I have argued that the *Treatise* is cast in narrative form and should be read, in part, as a philosophical drama, where the earlier sections gain in significance by being viewed in the light of later developments. One surprising turn of thought occurs in book II where Hume discovers the "general maxim, that no object is presented to the senses, nor image form'd in the fancy, but what is accompany'd with some emotion or movement of spirits proportion'd to it" (T, 373). And Hume is clear that this maxim applies to every idea, even to those of quantity: "Every part, then, of extension, and every unite of number has a separate emotion attending it, when conceiv'd by the mind" (ibid.). The principle is described as the "new discovery of an impression, that secretly attends every idea" (T, 375). None of this was available in book I because the self does not appear there as an explanatory entity. Perceptions may easily appear to be devoid of any meaning. But having discovered the principle, we are to read it back into book I and to view perceptions as having always had the properties it describes.

Viewed in the light of this "new discovery," the perceptions of book I jump to life. They no longer appear as meaningless phenomena but as emotionally charged existences which make up the emotional life of a self. The discussion of tenseless time in book I makes no reference at all to the self; although, of course, we now know that "the idea, or rather impression of ourselves is always intimately present with us" (T, 317, 320). A main point of book I is that of establishing, via the Pyrrhonian illumination, the reality of the world of common life with its internal and external aspects. The focus in book I is on the external. The self is discussed mainly under the problematic rationalistic conception of it. In book II, the self is the main object of study; it appears there as an empirically discernible psycho-physical system—"the qualities of our mind and body, that is *self*" (T, 303)—and it is the central explanatory entity in Hume's account of the passions. There was no need to employ the concept of the self in book I since the concepts Hume is concerned to explicate there are those which are necessary for understanding the spatiotemporal order of nature and which are not logically mind-dependent. These would include, of course, the tenseless concept of time. Given the absence of the self as an explanatory entity in book I, we can appreciate what otherwise might appear strange: why the discussion of tensed time had to await book II.

I have argued that tensed ideas register for Hume the self's awareness of its position in the order of tenseless time. Since every impression and idea is emotionally charged to some degree or other, the awareness of our position in tenseless time must also be "accompany'd with some emotion or movement of spirits." Feelings that arise from thinking about something Hume calls "impressions of reflection." These give rise to "ideas of reflection" which in turn may give rise to other impressions of reflection and so on indefinitely (T, 8). The impressions of reflection or feelings that arise when we reflect on our position in tenseless time we may call *temporal passions*. These in turn yield ideas of reflection: the idea of what it feels like to be in time. An initial statement of Hume's view on the idea of tensed time can now be given. (1) Tensed ideas refer to the self's awareness of its position in tenseless time. (2) These ideas, however, are always attended by temporal passions, which are special feelings we have about our location in time. (3) These temporal passions, in turn, give rise to temporally reflective ideas of the feelings we have about our location in time. The key to the whole analysis, however, is the notion of a temporal passion, for it is this notion that enables Hume to give an account of the qualitative difference between past and future time. The account comes in the form of answers to two questions: (1) Why, all things being equal, do we have a more lively conception of and greater passion for objects removed in the future than we do for those removed an equal distance in the past? (2) Why, all things being equal, does a great removal in the past cause a greater admiration and esteem for an object than a like removal in the future? We shall take them in turn.

Hume's answer to the first question is based on three properties of the fancy: (1) The imagination is essentially oriented towards the present: "however it may turn its attention to foreign and remote objects, it is necessitated every moment to reflect on the present" (T, 428). (2) When we reflect on temporally remote objects "we take them in their proper order and situation, and never leap from one object to another, which is distant from it, without running over, at least in a cursory manner, all those objects, which are interpos'd betwixt them" (T, 428). (3) Besides the propensity to a gradual progression through the points of time, "We always follow the succession of time in placing our ideas, and from the consideration of any object pass more easily to that, which follows immediately after it, than to that which went before it" (T, 430). The view here is that time as a tenseless order of succession has a direction or "arrow" which is causally reflected in a propensity of the imagination to order its ideas similarly. The direction of time is not a tensed property, not a direction from past to future. It is, rather, a structure inseparable from the "manner" in which untensed temporal objects are disposed, that is, it is internal to the notion of succession itself.

Given these propensities of the fancy, Hume answers the first question as follows. When the object is past, the progression of thought in passing to it from the position of the present is "contrary to nature" in proceeding from one point of time to the preceding one and from that to another preceding one "in opposition to the natural course of the succession" (T, 430). On the other hand, when we think of an object in the future, "our fancy flows along the stream of time, and arrives at the object by an order, which seems most natural, passing always from one point of time to that which is immediately posterior to it" (T, 430-31). "This *easy* progression" enables the imagination to "conceive its object in a stronger and fuller light, than when we are continually oppos'd in our passage, and are oblig'd to overcome the difficulties arising from the natural propensity of the fancy" (T, 431). In this way, Hume provides a ground for explaining our essential forgetfulness about the past and for explicating such future-referring passions as anticipation, hope, fear, regret, and feelings of destiny and fate.

Now the above may be taken as merely a bit of armchair psychology with Hume saying that because of the way the future and past are we have a tendency to think about objects in the future as opposed to the past. But he is in fact saying that because the imagination follows the "arrow" of tenseless time, we tend to think of events after now as *qualitatively* different from events prior to now. The former we call future, the latter past. In a word, Hume is trying to show how a property of the fancy determines our ideas of past and future. Past and future are understandable only through *ideas of reflection*. It is this "quality of the fancy, by which we are determin'd to trace the succession of time by a similar succession of ideas," that Hume is concerned to explicate. This fact is brought out by the following passage which amplifies the above account: "When from the present instant we consider two points of time equally distant in the future and in the past, 'tis evident, that, abstractedly consider'd, their relation to the present is almost equal. For as the future will *sometime* be present, so the past was *once* present. If we cou'd, therefore, remove this quality of the imagination, an equal distance in the past and in the future, wou'd have a similar influence" (T, 431).

This passage deserves several comments. First, it is especially clear here that Hume does not consider tensed time to be independent of the mind. Tenses are entirely relative to the self's awareness of its position in tenseless time or what Hume calls time "abstractedly considered." What is past to one person is at some other point in tenseless time future to another. The past is always somebody's past. But the tenseless order of succession is the same for all and is what it is independently of anyone's perception of it. Second, if the quality of the imagination in question were removed, the past and future would present themselves as trivially different distances on the same continuum. But as it is, we think of the past and future as *qualitatively* different. The qualitative indifference of the past and future, independent of the fancy, can be brought out in another way: "Nor is this only true, when the fancy remains fix'd, and from the present instant surveys the future and the past; but also when it changes its situation, and places us in different periods of time. For as on the one hand, in supposing ourselves existent in a point of time interpos'd betwixt the present instant and the future object, we find the future object approach to us, and the past retire, and become more distant" (T, 431). There is nothing, logically, in the order of tenseless time itself that requires us to order our thoughts about tensed time as we do. It is possible to direct our thoughts toward the past in the way that we now direct them toward the future.

Happily, though, how we think about time is not a matter of reason. The fancy, reflecting the arrow of tenseless time, has not left this matter to our choice. Without this propensity, we could fritter time away, pursuing the past with our backs, so to speak, turned toward the future, and this would be, to use the language of *Sein und Ziet*, an inauthentic mode of existence. Instead, "We advance, rather than retard our existence; and following what seems the natural succession of time, proceed from past to present, and from present to future. By which means we conceive the future as flowing every moment nearer us, and the past as retiring" (T, 432). The imagination, then, is essentially future-referring: any object we perceive or think about is going to be viewed in the light of some idea of what follows it in relation to some idea of *our* future. We can never think of any object as being merely past or present: "The fancy anticipates the course of things, and surveys the object in that condition, to which it tends, as well as in that, which is regarded as the present" (T, 432). Events in the present and past are viewed, however faintly, in the light of later events leading successively to the future and, hence, ordered by ideas of our future. When we view events under the future-referring propensity of the fancy, the past seems unreal, as something "continually diminishing" to nothingness. Although always present, this propensity does not always dominate. The thought of objects in the remote past gives rise to a different impression of reflection: the passion of veneration and esteem, a feeling we do not have for a correspondingly distant object in the future. A similar inequality holds regarding our admiration for objects remote in space as opposed to those remote in the past: "Antient busts and inscriptions are more valu'd than *Japan* tables: And not to mention the *Greeks* and *Romans*, 'tis certain we regard with more veneration the old *Chaldeans* and *Egyptians*, than the modern *Chinese* and *Persians*, and bestow more fruitless pains to clear up the history and chronology of the former, than it wou'd cost us to make a voyage, and be certainly inform'd of the character, learning and government of the latter" (T, 433).

To account for this turn in our thinking Hume brings in two more propensities in addition to those already mentioned. (4) "'Tis a quality very observable in human nature, that any opposition, which does not entirely discourage and intimidate us, has rather a contrary effect, and inspires us with a more than ordinary grandeur and magnanimity. In collecting our force to overcome the opposition, we invigorate the soul, and give it an elevation with which otherwise it wou'd never have been aquainted" (T, 433-34). (5) "'tis evident that the mere view and contemplation of any greatness, whether successive or extended, enlarges the soul, and gives it a sensible delight and pleasure. A wide plain, the ocean, eternity, a succession of several ages; all these are entertaining objects, and excel everything, however beautiful, which accompanies not its beauty with a suitable greatness" (T, 432). Now although it is difficult to conceive of a past object because of the future-referring propensity of the fancy, it is not impossible. The difficulty in connection with a small distance in time weakens the imagination but has a contrary effect when the distance is great. "The mind, elevated by the vastness of its object, is still farther elevated by the difficulty of the conception; and being oblig'd every moment to renew its efforts in the transition from one part of time to another, feels a . . .vigorous and sublime disposition" which by association of ideas is transferred to the idea of the distant past object and "gives us a proportionable veneration for it" (T, 436). Nor is it necessary that "the object shou'd be actually distant from us, in order to cause our admiration" An ancient "*Greek* medal, even in our cabinet, is always esteem'd a valuable curiosity. Here the object, by a natural transition, conveys our view to the distance; and the admiration, which arises from that distance, by another natural transition, returns back to the object" (T, 433). This is "the reason why all the relicts of antiquity are so precious in our eyes, and appear more valuable than what is brought even from the remotest parts of the world" (T, 436).

The remote past, then, is viewed as a realm of monumental greatness and authority. Hume metaphorically identifies this sublime view of the remote past with the notion of ascent. As we move in imagination away from the remote past to the present, objects descend in greatness and sublimity. It is "as if our ideas acquir'd a kind of gravity from their objects" (T, 435). Hence we "are not apt to imagine our posterity will excell us, or equal our ancestors." Rather, "we imagine our ancestors to be, in a manner, mounted above us, and our posterity to lie below us. Our fancy arrives not at the one without effort, but easily reaches the other" (T, 437). On this primitive passion of temporal piety are grounded the passions of veneration, love of antiquity, and, most important, the purely temporal standards framed in traditions, customs, precedent, and prescription. Even the standards of causal inference derive much of their authority from this normative manner of imagining the past.

Now it should be stressed that the greatness and normative character of the remote past are determined, as it were, a priori, by an original propensity of the imagination and are not the result of any empirical investigation using timeless standards. We may, of course, take a temporally neutral stance and find our ancestors inferior to us in many ways, e.g., in matters of health, morals, and scientific knowledge. But this cannot lead to a total rejection of the normative past unless we are prepared to think only in a tenseless way. And we can think in that way only in a state of nature. But, as it is, men are part of a historically determined society and are structured by its normative traditions and customs: "Time and custom give authority to all forms of government" and to the social norms that bind men together into common life (T,

566). The normative past constitutes an order of things. One may apply temporally neutral standards to make evaluations within this order, but one cannot eliminate all such order on pain of destroying a fundamental bond of common life.

Hume's full conception of time can now be stated. (1) Time is the order of objects in succession where the objects and the order are internally connected. Time, so conceived, is a structure of the physical world, is tenseless, and exists independently of the mind. (2) Tensed time presupposes tenseless time and in addition the self. I have argued that Hume's discussion of tensed structures in book II suggests the following analysis of tensed time: to say something is occurring *now* is to say that it occurs coexistent with our awareness of its occurrence. And with the aid of the tenseless idea of time, we can say that an object occurs in the past when it occurs before now and that an object occurs in the future when it occurs after now. Since tensed time presupposes the self, it is mind-dependent. (3) Tensed time is the self's awareness or idea of its position in tenseless time. But the idea of tenseless time is always attended with some feeling or impression of reflection. These temporal passions, as we have called them, give rise to temporal ideas of reflection: ideas of what it feels like to be in tenseless time. Temporal ideas of reflection are, experientially, the most developed and concrete of our temporal notions. They frame the idea of time as we live through it, which is the order of time that structures the moral world.

Hume is often pictured as having an unusually crude atomistic and mechanical method of analyzing experience, one that cannot do justice to the rich flow of experience as actually lived. Such criticism is misplaced insofar as it suggests that all analyses of experience are falsifications and that the only way to understand what we experience is through some sort of intuitive grasp. But extravagance aside, there is, in Hume's case, something to the criticism. It can, however, be mitigated by the following considerations. Hume's skepticism does not allow treatment of any analysis or principle as ultimate; the most we can do is take common perspectives and make comparative judgments relative to those perspectives. These common points of view are housed in the linguistic conventions that make up common life and include, among other perspectives, a point of view regarding the physical world, a causal point of view, and a moral and aesthetic point of view. These are so many islands of objectivity in a stormy sea of darkness and obscurity. The eternal temptation of philosophers is to imagine that these points of view are absolute: "There is one mistake to which they seem liable, almost without exception; they confine too much their principles, and make no account of that vast variety which nature has so much affected in all her operations. . . . Our own mind being narrow

126

and contracted, we cannot extend our conception to the variety and extent of nature, but imagine that she is as much bounded in her operations as we are in our speculation" (E, 161). So Hume was aware that there is more to experience than is captured by the associationist psychology of the *Treatise*, but we must have some sort of analysis to get started, however crude it might be.

Further, Hume's analysis of experience is not as "mechanical" or "atomistic" as it has sometimes been made out to be. For instance, he does not try to "construct" the rich notion of time as we live through it (the idea stated in [3] out of the simpler notions of time stated in (1) and (2). (3) is not a complex built out of (1) and (2) conceived as atomic building blocks; rather (3) is the representation of time as we experience it and (2) and (1) are arrived at by a process of progressive abstraction. (1), i.e. the idea of time in book I, is time "abstractedly consider'd" (T, 431). This fact is obscured by Hume's narrative mode of exposition in the *Treatise* and by the phenomenalistic preconceptions we bring to it, whereby we expect to find a system of complex ideas built out of indubitable sensory atoms. The temporal passions of the soul do not appear in book I but only because they would have gotten in the way. In book II, however, we see that they were presupposed all along.

Following Hume's own metaphorical use of the distinction between primary and secondary qualities, I have suggested that the properties of tenseless time are treated by Hume as primary qualities of objects and the properties of tensed time as secondary qualities, making them mind-dependent in roughly the same way that moral and aesthetic properties are mind-dependent. But there appears to be a significant difference between tensed properties on the one hand and moral and aesthetic properties on the other. The latter properties determine orders of sentiment; without certain sentiments there would be no moral or aesthetic properties. But tensed properties appear to hold independently of our sentiments (we appear to occupy the place we do in time whatever our feelings about it). And this raises the question of whether tensed properties should be thought of as mind-dependent in the way that moral and aesthetics properties are. Clearly they should not be if (2) is taken as the idea of tensed time, for the mere awareness of our position in tenseless time does not logically imply the idea of any feeling about time. Such feelings do, however, contingently arise from the idea of our location in time and *always* attend that idea. Indeed, these feelings or temporal passions are so intimately connected to the idea as to be virtually an internal part of it. I say "virtually" because Hume does hold that the feeling can be separated from the idea, however difficult it may be to do so: "however custom may make us insensible of this sensation, and cause us to confond it with the object or idea, 'twill

127

be easy, be careful and exact experiments, to separate and distinguish them" (T, 373). So tensed properties can be conceived independently of any passions we may have, but Hume is equally clear that this would be a very abstract conception of tensed properties, and one arrived at only by very careful analysis. Our ordinary notion of tensed time, then, is (3), which has reference to the temporal passions built into it. So when we think of past, present, and future under *temporal ideas of reflection*, we are thinking of them in light of the temporal passions and that is very much like thinking of a painting as beautiful or a character as just.

This can be brought out by considering Hume's account of moral and aesthetic properties. The basic idea is that there are certain kinds of objects which, if viewed in certain specifiable ways, cause normal people to have feelings of certain kinds. The sentiments aroused are called moral or aesthetic depending on the sort of object involved and the sort of viewpoint required. A property such as beauty (or virtue) "is not, properly speaking, a quality in any object, but merely a passion or impression in the soul" (T, 301). However, by an association of ideas and sentiments we read the idea of the sentiment of beauty that an object causes into the idea of the object, and then speak of the object having the property of beauty. Ascriptions of moral and aesthetic predicates are objective because there is a causal relation between certain features of the object and the sentiment of the perceiver and because the physical and cultural factors that determine the special viewpoint are objective. And Hume stresses the fact that these latter factors can be quite complex: "in many orders of beauty, particularly those of the finer arts, it is requisite to employ much reasoning, in order to feel the proper sentiment; and a false relish may frequently be corrected by argument and reflection. There are just grounds to conclude, that moral beauty partakes much of this latter species, and demands the assistance of our intellectual faculties" (EM, 173).

Likewise, when we view temporally disposed objects under temporal ideas of reflection we are, in effect, reading our temporal passions into the tensed properties of the objects. It is, of course, always possible by abstraction to ignore these temporal passions and to concentrate on time as stated in (2), the bare notion of the self's awareness of its place in tenseless time. For that matter, we can, by abstraction, ignore the self and concentrate on the idea of time as stated in (1), the idea of objects disposed in the tenseless order of succession. But in common life we rarely perform such abstractions. The temporal properties of the moral world have our temporal passions built into them in the same way that the ethical and aesthetic properties of the moral world have the corresponding sentiments built into them. To eliminate the temporal, ethical, and aesthetic passions from their respective properties would be to eliminate the moral world.

Hume did not explore the temporal passions as deeply as he did the moral and aesthetic passions. Only two passions are discussed: the future-referring propensity whereby we order temporally disposed objects in the light of some idea of our future, and the veneration we have for objects in the remote past. Hume discusses these passions in a very general way and treats them more as forms of the imagination than as objects. There are some hints, however, as to how these forms might receive content. For instance, Hume comments that we have a greater veneration for "the *Greeks* and *Romans*" than for "the old *Chaldeans* and *Egyptians*" even though the latter are more remote in the past than the former (T, 433). The reason might be that we also admire the Greeks for having achieved certain nontemporal values such as scientific knowledge and beauty, and the Romans for having established a superior political administration. So the purely temporal passion of veneration can be modified by nontemporal values. Or we may have a greater veneration for the Greeks and Romans because they are considered to be more closely connected to our history and traditions. And in this case the temporal passion of veneration is modified by other temporal values locked in traditions and stories we tell about ourselves. Similar remarks could be made about the passions arising from the future-referring propensity of the imagination.

And there may be other temporal passions which Hume does not discuss. Indeed, if every idea is emotionally charged (and Hume is prepared to carry this thesis very far: "Every part . . . of extension, and every unite of number has a separate emotion attending it, when conceiv'd by the mind" (T, 373), then there are temporal passions which Hume has not discussed. What feelings, for instance, do we have for objects disposed between the present and the remote past? We may have the temporal passion of regret for things done in our immediate past or the passion of nostalgia for a way of life not too far from the present. One may venerate the Romans but could hardly have nostalgia for them. Likewise nostalgia is something we might have for the "forties," but veneration would be impossible.

Although Hume does not fully develop his discussion of time, conceived of in the light of the temporal passions, what he does say is important for understanding his philosophy. Hume understands clearly that time, as we understand it in the moral world, is not the tenseless time of natural philosophy. It is rather time as we live through it: time that is *significant* for us. That Hume should have arrived at such a conception of temporality at all is an important philosophical achievement and one which was unusual for the time. Along with the work of Vico (which Hume did not know) it was one of the very first moves, in shifting philosophical inquiry away from an almost exclusive preoccupation with the epistemological and ontological problems of physics and mathematics to an investigation of the nature of historical knowledge and existence. But to bring out the full importance of Hume's discussion of the temporal passions, we must examine more closely the sort of significance they give to our understanding and experience of time. I shall now try to show that the sort of significance in question is that framed in narrative relations.

## NARRATIVE ASSOCIATIONS

Events take on narrative significance in a story by being viewed in the light of temporally separate events. Early events in a story gain meaning by being viewed from the perspective of later events, and later events are narratively unintelligible unless seen in the light of earlier events. In general, we may say that narrative relations occur when one set of events is viewed as significant in the light of some other temporally separated set of events. This, however, is only a minimum characterization of narrative order. We shall see shortly that other conditions are required, and, moreover, that Hume himself supplies them. In the meantime, the minimum characterization will serve as a convenient framework for interpreting Hume's conception of the temporal passions.

The idea of time and the self is always present to the imagination, and the self is always aware of its position in time. The self's awareness of its position in the present is the standard and focal point whereby prior objects are viewed as past and posterior objects as future. Moreover, the conception of any past or future object is associated with (1) the idea of the self's location in the present and (2) an idea of the correct empirical order of events lying between the temporally distant object and the self. In making this association, we are obliged not only to reach the distant object "by passing thro' all the intermediate space betwixt ourselves and the object, but also to renew our progress every moment; being every moment recall'd to the consideration of ourselves and our present situation" (T, 428). And the association is not a random one; events are viewed as significant in the light of ideas of temporally separate events one of which is always the self's awareness of its position in the present. Significance is constituted not only by the standard associating relations of resemblance, contiguity, and causation but more particularly by the ideas of the qualitative difference between past and future time which are generated by the temporal passions. Now the association of ideas in Hume's discussion of the temporal passions conforms exactly to the minimum characterization of narrative relations described above. The idea of any temporally disposed object is necessarily associated with at least one other time-separated object in the light of which the first is viewed as significant. These we may call *narrative associations*. All ideas, and not just temporally reflective ones, are associated narratively. The idea of any object will be thought of as existing in some temporal order of succession and so will be associated with temporally separate events and in the light of the self's awareness of its location in the present. For special purposes we may ignore these tensed features of our ideas, and in the standard Humean way, form an abstract, timeless idea of something. But for Hume, the tensed features are still there. Our primordial way of thinking about the world is through narrative associations.

Was Hume aware of the narrative character of the association relations? There is evidence to think he was to some degree. In the discussion of time in book II, for instance, Hume says of the propensity of the fancy "to follow the succession of time in placing our ideas" and to move "from the consideration of any object . . . more easily to that, which follows immediately after it, than to that which went before it" that it determines one of the main principles of historical narration: "We may learn this . . . from the order, which is always observ'd in historical narrations. Nothing but an absolute necessity can oblige an historian to break the order of time, and in his *narration* give the precedence to an event, which was in *reality* posterior to another" (T, 430). Since every object is conceived as being in time and related to ourselves and since the idea of our location in time triggers this propensity, Hume is committed to the view that a narrative order is built into all associations of ideas. But Hume does not develop this suggestion any further in these sections of book II. One reason, perhaps, is that Hume is aware that his discussion of the temporal passions is original and "pretty remarkable" (T, 432). He is not entirely sure of himself or of his rapport with what he imagines to be an increasingly impatient reader. Hence the apologetic tone: "The curiousness of the subject will, I hope, excuse my dwelling on it for some time" (T, 432). And: "These methods of thinking, and of expressing ourselves, are not of so little consequence as they may appear at first sight" (T, 434). However this may be, Hume did not abandon the subject of the temporal passions and their relation to narrative thinking; it occurs again and is developed more fully in the *Enquiry* on understanding.

In section III, "Of the Association of Ideas," Hume roughs out the theory of association in a page and a half and then spends the remaining seven pages discussing "the effects of this connection upon the passions and imagination; where we may open up a field of speculation more entertaining, and perhaps more instructive, than the other [confirming the thesis that there are only three principles of association]" (EUH, 33). This more entertaining and instructive subject matter is that of the temporal passions discussed in book II and entitled "Of contiguity, and distance in space and time." In the *Enquiry*, however, only the influence of temporal contiguity is discussed, and there it is limited exclusively to a discussion of the structure of narrative order in biography, history, epic poetry, and drama. There is a clear suggestion here that, for Hume, temporal associations are in some way fundamental and that the other relations—resemblance, cause-effect, and spatial contiguity—gain their significance by being part of a temporal order which from the point of view of "the passions and imagination" is best grasped in narrative form. All of this was implied in the discussion of the temporal passions in book II, but it is now made more explicit.

Hume lays it down as a rule that "admits of no exception" that the events or actions in a narrative composition "must be related to each other in the imagination, and form a kind of *unity* which may bring them under one plan or view, and which may be the object or end of the writer in his first undertaking" (EUH, 33). Although the principles connecting the events which form the subject of a poetic or historical narrative "may be very different according to the different designs of the poet or historian," in the end they are all grounded on one or a combination of the three principles of association: resemblance, contiguity, and cause-effect. "Ovid has formed his plan upon the connecting principle of resemblance. Every fabulous transformation produced by the miraculous power of the gods falls within the compass of his work" (EUH, 33-34). Contiguity in space and time would preside over the design of an "annalist or historian who should undertake to write the history of Europe during any century." All the events that occur in that chosen portion of space and time "though in other respects different and unconnected" would "have still a species of unity amidst all their diversity." But "the most usual species of connection among the different events which enter into any narrative composition is that of cause and effect" (EUH, 34).

Hume's remarks are worth quoting at length. The "historian traces the series of actions according to their natural order, remounts to their secret springs and principles, and delineates their most remote consequences. He chooses for his subject a certain portion of that great chain of events which compose the history of mankind: each link in this chain he endeavors to touch in his narration; sometimes unavoidable ignorance renders all his attempts fruitless; sometimes he supplies by conjecture what is wanting in knowledge; and always he is sensible that the more unbroken the chain is which he presents to his readers, the more perfect is his production" (EUH, 34). The ideal of perfect continuity should be distinguished from the demand for causal explanation. The first is based on that propensity of the fancy already discussed in book II of the *Treatise* whereby we "trace the succession of time by a similar succession of ideas," ordering events successively in the direction of our future. But events could be ordered in perfect succession without being causally connected, just as they could be causally connected but not arranged in perfect succession. This is why the historian must "remount" to the "secret springs and principles" of the events successively ordered. Causal laws, for Hume, are timeless structures that govern connections between events in a narrative order but are not themselves part of the order. A perfect narrative history, then, would contain a continuous succession of events, all causally connected, and ordered by some idea of the historian's future.[3] Hume refers to this ideal as that of tracing events "according to their natural order," but it is clear that he has in mind ordering them according to certain propensities of the fancy to associate ideas which, of course, does not take away from the order being a natural one.

The theory of association of ideas, then, may afford us "some notion of that *unity of action* about which all critics after Aristotle have talked so much, perhaps to little purpose, while they directed not their taste and sentiment by the accuracy of philosophy" (EUH, 34). The unity of action provided by the association relations is tenseless insofar as the association relations are grasped through abstract ideas and are considered independent of the self. This is, of course, how Hume considers them in book I, where no reference to the self's awareness of its position in time is made in explicating them. So there is a tenseless relation constituting the unity of action in any narrative context. In the light of this tenseless unity, a further unity is established by viewing the temporally disposed events in a narrative as significant by reference to each other so that their mutual dependence constitutes a unity of the whole. Hume sets the standard for this unity extremely high and applies it not only to epic poetry but to history and biography as well: "Not only in any limited portion of life a man's actions have a dependence on each other, but also during the whole period of his duration from the cradle to the grave; nor is it possible to strike off one link, however minute, in this regular chain without affecting the whole series of events which follow" (EUH, 34-35). This strict canon of narrative unity does not, however, apply to the stage: "As the author is entirely lost in dramatic compositions, and the spectator supposes himself to be really present at the actions represented, this reason has no place with regard to the stage." Consequently, "any dialogue or conversation may be introduced which, without improbability, might have passed in that determinate portion of space represented by the theater" (EUH, 37). The reason for this is that a spectator at a drama views things from a timeless point of view. Like God, he is not a part of the temporal process he observes, nor is the author part of the process; he is, as Hume says, "entirely lost in dramatic compositions." In history and epic poetry the case is otherwise. There a storyteller is present who is part of the temporal order he is relating: he exists and the reader must understand him to exist in a point of time after the events his story is about. It is for this reason that histories and epic poems are always in the past tense. The use of the past tense registers the fact that the events related are in the storyteller's and the reader's past. In a drama, the past tense cannot be used relative to the spectator since the events the drama is about are supposed to be occurring in his present.

The strict canon of narrative unity is necessary for history and epic poetry because of the special temporal point of view that the storyteller and the reader have on the events related. As Hume pointed out in the discussion of time in book II, when we think of objects in the past we view them in what we take to be the correct order of their temporal succession. But we must think "at least in a cursory manner" of each successively ordered event in relation to our present (T, 428). And when we do this, we are compelled to think through the chain of past events in opposition to "the natural course of the succession," passing from one event to that which precedes it and from that to another preceding, and so on, all along keeping our eye on our location in the present. When, thinking in this way, the historian "chooses for his subject a certain portion of that great chain of events which compose the history of mankind," he must necessarily view every event in his story in the light of every other event and so in accord with Hume's strict canon of narrative unity. In particular, since the historian will have before him the whole story he is relating, he must necessarily view the early parts of the story in the light of its conclusion. And by doing so, he will have a kind of *fated* perception of past actions, for he will be able to view them in the light of knowledge about their outcome. Hume writes that "none of our actions can alter the past" (T, 430). Insofar as we cannot change it, our view of the past is fatalistic. This is why narrative history necessarily communicates to the reader a sense of fate and destiny about the agents whose story is being told. In Hume's history of the Stuarts, we watch helplessly as Charles I moves with a steady, measured tread towards his inevitable trial and execution. To order events in this way is, Hume says, "contrary to nature" (T, 430), meaning that our usual tendency is to order events in accord with the future-referring propensity of the fancy, arranging them successively toward our future. Events ordered this way, whether in our present or past, open out into a future that is unknown and full of possibility.

They, consequently, cannot form a story the outcome of which is known and so cannot be a subject for narrative history as Hume understands it. We can view Charles's execution as inevitable precisely because *his* future is in *our* past. Past events narratively ordered can be thought of in a fated way, and it is for this reason that Hume's chain-link metaphor is an appropriate symbol of the past and also that Hume can insist it is impossible "to strike off one link, however minute, in this regular chain without affecting the whole series of events which follow" (EUH, 35).

Hume stresses that "history, biography, or any species of narration that confine themselves to strict truth and reality" have the same narrative form as epic poetry: "The unity of action . . . in biography or history differs from that of epic poetry, not in kind, but in degree" (EUH, 35). The main difference is that "poetry, being a species of painting, approaches us nearer to the objects than any other species of narration, throws a stronger light upon them, and delineates more distinctly those minute circumstances which, though to the historian they seem superfluous, serve mightily to enliven the imagery and gratify the fancy" (EUH, 35). Such intense imagery, however, is incompatible with a long time-scale and a slow development of action. "The Peloponnesian war is a proper subject for history, the siege of Athens for an epic poem, and the death of Alcibiades for a tragedy" (EUH, 38). Hume grants, however, that because the difference between history and epic poetry is one of degree, "it will be difficult, if not impossible, by words to determine exactly the bounds which separate them from each other. That is a matter of taste more than of reasoning" (ibid.). Consequently, a proper narrative unity "may often be discovered in a subject where, at first view, and from an abstract consideration, we should least expect to find it" (ibid.). Here as elsewhere Hume insists on paying close attention to examples. One interesting counterexample to the above rule is *Paradise Lost* where, by using the principles of resemblance and contiguity, Milton is able to establish a unity sufficient for an epic poem even though the train of events narrated is "both very long and very causal," encompassing the rebellion of the angels, the creation of the world, and the fall of man (EUH, 38-39).

Hume's interesting and insightful discussion in section III of the *Enquiry* of how the association relations constitute narrative unities in history, epic poetry, and drama lends support to the interpretation that, abstractions aside, the association relations are ordered in narrative form. But the analysis of narrative thinking given there is sketchy and not developed in any systematic way. There is the same awkwardness and retreat before the reader as in book II of the *Treatise*. The whole discussion of the narrative pattern of thinking in history and the arts is presented as "These loose hints I have thrown together in order to excite the curiosity of philosophers, and beget a suspicion at least if not a full persuasion . . . that many operations of the human mind depend on the connection or association of ideas which is here explained. Particularly, the sympathy betwixt the passions and imagination will, perhaps, appear remarkable" (EUH, 39). The sympathy mentioned here is that discussed in book II which is used to explain the temporal passions and which is used in the *Enquiry* to account for narrative passions and ideas. But unhappily the principle is not developed: "The full explication of this principle and all its consequences would lead us into reasonings too profound and too copious for these Essays" (ibid.). We shall never know clearly what Hume had in mind by these "reasonings too profound"; they were not fully developed in book II or in the *Dissertation on the Passions*, which is a brutally truncated version of book II, where the two-section discussion of the influence of space and time on the imagination and passion is reduced to one sentence: "What is distant, either in place or time, has not equal influence with what is near and contiguous" (DP, 166).

Hume, then, never found a place for a systematic treatment of his insights into the nature and value of narrative thinking. The discussion in section III of the *Enquiry* is the most explicit. The section is entitled "Of the Association of Ideas," and the analysis of narrative thinking is tacked on to a page-and-a-half summary of the theory of ideas. In all editions but the last, the two subjects were kept together. But in the last edition, Hume dropped the discussion of narrative thinking. The reasons were no doubt stylistic. The discussion does appear to be tacked on, but perhaps most important, it overwhelms the page-and-a-half sketch of the theory of association of ideas and threatens to absorb that theory into the theory of narrative thinking. What is surprising is that Hume kept it through three editions. He did so because he considered the subject of narration an important one (his plans for writing history go back to the period of the *Treatise*, and a first attempt at the composition of a history of England was made in 1745, three years before publication of the first edition of the *Enquiry* on understanding) but also, perhaps, because he recognized that the association relations, when not considered in abstraction, have narrative form and can be most easily grasped through their operation in narrative literature.[4]

## NARRATIVE EXISTENCES

Do historians really discover the narrative orders they claim to find in the world or do they put them there? Hume does not explicitly raise this question but a Humean answer can be inferred from the above discussion of his views on time and narrative structure. The answer given depends on what is understood by "world." If we mean the natural world as Hume presents it in book I, that is, a spatiotemporal world existing independently of the mind, then there are no narrative orders in the world. Narrative orders are tensed and always lie in the historian's past, but time in the natural world is tenseless and contains no stories. Narrative order exists only in the moral world, and in Hume's view the paradoxical answer would have to be that the historian both discovers and places narrative order there. The paradox is possible because the moral world, for Hume, is simply the natural world viewed in the light of our passions or impressions of reflection ordered from a certain point of view. Objectivity in the moral world is constituted by these points of view and is manifest in the conventions of common life and the language that informs them. The objective orders of morality and beauty are two such points of view. Moral and aesthetic properties are relational properties which apply to external objects on condition that a spectator have certain sentiments from a disciplined point of view. I have argued that tensed properties, if grasped concretely, that is, through ideas of temporal reflection, are parallel with moral and aesthetic properties in that all three determine an order to things dependent on a certain order of sentiment. Concretely understood, tensed properties are dependent on the temporal passions. But if we consider them more concretely still, we find that tensed structures are always grasped through narrative associations, so that our concrete experience of time is the experience of narrative order.

For Hume, the fundamental problem of moral philosophy is to bring order into the passions we have about the natural world and into the ideas of reflection about the world that these passions yield. This project is locked into Hume's famous dictum that " philosophical decisions are nothing but the reflections of common life, methodized and corrected" (EU, 162). Hume spent much effort analyzing our moral and aesthetic passions and ideas and sought to establish standards for thinking critically about them. There is a parallel problem of establishing standards for bringing order into our temporal passions and temporally complex ideas of reflection. Hume did not explore this problem as deeply as he did the parallel problems of morals and aesthetics, but it is a problem which runs throughout his thinking and at a very deep level since it has to do with how we should and do think of ourselves as temporal beings.

All of the standards that constitute the moral world, from the first principle itself through epistemological, moral, aesthetic, and political standards, have in one way or another a temporal content which constitutes part of their authority. To say that ideas are derived from past impressions is to tie the norms of understanding to a relation between present and past existences. To say that "Time and custom give authority to all forms of government" is to give time, as we think of it in politics, a normative content. And so it is with all standards in the moral world. Even tenseless standards are, for Hume, abstractions from temporal standards which alone have primordial authority. Tenseless standards are always viewed by Hume as codifications of existing temporal standards which have an authority of their own that is independent of the tenseless standards derived from them. Likewise, tenseless standards have no a-priori authority of their own that is independent of the temporal standards from which they are derived and to which they are supposed to be critically applicable. Tenseless aesthetic judgments are codifications of a tradition of critical taste that has withstood the test of time and, one believes, will continue to. Hume's method is always to codify critically the principles that govern a well-established practice in common life, and to render them as universal as possible. These principles enable us to be self-conscious about existing practices and serve as norms for critically continuing the practice. In this method, tenseless standards grow historically, as it were, out of existing practices and are reflections of them, a procedure contrary to the rationalist method of determining principles a-priori, independently of any authority that established institutions might have, and then using those principles as a grim measuring rod for judging those institutions. Here with institutions, as elsewhere, the paradigm of understanding is that ideas (the critical principles of a practice) are reflections on impressions (the unreflective practice itself).

This is not the place to evaluate Hume's method of determining standards. What I wish to show here is that Humean standards are held together by temporal relations which constitute much of the standards' authority. Time as it is built into standards is thought of as having a normative quality, which means that it is being viewed by the imagination in the light of some ordering of the temporal passions. To understand the nature and limits of Humean standards we must, among other things, understand the correct ordering of the temporal passions. As we have seen, there is a correct ordering of our moral passions of approval and disapproval of actions and characters. When this standard is ignored, " we find . . . many contradictions to our sentiments in society and conversation" (T, 583). In order to avoid "those continual *contradictions*" (T, 581), we must make explicit the moral standard which makes the contradictions possible and which also provides the method for removing them, that is, for "correcting our sentiments, or at least, of correcting our language, where the sentiments are more stubborn and inalterable" (T, 582). Similar remarks apply about a correct order for our aesthetic passions, or what Hume calls "the standard of taste." So there must also be a correct order for our temporal passions and for the ideas of reflection these passions generate. Hume was not explicitly aware of the problem of bringing critical order to the temporal passions, but because of the temporally normative quality he gives, in varying degrees, to all standards, he is forced in many contexts to deal with the problem. At times the awareness of the problem is more explicit than at others, but independently of Hume's awareness the problem is built into his philosophy. And because it is there, we can use it as a framework to interpret that philosophy. By reference to it, some unity can be given to Hume's scattered remarks on the nature of historical knowledge and existence. Certain aspects of Hume's philosophy can also be explored more deeply. For instance, social and political standards, for reasons that will appear later, have a greater saturation of temporal authority than moral or aesthetic standards. Underlying Hume's discussion of social and political standards are deep presuppositions about the correct ordering of the temporal passions which must be understood before we can adequately evaluate Hume's social and political philosophy. Finally, we shall be able to better appreciate the many conceptual connections that hold between Hume's philosophical and historical work. As we shall see later, one of the main points of the *History of England* is to show concretely how beings in time using temporal standards can make critical judgments about social and political institutions and what the limits of those judgments are.[5]

I want now to put together, from the above discussion of Hume's views on time in the *Treatise* and *Enquiry* and relevant remarks in other works, a rudimentary Humean theory of the correct ordering of the temporal passions and the temporally complex ideas of reflection which are derived from them. We have seen that tensed properties, concretely considered, like moral and aesthetic properties, pick out an objective order which is identified with an order of sentiment (in this case, the temporal passions). Moreover, to think of events temporally disposed under this tensed conception of time is to think of them under narrative associations where an event is viewed as significant in the light of some temporally separated event. The first step, then, in bringing some normative order into the temporal passions is to determine the nature and limits of narrative thinking. That Hume, in some way, saw the need for such a theory is clear from the discussion of the temporal passions in book II, his remarks on history and the novel elsewhere in the *Treatise* (T, 97-98, 121-23), and the more developed discussion of narrative order in the *Enquiry* on understanding and in "Of the Study of History."[6]

Narratives are ordered by a unity of action that requires every event in the narration to be mutually dependent on every other event. This unity of action is determined by the storyteller's "design." In addition, there is a temporal restriction on narratives. They apply only to events in the storyteller's past. And when we think of past events, we always think of them through narrative associations, necessarily viewing them in the light of *our* present and of all the events intervening. This enables us to have a kind of fated perception of past events, viewing them in the light of their consequences. It is this sort of perception that makes possible the tight unity of action that Hume requires of all narration, historical as well as fictional. But most important, it is this sort of perception that Hume considers the true point of view on past events. In recommending the study of history, Hume says: "what more agreeable entertainment to the mind, than to be transported into the remotest ages of the world . . . to see all the human race, from the beginning of time, pass, as it were, in review before us, appearing in their *true colours*, without any of those disguises which, during their lifetime, so much perplexed the judgment of the beholders" (E, 560, emphasis mine). Those who lived through past events were too involved in them to see them "as they stand in themselves" (E, 562). Philosophers take a "general abstract [timeless] view of objects" which takes them out of the tensed order, isolating them from the passions which have shaped events and which are to be viewed as an internal part of them. But "History keeps in a just medium between these extremes, and places the objects in their *true point of view*" (ibid., emphasis mine). As we have already observed, judgments for Hume presuppose a common point of view from which orders of objectivity are generated. For moral, aesthetic, and perceptual judgments about physical objects, the objective-making point of view is abstract and timeless. But any objective point of view on past events would have to be tensed and so part of a narrative order projected from the historian's present. The "true point of view" for considering past events "as they stand in themselves" is entirely relative to the historian's present.

Hume does not spell out how temporally distant the historian must be from past events, or what other circumstances are necessary, in order to see them correctly. Perhaps he had in mind that, when the effects of an action have run their course, we can view the action in true perspective by seeing it in the light of its consequences. But this means that we must consider the action and its consequences under the narrative principle of the unity of action, and the criteria for narrative unity are determined in part by the historian's "plan or design" and so is "a matter of taste more than of reasoning" (EUH, 37, 38). (What Hume could mean by good taste in historical narratives is examined in chapter 8, below). The remaining criteria are those laid out in Hume's official theory of identity in the *Treatise* which shows that "objects, which are variable or interrupted, and yet are suppos'd to continue the same, are such only as consist of a succession of parts, connected together by resemblance, contiguity, or causation" (T, 255). So the identity of narrative unities is acocunted for, in part, by "the same method of reasoning . . . which has so successfully explain'd the identity of plants, and animals, and ships, and houses, and of all the compounded and changeable productions either of art or nature" (T, 259). Historians may disagree on when the period known as the Renaissance began. The debate could be settled by discovering certain crucial resemblances, temporal relations, or causal relations between events, but that there was a Renaissance at all is a matter of the historian's "design" which means that the identity of narrative entities is determined primarily by the historian's interests and passions.

By making the historian's present the focal point for a true point of view on past events, Hume has made historical objectivity relative to a position in tensed time, and so is committed to a form of historical relativism. If time could be stopped, the historian's narrative point of view would be as fixed and absolute as the point of view we take on perceiving physical objects. But as it is, time moves on. New events occur and narrative associations generated by the historian's passions and interests are woven into the old narrative unities to produce new narrative unities in which the old are either transformed or destroyed altogether in the process. There is, however, no reason in the nature of things why a certain narrative point of view could not remain stable for an indefinite period of time. And this would be the case if the passions and interests which shape the narrative unities designed by historians were stable over a long period of time. Marx thought that narrative history was the result of class struggle, and that in a classless society there would be a sufficient uniformity of interest to establish one narrative point of view for all time. And this he thought would, in effect, be the end of history. Hume did not believe in any such radical transformation of society. But he did seem to think or at least hope that "the wise and learned," that elite group composing the "party of humanity," could arrive at a consensus of passion and interest so that a fairly stable narrative point of view on the past would be possible (EU, 110). It is some such view as this that Hume has in mind when he expresses hope and sometimes confidence that his own judgments on things will be in accord with those of posterity. As we shall see later, one of Hume's main philosophical and historical tasks was to supplant the traditional Christian story line of the creation, fall, and redemption of man by a new unity of action based along secular and humanistic lines.[7]

The historian, then, occupies a privileged position insofar as he can see past events as they really were without those appearances which "during their lifetime, so much perplexed the judgment of the beholders." But this privileged position has a limit. The historian must have the same perplexity about events in his present that historical agents had about events in their present. He could be liberated from this perplexity only if he could view events in his present in the light of events in his future. But this is impossible since events in the future have not yet occurred. If we could view our present in the light of our future, we would have to treat the future as, in some way, having already happened. And if this were to occur, our perception of the present would not be *like* a fated perception (as we have metaphorically characterized all narrative perceptions of the past), it would in fact *be* a fated perception of the present. For fatalism is the doctrine that the future can be thought of as we think of the past, that is, as unchangeable. And that is exactly how we would be treating it if we tried to view our present as narratively significant in the light of our future. In Humean terms, the error can be characterized as an attempt to apply the narrative principle of the unity of action, which holds only for events in our past, to events in our present. We wish to give a narrative unity of action to the disconnected and perplexing events in our present, and this can be done only by viewing them in the light of our future. We have before us the whole life of Charles I and can comprehend it under a unity of action; as the story unfolds we can view him struggling through events the significance of which he could not understand. Similarly, the significance of our own present is not clear to us, and so we can imagine ourselves living through a story which we cannot but would very much like to understand.

One metaphysical position that demands such an interpretation of the present is the providential and prophetic theory of history associated with certain forms of theism. In one form or another this vision of history was the dominant one in Hume's day. And one main effort of his philosophy is to show that it is false. "Of a Particular Providence and of a Future State" in the *Enquiry* on understanding and the *Dialogues* are attempts to show that natural theology is not possessed of any logical or causal arguments to believe in the existence of the God of providential history: "No new fact can ever be inferred from the religious hypothesis; no event foreseen or foretold" (EU, 146). "Of Miracles" attempts to show that the existence of a providential God cannot be known on the basis of miracles taken to be special revelations in history. And the elimination of miracles entails the elimination of a prophetic understanding of history: "What we have said of miracles may be applied, without any variation, to prophecies: and indeed, all prophecies are real miracles, and as such only, can be admitted as proofs of any revelation. If it did not exceed the capacity of human nature to foretell future events, it would be absurd to employ any prophecy as an argument for a divine mission or authority from heaven" (EU, 130-31). It should be noticed that Hume does not say that human nature is incapable of *predicting* future events; what we cannot do is "foretell future events," that is, project narrative unities of action into our future and use them to read significance into our present. Predictions, being in the future tense, are not definitely true or false and should they come true would, at that time, cease to be in the future tense. Predictions then can only be reasonable or unreasonable; never true or false. Consequently, the most rational of predictions is compatible with the nonoccurrence of the event it is about. But we cannot be said to foretell events if those events do not occur. The point of making rational predictions is to gain some control over the future, and this activity presupposes that the present is a scene of action and freedom; our ability to make rational predictions increases rather than diminishes our freedom. But the point of foretelling events is *not* to control the future; it is to give us that passive and fated understanding of the present and its relation to the future that is the central feature of narrative understanding. Its effect, then, is that the present is not viewed as a place of action from which we might with the help of causal laws shape the future; rather it is viewed in terms of future events thought of as, in some sense, already having happened and in the light of which our present is seen as a passing phase of a process. But this is to "so far reverse the whole course of nature, as to render this life merely a passage to something farther" (EU, 141).

In saying that the providential view of the present obliges us to "reverse the whole course of nature," Hume does not mean that we are thinking of history going in reverse like a motion picture being run backwards. Rather he means that the future is being given a narrative role to perform that is proper only for the past. Past events do gain narrative significance by being viewed in the light of later events up to and including the historian's present. But we cannot view our present as significant in the light of future events. To do so would be to apply the fated narrative pattern of understanding to relations between present and future events when it is properly applicable only to relations between past and present events. In the discussion of time in book II, Hume described any attempt to understand relations between the present and past as a pattern of thought "contrary to nature" (T, 430), by which he meant that in ordering past events we must, in imagination, turn the arrow of time away from the future and towards the past. In this way a new order of time, produced by the imagination, is woven into the real order of succession which is in the direction of our future.

Now it is just these two patterns of time running contrary to each other but unified in the imagination that makes possible the peculiar sort of fatalistic significance that is characteristic of narrative order. When we think narratively we are, in thought, able to stop time, and from that point, following the new direction of time produced by the imagination, read a unity of action back into the succession of events we have fixed on. Narrative thinking then is "contrary to nature" in that it presupposes the true order of succession but requires that we think of it with a pattern of ideas arranged in reverse order. It is, nevertheless, a pattern of thinking appropriate to the past and one, moreover, which deals with "strict truth and reality" (EUH, 35).

But when we extend this narrative pattern from judging the past in the light of the present, where it is applicable, to judging the present in the light of the future, where it is not, we indeed, as Hume says, reverse the course of nature. Our mistake is an ontological one, for we are now treating our present as if it were past. The future-referring propensity of the fancy whereby we view the present as a place of action which opens into a future of possibilities is frustrated, and we become spectators of our own present in the same way that we are spectators of some historical agent's present.

It is typical of Hume not merely to expose errors but to explain why it is we are led to make them. No explanation, however, is given why we are inclined to interpret our present providentially and prophetically. But from what he has said about the temporal imagination, we can offer the following. The unities of action framed in narrative thinking apply only to the past. But this means that our present must be seen as narratively disconnected and without any unity of action. To supply this unity, we extend the narrative pattern to our future and imagine ourselves now living through a story written by providence. This desire to experience a narrative unity in the present is a temporal passion which is understandable but which must, nevertheless, be restrained. Hume indulged it in his autobiography written shortly before his death: "To conclude historically with my own character. I am, or rather was (for that is the style I must now use in speaking of my self, which emboldens me the more to speak my sentiments)—I was, I say, a man of mild dispositions . . . [etc]" (MOL, 10). Hume has imagined his death to have already occurred; so his life now has the unity of action required for a full narrative comprehension. In addition, he has placed himself in the rank of historians of posterity who can view his life from the temporally correct perspective. This has, rhetorically, the effect of making it seem as though the judgment of posterity has already occurred, and if that were so, Hume's place in history would be fixed. But it is all a pleasing illusion which Hume himself shatters in the concluding last sentence of the paragraph where he presses home the poignant truth that no one can grasp the narrative significance of his own work; that is a question for historians of the future and one that admits of a nonarbitrary answer: "I cannot say there is no vanity in making this funeral oration of myself, but I hope it is not a misplaced one; and this is a matter of fact which is easily cleared and ascertained" (MOL, 11).

There is, then, a temporal limit within which narrative associations can be validly made. Narrative associations of ideas of relations holding between events in the spectator's past and present deal with "strict truth and reality" (EUH, 35). Those holding between events in the spectator's present and future (with the exception of predictions) are the result of the "conceit and imagination" of philosophers (EU, 141). The following are the four main narrative associations that are possible, along with examples of the sorts of judgments to which they may give rise.

(1) A narrative judgment is made about a past event which is associated with the idea of later events up to and including events in the spectator's present. (The assassination of the archduke Ferdinand opened up World War I.)
(2) A narrative judgment is made about a present event which is associated with the idea of events in the spectator's past. (Here now is the senator from North Carolina.)
(3) A narrative judgment is made about a future event which is associated with the ideas of events in the spectator's present (or past). (It will rain this afternoon given the look of the clouds.)
(4) A narrative judgment is made about a present event which is associated with the idea of events in the spectator's future. (Here now is the man who won two gold medals in the 1996 Olympics.)

It is a convenience of Hume's associationism that it pictures thought as a matter of combining conjuncts, and so easily lends itself to a truth-functional analysis. All of the above statements can be interpreted as truth-functional conjunctions of at least two statements, each describing events occurring at different points in time but united by the imagination into a whole statement which is taken to be *about* one of the time-separated events in the light of the other. All of the above examples are tensed, and so their truth conditions can be interpreted simply as the truth functions of the tensed statements that make them up. Statements (1) and (2) can be true since they are conjunctions of past- and present-tense statements. But (3) and (4) cannot be true since each contains a future-tense statement in conjunction with a present- or past-tense statement. Statement (3) is a prediction and although neither true nor false may be reasonable or unreasonable. Statement (4) is false because it is contradictory. It describes an event in the present, but what it says about the present is not true unless certain future events have, in some way, already happened. It is for this reason that the future event, winning two gold medals at the 1996 Olympics, is described in the past tense. The individual before us is thought of not as one who most likely will win the medals (that would be to make [4] a prediction like [3]) but as one who has somehow already won them. But it is contradictory to describe future events *now* in the past tense. Events cannot have happened before they have happened. Statement (4), then, is one of those cases where, as Hume says, we "reverse the whole course of nature," treating the future as related to the present in the way that only the past can be. Only narrative associations that conform to the patterns in (1) and (2) can lead to judgments about the world that are true. And since Hume accepts the correspondence theory of truth, whatever corresponds to a true narrative association may be thought of as a *narrative existent*.[8]

I would now like to show how narrative associations and narrative existences structure Hume's moral world. We have seen that for Hume tensed time is not thought of as a property of the natural world. Time as it exists, independently of the mind, is a tenseless order of succession. Similarly, natural objects such as men, women, trees, and mountains are thought of in a tenseless way. Hume accepted the Christian doctrine of creation as a logical possibility and often used it for analytical purposes as in the many passages in which he tries to explain the importance of experience by asking what Adam could or could not know, feel, or do shortly after his creation.[9] So Hume is committed to the thesis that it is logically part of the concept of a natural object that it could be created in an instant out of nothing, without a past, and still be just as it is. But not all concepts are logically tenseless. Past-entailing concepts, discussed earlier, apply to existences on condition that certain statements about the past are true. God could create "full-grown" adults such as Adam and Eve without a past, but not even God could create nephews, priests, thieves, legal precedents, a Botticelli, a U. S. senator without creating also a past of the appropriate length. An all-powerful being could, of course, produce forgeries, as it were, of such beings and have it so that we believe they exist. But no one could *be* a U. S. senator unless he were duly elected in accord with his state constitution and the U. S. Constitution ratified in 1789. So to have a U. S. senator, we must have a past going back at least to 1789 and even that might not be far enough.

Past-entailing concepts mark out the bounds of a specifically human world, inhabited by beings who are self-aware of their position in time, who think in a tensed way, and whose temporal passions permeate all their activities. But past-entailing concepts may be seen as special products of narrative associations: to say that someone in the present is a priest is to think of a present existent (a man) in the light of a whole set of past events (including not only some act of confirmation in the past but beliefs about the whole apostolic succession which gives the confirmation authority) and where the present and past events are bound together in the imagination by some principle constituting a unity of action. To those who constitute priests, the unity of action would presumably be God's revelation in a sacred tradition and his continued action in history. Hume, of course, rejected the notion of Divine Providence and so would tie together the relevant present and past events so as to constitute some sort of secular unity of action.

Hume emphasizes the artificiality of the moral world. Part of what he means by this is that the standards which constitute the moral world are derived not from any natural spatiotemporal distinction to be found in nature but in what natural objects mean to us in terms of the passions and thoughts we have about them. We have observed that the temporal passions are essential to all standards in the moral world. What Hume says about time constituting the standards of property relations holds for all standards: "But as 'tis certain, that, however every thing be produc'd in time, there is nothing real, that is produc'd by time; it follows, that property being produc'd by time, is not any thing real in the objects, but is the offspring of the sentiments, on which alone time is found to have any influence" (T, 508-9). Except for abstract purposes in natural philosophy we have little interest in "time, as it exists" (T, 31), that is, as a tenseless order of successive objects in nature. The time that is a category of the moral world is time as reflected in our feelings and thoughts about our location in tenseless time, and that is tensed time narratively ordered. The moral world is, ontologically, the product of thought and particularly of narrative associations.

Perhaps this can be brought out more clearly by considering the difference between the properties of the natural world and those of the narrative existences that populate the moral world. A woman is a natural object, and the criteria for applying the predicate "is a woman" are manifest to observation. There are, we may say, female properties which can be detected by direct inspection or, to use Hume's language, by having a certain sort of complex impression. But the same is not true of an entity such as a queen. Although all queens are women, there are no queen-like properties that can be directly observed. A queen disrobed looks like any other woman. The reason is that a queen is a narrative existent, a relation between present and past existences held together in the imagination by some principle constituting a narrative unity of action. No woman in the present is a queen unless certain statements about the past are true. Past existence is built into the ontology of a queen. There are no queen-like properties manifest to observation simply because the past that constitutes a queen cannot, in principle, be observed. And the unobservability of moral entities is more radical than that of theoretical entities in science. Theoretical entities like electrons do not have properties manifest to observation. But the presence of such entities can be detected by their effects, as when electrons are examined through the visible traces they leave in a Wilson cloud chamber. But queens leave no visible trace of their presence. The *being* of a queen is her narrative relation to the past. To understand this relation we would have to understand the principles governing the narrative unity of action that constitutes it. These principles determine a vast system of narrative relations which inform the rank, status, privileges, rights, and duties of an entire social and political order of which the queen is a part. Queens and the moral order internal to them, like property, are "produc'd by time" and so are "the offspring of the sentiments, on which alone time is found to have any influence."

Because moral entities are narrative existences and so, unlike natural entities, are devoid of manifest properties, it has been necessary to devise visible symbols and rituals to indicate their reality, hence the symbolic dress of the clergy, judges, the military, the police, the monarchy, the ritualistic performance of promises, and countless other symbols of our station, duties, and privileges in the moral world. As a further indication of the nonnatural properties of moral entities, Hume compares the use of these symbols and rituals to the use of those in sacramental religious systems which establish supernatural beings and miracles: "Had I worn this apparel an hour ago, I had merited the severest punishment; but a man, by pronouncing a few magical syllables, has now rendered it fit for my use and service" (EM, 199). The rhetorical point here is that a moral entity like property is like a supernatural being in that its essential properties are not those of the natural world. So close does Hume draw the analogy between the sacramental world of religion and the moral world that he is occasionally forced to make clear that there *is* a fundamental distinction between the two: "But there is this material difference between *superstition* and *justice* . . ." (ibid.). The comparison is useful to Hume because it brings out sharply the fact that moral philosophy is an inquiry with its own objects and methods which is quite distinct from natural philosophy. And as we shall see in a later chapter, it is a comparison that points out the great difference between Hume's analysis and that of the rationalists and naturalists of his day who think of the moral world in a tenseless way.

The moral world, then, as Hume understands it is woven together by the narrative imagination which registers the passions and thoughts we have about our temporal involvement with natural objects and with each other. It is a world of narrative associations, that is, of stories having varying degrees of significance and generality. And the question arises whether these stories might form a system of stories, whether the unities of action that constitute there are, in turn, part of some larger unities of action that constitute them are, in turn, part of some larger The providential and prophetic view of history is just such a story, and Hume most explicitly rejected it. Whether he thought some other story could take its place is a question taken up in chapters 8 and 11.

# 6

# Causal Explanation in Science and Metaphysics

> But allow me to tell you, that I never asserted so absurd a
> Proposition as *that any thing might arise without a Cause:* I
> only maintain'd, that our Certainty of the Falsehood of
> that Proposition proceeded neither from Intuition nor
> Demonstration; but from another Source.
>
> Hume, letter to John Stewart, 1754

## THE POSITIVIST INTERPRETATION

Hume is best known for his analysis of causality and the theory of
causal explanation that follows from it. And there has always been a
remarkably uniform opinion as to what that analysis is. It is generally
believed that, in Hume's view, to say that A causes B is to say (1) that
A-like things and B-like things are constantly conjoined and (2) that the
mind on the appearance of an A feels a determination to expect that a B
will occur and on the appearance of a B feels a determination to believe
that an A has occurred. This interpretation is usually given a phenomenalistic twist to include the thesis (3) that the events conjoined
must be analyzable without remainder into impressions. From these
theses a theory of causal explanation follows: to give a causal explanation of an event is to cover it with an empirical regularity.

We may call this the positivist interpretation not only because it resembles very closely the concept of causality and causal explanation
given by contemporary positivists and logical empiricists but also because contemporary positivists have presented Hume as a precursor of
their own view and have been influential in establishing the interpretation. There is, as we shall see, much in the text that appears to support
it, but, in the end, it must be rejected because too much is left out. In
this and the next chapter, I want to explore the evidence for the positivist interpretation in the light of what has been left out. I shall not be

150

arguing that Hume holds some view, equally clear, but contrary to that ascribed to him by the positivist interpretation. Rather, what we shall find is that Hume's account is not at all a clear and simple one. His thinking on causality and causal explanation is a difficult path to follow. At times the way seems clear enough, but then the trail breaks off only to be picked up later in the most unexpected place. These changes are not to be interpreted as inconsistencies but as gaps left by insights won but not systematically developed. It is just these insights and their relation to Hume's more established doctrines that I wish to examine. To bring them out in an orderly way, it will be convenient to use the positivist interpretation as a background. In this chapter I shall examine Hume's doctrine of causality as applied to science and metaphysics. In the next chapter I shall examine its application to the explanation of human action.

Let us begin with (3), the thesis that causal relations hold only between objects that can be experienced. In this interpretation, theoretical entities such as gravitational forces, energy, and other causal powers thought to be productive of phenomena would be excluded from our understanding of what causal relations are. The reason is that theoretical entities of this sort are thought of as being logically unobservable. As such they cannot enter our experience, and so cannot enter into the experienced constant conjunctions that constitute causal relations. Many passages can be deployed to support this interpretation. After searching diligently for an empirical origin of the ideas which we associate with "the terms of *efficacy, agency, power*," Hume concludes that "Upon the whole . . . 'tis impossible in any one instance to shew the principle, in which the force and agency of a cause is plac'd; and that the most refin'd and most vulgar understandings are equally at a loss in this particular" (T, 157-59). The same conclusion is reached in the first *Enquiry*: "In all single instances of the operation of bodies or minds there is nothing that produces any impression, nor consequently can suggest any idea, of power or necessary connection" (EU, 78). The next step is to show that although the idea of necessary connection cannot be derived from an experience of objects, it can be derived from the effects the experience of objects has on the imagination, and this yields Hume's two famous definitions of cause: "we may define a cause to be an object followed by another, and where all the objects, similar to the first, are followed by objects similar to the second. Or, in other words, where, if the first object had not been, the second never had existed." And we may also think of a cause as "an object followed by another, and whose appearance always conveys the thought to that other" (EU, 77; cf. T, 169-70). I shall refer to the first as the objective definition and to the second as the subjective definition.

151

Hume appears to present these as real definitions of the same structure, namely the causal relation. But they cannot function together as real definitions for they are neither intentionally nor extensionally equivalent. What role, then, do they play in Hume's understanding of causality? The answer is a very complicated one, but we may begin with a few remarks which will be developed more fully later. The first thing to appreciate is that Hume is not really trying to give a definition of "cause" at all. He understood by "cause" essentially what his contemporaries understood by it: a cause is a power productive of phenomena where "the terms of *efficacy, agency, power, force, energy, necessity, connexion*, and *productive quality*, are all nearly synonymous (T, 157). Hume's problem is not that of defining "cause" so much as it is framing an empirical standard for applying the predicate to the world. And this he sets up as the question of whether the idea of "cause" can be derived from impressions. To take a parallel example: we may define metric concepts in terms of other metric concepts and so be able to understand all expressions in the metric system without knowing at all how to apply such terms to the world. What is needed is an empirical standard for applying the metric system to the world, and that is the iridium bar in Paris which is taken as the standard meter. Likewise, Hume is looking for a nonarbitrary empirical standard for applying the predicate "is a cause" to the world, and this he presents as the problem of whether the idea of "causal power" as we ordinarily understand it can be derived from impressions: "we reject at once all the vulgar definitions, which philosophers have given of power and efficacy; and instead of searching for the idea in these definitions, [which define 'causal power' in terms of other power words] must look for it in the impressions, from which it is originally deriv'd" (ibid.).

Hume argues that causal power, as we ordinarily understand it, is not an object of experience, roughly in the way one might argue that metric length is not an object of experience. He then turns to an examination of the linguistic convention of making causal ascriptions, in an effort to determine the empirical conditions under which we apply causal predicates to the world. What he comes up with are the "two definitions" which (1) serve to specify the conditions for applying causal predicates to the world, and (2) which are part of a causal theory that explains *why* we apply causal predicates to the world. The reason why the two definitions of "cause" are not equivalent is that they are empirical conditions for applying the term "cause" to the world, and empirical conditions not only can but must be nonequivalent if they are not to be vacuous.

Failure to appreciate this can easily lead to the positivistic interpretation. Hume's own language disposes one to believe that he is offering something like an analysis of the causal relation in the manner of contemporary analytic philosophy. Those who read Hume this way typically reject the subjective definition as irrelevant to the analysis of cause. One is left, then, with the view that a cause, for Hume, is nothing but a constant conjunction of like events: necessity simply is uniformity. But this is not Hume's view.

First, it fails to explain why Hume thought the subjective conditions of the two definitions are important. He says plainly that "This therefore [the felt determination of the mind] is the essence of necessity" (T, 165). It is not through experience or demonstrative reasoning that we make causal judgments. Consequently, if constantly conjoined events were not experienced passionately and the felt determinations of the mind projected onto the world, we would not have the idea of causal necessity at all. If we were listless about the regularities we experience, there would be no causal judgments, and science as well as common life would cease. Second, even if, in spite of this, we ignored the subjective conditions, it would still be wrong to view the remaining objective conditions as Hume's analysis of what the causal relation is. Hume is clear that the two definitions are the conditions under which a person who has experienced a constant conjunction of like events "*pronounces* them to be *connected*" (EU, 75 first emphasis mine). Likewise in the *Treatise:* without these two conditions, we would not "be able to *attribute it* [power and necessity] either to external or internal objects, to spirit or body, to causes or effects" (T, 165, emphasis mine). Moreover, "both these definitions" are "drawn from circumstances foreign to the cause," which implies that Hume does not think he has given an analysis of *what* the causal relation is, in itself, but rather has exposed the conditions under which we apply causal predicates to the world (EU, 77, cf. T, 170).

Third, the positivist interpretation appears to rest on the assumption that, having explained the origin of the belief that there are causal powers in nature by reference to the contingent workings of the imagination, Hume could not have taken the belief seriously or have given it any ontological weight. He must have thought, then, that causal necessity simply is observable regularity. But this, most decidedly, is not Hume's view. It is the propensity of the imagination to project into nature the felt determination of the mind set up by experience of constant conjunctions that Hume takes to be the origin of our unshakable belief that there are unobservable powers in nature. To be sure, the belief is not certified by sense or reason, but, then, neither is our belief in external objects. Both beliefs are categorical and are part of the popular system transcendentally conceived. The imagination "dignifies" the objects of both "with the title of *realities*" (T, 108). And it should be stressed here that Hume's position is not a form of fictionalism, a view held by some contemporary empiricists: he has not argued that sense and reason show us that there are no causal powers but that we believe in them anyway. The case here is the same as with the popular system discussed in chapter 1. Hume's position is skepticism. All the central doctrines of common life, that there are natural objects with sensory properties, other minds, and causal powers, are consistent. All such entities *could* exist (and, of course, we believe they do exist); it is just that philosophy guided by the autonomy principle cannot show that they do or that they do not exist. The matter is decided on other grounds which Hume has tried to bring out by logical and psychological analysis. But it is decided.

To know the origins of the belief that there are causal powers in the world is not to cease having the belief, and if the belief really is absolute, we cannot, on pain of bad faith, ask whether we ought to have it. But, given that we do have it, it is still possible to formulate norms and to think critically about it.[1] And it is this aspect of Hume's thought on causal necessity that I would now like to examine.

Other than the two "definitions," Hume concludes that "we have no idea of connection or power at all, and that these words are absolutely without any meaning, when employed either in philosophical reasonings or common life" (EU, 74). From such passages, Hume does seem to be committed to a radical form of empiricism: that all terms purporting to be about causal powers and other such theoretical entities are meaningless. And this, in turn, is very close to the ontological thesis embraced by many twentieth-century empiricists that theoretical entities are not real and that theoretical expressions in science must, in some way, be translatable into expressions referring only to observable entities on pain of being meaningless. But however plausible this interpretation might appear, it must be abandoned, for Hume does hold that there are logically unobservable powers in nature which are productive of phenomena: "It must certainly be allowed, that nature has kept us at a great distance from all her secrets, and has afforded us only the knowledge of a few superficial qualities of objects; while she conceals from us those powers and principles on which the influence of these objects entirely depends" (EU, 32-33). The "superficial qualities" Hume refers to are observable properties produced by "powers and principles" which are unobservable. The point is illustrated by contrasting the sensory properties of motion with the Newtonian forces which produce them: "Sight or feeling conveys an idea of the actual motion of bodies" but the "force or power, which would carry on a moving body forever in a continued change of place, and which bodies never lose but by communicating it to others, of this we cannot form the most distant conception" (ibid.). This is a paradoxical saying, for the Newtonian force Hume has just described (albeit in a simplified way) and so *conceived* is the very thing of which "we cannot form the most distant conception." Is it possible to reconcile Hume's conflicting claims that we have no idea of power at all and that unobservable powers are productive of all phenomena?

## SECRET AND UNKNOWN CAUSES

Hume no more questioned the existence of causal powers than he questioned the existence of body (T, 187). "But notwithstanding this ignorance of natural powers and principles [that they are unobservable], we always presume, when we see like sensible qualities, that they have like secret powers, and expect that effects, similar to those which we have experienced will follow from them. . . . The bread, which I formerly ate nourished me; that is, *a body of such sensible qualities was, at that time, endued with such secret powers*" (EU, 33-34, emphasis mine).

So we do believe there are unobservable causal powers which are productive of the things we experience. The question is what can be known about them if we have no idea of them. When Hume says we have no idea of causal power, he means that we do not have an internal mastery of the concept; that is, we have no image of power. This does not prevent us, however, from having an external grasp of the concept, that is, knowing the public criteria for applying the expression "causal power" in some linguistic convention. And we do have this external understanding of the concept as specified (a) in the two definitions and (b) in the conditions for causal ascription worked out in the linguistic conventions of theoretical science.

Unhappily, Hume does not systematically develop (b). In the *Treatise*, it is hardly broached at all. The most he presents are (1) the eight "Rules by which to judge of causes and effects" (T, 173-75) which apply indifferently to causes conceived as observable events or as unobservable secret powers, and (2) a number of hints about relative ideas (see the discussion of Hume's conception of relative ideas in chapter 3, above). Relative ideas, we may recall, are constituted by the idea of perceivable objects related through one or more of the seven philosophical relations to an entity specifically different from perceptual objects. Unobservable causal powers, being specifically different from perceptions, would qualify as the object of a relative idea. Yet nowhere in the *Treatise* does Hume explicitly apply the doctrine of relative ideas to causal powers. Indeed, most of his effort there is directed to the negative task of showing that we have no experience of causal power. But what Hume objects to is not the notion of unobservable causal powers but rather the notion that these can be known a priori through a formal and necessary connection between cause and effect. Hume has no objection as long as the causal powers are known empirically through their effects and presumably through relative ideas. The point is made clearly in the Introduction to the *Treatise*: "the essence of the mind being equally unknown to us with that of external bodies, it must be equally impossible to form any notion of its powers and qualities otherwise than from careful and exact experiments, and the observation of those particular effects, which result from its different circumstances and situations" (T, xvii).

In the *Enquiry* on understanding a change of emphasis occurs. Hume seems to have recognized that what had been taken for granted about the scientific investigation of causal powers in the *Treatise* had to be made more explicit and in particular that something had to be said about references to causal powers in the theoretical physics of his day. This change is manifest in several places. The problem of causality is introduced as the problem of how "we *infer* a connection between the sensible qualities and the secret powers [which have unobservable qualities]" (EU, 36). Similarly, the problem of induction is formulated by reference to the existence of causal powers: "When a man says, *I have found, in all past instances, such sensible qualities conjoined with such secret powers:* And when he says, *Similar sensible qualities will always be conjoined with similar secret powers*, he is not guilty of a tautology" (EU, 37). In a footnote, added to the second edition, Hume observes that "The word power is here used in a loose and popular sense" and that a "more accurate explication" is given in section VII. The more precise account includes mainly a restatement of the thesis of the *Treatise* that we can have no imaginary grasp of causal power. In addition, he makes an attempt, though a modest one, to give some account of what theoretical physicists can mean when they talk of causal powers: "I need not examine at length the *vis inertiae* which is so much talked of in the new philosophy, and which is ascribed to matter. We find by experience that a body at rest or in motion continues forever in its present state, till put from it by some new cause; and that a body impelled takes as much motion from the impelling body as it acquires itself. These are facts. When we call this a *vis inertiae*, we only mark these facts, without pretending to have any idea of the inert power; in the same manner as, when we talk of gravity, we mean certain effects without comprehending that active power" (EU, 73). Here it is quite clear that Hume believes there are powers in nature; bodies are "impelled"; motion is communicated from one body to the next; and gravity is a real power known indirectly through its effects. But again, of course, we have no internal grasp of "that active power" which produces these effects.

In another footnote, introduced in the second edition, Hume is even more explicit about the existence of causal powers and adds some re-marks about how they can be known through relative ideas: "Accord-ing to these explications and definitions, the idea of *power* is relative as much as that of *cause;* and both have a reference to an effect, or some other event constantly conjoined with the former. When we consider the *unknown* circumstance of an object, by which the degree or quantity of its effect is fixed and determined, we call that its power: And accord-ingly, it is allowed by all philosophers, that the effect is the measure of the power" (EU, 77n). By "the unknown circumstances" Hume means circumstances that are unobservable, and these are known indirectly through experience of their effects. But what he really wants to stress is that scientists have no *direct* acquaintance with power. That there are powers and that they can be measured indirectly he takes to be obvious: "But if they had any idea of power, as it is in itself, why could they not measure it in itself? The dispute, whether the force of a body in motion be as its velocity or the square of its velocity, this dispute, I say, need not be decided by comparing its effects in equal or unequal times; but by a direct mensuration and comparison" (EU, 77n).

Here Hume is suggesting that a more sophisticated codification would involve an analysis of how theoretical concepts of such causal powers as gravitational forces are mathematicized and connected with observable phenomena thought of as their effects. We can, for instance, individuate powers and discover that there is really one power operat-ing and not two: "Why do philosophers infer, with the greatest certain-ty, that the moon is kept in its orbit by the same force of gravity, that makes bodies fall near the surface of the earth, but because these effects are, upon computation, found similar and equal?" (EM, 236). But these are only hints. Hume never undertook a systematic examination and codification of our higher and theoretically governed inductive prac-tices. And this must take away considerably from the reputation he has gained from the positivist interpretation as a philosopher of science. If Hume had held that a cause simply is an experienced constant conjunc-tion of like events, along with a determination of the mind to believe that the conjunction will continue, he would have been proposing a radical thesis in the philosophy of science, requiring an extensive modi-fication of our conception of theoretical language along with, perhaps, the favorite project of early twentieth-century empiricism, that of re-ducing theoretical terms that purport to be referential to observation terms. As it is, Hume did not hold such a view. What he did was to codify our most elementary inductive practices, leaving the higher cod-ifications to others. But just here Hume abandoned the central problem of philosophy of science, which is to give an account of the status of theoretical language and its relation to common language.

Another difference of emphasis between the accounts of causality in the *Treatise* and *Enquiry* is in the handling of the two "definitions." In the *Treatise*, the definitions are presented boldly and with full relish of the paradoxes they might generate. In the *Enquiry*, they are presented with more humility and in full recognition that unobservable causal powers are presupposed. Owing to the fact that our ideas of causal connection are "so imperfect," "it is impossible to give any just definition of cause, except what is drawn from something extraneous and foreign to it" (EU, 76). And immediately after the definitions are presented, both are said to be "drawn from circumstances foreign to the cause" Hume characterizes this as an "inconvenience" which cannot be remedied, for we cannot have the sort of internal understanding of causal power that we want. All we can have is an indirect understanding by postulating a productive power and by measuring its observable effects in the context of some theory.

Again, the two definitions should not be taken together as a real definition of causality. A cause, for Hume, is not a constant conjuction of like objects along with a habit of expectation that the conjunction will continue. These are circumstances "foreign to the cause." Causes are unobservable productive powers which have observable and measurable effects. The purpose of the dual definitions is to show how our belief in causal power arises and what criteria we actually use in making causal ascriptions, that is, the conditions under which, given two events, one "pronounces them to be *connected*" (EU, 75). Here, as elsewhere, Hume is simply codifying an already established normative practice of common life; in this case, inductive practices. And the practices codified operate at a very deep level; indeed, so deep as to include the inductive practices of animals, children, and the vulgar. Hume, understandably, delights in uncovering causal judgments at this level because it opens a point of view on the concept of causality that cannot be accounted for by the rationalist. This is why he tends to ignore the scientific importance of causal power in the *Treatise* and treats the whole problem of our knowledge of causes as "such an affair as this, which must be an object of the simplest understanding, if not of the senses" (T, 158). But though the two definitions may be an adequate codification of our simplest inductive practices, they do not capture the more sophisticated practices of theoretical physics.

There are, I think, two main reasons why Hume did not explore the higher inductive practices of theoretical science. First, such a study would have taken him out of his proper field as a moral philosopher into natural philosophy, a move that Hume is careful to avoid (T, 275-76). Second, and most important, Hume is mainly concerned with the negative task of purging rationalism from our causal conceptions. Once this illusion is removed, inductive practices in science and common life can emerge and operate freely without conceptual confusions brought on by rationalistic interpretations of them. When this conceptually therapeutic task is accomplished, there is little need for codification, especially to any refined degree. It is a central thesis of Hume's that the codification of rules presupposes a practice operating with an authority of its own independent of the rules. The discovery of the rules does little to advance the practice except in the case where there is conceptual confusion about what the practice is, confusion that misdirects the practice or places us in danger of losing it altogether. Such confusion is typically brought on by philosophical interpretations guided by the autonomy principle. The discovery of the rules which inform a practice raises the practice to the level of self-consciousness and enables us to break free of philosophical distortions of it. But beyond this, there is little practical value in codification. For this reason Hume was diffident about laying out rules for judging causes and effects: "Our scholastic headpieces and logicians shew no such superiority above the mere vulgar in their reason and ability, as to give us any inclination to imitate them in delivering a long system of rules and precepts to direct our judgment, in philosophy" (T, 175). Hume includes natural philosophy along with the causal judgments of the vulgar as a practice not in need of special codification.

Hume's own criteria (the two definitions) for making causal ascriptions enable us to see, at the deepest level, what is essential about our inductive practices and how they exist at all. This will be sufficient, he thinks, to show that rational analysis is not what gives authority to causal judgment and that is really all Hume wants to show. It is, as he says, "the main question on which I would insist" (EU, 34). He is confident that he has discovered the basic form and authority behind our inductive practices and that, however complicated they may become in the higher reaches of theoretical physics, they must be instances of the same constant-conjunction *form* and so can afford no comfort to the rationalist. He points out, for instance, that even mathematical physics, which might be thought to afford some "insight" into the necessary connections of things, is merely a more sophisticated case of the same practice: "Thus, it is a law of motion, discovered by experience, that the moment or force of any body in motion is in the compound ratio or proportion of its solid contents and its velocity; and consequently, that a small force may remove the greatest obstacle or raise the greatest weight. . . . Geometry assists us in the application of this law . . . but still the discovery of the law itself is owing merely to experience" (EU, 31-32). And more generally, "Every part of mixed mathematics proceeds upon the supposition that certain laws are established by nature in her operations; and abstract reasonings are employed either to assist experience in the discovery of these laws, or to determine their influence in particular instances, where it depends upon any precise degree of distance and quantity" (EU, 31).

Hume's failure to explore adequately the question of how knowledge of theoretical entities is possible should not obscure his real contribution to the philosophy of science. As a moral philosopher, Hume presented a vision of science as a human convention spawned by the imagination through its primordial involvement with the world. (Hume's views on the history of this convention and of causal judgment are discussed below, in chapter 9.) Although self-corrective and objective, science is inescapably anthropomorphic. The association relations of the imagination are for us the "cement of the universe." As a human activity science is intelligible only by reference to common life. We cannot have an internal understanding of most theoretical concepts in science, but we can and do have an internal grasp of science itself as an activity of the imagination. The theory of science framed in Kant's revolution in philosophy was already firmly established in Hume's writings.

Henceforth, science would be seen not as a rationalistic investigation of things as they are in themselves through a mind thought to be cognate with reality but as an empirical study of things as constituted by the imagination. The point of the two "definitions" of causality and the arguments leading to them is to confound the rationalist, to expose the essential nature of our inductive practices, and to show how science is rooted in the prejudices and habits of common life. Having located science in human nature, Hume could leave the details of a philosophy of science to others. For his own purposes he did not think any more needed to be said. At the end of the discussion on the idea of necessary connection he remarks: "In all abstract reasonings there is one point of view which, if we can happily hit, we shall go farther toward illustrating the subject than by all the eloquence and copious expression in the world" (EU, 79). The subsequent history of philosophy shows that Hume artfully found just that point of view.

## ULTIMATE CAUSAL EXPLANATIONS

Hume uses the term "causal power" in two senses: a causal power is an ultimate and necessary connection between events (T, 161; EU, 67-68); a causal power is a contingent connection between observable and unobservable events (EU, 32-34, 36-39). We have indirect knowledge of causal power in the second sense (gravitational forces), but no knowledge of it at all in the first sense (the ultimate reason why gravity is a causal power). Yet Hume is rarely explicit in distinguishing the two meanings, and the result is that in vigorously denying that we have knowledge of causal power in the first sense, he seems also to deny that we have knowledge of causal power in the second sense. It is largely for this reason that it has been easy to read Hume as denying the reality of unobservable theoretical entities such as gravitational forces. But although Hume denies that we have knowledge of ultimate causal connections, he does not deny that there are such connections. In fact, he believes there are, and, as we shall see, this belief is fundamental to understanding his conception of causality and causal explanation. It is this belief that makes Hume's criticism of the rationalist doctrine of ultimate causation a form of skepticism rather than positivism. If we take logical positivism as the paradigm of the positivist way of looking at things, then the doctrine of ultimate causation would be rejected on the ground that it is cognitively meaningless. One would be in a position to claim that there are and can be no ultimate causal connections. The positivist would be nihilistic, not skeptical, about ultimate causation. Hume's strategy is different. It is to lead one to skepticism about ultimate causal connections. But, logically, one cannot doubt that we can have knowledge of ultimate causes unless there could be such causes. And Hume holds not only that such causes could exist but also that we believe they do exist, although there is no reasonable hope that we can know anything in particular about them. Here, as elsewhere, Hume's criticism of rationalism is developed dialectically within the very rationalistic framework he is examining, and this because Hume's own thinking is still very much part of the rationalist tradition.

The rationalist goal of science is to enable us to see ultimately why things must be as they are. To accomplish this goal, science must be in possession of principles which satisfy an a-priori criterion of intelligibility. The master example was given by Descartes, who held that the acceptability of a scientific principle is whether it is "clear and distinct." And we know a proposition is clear and distinct if it is necessary in the same way that our existence necessarily follows from the fact that we are conscious. It was on the basis of this criterion that Descartes ruled out the possibility of causal power in matter: it is not necessary that matter be in motion, and so motion is not an essential property of matter. This, in turn, led Descartes to place the productive power of motion outside of the material universe in God's creative and sustaining power. The idea that scientific principles must be in some way "understandable" was challenged by Bacon. In an early statement of the positivist outlook he writes: "the most general principles of nature ought to be held merely positive, as they are discovered, and cannot with truth be referred to a cause."[2] By a "cause" Bacon means a reason which would explain why the "merely positive" regularities must be as they are. Like Bacon, Newton rejects the notion that "understanding" is an essential feature of scientific principles. *Any* theory, whether self-intelligible or not, may be accepted if sufficiently established by experimental evidence: "If no exception occur from phenomena, the conclusion may be pronounced generally."[3] But Newton has not abandoned the rationalist ideal of scientific explanation. It is not enough that general regularities are discovered; in addition, they should be made understandable by uncovering their "cause": "For we must learn from the phaenomenon of nature what bodies attract one another, and what are the laws and properties of the attraction, before we enquire the cause by which the attraction is performed."[4] The cause Newton is after here is not just another, more general regularity under which the regularities of attraction can be subsumed; he is looking for an explanation of a formally different sort. He would like to discover principles inherent in the nature of matter which would explain, in a rationally satisfying way, why bodies must attract as they do. For Newton, nature is an intelligible system, hierarchically ordered, and it is the ideal task of science, through experimental means, to grasp the rationale of that system: "The main business of natural philosophy is to argue from phenomena without feigning hypotheses, and to deduce causes from effects, till we come to the very first cause."[5]

Hume, like Newton, believes that there are ultimate causal principles. The difference is that Newton conceives of science as progressing, however modestly, towards the discovery of ultimate causes, whereas Hume does not think any significant progress has been or ever will be made. It is because Hume holds both of these views that he could be skeptical about the explanatory value of even the most established causal explanations: "we cannot give a satisfactory reason, why we believe after a thousand experiments, that a stone will fall, or fire burn" (EU, 162). Even the most advanced causal explanations in natural philosophy do not really explain anything: "The most perfect philosophy of the natural kind only staves off our ignorance a little longer" (EU, 31). But precisely why are the causal explanations of natural philosophy inadequate?

In the *Enquiry* on understanding, Hume lists what he considers the main causal principles discovered by natural philosophy: "Elasticity, gravity, cohesion of parts, communication of motion by impulse" (EU, 30), all of which are contingent regularities between unobservable powers and observable effects. As constant-conjunction regularities, they are equally intelligible or unintelligible; that is, they are simply brute facts. To render them understandable, we should have to uncover the rationale or "cause" behind them which would show us in an intuitively satisfying way why they must be as they are. A more general regularity including them all will not do because it too would have constant conjunction *form* and so would be in need of explanation. Newton would and did view the four causal principles mentioned above as departures for scientific research into their underlying rationales. Hume, however, views them in a more conservative way as contingent limits to inquiry. Of the four causal principles, he says that they "are probably the ultimate causes and principles which we shall ever discover in nature; and we may esteem ourselves sufficiently happy, if, by accurate inquiry and reasoning, we can trace up the particular phenomena to, or near to, these general principles" (EU, 30). Hume's suggestion that the four causal principles be treated as "ultimate" could lead to an attitude that would hinder scientific progress in a way that Newton's idealistic pursuit of ultimate causes would not. However, the obvious point Hume wishes to make is that all empirical regularities (no matter how general) have constant conjunction form and so are inadequate relative to the ideal of ultimate explanation. Since all empirical regularities are and always will be inadequate in this way, there is no special reason to lament the inadequacy of the regularities we have discovered.

Here, as elsewhere, Hume is combatting that melancholy philosophical mentality, governed by the autonomy principle, which cannot accept any limit not imposed by its own consciousness. Such a frame of mind is logically emancipated from the ordinary canons of common life: "We are got into fairy land, long ere we have reached the last steps of our theory; and *there* we have no reason to trust our common methods of argument, or to think that our usual analogies and probabilities have any authority" (EU, 72). Such alienated philosophical consciousness can be a barrier to the improvement of empirical science by discouraging it, misdirecting it by virtue of some favored a-priori scheme, or halting it by hardening some contingent principle into a metaphysical absolute and making it impervious to empirical test. To avoid these consequences we should clearly recognize the nature and limits of the causal regularities we have discovered and celebrate them as such. This is what Hume has in mind, I think, when he says that we should treat the four causal principles above as "ultimate." We should take them seriously in full appreciation of their limits. But we cannot perceive their limits and, hence, their nature, and, consequently, their value without the background idea of ultimate causes. This is the dialectical sting in Hume's skeptical analysis of causality. And this is why praise of the achievements and value of empirical science is, in Socratic fashion, internally connected to a celebration of "our profound ignorance" of ultimate causes (EU, 73; cf. 31, 70, 72, 75-77).

Passmore has remarked that "Empirical science, to Hume, is the discovery that things in fact behave in certain ways; and it is not our incapacity which prevents us from discovering ultimate causes, but the fact that there are no such causes to discover." Certainly Hume did hold that the task of empirical science is to discover how things in fact behave, and he does not think, as Newton did, that science can be viewed as making progress towards the discovery of ultimate causes. But he does not hold these views because he believes there are no ultimate causes. As we have seen, he believes there are such causes, although he is skeptical about our ever discovering anything in particular about them. Moreover, Hume uses this belief as a necessary background for illuminating the nature and value of empirical science.

Hume's frequent remarks that we have no idea of ultimate causation are the main reason for believing that he denies the existence of ultimate causes, for if we really have no idea of ultimate causes, then it would be meaningless to say either that they do or do not exist. But Hume's assertion that we have no idea of ultimate causes must be understood with a limitation which he is careful to point out: "as we can have no idea of anything which never appeared to our outward sense or inward sentiment, the necessary conclusion *seems* to be that we have no idea of connexion or power at all, and that these words are absolutely without any meaning, when employed either in philosophical reasonings or common life" (EU, 74, Hume's emphasis). Hume then goes on to explain how the idea of ultimate causal connection originates, using the conditions specified in the dual definition: objects constantly conjoined, along with a determination of the mind to infer the existence of the one from the occurrence of the other. When these conditions are satisfied, "We then call the one object, *Cause;* the other *Effect.* We suppose that there is some connection between them, some power in the one by which it infallibly produces the other, and operates with the greatest certainty and strongest necessity" (EU, 74-75). This is our idea of ultimate causation; it is a supposition determined by the imagination, arising out of a certain sort of experience but one which we, nevertheless, attribute to objects in the world: "Without considering it [necessity] in this view, we can never arrive at the most distant notion of it, or be able to attribute it either to external or internal objects, to spirit or body, to causes or effects" (T, 165). The supposition is that objects which appear only conjoined in experience are in reality connected by the "strongest necessity." And Hume is clear that the connection we suppose to exist is metaphysical and absolute; it is described as an "inseparable and inviolable connexion" (EU, 31). Every material object, we suppose "is determin'd by an absolute fate to a certain degree and direction of its motion" (T, 400). It is the sort of connection which, if we could discover it, would enable us to "account ultimately for the production of one thing to another" (EU, 77n).

However, Hume also insists that our belief in ultimate causal connections is empirically vacuous and that we should avoid the conceptual confusion brought on by identifying our experience of what we consider causal regularities with ultimate causes. Two sorts of confusion should be guarded against; one is due to the vulgar, the other to philosophers. The vulgar believe that in their experience of causal regularities, "they perceive the very force or energy of the cause by which it is connected with its effect, and is forever infallible in its operation" (EU, 69). But in fact they perceive objects conjoined, not connected. Philosophers using "reasonings from analogy, experience, and observation" with the help of "mixed mathematics" treat causal regularities as relations between unobservable "secret powers," such as gravity, and their observable effect (EU, 30). Natural philosophers often treat such "secret powers" as ultimate or as providing *partial* insight into some ultimate causal connection. But the relation holding between such powers, which we indirectly experience, and their observable effects is as contingent as that holding between sets of directly observable objects (EU, 36-37). So the secret powers discovered by natural philosophy are not ultimate nor are they partial revelations, as Newton thought, of ultimate causal connections: "The most perfect philosophy of the natural kind only staves off our ignorance a little longer" (EU, 31).

Our belief in ultimate causal connections is empirically vacuous because we cannot derive the idea of ultimate causal connections from impressions. Over and over Hume insists that we have no idea of ultimate causal connections, but, as we have mentioned, he does not mean that talk about such connections is meaningless in the way that twentieth-century empiricists might mean if they were to say the same thing, for neither his remarks on meaning nor his theory of language is developed in such a way as to make possible, for instance, the logical positivist claim that metaphysical statements are meaningless. What he means is that we do not and cannot have an internal mastery of the concept. But we do have an external understanding of it, and it is this understanding that makes possible a belief in ultimate causes. I would now like to examine Hume's reflections on the content of this external understanding.

We have some understanding of what it would be like to know an ultimate causal connection: "it must be allowed that when we know a power, we know that very circumstance in the cause by which it is enabled to produce the effect" (EU, 67). And this means knowledge of the *nature* of the cause and the effect and "the aptitude of the one to produce the other" (ibid.). To have such knowledge, we must "be able to pronounce, from a simple view of the one, that it must be follow'd or preceded by the other. This is the true manner of conceiving a particular power in a particular body" (T, 161). This, then, is our external understanding of what it would be like to have knowledge of an ultimate causal connection. Under what conditions could we be said to know from the nature of cause and effect that the two are connected by the strongest necessity? Hume characterizes such knowledge in various ways. It would be to know "the manner in which bodies operate on each other" (EU, 72); it would be to grasp a "real intelligible connexion betwixt" cause and effect (T, 168); it would be to have "insight into the essence of bodies" (T, 400; cf., 169), or to "penetrate into the intimate nature of bodies" (D, 191). It would be a case of giving "the ultimate reason why milk or bread is proper nourishment for a man, not for a lion or tiger" (EU, 28). The problem is specifying nonarbitrary criteria for applying these terms. The doctrine of innate ideas is an obvious candidate, but it "has been already refuted, and is now almost universally rejected in the learned world" (T, 158). The next most likely suggestion is to say that "Such a connexion wou'd amount to a demonstration, and wou'd imply the absolute impossibility for the one object not to follow, or to be conceiv'd not to follow upon the other" (T, 161-62). But we know of no connection between matters of fact the denial of which is inconceivable. And since no other connection seems available, it appears that we have very little idea of what knowledge of ultimate causation would be like: "We have no idea of this connection, nor even any distinct notion what it is we desire to know when we endeavour at a conception of it" (EU, 77). This is not the remark of someone standing, ironically, outside the tradition of belief in ultimate causal connections; it is rather the result of a searching examination of one who is still within that tradition.

One important and very tight restriction that Hume places on knowledge of ultimate causation is that we must first be acquainted with a particular case of the connection on the basis of which, and in line with Hume's theory of abstract ideas, a general abstract idea of the ultimate connection can be formed: "If we be possest, therefore, of any idea of power in general, we must also be able to conceive some particular species of it . . . we must be able to place this power in some particular being" (T, 161). But belief in particular ultimate causal connections presupposes belief that reality is ultimately an intelligible scheme of things which determines these particular connections. As we shall see in the next section, Hume spends some effort speculating about what the ultimate system might be. Even if correct, however, such speculations, in his view, could bring us no closer to understanding any particular ultimate causal connection. They are, nevertheless, of intrinsic philosophical interest, and can, at least, bring us closer to "what it is we desire to know when we endeavor at a conception of it" (EU, 77).

## NEO-EPICUREANISM

Two candidates for ultimate causal systems are to be found in Hume's writings: materialism and theism. Throughout Hume's philosophical works are passages which suggest that he was inclined to some form of materialism. In *The Natural History of Religion*, he writes that "We are placed in this world, as in a great theatre, where the true springs and causes of every event are entirely concealed from us" (NHR, 28). Primitive people and "the ignorant multitude" typically impose a religious interpretation on these unobservable causes. But could they "anatomize nature, according to the most probable, at least the most intelligible philosophy, they would find, that these causes are nothing but the particular fabric and structure of the minute parts of their own bodies and of external objects; and that, by a regular and constant machinery, all the events are produced, about which they are so much concerned" (ibid., 29). Here materialism appears as "the most intelligible philosophy" and "the true springs and causes of every event" are the mechanical operations of the unobservable structure of matter. In the *Treatise*, although Hume distinguishes between mental and physical phenomena, he also says that matter in motion "may be, and actually is, the cause of thought and perception" (T, 248). Hume also appears to identify ideas and the association relations with brain states in a way similar to that of the contemporary identity theory (ibid., 60-61). In "Of the Immortality of the Soul," physical causes are said to be the causes of anything that can be known: "The physical arguments from the analogy of nature are strong for the mortality of the soul; and are really the only philosophical arguments which ought to be admitted with regard to this question, or indeed any question of fact" (E, 602). In the dialogue "Of a Providence and a Future State," Epicurus speaks for Hume in criticizing the providential view of the world. And in the *Dialogues*, Hume has Philo, after running through several metaphysical systems, "revive the old Epicurean hypothesis" (D, 182). It is given an up-to-date Newtonian interpretation, and presented as "a plausible, if not a true solution of the difficulty" of choosing an ultimate explanatory system (ibid., 185).

In contrast to traditional theism, which places the source of order of the material world in a transcendent deity, Philo "ascribes an eternal, inherent principle of order to the world; though attended with great and continual revolutions and alterations" (ibid., 174). The principle that order is internal to the world is a belief that Philo treats as categorical to any explanation whatsoever and is part of what we mean when we say there are ultimate causes: "This at once solves all difficulties; and if the solution, by being so general, is not entirely complete and satisfactory, it is, at least, a theory, that we must, sooner or later, have recourse to, whatever system we embrace. . . . Every thing is surely governed by steady, inviolable laws. And were the inmost essence of things laid open to us, we should then discover a scene, of which, at present, we can have no idea. Instead of admiring the order of natural beings, we should clearly see, that it was absolutely impossible for them, in the smallest article, ever to admit of any other disposition" (ibid., 174-75). Here Philo has stated in the clearest terms that belief in an ultimately intelligible scheme of things is a presupposition of all attempts at explanation: "How could things have been as they are, were there not an original, inherent principle of order somewhere, in thought or in matter? And it is very indifferent to which of these we give the preference" (ibid., 174).

Still a preference can be given to matter insofar as we have considerable experience of thought arising from matter, but "thought has no influence upon matter, except where that matter is so conjoined with it, as to have an equal reciprocal influence upon it" (D, 186). But an even stronger case can be made. Philo asks: "Is there a system, an order, an oeconomy of things, by which matter can preserve that perpetual agitation, which seems essential to it, and yet maintain a constancy in the forms, which it produces? There certainly is such an oeconomy: For this is actually the case with the present world" (ibid., 183). Moreover, were this form of materialism true, the world would appear just as it is now complete with what appear to be cases of design: "But whenever matter is so poised, arranged, and adjusted as to continue in perpetual motion, and yet preserve a constancy in the forms, its situation must, of necessity, have all the same appearance of art and contrivance which we observe at present" (ibid.). If so, then utilities in nature are the result of a process akin to *natural selection* and not of thought: "It is in vain, therefore, to insist upon the uses of the parts in animals or vegetables, and their curious adjustment to each other. I would fain know how an animal could subsist, unless its parts were so adjusted?" (ibid., 185).

But even if matter possessed the internal principle of order which Philo ascribes to it and all observable phenomena could be accounted for in terms of the regularities of matter in motion, one would still not have an ultimate account of things. Regularities, no matter how general and no matter how systematically ordered, are still just brute facts. An ultimate understanding is achieved only when we know the "cause" or rationale of these regularities and thus see why, in an intuitively satisfying way, they could not be otherwise. Accordingly, Philo speculates about what it might be like to comprehend the ultimate causes implied in the materialistic cosmology: "It is observed by arithmeticians, that the products of 9 compose always either 9 or some lesser product of 9; if you add together all the characters, of which any of the former products is composed. . . . To a superficial observer, so wonderful a regularity may be admired as the effect either of chance or design; but a skilful algebraist immediately concludes it to be the work of necessity, and demonstrates, that it must for ever result from the nature of these numbers. Is it not probable, I ask, that the whole oeconomy of the universe is conducted by a like necessity, though no human algebra can furnish the key which solves the difficulty?" (D, 191).

We should perhaps read for Philo's "probable" the weaker "plausible" or even "possible." In any case, Hume is making an effort to say something about what could count as an ultimate causal connection and what it could be like to have knowledge of it.[6] There could be a kind of algebra of the operations of matter, understandable in mathematical terms. This analogy between ultimate causal connections and mathematical necessity is something more than a play of words because its possibility is grounded in Hume's conception of mathematics.

Mathematical propositions, for Hume, as we saw in chapter 1, are not analytic. They are about the world, yet are necessarily true or false. Some sense, then, can be given within Hume's conception of mathematics to Philo's suggestion that mathematical necessity can be used as a model to throw light on what we might have in mind when we wonder about ultimate causation.

The claim Hume has Philo make is that it is "probable" that there is something *like* mathematical necessity governing the operations of matter which "no human algebra" can decipher. To say that this view is probable is simply to underscore the strong case that can be made for materialism as opposed to theism. In *The Natural History of Religion* materialism, as we have seen, is characterized as "the most probable, at least the most intelligible philosophy" (NHR, 29). But in saying it is the "most intelligible philosophy." Hume is not saying, for instance, that the laws of Newtonian mechanics are "intelligible" in the rationally satisfying way that ultimate causal connections are supposed to be. They are still brute facts in need of explanation. The laws of natural philosophy are the "most intelligible" because they are the most comprehensive and best established. This being so, any attempt to establish theism using the concept of necessary existence, as in the case of the ontological argument, immediately gives rise to the challenge: "why may not the material universe be the necessarily existent Being, according to this pretended explication of necessity?" (D, 190). Materialism has the advantage, given the present state of scientific knowledge, of offering the most likely cosmology, and, because it is susceptible of a mathematical interpretation, of enabling us plausibly to imagine what the ultimate causal connections might be like. Neither advantage is afforded by theism.

But in the end, Hume rejects materialism as a cosmology and the mathematical model of ultimate causation as having any scientific value. In the *Enquiry* on understanding, he writes: "Nor is geometry, when taken into the assistance of natural philosophy, ever able to remedy this defect or lead us into the knowledge of ultimate causes, by all that accuracy of reasoning for which it is so justly celebrated." The application of mathematics to natural philosophy "proceeds upon the supposition that certain laws are established by nature in her operations; and abstract reasonings are employed, either to assist experience in the discovery of these laws, or to determine their influence in particular instances, where it depends upon any precise degree of distance and quantity" (EU, 31). In *The History of England*, while assessing the achievements of Boyle and Newton, Hume suggests why materialism has had such a seductive appeal: "Boyle was a great partizan of the mechanical philosophy; a theory which, by discovering some of the secrets of nature, and allowing us to *imagine* the rest, is so agreeable to the natural vanity and curiosity of men. . . . While Newton seemed to draw off the veil from some of the mysteries of nature, he showed at the same time the imperfections of the mechanical philosophy, and thereby restored her ultimate secrets to that obscurity in which they ever did and ever will remain" (H, VI, 1xxi, 374, emphasis mine). Mechanical connections are easy to imagine. Given two gears meshed, if one goes clockwise, the other must go counterclockwise. This is not simply an empirical regularity, it is also in some way necessary and so motivates our curiosity to discover principles in nature that are "intelligible." Given some significant mechanical explanations, it is easy to imagine that all bodies must be connected by some such intelligible principles. Morever, since mechanical causal connections can be given a geometrical representation, it is also easy to believe that we may be able to analyze them as being ultimate in the way that mathematical propositions are ultimate. Newton destroyed this pleasing metaphysical vanity with the doctrine of gravitational forces which required accepting the counterintuitive principle of action at a distance. If there can be action at a distance, then there is no way to imagine how bodies must act in relation to each other, and the whole mechanical framework for scientific research falls to the ground. It was Newton's ability to frame such bold hypotheses about powers which cannot be imagined that in Hume's eyes made him superior to Boyle, whose scientific understanding was hardened by a fixation on what could be imagined. Newton was "Cautious in admitting no principles but such as were founded on experiment, but resolute to adopt every such principle, however *new or unusual*" (ibid., 374, emphasis mine).

But Newton was not entirely emancipated from the mechanical imagination. He still hoped to find a medium holding between all bodies which would account for their movement. Nor for that matter was Hume so emancipated. The analysis of causal relations in the *Treatise* requires that cause and effect be spatially contiguous, a concession to the mechanical paradigm which flatly contradicts his claim elsewhere in the *Treatise* that most perceptions have no spatial location and yet can enter into causal relations (T, 235). This contradiction is due to a larger tension in Hume's thinking between (1) the view that we do not have an *adequate* grasp of a concept unless we can have a narrative encounter with what it purports to be about and (2) the recognition that we, nevertheless, do have some understanding of theoretical concepts which purport to be about entities which cannot be experienced. I have called these, respectively, the internal and external understanding of concepts. Hume does not, except in a cursory way, take up the question of how (2) is possible, and without that it is not clear why he insists on (1). But both (1) and (2) are required for Hume's characteristically skeptical and paradoxical conclusion: that since there are empirical conditions for applying the term "gravitational power," it is intelligible to talk about gravity and to assert its existence, but that we still have no idea of what gravity is.

We should observe, though, a certain progress in Hume's thinking about the status of theoretical concepts. In the *Treatise*, although not failing to recognize (2), Hume stresses (1), leaving the impression of a very restrictive imagistic account of theoretical activity. This is especially clear in his treatment of concepts like that of infinite divisibility and the vacuum (T, I, II, i-v). In the *Enquiry* on understanding, more recognition is given to the importance of (2). Unobservable causal powers are clearly affirmed, and some attempt is made at explicating how talk about them can have empirical content. The passage from the *History* quoted above sounds the same theme and stresses the rule that theoretical activity must be free of any imagistic constraints and allowed to embrace any principle, however counterintuitive. Newton's system, though theoretically more successful than Boyle's, has made it more difficult to imagine the manner in which bodies operate. And in the *Dialogues* the principle of the priority of impressions to ideas is not deployed; no restriction from a theory of meaning is placed on talk about unobservable causal powers and principles (in nature or in the Deity), the only requirement is that the evidence for the truth of what we say must be based, indirectly, on experience of their effects.

Hume rejects materialism as the ultimate explanatory system because there is not sufficient data to establish it. "I have still asserted," says Philo, "that we have no *data* to establish any system of cosmogony. Our experience, so imperfect in itself, and so limited both in extent and duration, can afford us no probable conjecture concerning the whole of things" (D, 177). Although Hume rejects materialism, it still "affords a plausible, if not a true solution" to the problem of choosing the best cosmology. Indeed, Hume appears to have thought of materialism as the system that most readily comes to mind if one tried to stretch the scientific knowledge of his time to fit the whole of reality.

## PHILOSOPHICAL THEISM

The ultimate system which Hume officially adopts is "pure theism" (NHR, 23), and it is the content and justification of this belief that we must now examine.[7] At the end of the *Dialogues* Philo explicitly affirms his own belief in "the divine Being, as he discovers himself to reason, in the inexplicable contrivance and artifice of nature. A purpose, an intention, or design strikes everywhere the most careless, the most stupid thinker; and no man can be so hardened in absurd systems, as at all times to reject it" (D, 214). The same opinion is expressed in *The Natural History of Religion*: "The whole frame of nature bespeaks an intelligent author; and no rational enquirer can, after serious reflection, suspend his belief a moment with regard to the primary principles of genuine Theism and Religion" (NHR, 21). These passages show that Hume accepted, in some form, the argument from design.

In a letter defending the *Treatise* from the charge of atheism, Hume insists that while he has rejected the a-priori ontological argument for God's existence, he accepts the empirical argument from design: "all the solid Arguments for Natural Religion retain their full Force upon the Author's Principles concerning Causes and Effects, and that there is no Necessity even for altering the common Methods of expressing or conceiving these Arguments. . . . Wherever I see Order, I infer from Experience that *there*, there hath been Design and Contrivance. And the same Principle which leads me into this Inference, when I contemplate a Building, regular and beautiful in its whole Frame and Structure; the same Principle obliges me to infer an infinitely perfect Architect, from the infinite Art and Contrivance which is display'd in the whole Fabrick of the Universe. Is not this the Light in which this Argument hath been placed by all Writers concerning Natural Religion?" (LG, 24-26). And as early as the *Treatise* itself Hume had argued that "The order of the universe proves an omnipotent mind" (T, 633n).

How do we come to a belief in philosophical theism and how is that belief justified? First of all, Hume distinguishes sharply between philosophical theism and the theism of traditional religion. This is best brought out by reviewing his account of how religious beliefs originate. Religion arises "chiefly from an anxious fear of future events" and by the way in which men try to understand the unknown causes of these events (NHR, 65). Religion arises out of the problem of causality, and Hume's account of it illuminates his conception of causality. Primitive man, faced with the dreadful chaos of life in which "life and death, health and sickness, plenty and want . . . are distributed amongst the human species by secret and unknown causes," attempts to form "ideas of those powers, on which we have so entire a dependence" (NHR, 29). Men would never have been led to continue the search for the causes of their destiny, especially after repeated failures, "were it not for a propensity in human nature, which leads into a system, that gives them some satisfaction" (ibid.). So there is in human nature on original propensity to work our a satisfying system which can explain why things are as they are. There is also a propensity among men to believe there is "invisible, intelligent power in nature" and a contrary propensity "equally strong to rest . . . attention on sensible, visible objects; and in order to reconcile these opposite inclinations, they are led to unite the invisible power with some visible object" (NHR, 38). These three propensities structure the origin not only of all religious belief but of all causal beliefs as well. They do not, however, have the stability of an "original instinct or primary impression of nature, such as gives rise to self-love, affection between the sexes, love of progeny, gratitude, resentment . . . . every instinct of this kind has been found absolutely universal in all nations and ages, and has always a precise determinate object, which it inflexibly pursues." The propensities from which religion arises "must be secondary; such as may easily be perverted by various accidents and causes, and whose operation too, in some cases, may, by an extraordinary concurrence of circumstances, be altogether prevented" (NHR, 21).

Given these propensities, along with the contrariety of events, it is natural, Hume thinks, that polytheism would have been the first religion, one in which the whole visible world is viewed as a system of warring and capricious deities. Popular theism arises out of polytheism not by recognizing the rational necessity of one supreme deity but out of the "adulation and fears of the most vulgar superstition." To worship is to praise, and in proportion as the fears of men become more urgent, they invent new strains of adulation "till at last they arrive at infinity itself, beyond which there is no farther progress" (NHR, 43). In this way men stumble on to the idea of an all-perfect creator of the world, characterized by "unity and infinity, simplicity and spirituality"

(NHR, 47). But the seeds of polytheism are still contained in the idea of an all-perfect being, an idea that cannot be sustained without the notion of inferior mediators which interpose between man and the supreme deity. These middle beings, partaking more of human nature and being more familiar to us, gradually usurp the devotion due to the supreme deity. There is, then, a dialectical tension, what Hume calls a "flux and reflux," in all religion—a tendency in polytheism to become theistic and a tendency in theism to collapse back into polytheism.

Genuine, or philosophical, theism has a quite different origin and so a different significance. It comes about only after men have acquired the habit of making inductive inferences and of viewing nature in a lawlike way. The motives which carry men beyond the visible world to construct theories about the invisible causes of events are different as between philosophical and popular theism. The latter begins in and is always guided by an anxious *fear* about events that affect human life. The former is guided by an *appreciation* of the beauty and fitness of order. "Even at this day, and in Europe," says Hume, if we ask any vulgar theist "why he believes in an omnipotent creator of the world; he will never mention the beauty of final causes. . . . To these he has been long accustomed; and he beholds them with listlessness and unconcern. He will tell you of the sudden and unexpected death of such a one. . . The excessive drought of this season: The cold and rain of another. These he ascribes to the immediate operation of providence: And such events, as with good reasoners, are the chief difficulties in admitting a supreme intelligence, are with him the sole arguments for it" (NHR, 41). What astonishes the vulgar theist is not the order and regularity of the world but what is disorderly and irregular relative to his expectations and interests. His is a providential and miraculous universe.

What fascinates the philosophical theist is simply the lawlike order of the world as discovered in empirical science. But this passion of wonder is possible only because philosophers are able to view empirical regularities themselves as, in some way, "unexpected" or "astonishing." And, for Hume, this is possible because of his concept of knowledge: a proposition is known to be true just in case its denial is inconceivable. Bringing this strong conception of knowledge to the world, philosophers may not only be logically surprised that things are ordered the way they are but also that there *is* anything at all, for a priori nothing has to be: "It will still be possible for us, at any time, to conceive the nonexistence of what we formerly conceived to exist" (D, 189). Hume's principle of the radical contingency of the world is one he owes to the Christian tradition and specifically to the doctrine of creation *ex nihilo*. Hume recognized this debt in the *Enquiry* on understanding: "That impious maxim of the ancient philosophy, *Ex nihilo, nihil fit*, by which the creation of matter was excluded, ceases to be a maxim, according to this philosophy. Not only the will of the supreme Being may create matter; but, for aught we know *a priori*, the will of any other being might create it, or any other cause that the most whimsical imagination can assign" (EU, 164n). Coming to the world with this presupposition, the Humean philosopher is conceptually astonished that there is anything at all and that things are ordered the way they are. He, therefore, has a special appreciation for the fact that things simply exist and that they are ordered, and out of this wonder he is led to inquire into the ultimate causes of order.

We have seen that there is an original propensity to give a systematic account of events and that this is one of the causes of religion (NHR, 29). But it is also a cause of science. Hume did not write the natural history of science that would be parallel to the natural history of religion, but he left room and, indeed, a need for such a history. In the course of their causal involvement with the world and critical reflection upon it, men gradually come to believe in the lawlike order of the world; regularities themselves become an object of wonder. And with this belief and attitude, the scientific outlook is established. The original religious propensities persist, though transformed, in the new outlook. The primitive polytheistic belief and anxiety about capricious gods grows into the later theistic doctrine of creation out of nothing, and both are logically reconstituted in the modern doctrine that the world of experience is conceptually contingent. So scientists believe that the world as we experience it and imagine it is contingent but that behind this apparent contingency and connected to it is an ultimately intelligible system of laws. The universal propensity to believe in the existence of intelligent power as the cause of things is manifest in the modern doctrine common to philosophers and theists alike that there is a "Sovereign mind or first principle of all things" who has "fixed general laws, by which nature is governed" (NHR, 42, 75).

But there is a great difference between the philosophical theist and the traditional religious theist. The latter requires the doctrine of a "*particular* providence," that God has a plan for his creatures and will intervene personally and miraculously to accomplish it. The philosophical theist believes in a universe of inflexible law where God is the ultimate principle of order. And with this a sharp break has occurred in the natural history of religious belief, one that effectively places the philosophical theist outside the religious tradition in which his own thought has developed. Hume's *Dialogues Concerning Natural Religion* is, in part, an attempt to dramatize the rationale of this break. Both Philo and Cleanthes believe in God as the supreme author of the universe and both believe that God is known through "the inexplicable contrivance

and artifice of nature" (D, 214; NHR, 24). The difference is that Cleanthes is not entirely emancipated from the primeval religious tradition
that conceives of the Deity in a providential way. Philo's main role in
the *Dialogues* is to show that the argument from design, so fashionable
among the moderate clergy of Hume's time, cannot support inferences
to the anthropomorphic conceptions of God which are a carryover from
the superstitious origin of religion. The difference in meaning between
the theism of Philo and that of Cleanthes was, in effect, sketched out in
*The Natural History of Religion* which was written about the same time as
the *Dialogues*. Traditional theists, says Hume, while "they confine
themselves to the notion of a perfect being, the creator of the world,
they coincide, by chance, with the principles of reason and true philosophy; though they are guided to that notion, not by reason, of which
they are in a great measure incapable, but by the adulation and fears of
the most vulgar superstition" (NHR, 43).

Cleanthes' theism, although more refined and rational than that of
the first theists, is nevertheless still governed by the superstitious motives of the primeval tradition. Philo's task is to expose the tension in
Cleanthes' thought between the rational and the traditional content of
his religious belief. In the next to the last section, just before Philo's
open confession of belief in the soundness of the design argument,
Cleanthes is brought to recognize that "vulgar theology" has governed
much of his own thinking (D, 213). But in the last section, after having
reached what appears to be complete agreement, Cleanthes backslides
into a providential interpretation of God, although one of considerable
refinement: "Take care, Philo. . . . Push not matters too far: Allow not
your zeal against false religion to undermine your veneration for the
true . . . which represents us as the workmanship of a Being perfectly
good, wise, and powerful; who created us for happiness, and who,
having implanted in us immeasurable desires for good, will prolong our
existence to all eternity, and will transfer us into an infinite variety of
scenes, in order to satisfy those desires, and render our felicity complete and durable" (D, 224). Granting that such a conception may be
edifying to "the true philosopher," Philo stresses again that it is not
warranted by the design argument and in any case would, for the generality of mankind, bring into play the superstitious passions of terror
and hope about a future state which have had such a disastrous effect on
morals and civil order. In a word, any providential conception of God
will trigger the whole absurd and socially destructive dialectic of passions and thoughts that Hume traced out in *The Natural History of
Religion*.

What, then, is a rationally acceptable belief in God, and how do we
come to it? First of all, "contrivance and artifice" are manifest in nature

upon the least reflection: "A purpose, an intention, or design strikes everywhere the most careless, the most stupid thinker; and no man can be so hardened in absurd systems, as at all times to reject it" (D, 214; NHR, 74). But only those who have acquired to some degree the inductive habit of lawlike thinking can appreciate what the order manifest in the universe means. "Barbarous and uninstructed" men and even the superstitious in civilized societies are so caught in the grip of their own hopes and fears about the unknown causes that affect their destiny that they pay little attention to what the order of the universe suggests to "any one of good understanding." But "when our comprehension is so far enlarged as to contemplate the first rise of this visible system, we must adopt, with the strongest conviction, the idea of some intelligent cause or author" (NHR, 74; D, 214-17). Belief in "a first intelligent Author" of the universe is, then, a natural belief like that of belief in external objects and unobservable causal connections. But it is unlike those beliefs in that it requires historical and cultural preparation (scientific development) for its appearance, and it does not have the brute animal stability of the other beliefs: human nature would not "immediately perish and go to ruin" if men ceased to believe in an intelligent author of the world, as it would if they ceased to believe in external objects and ceased to make causal judgments (T, 225).

But philosophical theism is more than a natural belief, it also has a special sort of rational justification. It is so firmly entrenched in the conceptual framework and methodology of the scientific community that it may be treated as a category or fundamental presupposition of scientific thinking: "*that nature does nothing in vain*, is a maxim established in all the schools, merely from the contemplation of the works of nature, without any religious purpose; and, from a firm conviction of its truth, an anatomist, who had observed a new organ or canal, would never be satisfied till he had also discovered its use and intention. One great foundation of the Copernican system is the maxim, *that nature acts by the simplest methods, and chooses the most proper means to any end;* and astronomers often, without thinking of it, lay this strong foundation of piety and religion. The same thing is observable in other parts of philosophy: And thus all the sciences almost lead us insensibly to acknowledge a first intelligent Author; and their authority is often so much the greater, as they do not directly profess that intention" (D, 214-215). Another presupposition of science is that God is a unity and that the world he created forms one consistent system: "The uniform maxims . . . which prevail throughout the whole frame of the universe, naturally, if not necessarily, lead us to conceive this intelligence as single and undivided, where the prejudices of education oppose not so reasonable a theory. Even the contrarieties of nature, by discovering themselves everywhere, become proofs of some consistent plan, and establish one single purpose or intention, however inexplicable and incomprehensible" (NHR, 74). Human nature would not perish if men ceased to believe in philosophical theism, but advanced scientific thinking might well collapse without that belief. This is a new and specifically Humean insight. Newton, Boyle, and others had argued that scientific reasoning can provide independent grounds for belief in a supreme intelligent author, but Hume is arguing the other way, that belief in a supreme intelligent author is a ground for scientific thinking. This sort of "transcendental" justification of philosophical theism is typical of Hume's method of justifying beliefs by showing they are in some way grounded in human nature. As we saw in the first chapter, Hume argues that we are going to believe in external objects as conceived by the popular system as a matter of brute psychological fact. But he also offers a logical justification: that all philosophical criticism of the popular belief in external objects presupposes it, and so is incoherent.

If philosophical theism is in some way a presupposition of science, then it has an authority greater than theists in Hume's day had supposed. So great was the authority and prestige of scientific thinking that liberal theologians were no longer content to base theism on the revelation of a sacred tradition; nothing less than a scientific argument based on experience would do. But if philosophical theism is a necessary presupposition of scientific thinking, it has a greater authority than it would have if it were a contingent conclusion of an inductive argument. Science was supposed to ground theism, but it turns out that theism grounds and guides science. However, a price must be paid for this conceptual turn of affairs. Theism must be cut free from the primeval religious tradition out of which it grew. Hume recognized that the religious tradition had unwittingly spawned a scientific community which had a rationale of its own. Early scientific thinkers such as Kepler, Descartes, Galileo, Newton, Boyle, Hartley, and Priestley saw no conflict between the revelation of sacred tradition and an empirical study of the world. Newton, Hartley, and Priestley used scientific knowledge to clarify and systematize biblical prophecies and used biblical prophecies as a guide to their actions in the providential scheme of things.[8] For these thinkers and for the vast majority of Hume's contemporaries, the religious and scientific traditions were wholly of a piece. Hume tried to show that religion originated in and had been perpetuated by a superstitious hope and fear about the unknown causes of human life. He thought that such superstition was just under the surface of the scientific facade covering the fashionable natural theologies of his time and was manifest in the widespread belief in prophecy and providential history.[9] He was concerned to show that the new scientific attitude that was being pressed into the service of revealed religion presupposed a universe "governed by steady, inviolable laws" (D, 174), but that such a universe was incompatible with a mysterious providential universe of miracles and prophecies. In "Of Miracles," Hume argues that belief in a universe governed by law is incompatible with testimony that a miracle has occurred which could found or support a system of religion. Prophecies are classed as miracles and rejected for the same reason (EU, 130). The same line of reasoning is used in the *Dialogues*, where Philo tries to show Cleanthes that his belief in a universe of law known through empirical means is incompatible with his belief, however refined, in a providential universe (it is not clear whether Cleanthes would use the providential theory of God to support claims about miracles and prophecies as, say, Priestley did). But Cleanthes must have both beliefs, since it is only through empirical methods that he claims to know the Deity. And it is here that Philo is able to argue that the evidence cannot support Cleanthes' anthropomorphic hypotheses and, in fact, provides better support for materialism.

Science developed out of religion insofar as both are attempts to explain the causes of things, and Hume's lesson is that they now operate in the world with incompatible presuppositions. But there is still a continuity between them. In fact, we may say that for Hume science is (or ought to be) religion come of age. This is why he insists on philosophical theism as a presupposition of science (the very expression "philosophical theists" suggests a dialectical union of the two) (D, 226), and why he thinks he can show that the dispute between atheists and theists is, in reality, a verbal dispute: they agree on all the issues that are rationally decidable (D, 218).

Philosophical theism is rational insofar as it is a presupposition of scientific thinking and so has whatever rational authority science has. But philosophical theism is also rational in that it is supported by the argument from design, and, as such, it is not merely a presupposition of science but a conclusion *in* science as well: "That the works of nature bear a great analogy to the productions of art is evident; and according to all the rules of good reasoning, we ought to infer . . . that their causes have a proportional analogy. But as there are also considerable differences, we have reason to suppose a proportional difference in the causes. . . . Here then the existence of a Deity is plainly ascertained by reason" (D, 216-17). Reasoning from analogy, we may conceive of "the supreme cause" as "*mind* or *intelligence*, notwithstanding the vast difference, which may reasonably be supposed between him and human minds" (D, 217). We may also "attribute a much higher degree of power and energy to the supreme cause than any we have ever observed in mankind" (ibid.). But beyond this we cannot go. We cannot, for instance, infer anything by analogy about God's moral attributes because the "benevolence and justice" revealed in the works of nature are so vastly different from ours (D, 219). But a being without moral attributes cannot properly be thought of as a person, certainly not as a person who could bear a particular providential relation to mankind. Our knowledge of the Deity, then, based on the analogy of design, is very weak; the whole resolves itself into "one simple, though somewhat ambiguous, at least undefined proposition, *that the cause or causes of order in the universe probably bear some remote analogy to human intelligence*" And this proposition must be understood with the limitation that it is not "capable of extension, variation, or more particular explication," that it can afford "no inference that affects human life, or can be the source of any action or forbearance," and that "the analogy, imperfect as it is, can be carried no farther than to the human intelligence; and cannot be transferred, with any appearance of probability, to the other qualities of the mind" (D, 227).

This is the Deity that is "plainly ascertained by reason." It is a Deity with no providential content whatsoever, and is incompatible with traditional theism whether of ancient or modern form. Accordingly, Philo suggests that the language should be changed from "God or Deity" to the more abstract "Mind or Thought" (D, 217). God as revealed in the presuppositions of science and in the argument from design is simply the ultimate cause of all order in the universe. Hume's philosophical theism, then, is an essential part of his theory of causality. We come to believe in an ultimate cause in roughly the same way that we come to believe in the existence of any cause, namely, by an interplay of human propensities and by "reasonings from analogy, experience, and observation" (EU, 30). The constant conjunction of like events triggers a propensity to believe that those events are necessarily connected, so that upon the appearance of the one the other must also occur, even though we can imagine some other or no event at all occurring. There is also a "universal propensity to believe in invisible, intelligent power," which although "not an original instinct, being at least a general attendant of human nature, may be considered as a kind of mark or stamp, which the divine workman has set upon his work" (NHR, 75). At first this propensity is put to the ends of superstition, and a system of theological powers is put forward to account for things. But after men come to recognize and appreciate the regularities of the universe (especially after the establishment of the Newtonian world view), they conceive of the invisible powers productive of phenomena not in theological terms but in terms of natural regularities unobservable in principle, such as "Elasticity, gravity, cohesion of parts, communication of motion by impulse . . ." (EU, 30).

The first modern philosophers were not entirely emancipated from the primeval theological systems in which the Deity is viewed as the direct cause of all observable phenomena: "Descartes insinuated that doctrine of the universal and sole efficacy of the Deity, without insisting on it. Malebranche and other Cartesians made it the foundation of all their philosophy." But it had no authority in England. "Locke, Clarke, and Cudworth never so much as take notice of it," and it "was never the meaning of Sir Isaac Newton to rob second causes of all force or energy, though some of his followers have endeavored to establish that theory upon his authority." On the contrary, Newton postulated "an etherial active fluid to explain his universal attraction, though he was so cautious and modest as to allow that it was a mere hypothesis not to be insisted on without more experiments" (EU, 73n).

The universal propensity to believe in invisible, intelligent power can be modified by critical reflection but hardly done away with altogether. Hume rejects the Cartesian superstition of the universal and sole efficacy of the Deity. But he does not reject the notion of intelligent causal power. First of all, Hume believes there are unobservable powers such as gravity and elasticity which are productive of observable phenomena. Reflection shows, however, that the unobservable relation between the power and the observable phenomena is merely that of constant conjunction. All such conjunctions, no matter how universal, are, for Hume, brute facts in need of being rendered "intelligible." Philosophical theism is the doctrine that reality is the work of "a first intelligent Author" and that, consequently, reality is a single intelligible system "however inexplicable and incomprehensible" its appearances may be (D, 215; NHR, 74).

Hume's conception of causality as discussed so far can be summed up as follows. The experience of the constant conjunction of an event of kind A followed by an event of kind B produces in us, owing to an original and invariable propensity of the fancy, the belief that the two events are *necessarily* connected. But there is another propensity (no less universal but not as stable and more subject to the influences of education and prejudice) to believe in a *system* of invisible, intelligent power as the cause of things. Since this propensity is culturally variable, its operation in causal thinking has a history the broad outline of which is sketched out in Hume's writings. For primitive man, the first causal powers were unobservable gods who controlled events affecting the immediate destinies of men. The knowledge of empirical regularities that primitive man had insensibly acquired, owing to the first propensity, and that he shared with the brutes, was placed in the background in favor of the specifically human fascination with intelligent causal power: "in this disordered scene, with eyes still more disordered and astonished, they see the first obscure traces of divinity" (NHR, 28). But as men developed, especially as they developed the mechanical arts and reflected upon themselves as productive agents relying upon the lawlike regularities of nature, they turned attention to these forgotten regularities and began to wonder about their causes. This led to the concept of *nature*, "to which the vulgar refer everything" (D, 178), and the idea that visible phenomena are directly produced not by intelligent powers but by powers that are nonetheless intelligible. This was the view of the ancient philosophers, and it has survived on into the modern period along with the remarkable revival in Cartesianism of the superstitious doctrine of "the sole efficacy of the Deity."

An important part of Hume's natural history of scientific thinking is to be found in the *Treatise*, I, IV, III-IV, entitled respectively "Of the Ancient Philosophy" and "Of the Modern Philosophy." In these sections, Hume explores the rationale in human nature that has led philosophers to postulate the existence of natural powers to explain visible phenomena. He follows "an excellent method," recommended by several moralists for "becoming acquainted with our own hearts," that we "recollect our dreams in a morning, and examine them with the same rigour, that we wou'd our most serious and most deliberate actions" (T, 219). In like manner, he is "persuaded, there might be several useful discoveries made from a criticism of the fictions of the ancient philosophy, concerning *substances, and substantial forms, and accidents, and occult qualities;* which, however unreasonable and capricious, have a very intimate connexion with the principles of human nature" (T, 219). In *The Natural History of Religion*, Hume regarded the religious explanations of things as "sick men's dreams" the rationale of which he, nevertheless, tried empathetically to understand. Similarly, Hume attempts to understand the metaphysical illusions, the "sympathies, antipathies, and horrors of a vacuum," put forth to explain phenomena, not by men who attempt to be pious, but by men who attempt to be rational. And this includes Hume himself and his enlightened contemporaries. As a strenuous effort at self-examination, it will be "worth while to consider the *causes*, which make us almost universally fall into such evident contradictions, as well as the *means* by which we endeavour to conceal them" (T, 219). The common error behind the occult powers of theologians and metaphysicians is the "very remarkable inclination in human nature, to bestow on external objects the same emotions, which it observes in itself; and to find every where those ideas, which are most present to it" (T, 224). If religious causal explanations resemble "sick men's dreams" and "the playsome whimsies of monkies in human shape," the metaphysical explanations of virtually all philosophers, ancient and modern, are to be compared to "spectres in the dark" and to the "punishment of Sisyphus and Tantalus" (T, 223, 226).

Hume's analysis so far resembles Comte's law of the three stages of history: the theological age, the metaphysical age, and the positivistic age. Hume, however, did not think it possible to break entirely from the metaphysical stage. That is why he is a skeptic rather than a positivist. And in this Hume appears to be right. No form of positivism, whether Comtean or logical, has succeeded in avoiding metaphysical assumptions or statements about ultimate reality. Contemporary philosophers talk as freely about ultimate metaphysical entities, possible worlds, and the like as they ever did in the seventeenth century. One may observe, though, that they are more diffident about their metaphysical opinions than previously, a state of affairs traceable directly to the influence of Hume's skepticism.[10] For Hume had argued that, notwithstanding the full recognition of our ignorance, we must make judgments about ultimate reality. Nevertheless: "A true sceptic will be diffident of his philosophical doubts, as well as of his philosophical conviction" (T, 273). Following out the analogy with Comte, Hume's third stage would be the dialectical one of post-Pyrrhonian philosophy.

Hume rejects the notion of occult powers but affirms the idea of causal power insofar as it can be given empirical content; that is, we must be able to infer empirically testable consequences from a hypothesis about the power. As long as these conditions are met, Hume is prepared to countenance and even to encourage the boldest hypotheses, "however new or unusual," concerning causal power. The repeated insistence that we have no idea or image of power is not intended to show that talk about power is unintelligible. On the contrary, it is an attempt to show what the empirical content of such talk amounts to. We cannot have experience of the internal structure of gravitational forces, but we can experience the events that could confirm or falsify a hypothesis about gravitational forces. To insist that we have no experience of gravity is to keep the concept free of anthropomorphic elements and to set up a barrier against the entry of occult interpretations. If we thought we could experience gravity, it would be easy to read the emotions attending that experience into the power and so have the emotionally satisfying conception of power that, Hume thinks, so often satisfies the metaphysician's illusory search for "intelligible" relations between events.

So we can claim there are gravitational forces "without comprehending that active power" (EU, 73n). Likewise, without having a clear notion of the nature of the divine power, we can know that the Deity, as the ultimate cause, exists: "The same imperfection attends our ideas of the Deity. . . . The order of the universe proves an omnipotent mind; that is, a mind whose will is *constantly attended* with the obedience of every creature and being. Nothing more is requisite to give a foundation to all the articles of religion, nor is it necessary we shou'd form a distinct idea of the force and energy of the supreme Being" (T, 633n). But there are two important differences between the "religious hypothesis" of a supreme, intelligent cause of order and an ordinary scientific hypothesis about physical powers. We cannot draw any inference from the nature of the supreme cause to a conclusion about any particular phenomena, as we can and must be able to do with a hypothesis like that of gravity. The knowledge we have of the supreme cause is simply that reality is ultimately a system of "inviolable laws." This is why Hume stresses that God's will is "constantly attended" with the obedience of every creature. The only effect the religious hypothesis has on the world is in the mind of the scientist, where it produces an absolute conviction that the search for laws is not in vain and will not be frustrated by the occurrence of miraculous interventions. A second difference is that we have, in a way, a better understanding of the nature of the ultimate cause than we do of ordinary causal powers like gravity. We have no internal understanding of gravity at all, but we do have some internal understanding of ultimate causal power insofar as it is supposed to bear a remote resemblance to the human intelligence with which we are familiar. Although our knowledge of the supreme cause is not as concrete as our knowledge of gravity, it is rationally and emotionally more satisfying because of the analogy that can be drawn between ourselves as causal agents and the supreme cause. But here there is a danger of vulgar anthropomorphism and idolatry; men may read some favored image of human intelligence into the nature of the Deity and vainly imagine themselves to know more than they do.

To this inevitable temptation, Hume sets up two barriers. First, he stresses the weakness of the analogy. This is done through Philo's imaginary cross-examination of a theist and an atheist. The theist must admit that "there is a great and immeasurable, because incomprehensible difference between the *human* and the *divine* mind," and "the more pious he is . . . the more will he be disposed to magnify the difference." The atheist, on the other hand, must admit "from the coherence and apparent sympathy in all the parts of this world" that there is an analogy between "all the operations of nature, in every situation and in every age"; he is asked whether "the rotting of a turnip, the generation of an animal, and the structure of human thought be not *energies* that probably bear some remote analogy to each other" (D, 218 emphasis mine). The atheist also agrees that "the principle which first arranged, and still maintains, order in this universe, bears . . . also some remote inconceivable analogy to the other operations of nature, and among the rest to the oeconomy of human mind and thought" (ibid.). The conceptual lesson is that the theist and atheist are dialectically related, the one stressing the difference between the original intelligence and human reason, and the other admitting a remote analogy between the two. Moreover, the theist will, typically, tend to magnify the difference while the atheist, especially one of a scientific turn of mind, will tend to magnify "the analogy among all the operations of nature" and view the whole as a unity resembling the structure of human reason. In this way, the theist and atheist "insensibly change sides," and any vulgar anthropomorphic interpretation of the Deity must appear absurd (ibid.).

The second barrier that Hume sets up against idolatry and anthropomorphism is that the analogy between the operations of human reason, other natural processes, and the supreme cause is *unimaginable*. The theist and atheist admit that these analogies are "incomprehensible" and "inconceivable." This is Hume's usual language (confusing to his readers and, perhaps, to himself) for saying that we have no direct experience of and can form no image of the causal power by which human reason or any other process operates. It must be kept in mind that the analogy employed in the argument from design is one that holds between unobservable productive powers (ibid.). But to know that we can have no image of causal power discourages the anthropomorphic tendency of the vulgar and philosophers alike to read emotionally satisfying images into the causal structure of things. Hume was as strict as any rationalist or idealist in insisting that the theoretical concepts of science having to do with productive processes can be given no imaginary representation at all. He differs only in his account of the origin of such concepts. The strategy for purging natural theology of idolatry is the same as that for purging the concepts of theoretical science of imaginary representations.

The analogy on which the design argument rests is very weak and stated in such a way as to discourage any robust anthropomorphic interpretation, whether vulgar or philosophical, of the supreme cause. The operation of the supreme cause is like the operation of human reason but only in the way that the latter is like the operation manifest in "the rotting of a turnip" and "the generation of an animal." This comparison weakens the analogy, but it does not upset the analogical heirarchy. Human reason is still the paradigm of order, not the rotting of a turnip, though the analogy between the two must humble the vain pretensions of the age of reason. In the end, Hume does not (and could not) absolutely reject an anthropomorphic interpretation of the supreme cause. Both the theist and the atheist are forced to view the world, however vaguely, as the operation of an ultimate principle analogous to "Mind or Thought," that is, as a unified system of "inviolable law." This conviction is due mainly to that "universal propensity to believe in invisible, intelligent power" as the cause of phenomena. This principle though "a general attendant of human nature" is capable of modification by "the prejudices of education" (NHR, 74-75). Hume's theory of causality, in its widest context, is an attempt to bring systematic and critical order to the religious *and* scientific beliefs spawned by this principle of human nature.

# 7
# Causal Explanation in the Moral Sciences

A Proof that natural Philosophy has no Truth in it, is, that
it has only succeeded in things remote, as the heavenly
Bodys, or minute as Light.
Hume's "Early Memoranda," 1729–1740.

## THE COVERING-LAW MODEL

We have now to examine Hume's views on the structure of causal explanation in the moral sciences. Here, as in the last chapter, it will be helpful to introduce Hume's actual views by contrasting them with the positivist interpretation. Indeed, nowhere in Hume's work does that interpretation seem more appropriate than here. It is easy to read Hume as a precursor of the famous covering-law model of explanation defended by Hempel and others in the positivist tradition. But, as we shall see, there are passages that frame a form of causal explanation contrary to that of the covering-law model. For reasons that will appear later, we may call these "moral causal explanations." I wish now to explore in some detail the structure of moral causal explanations and the deep logical place they occupy in Hume's general account of causal explanation.

The covering-law model of explanation is structured around three theses, all of which have roots in Hume's thinking. The first is *the unity of science thesis:* that all the empirical sciences, whether natural or moral, have the same methodology and the same form of explanation. Hume certainly appears to accept the unity of science thesis. He considered it a strong systematic point in favor of his own analysis of causality that it unified the conception of causal explanation in the moral and natural sciences: "there is but one kind of *necessity*, as there is but one kind of cause, and that the common distinction betwixt *moral* and *physical* necessity is without any foundation in nature. . . . 'Tis the constant con-

187

junction of objects, along with the determination of the mind, which constitutes a physical [and a moral] necessity" (T, 171). The same view is expressed in the *Enquiry:* "when we consider how aptly *natural* and *moral* evidence link together and form only one chain of argument, we shall make no scruple to allow that they are of the same nature and derived from the same principles. . . . The same experienced union has the same effect on the mind, whether the united objects be motives, volitions, and actions, or figure and motion. We may change the name of things, but their nature and their operation on the understanding never change" (EU, 90–91).

Another point at which Hume's theory of causal explanation seems isomorphic with the covering-law theory is *the symmetry thesis* of explanation and prediction: the thesis that what serves to explain an event could have served, if presented earlier, to have predicted it. If we know that John died because he consumed a certain amount of arsenic, then we could have predicted prior to the event that consuming that amount would lead to death. And our prediction would have been as certain then as our explanation of why he died is now. Explanation and prediction have, logically, the same form, the only difference being the temporal one of whether the justifying statements are presented before or after the event has occurred.

Underlying the symmetry thesis of explanation and prediction is what might be called *the existence thesis:* the view that any adequate causal explanation must provide good reasons to believe that the event to be explained occurred rather than did not occur. Hempel writes: "It seems to me beyond dispute that in any adequate explanation of an empirical phenomenon the explanans must provide good grounds for believing or asserting that the explanandum phenomena did in fact occur."[1]

Although Hume does not explicitly state either of these theses, he is clearly committed to them from what he does say about the structure of causal arguments. Causal arguments are inductive arguments and so must provide good reasons to believe the event to be explained occurred rather than not: "The first question that occurs on this subject is always, *whether* the object shall exist or not: The next, *when* and *where* it shall begin to exist" (T, 80). Likewise, Hume is committed to the symmetry thesis of explanation and prediction. A priori, all events appear loose and disconnected; anything could cause anything. Were it not for memories and written records, our knowledge of the past would be as abstract and uncertain as our knowledge of the future is now.

Covering-law theorists have distinguished two types of scientific explanation based on the nature of laws and of their relation to the event to be explained. Deductive nomological explanations are those with strictly universal laws which assert that in all cases in which certain specified conditions are realized an occurrence of such and such a kind results. Along with a statement of initial conditions, the laws are deductively connected to a description of the event to be explained. Inductive-statistical explanations contain laws of statistical form which, along with a statement of initial conditions, are connected to the event to be explained, not deductively, but with a high degree of inductive probability. These two forms of causal explanation are roughly parallel to Hume's distinction between causal arguments which amount to "a full *proof* of the future existence of . . . [the] event" and those which amount to a "probability" (EU, 110; cf. T, 124).

The regularities that go into Humean causal explanations are *lawlike*. We may leave aside the question of whether Hume has an adequate account of lawlikeness, for the covering-law theory does not depend on any solution to the vexing problem of lawlikeness.[2] All that is required is that covering laws have empirical content which, of course, Hume allows. One agreed-upon criterion for a law is that it be capable of supporting subjunctive conditional statements; that is, genuine laws must be capable of supporting claims about what would happen under certain circumstances whether or not those circumstances are in fact ever realized. Laws must be capable of determining what is factually possible, impossible, and necessary. That Hume thinks of laws as having this characteristic is evident from the essay on miracles where he argues that laws must be capable of ruling out as impossible in fact purported counterexamples (miracles) even when supported by strong independent testimony.

There is considerable evidence, then, for the interpretation that Hume's views on causal explanation are an early statement of the covering-law theory. But there are a number of other passages which imply a quite different conception of explanation, one which is incompatible at every major point with the covering-law model.

## MORAL CAUSAL EXPLANATIONS

In "Of Some Remarkable Customs," Hume goes out of his way to argue that moral philosophers have a privileged way of explaining human actions which is not available to natural philosophers.[3] He examines three counterexamples to what are considered well-established empirical generalizations about political behavior. The explicit purpose of the essay is to establish two theses: (1) "[that empirical laws] in politics ought to be established with great caution; and that irregular and extraordinary appearances are frequently discovered in the moral as well as in the physical world" and (2) that "we can better account

for . . . [human actions] after they happen, from springs and principles, of which every one has, within himself, or from observation, the
strongest assurance and conviction: but it is often fully as impossible for
human prudence, beforehand, to foresee and foretell them" (E, 372).

The sort of explanation Hume has in mind is incompatible with the
three central theses of the covering-law model. It violates the unity of
science thesis because it allows that moral philosophers have a special
form of causal explanation not available to natural philosophy and one
which, purportedly, can account for "extraordinary and irregular" occurrences inconsistent with existing regularities and not covered by any
new regularities. It violates the symmetry thesis of explanation and
prediction because explanations of past actions can be given which
could not have been used beforehand to have predicted those actions.
And it violates the existence thesis because, not employing empirical
laws and not having predictive power, it cannot satisfy Hume's require-
ments for an existential argument, and thus cannot provide good
grounds to believe the event to be explained occurred rather than did
not occur.

Let us now examine the moral causal explanation Hume gives for the
first of the three extraordinary practices. The explanation is introduced
against the background of three "indisputable" axioms of political science: (1) that it is "essential to every supreme council or assembly
which debates, that entire liberty of speech should be granted to every
member, and that all motions or reasonings should be received, which
can any way tend to illustrate the point under deliberation" (ibid.). (2)
"after a motion was made, which was voted and approved by that assembly in which the legislative power is lodged, the member who made
the motion must for ever be exempted from future trial or enquiry"
(ibid.). (3) But should a trial result for such a member, "he must, at
least, be secured from all inferior jurisdiction; and that nothing less
than the same supreme legislative assembly, in their subsequent meet-
ings, could make him accountable for those motions and harangues, to
which they had before given their approbation" (ibid., 372–73). Although these principles appear "irrefragable," Hume, nevertheless,
finds a counterexample in the ancient Athenian "law of indictment of
illegality." This law states that "any man was tried and punished in a
common court of judicature, for any law which had passed upon his
motion, in the assembly of the people, if that law appeared to the court
unjust, or prejudicial to the public" (E, 373).

Hume's task is to show how the "irregular" behavior of the Athenians can be explained even though it is not covered by the available
regularities of political science. The explanation runs as follows: (1)
"The Athenian Democracy was . . . a tumultuous government. . . .

The whole collective body of the people voted in every law, without any limitation of property, without any distinction of rank, without control from any magistracy or senate; and consequently without regard to order, justice, or prudence" (E, 374). (2) "The Athenians soon became sensible of the mischiefs attending this constitution: but being averse to checking themselves by any rule or restriction, they resolved, at least to check their demagogues or counsellors, by the fear of future punishment and inquiry. . . . they justly considered themselves as in a state of perpetual pupilage, where they had an authority, after they came to the use of reason, not only to retract and control whatever had been determined, but to punish any guardian for measures which they had embraced by his persuasion" (ibid., 374–75). (3) The Athenians considered the law of indictment of illegality "essential to their form of government," so that "Aeschines insisted on it as a known truth, that were it abolished or neglected, it were impossible for the Democracy to subsist" (ibid., 374). (4) The Athenians "accordingly instituted this remarkable law" (ibid.).

In order to count as a Humean covering-law explanation (1)–(4) would have to frame either an empirical proof or an empirical probability (EU, 110; T, 124). If the former, (1)–(3) would have to be connected to (4) by a statement of universal form, specifying what always happens under certain circumstances, what Hume calls "inviolable laws" based on a "firm and unalterable experience" (D, 174; EU, 114). If the latter, the connection must be made by a statistical statement of what usually happens under certain circumstances. But none of the statements in (1)–(3) is an empirical law; nor is that set connected to (4) by an empirical law, whether universal or statistical. All are particular statements about the circumstances and thoughts of the Athenians. (1) is a statement about the situation the Athenians were in. (2) and (3) are statements about how they conceived that situation and what they were resolved to do about it. Hume would have us see that (1)–(3) provided the Athenians with a good reason for instituting the law and that this explains why the law was established. "The same law had place in Thebes, and for the same reason" (E, 375).

We may call these "moral causal explanations" because they explain an act not by covering it with an empirical law but with what Hume calls a "moral cause," the reasons the agent had for acting. But how can covering an act with a reason explain it? Explanation, in general, is designed to rescue an event to be explained from being unintelligible. To understand the sense in which a model of explanation explains we must identify the principle of intelligibility which it frames *and* the principle of unintelligibility or absurdity which it rebuts. In his moral explanation of the Athenian law, Hume has explained what appears, from our point of view, to be an irrational law by showing that, relative to their intentions and their conception of their situation, the Athenians had a good reason to enact the law and no good reason to do otherwise. For moral explanation, then, the principle of *intelligibility* is that an act is intelligible just in case it can be covered by a good reason the agent had for acting. The principle of absurdity, to be rebutted in particular cases, is that acts are not covered by good reasons. Since moral accounts explain not by covering the act with an empirical law but by a good reason the agent had for acting, they do not, as Hume saw, have predictive force. We may think of them, therefore, as specifically historical explanations. And, indeed, as we shall see in the next chapter, moral explanations constitute the most important pattern of explanation in Hume's historical work.

But if moral explanations lack predictive force, are they merely ad hoc explanations and thus vacuous? They need not be. Consider a world in which, whenever an agent has good reasons for doing some act x and only x, he does non-x; and whenever an agent does x, he had good reasons for doing non-x and only non-x. In such a world, covering-law explanations could be given, but moral explanations would be impossible because the actions in this world would be absurd. Moral explanations, therefore, are not vacuous because they cannot always be given. The point of giving a moral account is to show that what appears "irregular" and "irrational" (because it is inconsistent with established generalizations about human action) is, indeed, irregular but not irrational. This is done not by covering the act with a new empirical regularity but by discovering the point or rationale behind the act. Moral explanations enable us to see how an action which would otherwise appear unintelligible is rationally satisfying. The existence of moral explanations in history is a certification that history is not wholly absurd or morally unintelligible. Nor is this a trivial matter, for there is no a-priori reason why history should be intelligible in this way.

Moral accounts, then, frame a different sort of intelligibility from that available in official Humean covering-law explanations. And it is for this reason that they can be given, even though covering-law explanations are not available (as Hume stresses in "Of Some Remarkable Customs"); this is also why they may be required even *after* a covering-law explanation has been given. For instance, throughout his writings, Hume describes the practices of popular religion as absurd and unintelligible. In section xi of the *The Natural History of Religion*, entitled "With regard to reason or absurdity," Hume argues that the religious man does not have good reason to follow the absurd practices of popular religion since, from the point of view of the religious man himself, those practices are often contradictory and incoherent. Moreover, the more systematic and rational a religion becomes (such as Christianity) the more absurd are its practices (NHR, 53, 75). In the same work Hume claims to have given a covering-law causal explanation of the origins of religious beliefs and practices as well as of important changes that have occurred in the history of religion. Still, at the end of the essay, he could lament that he had really failed to explain those beliefs and practices: "The whole is a riddle, and aenigma, an inexplicable mystery" (ibid., 76). These are indeed strange and paradoxical words for a social scientist whose task is to give a causal explanation in terms of empirical regularities. If Hume has given a causal explanation, as he claims to have done, why should an "inexplicable mystery" remain? The suggestion is that a moral account of popular religious practices (of the sort Hume gave of the seeming irrational behavior of Athenian politics) is needed but is not available. It is for this reason that Hume is forced to describe the practices of popular religion pathologically as "the playthings of monkeys or sick men's dreams" (ibid., 75).

## MORAL AND ULTIMATE CAUSAL EXPLANATION

I have argued that Hume believes there are ultimate causal connections which, if we could grasp them, would render intelligible the brute regularities of natural philosophy. These regularities are brute because, no matter how general they are, they all have a constant conjunction form; their denials are conceivable, and so there is no rationally satisfying way to explain why they must be as they are. Hume describes the project of providing such an explanation as the problem of discovering the "causes of these general causes," that is, the reason why the conjunction is as it is. Hume, of course, does not think we will ever discover such reasons: "But as to the causes of these general causes, we should in vain attempt their discovery. . . . Elasticity, gravity, cohesion of parts, communication of motion by impulse; these are probably the ultimate causes and principles which we shall ever discover in nature" (EU, 30). We do believe, however, that there are principles that could render the regularities of natural philosophy "intelligible," and this belief, as we saw in the last chapter, is a guiding presupposition of science. Hume makes that presupposition clear in a passage of the *Treatise* that deserves special comment. After the usual skeptical remarks about discovering the intelligible cause of such regularities as the "cohesion of parts," Hume says: "We must certainly allow, that the cohesion of the parts of matter arises from natural and necessary principles, whatever difficulty we may find in explaining them: And for a like reason we must allow, that human society is founded on like principles; and our reason in the latter case, is better than even that in the former;

because we not only observe, that men *always* seek society, but can also explain the principles, on which this universal propensity is founded" (T, 401–2, Hume's emphasis).

Here Hume has distinguished two sorts of regularities: those in natural philosophy, such as "Bodies always attract as the inverse square of the distance," and those in moral philosophy, such as "men always seek society." Both are thought of as lawlike and both may be used in covering-law explanations. Both, however, have a constant-conjunction form and so need to be rendered intelligible by "natural and necessary principles" (that is, ultimate principles) which, Hume says, we absolutely believe to exist, however difficult it may be to explain them. But what is especially important about the passage is Hume's claim that explanations in moral philosophy provide us with a better reason to believe in ultimate causal principles than do explanations in natural philosophy.

In this way Hume is again abandoning the unity of science thesis, holding that in some way explanations in moral philosophy are superior to those in natural philosophy. He does not, of course, mean that explanations in moral philosophy are superior to those in natural philosophy in being more general, or systematic, or in having greater predictive power, for he regularly maintains the contrary. The superiority of moral philosophy consists rather in the fact that moral philosophers can render their empirical regularities "intelligible" by giving moral accounts of them, whereas natural philosophers cannot. Hume does not mention the explanation he has in mind, perhaps because he thought it too obvious to mention; but from what he has said elsewhere about society, it is fairly clear what the explanation must be. The regularity that "men always seek society" is explained by the fact that, given the necessitous condition of men, both psychological and physical, they have a good reason to form society and no good reason to do otherwise. "Men always seek society" is understandable in a way that "Bodies attract as the inverse square of the distance" is not. The denial of neither would lead to a logical absurdity. The denial of either would lead to an empirical absurdity in that our expectations would be radically upset. But only a denial of the first would lead to a moral or rational absurdity. Logically, there could be a world in which men had a good reason to form society and no good reason to do otherwise, but, in fact, did otherwise. Such a world could have regularities and so could be empirically intelligible (D, 182). Covering-law explanation and predictions could be given. Such a world, however, would be morally unintelligible. But as things are, this is not the case. The existence of society is both empirically and morally understandable.

Another important point in the passage quoted above is the analogy that is made between moral accounts and ultimate causal explanations.

Hume takes the fact that we can sometimes render the empirical regularities of moral philosophy intelligible by giving moral accounts as providing some content to the idea of ultimate causal explanation. Indeed, the existence of moral explanations is said to provide us with a reason to believe in ultimate causal principles that is better than the reason provided by covering-law explanations in natural philosophy. Hume is not saying, of course, that moral explanations are ultimate explanations; he is saying only that they resemble them, and may serve to give some analogical content to the idea of ultimate causal explanation. Moral philosophers can succeed in doing something similar to what natural philosophers have wanted to do but have not been able to do. The natural philosopher wants "*insight* into the internal structure or operating principle of objects" (T, 169, emphasis mine). But all he finds is a constant conjunction, and "We cannot penetrate into the *reason* of the conjunction" (T, 93, emphasis mine). But this is just what we can do in moral philosophy. We understand the reason for the universal conjunction of man and society. We understand the rationale behind the irregular action of the Athenians. And we can have such insight because of "springs and principles, of which everyone has, *within himself*, or from observation, the strongest assurance and conviction" (E, 372, emphasis mine). The same point is made in the *Treatise*. In understanding moral phenomena, we are "guided by common experience, as well as by a king of *presentation*; which tells what will operate on others, by what we feel immediately in ourselves" (T, 332 Hume's emphasis). Hume does not explain here or elsewhere in the *Treatise* what he means by this inner "presentation," but it is reasonable to assume that he had in mind the "springs and principles . . . within," explicated in "Of Some Remarkable Customs," as the good reasons the agent had for acting as he did and which the moral philosopher must be able to reconstruct in his own mind. This essay was published in 1752, some thirteen years after the publication of the *Treatise*, but the thesis of the essay is evident in what remains of Hume's early memoranda and was probably worked out during the period in which he was writing the *Treatise*.

Hume's remarks on moral explanation should be viewed as an integral part of his famous problem of explicating our idea of necessary connection and of ultimate explanation. In the last chapter, we saw that, for Hume, God is the ultimate cause of things and that the idea of necessary connection cannot be understood without reference to the idea of God. But we understand very little about God. We do understand, however, that God, as first cause, is "*mind* or *intelligence*" (D, 217). This view is corroborated by Hume's remark in the *Treatise* that moral explanations resemble and throw light on the idea of ultimate explanation. Moral accounts render actions and regularities intelligible by exhibiting their point or rationale, that is, by showing that they are the result of the activity of mind.

We have discovered three patterns of explanation in Hume's writings: (1) covering-law accounts which frame a univocal form of intelligibility for both moral and natural philosophy (constant conjunction along with a tendency to infer the existence of the one from that of the other); (2) moral explanations which frame a form of intelligibility unique to moral philosophy and incompatible with the covering-law model; more specifically, moral accounts violate the unity of science thesis, the existence thesis, and the symmetry thesis of explanation and prediction; and, finally, (3) ultimate explanation which bears a remote affinity to moral explanation and the understanding of which is locked into the mysteries of "philosophical theism." These three patterns are merely sketched out by Hume and are not systematically developed. Even the covering-law model about which Hume has most to say is not adequately developed. As we have observed, he has virtually nothing to say about the status of theoretical entities which are referred to in the covering-law explanations of theoretical science. Hume does not explore the obvious conflicts that seem to hold between these three patterns of explanation, nor does he try to order them into a coherent theory. Indeed, he does not seem to be aware that the three forms of explanation are not coherently related. Moral accounts, for instance, are presented not so much as a special form of explanation but as a certain feature of moral philosophy which gives it an explanatory advantage over natural philosophy. Hume, however, does not recognize that, if moral philosophy has these advantages, its explanations no longer need have the covering-law form, and so the covering-law conception of causal explanation will have to be either abandoned or reformed.

One reason why Hume was not as sensitive to the conflict as we would like for him to have been is that the question of whether the form of explanation is the same for the moral and natural sciences had not really been asked in Hume's time. That question, as we understand it, belongs to the context of nineteenth-century German idealism with its distinction between the sciences of nature and the sciences of spirit and the claim that the latter require a special methodology owing to the special form of understanding or *verstehen* which they yield. This question has, in one shape or other, dominated discussion in the philosophy of history and the social sciences during the last three decades. The disputants have fallen into two camps: those such as Hempel, White, and Danto who support some version of the covering-law model and those such as Collingwood, Donagan, and Dray who support some version of what might be called the covering-reason model. The issues involved are far-reaching, touching not only philosophy of science and history but also the theory of human action, our metaphysical image of what man is, ethics, and even theology. With some such consideration in mind, Donagan has said: "Whether human action may be fruitfully studied by one or more of the natural sciences, or only by sciences of a different kind, is perhaps the most important question in the intellectual life of our time. A wrong answer could be disastrous."[4] This comment indicates something of the passion and high purpose that has informed the debate.

Hume was the first to broach the question, in the form we have it today, of the status of causal explanation in the natural and moral sciences, and what appears to be his "official" answer is on the side of the covering-law theorists. But the claims he makes for moral philosophy entail a quite different model of explanation, one which has obvious affinities with the covering-reason model. So Hume not only first broached the question, his answer revealed a conflict in his own mind between two models of explanation, a conflict remarkably parallel to the contemporary debate between covering-law and covering-reason theorists.

Another reason why Hume failed to appreciate the conflict in his account of explanation is that he was trying to introduce the experimental method of reasoning into the moral sciences and to show that moral subjects admit of scientific treatment. Throughout his writings Hume is anxious to present moral philosophy in a favorable light: to show that this or that difficulty occurs in natural philosophy, or that moral philosophy is equal to natural philosophy in this or that respect, or that it is even superior in certain respects. Thus Hume can triumphantly point out in "Of Some Remarkable Customs" that moral philosophers can give nonpredictive explanations of events that are contrary to established regularities and, in the *Treatise*, that moral philosophers can explain established regularities in a way that invites comparison with ultimate causal explanations, whereas natural philosophers cannot. In his eagerness to score points on behalf of moral philosophy, Hume was not always aware of the difficulties he was creating for his version of the covering-law model of explanation.

Concentration on Hume as the would-be Newton of the mind makes it easy to overlook those passages where he insists on the superior intelligibility of moral philosophy. Early in his career, during the time he was writing the *Treatise*, Hume wrote himself this note: "A Proof that natural Philosophy has no Truth in it, is, that it has only succeeded in things remote, as the heavenly Bodys, or minute as Light" (HEM, 499). This dark saying is made on behalf of moral philosophy at the expense of natural philosophy. The former can succeed in having an internal grasp of the world of common life, a world that is not "remote," and so is capable of truth. It is a favorite theme of Hume's that the moral world, being the result of human feeling and opinion, can be understood by men without the need to posit the existence of exotic theoretical entities such as light waves and gravitational forces. In determining structures of the moral world such as justice, the nature of promise-keeping, the nature of political allegiance, and the like, Hume often opposes "the sentiments of the rabble to any philosophical reasoning. For it must be observ'd, that the opinions of men, in this case [the nature of political, allegiance] carry with them a peculiar authority, and are, in a great measure, infallible" (T, 546). And elsewhere: "The general opinion of mankind has some authority in all cases; but in this of morals 'tis perfectly infallible" (T, 552). And Hume adds significantly: "Nor is it less infallible, because men cannot distinctly explain the principles, on which it is founded" (ibid.).

The sort of knowledge Hume is talking about here is independent of theoretical thinking. Traditionally, opinion was contrasted with knowledge and appearance with reality. Hume, however, is pointing out a way in which opinion in the moral world constitutes a kind of knowledge. The Italian language is really whatever the Italians believe it is. The legitimate government is whatever government people think is legitimate, because all authority in the moral world is founded on opinion. For entities of this sort there is no room for the traditional philosophical distinction between appearance and reality. But though the Italian language is necessarily what the Italians think it is, matter is not necessarily what the vulgar think it is or even what philosophers think it is. The natural world is an *alien* world, we have no internal grasp of it as we do of the world of common life, and therefore it requires the postulation of theoretical entities for its comprehension.

Only God who created the world could have an internal grasp of it, which is why Hume has made knowledge of God's acts a necessary condition for understanding what a causal connection really is. But the moral world is constituted by the deeds of men, and so can be understood by men. From this point of view, the moral world is supremely intelligible: "our internal perceptions, and the nature of the mind . . . . tho' involv'd in infinite obscurities, is not perplex'd with any such contradictions, as those we have discover'd in the natural" (T, 232). There is much greater agreement in moral philosophy than there is about the objects of theoretical inquiry: "Theories of abstract philosophy [including natural philosophy] have prevailed during one age: in a successive period these have been universally exploded . . . other theories and systems have supplied their place. . . . The case is not the same with the beauties of eloquence and poetry" (E, 248). He contrasts the "studies of logic and metaphysics [including natural philosophy]" with "the practical and more intelligible sciences of politics and morals" (EM, 214). Because the moral world is more intelligible, Hume considers it more important than natural philosophy: "All these [religion and politics, metaphysics and morals] form the most considerable branches of science. Mathematics and natural philosophy, which only remain, are not half so valuable" (E, 127). This position is corroborated by Hume's remark in the *Treatise* that mathematics and natural philosophy depend for their existence on moral philosophy "since they lie under the cognizance of men, and are judged of by their powers and faculties" (T, xv). Hume is here recasting Descartes' insight from "The Second Meditation" that the mind is better known than the material world because any knowledge of the physical world must be organized by thought structures which are cognitively certified by higher-order thought structures. The difference is that, for Hume, the mind is public and historical; for Descartes, it is logically private and timeless.

Hume thought that philosophy requires greater intellectual capacity and genius than any other human activity, and he places natural philosophers at the top: "So rare is this character, that perhaps there has not as yet been above two in the world who can lay a just claim to it. At least, Galileo and Newton seem to me so far to excel all the rest, that I cannot admit any other into the same class with them" (E, 584). Great poets may challenge the second place and great historians the third (ibid.). Hume perhaps chooses natural philosophers because for their study of an alien world a greater theoretical capacity is required than for the world of common life with its internal certainties that even the "rabble" can grasp and nonpredictive explanations from "springs and principles, of which everyone has, within himself . . . the strongest assurance and conviction . . ." (E, 372).

Hume came to see, however, in the *Appendix* that the sense in which moral philosophy is more intelligible than natural philosophy could not preclude conceptual confusion brought on by the alienating distance that autonomous philosophy brings to *any* object of reflection. Thus although moral philosophers may be in possession of many truths, they appear to be no better off when they attempt a philosophical theory of these truths: "I had entertain'd some hopes, that however deficient our theory of the intellectual world might be, it wou'd be free from those contradictions, and absurdities, which seem to attend every explication, that human reason can give of the material world" (T, 633). Hume goes on to say that his theory of personal identity is neither "correct" nor "consistent." And so the *Treatise* ends dialectically with Hume throwing into question what he had said about the superior intelligibility of moral philosophy (in T, 232, quoted above), leaving the whole as a problem for the reader.

Hume's views on the relation between causal explanation in moral and in natural philosophy are not systematically organized. They have more the status of isolated insights, the implications of which Hume does not pursue. To adequately appreciate Hume's thought on causality, we must examine more closely the tensions that exist between the three patterns of explanation we have uncovered and the conflicting presuppositions that make them possible.

## THAT IMPIOUS MAXIM OF THE ANCIENTS

Every explanation is an answer to some question, and we cannot understand how one form of explanation differs from another until we have grasped the question to which it is an answer and the presuppositions which make the question possible. Causal explanations are answers to the question "Did E occur?" But exactly what perplexity does this question purport to eliminate? Let us begin with Hume's version of the covering-law model. All Humean causal explanations yield conclusions about matters of fact and existence and so satisfy the existence thesis. Humean causal arguments, then, are inductive arguments which provide by virtue of their form an answer to the question "Whether or not E occurred?" Causal explanations are prompted by existential perplexities.

But why should we write an answer to the question "Did E occur?" into the very from of causal explanation? Why should the existence of E be a problem? The answer, as Hume suggests, cuts deeply into the principles of ontology and intelligibility presupposed in modern philosophy: "That impious maxim of the ancient philosophy, *Ex nihilo, nihil fit*, by which the creation of matter was excluded, ceases to be a maxim, according to this philosophy. Not only the will of the Supreme Being may create matter, but, for aught we know *a priori*, the will of any other being might create it, or any other cause that the most whimsical imagination can assign" (EU, 164n). The ontological principle of the ancients is impious because it denies that the Christian doctrine of creation is intelligible. But in Hume's view, the modern conception of what it means to render existence intelligible is locked into this deep theological belief. For modern philosophers, it is intelligible to say that the world could have come from nothing. If so, then not the nature but the very existence of the world becomes the first problem of philosophy.

Descartes' methodological dictum that, since all his former opinions could be false, he should treat them as being in fact false is supporting evidence for Hume's thesis about the moderns, for if it is intelligible to say that any belief which one has had could be false, it is intelligible to ask whether anything at all exists or could exist in light of the fact that we have had those beliefs. But it is Leibniz who first clearly writes the principle of the moderns into the problem of explanation. For Leibniz, the task of scientific explanation is to explain why "something exists rather than nothing."[5] And this means that one must veiw the actual world as a member of a set of possible worlds, and then show that it is logically necessary for this world to exist rather than not exist. Given this conception of the rationale of explanation, one must, in Cartesian fashion, throw into question the actual existence of the world, and then show that it exists because its nonexistence is logically impossible.

The Leibnizian and the Humean scientists find it logically strange that anything exists at all. For both, as for St. Augustine, the world cries out its contingency, and the problem of explanation is why "something exists rather than nothing." Any adequate explanation, then, must satisfy the existence thesis. The two differ only on the epistemological status of the grounds which support existence-claims. Leibniz requires an ontological argument, the denial of which yields a contradiction. Hume requires only an inductive argument, the denial of which entails no contradiction but which runs counter to our most established and reliable expectations. But a problem arises. It does not seem that the question "Why did E occur?" is exhausted by the question "Did E occur?" These appear to be different questions. Providing good grounds to believe that E occurred may be a necessary condition for answering the question of why E occurred, but it is not sufficient. The testimony of reliable eyewitnesses may provide excellent inductive grounds for believing that E occurred, but such an argument cannot be used to explain why E occurred. Other conditions must be satisfied if existential arguments are to be transformed into explanatory arguments.

To see what these conditions might be, let us consider the Leibnizian model of explanation: to explain the occurrence of E is to show that its nonexistence is contradictory. In this way, the question about the existence of E is answered absolutely in that no *logically* stronger answer is possible. Humean causal explanations are, of course, inductive arguments, and the denials of their conclusions are conceivable. Hence, a logical doubt can always arise about the existence of E. Because Leibnizian explanations remove this logical doubt, they provide the best answer to the question about the occurrence of E. But if we now have the most powerful answer to the existential question, we can say that no further explanatory problems arise by asking, in addition, "Why does E exist rather than not?" So the Leibnizian model of explanation, by answering in the best possible way the question "Did E occur?" has also answered the question "Why did E occur?" In this way, the existential and explanatory questions can be seen to be the same.

Hume, of course, rejects the Leibnizian model of explanation; in particular, he rejects the possibility of an ontological argument: "Whatever we conceive as existent, we can also conceive as non-existent. There is no Being, therefore, whose non-existence implies a contradiction" (D, 189). But both accept the existence thesis as a condition for an adequate causal explanation. Moreover, Hume could follow something like the Leibnizian strategy for converting the existential question into an explanatory question by defining the latter as that which provides the *best answer* to the former. For Leibniz, the best answer to an existence question would be an ontological argument. For Hume, it would have to be some sort of inductive argument. He holds, for instance, that empirical "proofs" are better inductive arguments than empirical "probabilities." "One wou'd appear ridiculous, who wou'd say, that 'tis only probable the sun will rise to-morrow, or that all men must dye; tho' 'tis plain we have no further assurance of these facts, than what experience affords us" (T, 124). Since inductive arguments admit of degrees of acceptability, Hume could explicate the question "Why did E occur?" as a request for the *best* inductive argument. An answer to this question based on historical testimony could not be explanatory, whereas an answer based on laws of nature could be, because it is a better answer to the existence question. The standard or ideal governing this scale of acceptable causal arguments would be the idea of an ultimate causal explanation. But since the ideal of ultimate causal explanation is not clear, the scale for ranking inductive arguments in respect to the degrees of adequacy in providing answers to the question "Did E occur?" is also unclear. Is there some way of specifying what the best induction would be, independently of the idea of an ultimate causal explanation?

The best induction is what Hume calls an empirical "proof." Such proofs, in turn, are justified inductions in that they are supported by established laws of nature. Hume has been criticized for having a grossly inadequate conception of lawlikeness. For Hume, it is thought, a law expresses (a) an experienced constant conjunction of events along with (b) a feeling of expectation that the conjunction will continue. Leaving the feeling aside, the objective content of a law boils down to mere constant conjunction, and this is not sufficient to distinguish lawlike regularities from accidental regularities. Laws must be capable of supporting subjunctive conditional statements about what is possible and impossible in fact, and only lawlike regularities can provide such support. This interpretation, however, is mistaken insofar as it treats (a) and (b) as Hume's analysis of what a causal relation is, whereas they are really the causal conditions which make possible the belief that there is unobservable causal power in the world.

In the last chapter, we observed Hume's historical analysis of how the idea of causal power has evolved, passing through the idea of unobservable deities, to the occult powers of ancient and medieval metaphysics, to the secondary causes of modern science (gravitational forces, radiant energy, etc.), and finally to the obscure order of these causes in the mind of God as ultimate cause. But all of this is no more than a sketch of the history of the idea of causal power, the details of which Hume never fills out. In particular, he does not explore (beyond the few hints discussed in the last chapter) the question of how modern scientists individuate unobservable causal powers. The upshot is that Hume does not have an explicitly stated theory of lawlikeness. Any Humean theory of lawlikeness would be the result of a critical examination of the actual conventions in natural philosophy of making theoretical judgments about powers. This project would carry Hume too far into natural philosophy itself and away from his task as a pioneering moral philosopher, a task which, in this case, is to provide a naturalistic account as opposed to the traditional rationalistic one of how there are any causal judgments about powers at all.

This does not mean however, that Hume has nothing to say about lawlikeness; it is just that what he does say is not systematically ordered. To begin with, Hume would agree that laws must be capable of supporting subjunctive conditional statements about what is possible and impossible in fact.[6] This point is brought out clearly in "Of Miracles" where Hume argues that empirical laws serve as canons of what is factually possible, and so have the authority to rule out miracles as impossible in fact even if they are certified by otherwise acceptable testimony (EU, 125, 128).

Under what conditions does a generalization become lawlike? Scattered throughout Hume's writings, a number of fairly obvious conditions emerge. (1) Laws describe a contingent relation between phenomena and unobservable theoretically determined powers (EU, 37–38). (2) Laws must be universal and unfalsified (EU, 114–15). (3) Laws must have been critically tested and subjected to a variety of strains in accord with the eight "Rules by which to judge of causes and effects" (T, 173–75). (4) Laws must have empirical content, that is, it must be possible to discipline theoretical talk about unobservable causal powers with empirical observations (EU, 77n). And finally, (6) laws must be part of a *system* of knowledge. This point needs some comment, because in the positivist interpretation a Humean law of nature is typically viewed as a universal conjunction arrived at phenomenally and independently of the rest of our knowledge.

To begin with, a miracle is rejected not because it violates a particular generalization that is well established but because it violates "the laws of nature" (EU, 114, 128). Miracles are incompatible with the whole system of natural knowledge. Hume is willing to allow that there could be acceptable testimony to the occurrence of an event contrary to what has been universally confirmed in our experience, if the testimony did not violate other systematically connected statements that we have good reason to believe are true. A tradition that "from the first of January 1600, there was a total darkness over the whole earth for eight days" falls within the bounds of testimony because the "decay, corruption, and dissolution of nature is an event rendered probable by so many analogies that any phenomenon which seems to have a tendency toward that catastrophe comes within the reach of human testimony if that testimony be very extensive and uniform" (EU, 127–28). But that "a dead man should come to life" must be viewed as an "absolute impossibility" not because it is incompatible with an isolated empirical regularity that dead men do not come to life but because it is incompatible with much else besides. Likewise, miracles are rejected because we already know by reference to the laws of nature that many of them are frauds or the result of certain tendencies in men to delusion. With this knowledge, a "strong presumption" against miracles can be established. Finally, "Of Miracles" is addressed to a certain class of people: "the wise and learned," "the judicious and knowing," "reasonable people," and the man who is a "just reasoner." These are people who take seriously the whole system or convention of inductive practices and are determined to guide themselves by it in their inferences from observed to unobserved cases.

Hume appreciated the fact that the authority of empirical laws derives in part from their location in a theoretical system. This is evident from the *Treatise* itself, which is presented as "a complete system of the sciences," one that is free from the defects of previous systems: "want of coherence in the parts, and of evidence in the whole" (T, xiii). Hume hopes that "the present system of philosophy will acquire new force as it advances; and that our reasonings concerning *morals* will corroborate whatever has been said concerning the *understanding* and the *passions*" (T, 455). Throughout the *Treatise*, Hume remarks on the rational authority that is generated by his system: "What principally gives authority to this system is, beside the undoubted arguments, upon which each part is founded, the agreement of these parts, and the necessity of one to explain another" (T, 154). There is also "that simplicity" of the system which is "its principal force and beauty" (T, 367). Hume occasionally and notoriously brushes aside counterexamples as having no force against a proposition (for instance, his treatment of the famous missing shade of blue). This procedure seems strange only if we view Hume as a "radical" empiricist whose task is to look for confirming cases of some isolated empirical generalization and to abandon this when counterexamples appear. But Hume saw himself, when he wrote the *Treatise*, as a "Newtonian," and this meant to him and to his contemporaries one who was the founder of a daring theory whose authority lay in its systematic and predictive power.[7] Perhaps this also explains why Hume considered Galileo and Newton to be the greatest philosophers of all time; both were men who had established important systematic frameworks for understanding the world (E, 584).

The above hints were never developed by Hume into a theory of what constitutes a law of nature, but it is clear enough that the essential function of a law or a system of laws is to support an inductive argument, that is, to answer the existence question. Since covering-law explanations are inductive arguments, the deep rationale behind covering-law explanation, whether of Humean or contemporary form, is that of providing the best answer to the existence question. Contemporary covering-law theorists consider a deductive-nomological argument to be a better answer to the question "Why did E occur?" than an inductive-statistical argument. Likewise, Hume considers an empirical "proof" to be a better answer to the same question than an empirical "probability." A system of empirical proofs would constitute a better answer still.

I have suggested that the rationale of explanation locked into the covering-law model is that of providing the best answer to the question "Did E occur?" and that it is open to Hume to explicate the rationale of explanation in the same way. But that is not Hume's approach to the problem. He does not think an answer to the question "Did E occur?" supported by empirical laws (no matter how good it might be) exhausts the meaning of the question "Why did E occur?". A problem still remains. That is why the concept of ultimate causal explanation remains alive in Hume's thinking, and why he can make skeptical remarks about the explanatory power of even the best-established explanations in natural philosophy: "we cannot give a satisfactory reason why we believe, after a thousand experiments, that a stone will fall or fire burn" (EU, 162). Hume, of course, does not deny that there are empirical "proofs" for the *existence* claims that "a stone will fall or fire burn," or, for that matter, that miracles cannot be. His point is simply that no empirical proof really *explains* why anything is the way it is.

The doctrine of moral explanations presupposes a quite different rationale for explanation. The principle undergirding this rationale is not that pious maxim of the moderns that something can come from nothing but that "impious maxim of the ancient philosophy, *Ex nihilo, nihil fit*" (EU, 164n). Since the moderns deny this principle, it is possible for them to be logically surprised that anything exists at all. Against this conceptual background, Leibniz's problem of why "something exists rather than nothing" becomes the first problem of explanation, requiring that the existence thesis be written into the *form* of explanation. But if the maxim of the ancients were accepted, that there is something rather than nothing could not be the central problem of explanation. The maxim is illustrated in the *Phaedo* where Plato has Socrates recall the rationale of explanation learned in his youth: "if anyone wished to discover the reason why any given thing came or ceased or continued to be, he must find out how it was best for that thing to be, or to act or be acted upon in any other way. On this view, there was only one thing for a man to consider, with regard both to himself and to anything else, namely the best and highest good although this would necessarily imply knowing what is less good, since both were covered by the same knowledge."[8]

Here the rationale of explanation is that of showing how it is best for something to be as it is, and this requires the application of a standard of valuation. Plato presents this model of explanation in contrast to that of Anaxagoras's naturalistic type of explanation which is remarkably similar to Hume's empirical "proofs." The fact that Socrates is in prison is explained not by his reasons for being there but by reference to his environment and physical state. Plato does not deny that such explanations could provide good grounds to believe that the event to be explained occurred rather than not. What he rejects is Anaxagoras's conception of the *rationale* of explanation: "Fancy being unable to distinguish between the cause of a thing and the condition without which it could not be a cause! It is this latter, as it seems to me, that most people, groping in the dark, call a cause—attaching to it a name to which it has no right."[9] But, if Hume is right, this is exactly the view of those who are walking in the full daylight of modern philosophy.

For Plato, the problem of explanation is not that of providing the best inductive support for claiming that the event to be explained occurred rather than not—that claim is justified on grounds that are independent of the form of explanation. The problem is to specify, relative to some standard of evaluation, that it is best for the event to be explained to have occurred rather than not. There is a relative and an absolute form of Platonic explanation. The former would be an argument that an act is best relative to the agent's intentions and beliefs about his situation, showing that the act conforms to the good reasons the agent had for acting. The latter would be an argument that the act is absolutely the best, independently of the reasons the agent had for acting. Socrates' own explanation that he is in prison because he has good reasons for being there is a case of the relative form, as is Hume's moral account of the Athenian law. Socrates' demand that the position of the sun and the moon be explained "in the same way" is a case of the absolute form.

The Humean or modern scientist who views the world against the conceptual background of the Hebrew-Christian doctrine of creation must find it logically odd that anything exists at all. Hume's covering-law-type theory of explanation is designed to resolve this perplexity (as is the modern covering-law model) by logically writing into the form of explanation empirical reasons (laws and initial conditions) for believing that the event to be explained occurred. The case is quite otherwise when an ancient scientist attempts to explain things. Since he considers it unintelligible to suppose that something could come from nothing, he cannot be logically perplexed that anything exists at all. His problem is, rather, to determine whether what admittedly exists makes sense or has any rational point by reference to some standard of valuation which is at the same time a standard of intelligibility. Essentially the same pattern of thought governs the Humean moral philosopher who would explain things by giving moral accounts of them. But such accounts, having no predictive force, apply uniquely to the past and so may be called historical explanations. The moral philosopher giving moral accounts is essentially a historian.

When the Humean historian views the world of past human action in order to understand it, he is not logically perplexed that there are any past events at all. That there are past events is determined on grounds that are independent of the form of moral causal explanation, for example, by historical testimony and records. What puzzles the historian when he attempts to explain past events is not the existence of the event, but rather whether these events make any moral or rational sense. Hume's conception of moral accounts is worked out to resolve this perplexity since it explains an act by uncovering its rationale or point.

The ancient Platonic model of explanation was applied not only to human actions but to all things, reality being viewed as the activity of mind. This model survives on into the modern period and guides the thinking of early modern science. Kepler thought of science as "sacred madness" and viewed the solar system as ordered by God not only mathematically but musically as well. Galileo viewed nature as a book written by God in the language of mathematics, as did Descartes. Boyle, Newton, Hartley, Priestley, and indeed almost all of the early modern scientists viewed science as a matter of working through the rationale of God's creative acts. Hume too accepts this pattern of explanation and, in the end, through "philosophical theism" views reality as the activity of mind. Since philosophical theism is neither demonstrably nor empirically justified, Hume gives a causal account of its origin. As we have observed, it is an idea that comes about only after men gain some measure of control over their environment and acquire the habit of making causal judgments, a habit that along with other propensities leads to the idea of a single intelligent author of all things.

Although we have this idea as a matter of fact, Hume also points out that the empirical laws discovered by science amount to no more than ideas of constant conjunction and habits of expectation, or systems of such ideas and habits, and could never formulate the kind of causal understanding required by the idea of God as first cause. Hume, then, did not abandon the ancient Platonic model of explanation for the sciences; scientifically minded men cannot avoid having such an ideal. In that ideal, reality is rationally ordered and the impious maxim of the ancients, "nihilo ex nihil fit," reigns. However, we can know this universe only through experience, which we view as logically disconnected but united by the imagination as far as our existence beliefs are concerned. Looked at this way, our scientific pursuits are carried out against the conceptual background of a radically contingent universe in which anything may cause anything. It is entirely characteristic of Hume's peculiar philosophical perception to point out that this radical contingency is a presupposition of scientific inquiry and that the presupposition has a history and is grounded not in reason but in the deepest dogmas of Hebrew-Christian theology. We are all heirs to this theological tradition, but we are also heirs to the pagan Platonic tradition. We think in both ways. Hume accepts the radically contingent universe of the former (as the universe presupposed by scientific methodology) and places it against the broader conceptual background of the latter. It is the latter that makes Hume's skepticism possible. Without it, his conception of science would collapse into positivism: the systematization of contingent existence beliefs without any conception at all of alienation from an ultimate ordering of things. It is because we also accept that impious maxim of the ancients that we can experience the skeptical alienation from reality that Hume constantly points out.

If we view the progress of modern science as, in part, the stripping away of layer after layer of the ancient Platonic model of explanation until finally the last vestige is cleared, then Hume is not in the main stream of modern science. He does not eliminate the ancient model of explanation from our concept of natural philosophy, he simply sets it at a remote, skeptical distance as the ideal of natural order locked into philosophical theism. For moral philosophy, however, the model is accepted wholeheartedly, the only problem being that Hume does not explain how moral explanations are connected with covering-law explanations in moral philosophy or, for that matter, in natural philosophy. The ground of the tensions in Hume's thought about causal explanation is due to his having embraced the two incompatible maxims we have discussed: that of the moderns and that of the ancients. He somehow recognized that his skeptical purge of the principle of the ancients from natural philosophy could not extend to moral philosophy without difficulty. The unity of science thesis, the existence thesis, and the symmetry thesis of explanation and prediction are internal to the modern conception of scientific intelligibility. But, as Hume found, they cannot be forced all the way into moral philosophy without rendering what is essential to it unintelligible, and so he is compelled to make special concessions to moral philosophy in his conception of causal explanation.

# 8
# *Historical Understanding*

I believe this is the historical Age and this [Scotland] the historical Nation.
                        Hume, letter to William Strahan, 1770

Hume is unique in being both a great philosopher and a great historian. Philosophers have often made contributions to other fields, but these contributions have typically been to the nonhistorical inquiries of theoretical science and mathematics. No philosopher of Hume's stature has made a contribution to history equal to that of his monumental *History of England*. Over half of Hume's production as a writer was in history, and most of the rest of it was in the fields of social, political, economic, and moral studies which, as he treated them, leaned heavily on historical research and interpretation. In his own time, Hume was appreciated not as a philosopher but as a historian and as the author of the historically oriented *Essays, Moral, Political, and Literary*. The *History* went through six editions during his lifetime and through at least 165 posthumous editions. It remained the standard work on the subject for over a hundred years, until Macaulay's *History of England* began to replace it in 1849. Even so, Hume's *History*, fortified now by a classical dignity, continued to be published into the last decade of the nineteenth century.[1] This was about the time when philosophers began to take serious notice of Hume's philosophical work, interest in his philosophy increasing almost in proportion as interest in his historical work decreased. Today Hume is thought of primarily as a philosopher, and his *History* is virtually forgotten.

That Hume made contributions to both fields raises the question of whether there are any interesting conceptual connections between his philosophical and historical works. The philosophical and mathematical works of Descartes, Leibniz, and Russell are recognized as mutually illuminating, but a parallel recognition is not generally accorded Hume's historical and philosophical works. Indeed, the prevailing attitude has been that expressed by Collingwood, that Hume "deserted philosophical studies in favor of historical at about the age of thirty-five," and that these areas were, in Hume's mind, completely independent.[2] Laird dismisses Hume's historical writings as being of no philosophical value; Hume was, he says, not a "philosophical historian . . . he was only a philosopher turned historian—a very different being."[3] John Stewart has judged the *Treatise* to be an "anti-historical" work because Hume's "theory of the understanding either neglects or misrepresents the historical world."[4] More recently, Haskell Fain has taken Hume to be the paradigm case of an antihistorical outlook which Fain thinks has dominated British and American philosophy: "The divergence between history and philosophy in England and America is perhaps best personified by David Hume, a philosopher and a historian but not both at once. His principle ideas in philosophy did not stem from his concern with history; rather, when he turned to history, he had already completed his philosophical system."[5]

It is difficult to know what to make of these interpretations. They are not interpretations that can be evaluated by a fairly straightforward reading of the texts. To say that Hume's historical works are not sufficiently philosophical, or that his philosophy cannot account for or misrepresents the historical world, or that his *History* is, at bottom, an antihistorical work, presupposes a view of what is to count as a specifically "historical" work, and this, in turn, presupposes a philosophy of history: a theory of what history is both as an inquiry and as an order in the world. The matter is further complicated by the fact that the philosophy of history, unlike the philosophy of science, is a relatively new discipline. It did not appear in anything like systematic form until the nineteenth century, when Hegel built an entire metaphysical system around historical categories, and into the twentieth century it remained largely the activity of German Idealism and its offshoots in such thinkers as Marx, Dilthey, and Croce. From this tradition, it passed into Anglo-American philosophy, largely through Croce's influence on Collingwood. During the last three decades a number of philosophers in the analytic tradition have brought history to light as a discipline with philosophical problems all its own. There is still, however, no generally agreed upon framework for thinking about history, as there is for thinking about science. The philosophy of science reaches back to the seventeenth century and has a well-established framework to guide philosophical inquiry: the problem of induction, the problem of the relation between theoretical and observational predicates, the problem of the status of primary and secondary qualities, the status of scientific theories, the application of mathematics to the world, and so on. There is no established parallel framework of problems for the philosophy of history. As a consequence, the philosophical vocabulary of reflection on history is not fixed. There is and may always be disagreement about how to use expressions such as "scientific theory," "scientific explanation," "induction," and the like, but none of these are as chaotic as the expression "historicist," "historicity," "historical change," and "historical process" (as distinct from some other kind of change or process).

Something of this conceptual anarchy has been carried over into the sparse commentary that exists on the relation between Hume's historical and philosophical works. We cannot well understand or evaluate claims about Hume's "anti-historical" philosophical or historical works until some decision is made about how to explicate the concept of history. Nor is this a decision that can afford to ignore Hume's work, for Hume was one of the very first philosophers of history and his own work can be useful in reaching conceptual decisions about the concept of history.

With these considerations in mind, I would like to examine the relation between Hume's philosophical works and his historical works. I hope to show that both sets of works are mutually illuminating and that neither is, in any philosophically interesting way, antihistorical. They are tied together by a mind deeply involved in the problems of what has come to be known as the philosophy of history. The insights Hume achieved and the problems he raised are still philosophically suggestive and move easily into contemporary debates in philosophy of history.

The best place to begin is with Collingwood's claim that Hume deserted philosophy for history, suggesting that the two were, in Hume's mind, logically independent inquiries. This view receives some confirmation from Hume's remark in *My Own Life* that the plan of writing a history of England occurred to him in 1752 when he became librarian to the Faculty of Advocates. But this statement is only partially correct and certainly should not be taken as marking the date when he first became interested in history. During the period from 1745 to 1749, while he was very much engaged in writing philosophy, he produced four large manuscripts of notes on English history, chronologically arranged, and an abridgement of English history from the Roman invasion through the reign of Henry II. These early attempts at a history of England are no doubt part of the "historical projects" Hume was contemplating in a letter of 1747, and for which he thought a military expedition with St. Clair would be a benefit (L, I, 99). These manuscripts also throw light on Hume's confession in a letter of 1748 that he had long "had an intention, in . . . [his] riper years, of composing some

History" for which he "had treasured up stores of study and plans of thinking for many years" (L, I, 109).

Hume's interest both in the writing of history and in philosophical problems of history dates from the very beginning of his career as a writer. His earliest extant essay, "An Historical Essay on Chivalry and Modern Honor," written shortly before or during the writing of the *Treatise*, reveals a serious theoretical interest in history. His "Memoranda" (1729–40) is illuminating as an illustration of the detailed historical research he was engaged in before, during, and after the writing of the *Treatise*. In addition, the "Memoranda" contains philosophical reflections on the nature of historical methodology, one of which (the concept of moral causal explanation) Hume developed about twenty years later in "Of Some Remarkable Customs" (1752). At about the same time, when he was doing the reading and thinking for the *Treatise* (1729–34), he wrote an essay on the problem of miracles and historical methodology which eventually became the famous "Of Miracles" first published in *Philosophical Essays Concerning Human Understanding* (1748).

The first two Books of *A Treatise of Human Nature* appeared in 1739, the third in 1740. The *Treatise* manifests evidence of considerable historical research and reflection, particularly in books II and III. Indeed, it would be difficult to find, in this period, any work of comparable philosophical value that contained as many references to history. Many philosophical arguments and analyses are made to depend on "history and common experience," and, conversely, "the study of history confirms the reasonings of true philosophy" (T, 379, 562). Scattered throughout the *Treatise* are reflections on the nature of historical knowledge and existence. To mention just a few: Hume raises and rebuts a special form of historical skepticism (T, 145–46), and discusses the peculiar nature of historical evidence and the origin of historical knowledge (T, 113, 106–8); the influence of temporal ideas on the imagination is discussed (T, 427–37), along with the related topics of the origin of narrative thought and the different effects that novels and histories have on the imagination (T, 430, 97–98, 121–23). The two *Enquiries* also contain important reflections on the nature of history, most notably the discussion on narration, historical evidence, and the critique of providential history in the first *Enquiry* (EU, III, X, XI) and the problem of reconciling laws of human nature with historical relativism in the second *Enquiry* (EM, 324–43).

Hume published the *Essays Moral and Political* during the years 1741–42 and the *Political Discourses* in 1752. He considered these essays part of his philosophical work, but many of them could be classed as works of history. Many also contain philosophical reflections on the nature of historical knowledge. Notable in this class are "Of the Study of History," "That Politics may be Reduc'd to a Science" (1741); "Of the Rise and Progress of the Arts and Sciences," "Of Eloquence" (1742); "Of the Original Contract," "Of National Characters" (1748); "Of the Populousness of Ancient Nations," "Of Some Remarkable Customs," and "Of Commerce" (1752).

While Hume was writing the philosophical *Essays* (1741–52), he was also busy (at least from 1745 to 1749) with the research and composition of a history of England.[6] By 1752 he was composing in earnest his projected *History of England*, which appeared in six volumes from 1754 to 1762. While he was writing the *History*, he published *The Natural History of Religion* (1757), a work important for understanding his conception of historical change. Except for *My Own Life* (April 1776), Hume's last compositions were concerned with problems of history. In 1773, he wrote "Of the Origin of Government" and "Review of Robert Henry's History of Great Britain," in which he was forced to modify some of his earlier views about historiography, and in the spring of 1775 he wrote "Of the Authenticity of Ossian's Poems."

Finally, Hume considered his historical writings as an application and extension of his philosophical work. Commenting on the composition of his *History of England*, Hume wrote to the Abbé Le Blanc: "the philosophical Spirit, which I have so much indulg'd in all my Writings, finds here ample Materials to work upon" (L, I, 193).

From this brief survey of his writings, it is clear that Hume at no time abandoned philosophy for history. From the beginning and throughout his career as a writer, he was engaged in historical work as well as in the philosophical problems to which such work gives rise. We have yet to determine, however, in precisely what way Hume's historical and philosophical thought are connected and, in particular, whether what his philosophy teaches about the historical world is "anti-historical."

## HISTORY AND HUMAN NATURE

Perhaps the most influential discussion of the alleged failure of Hume's philosophy to account for the historical world is that of J. B. Black in *The Art of History*. Unlike most commentators, Black believes that the *History* is an extension of Hume's philosophy: "the philosophy is so subtly insinuated into the texture of the work, so artistically blended with it, that the task of effecting a separation between them is by no means easy." But "until this separation has been accomplished, the true bearings of the *History* cannot be appreciated."[7] Black views Hume's attempt to introduce the experimental method of reasoning into moral subjects as an antihistorical project: the attempt to isolate the timeless laws of human nature, that is, the laws governing the mind and passions. When Hume came to write history, he was conceptually forced by this timeless model of human nature to overlook the uniqueness of historical events and so failed to understand the sort of unity required to account for them. Black quotes, with approval, Leslie Stephen's judgment that "History . . . was to Hume an undecipherable hieroglyphic."[8] In this case, he was typical of his age: "Hume did not grasp the elements of the problem, because he was dominated, as indeed were all the eighteenth century *philosophes*, by the belief that human nature was uniformly the same at all times and places. Why trouble to differentiate if there were no differences worth considering?"[9] There is a famous passage in the first *Enquiry* which appears to support this interpretation that Hume's conception of human nature and history is deeply antihistorical:

> It is universally acknowledged that there is a great
> uniformity among the actions of men, in all nations and
> ages, and that human nature remains still the same in its
> principles and operations. The same motives always
> produce the same actions. The same events follow from
> the same causes. Ambition, avarice, self-love, vanity,
> friendship, generosity, public spirit—these passions,
> mixed in various degrees and distributed through society,
> have been, from the beginning of the world, and still are,
> the source of all the actions and enterprises which have
> ever been observed among mankind. Would you know the
> sentiments, inclinations, and course of life of the Greeks
> and Romans? Study well the temper and actions of the
> French and English: you cannot be much mistaken in
> transferring to the former *most* of the observations which
> you have made with regard to the latter. Mankind are so
> much the same, in all times and places, that history
> informs us of nothing new or strange in this particular. Its
> chief use is only to discover the constant and universal
> principles of human nature by showing men in all varieties
> of circumstances and situations, and furnishing us with
> materials from which we may form our observations and
> become acquainted with the regular springs of human
> action and behaviour (EU, 83–84, Hume's emphasis).

The antihistorical character of this passage appears undeniable and lends support to Black's harsh interpretation that, for Hume, "history is a repeating decimal. The great drama is transacted on a flat and uniform level."[10]

Yet the passage cannot be properly understood unless read in context. It occurs in the section entitled "Of Liberty and Necessity" where

Hume is arguing for the compatibility of freedom and determinism. In particular, he wants to show that, if we allow that causal connections are identified by resembling constant conjunctions, then everyone really believes that human actions admit of causal analysis insofar as everyone believes that resembling constant conjunctions "take place in the voluntary actions of men and in the operations of mind" (EU, 83). The contrast is between a human nature exhibiting some resembling constant conjunctions and a human nature exhibiting none at all: the latter would be a world in which all events and actions "were continually shifted in such a manner that no two events bore any resemblance to each other, but every object was entirely new, without any similitude to whatever had been seen before" (EU, 82). The degree of uniformity in human nature that Hume is defending here is extremely modest and is of the sort that everyone can and, indeed, must admit, as is obvious from the examples he gives: the "characters" of the sexes tend to be different, "the actions of the same person [are] much diversified in the different periods of his life from infancy to old age," the force of custom and education can "mold the human mind from its infancy and form it into a fixed and established character," and so on (EU, 86).

There is no doubt that Hume considered human nature to be unchanging. But it is unchanging only in the sense in which the empirical laws of nature are thought of as unchanging. Human nature is not a kind of immutable substance. It consists of a set of powers, dispositions, and tendencies picked out by a uniform experience of their effects. These include the principles of association, the principles of sympathy, and a set of motives for action which depend upon these principles. Among these motives are: "Ambition, avarice, self-love, vanity, friendship, generosity, public spirit . . . mixed in various degrees and distributed through society" (EU, 83). These "regular springs of human action and behavior" are thought of like the principles of gravity and are thought to hold at all times and places: "Nor are the earth, water, and other elements examined by Aristotle and Hippocrates more like to those which at present lie under our observation than the men described by Polybius and Tacitus are to those who now govern the world" (EU, 84). But the men of the eighteenth century and those described by Tacitus are the same only at a very high level of abstraction. Hume does not mean that the qualitative effects of the passions will always be the same, that friendship, for instance, will have the same manifestations or the same prevalence in one society as in another; allowances must be made for different customs and values: "We must not, however, expect that this uniformity of human actions should be carried to such a length as that all men, in the same circumstances, will always act precisely in the same manner, without making

216

any allowance for the diversity of characters, prejudices, and opinions. Such a uniformity, in every particular, is found in no part of nature. On the contrary, from observing the variety of conduct in different men we are enabled to form a greater variety of maxims which still suppose a degree of uniformity and regularity" (EU, 85).

So the principle of the uniformity of human actions, like the principle of gravity, is to be thought of as holding on a very general level of abstraction. A more concrete understanding would require reference to external conditions which modify and give concrete content to the principle. Hume gives this example to illustrate his own methodology of how to study human nature: "The Rhine flows north, the Rhone south; yet both spring from the *same* mountain, and are also actuated, in their opposite directions, by the *same* principle of gravity. The different inclinations of the ground, on which they run, cause all the difference of their courses" (EM, 333). *Ceteris paribus* clauses are required for application of the principles of human action as well as for application of the principles of gravity.

The most significant modification of the principles of human nature is due to social and historical circumstances. Man, for Hume, is a social being. More so than other animals, he cannot readily survive as an individual: his physical wants are greater and his physical ability weaker. But men are not just physically dependent upon each other. There is also an epistemological and ontological dependence. As we observed in chapter 2, Hume rejects the Cartesian introspective method of examining mind in favor of a public, social, and historical approach. He explicitly denies that there is a privileged introspective avenue to knowing ourselves (T, xviii-xix). Self-knowledge presupposes a relation to physical objects: "Ourself, independent of the perception of every other object, is in reality nothing: For which reason we must turn our view to external objects" (T, 340). But most important, self-knowledge requires reference to other selves and their opinion of us: "Men always consider the sentiments of others in their judgment of themselves" (T, 303), and "the minds of men are mirrors to one another" (T, 365). The means of this mutual self-comprehension is Hume's famous principle of sympathy, which is a principle of communication whereby we gain an internal understanding of the thoughts and feelings of others. So tightly drawn are the social bonds among men that "We can form no wish, which has not a reference to society" (T, 363). Man is essentially an internal part of a social whole where both the parts and the whole exist in mutual epistemological and ontological dependence. Human nature, then, necessarily manifests itself in different forms depending on the different social circumstances which modify it.

Nor can these social circumstances remain, concretely, the same, for human nature is not only socially variable it is historically variable as well. The social world, for Hume, is an order of passion and thought, and of the *reflective* passions and thoughts men have about that order. Physical objects are, strictly speaking, not part of the social world. They become part of it only when they take on meaning to someone, that is, only when they become an object of some passion. And, as we observed in chapter 5, the passions of reflection are temporally reflective, that is, we think of the objects of our passions in tensed and narrative time. The social world, then, will have some sort of narrative unity woven together by the temporally reflective imagination. People are held together not merely by passions, unreflectively felt and tenselessly ordered, but by narrative associations, i.e., by the stories they tell about themselves. The legal, moral, social, political, aesthetic, and religious standards that constitute the moral world are the products of narrative associations of ideas, and so are part of some narrative unity. The moral world is a system of stories.

Human nature has two dimensions. (1) As a part of nature and as unreflective, man may be viewed in a timeless way and comprehended under whatever universal empirical regularities may be at hand: that men always form society, that the sexes are attracted to each other, that old men do not experience the world as young men do, that power tends to corrupt, and so on. It is in this sense that human nature is thought of as unchanging. (2) Man is a being in time who reflects, through narrative associations of ideas, on the significance of his deeds. These narrative ideas constitute a moral universe through which man understands himself as part of some narrative order. But narrative ideas, like all ideas of reflection, give rise to impressions of reflection (what was discussed in chapter 5 as temporal or narrative passions), and these enable men not only to *comprehend* themselves as inhabiting a narrative order but to *act* in the light of it as well. From this perspective, the moral world is constantly changing. Our narrative ideas and passions not only do not but cannot remain constant: to be "inconstant and irregular . . . is, in a manner, the constant character of human nature" (EU, 88). The unchanging principles of human nature will manifest themselves concretely in qualitatively different ways. Modern friendship is not the same as medieval friendship or ancient Greek friendship; yet each is friendship of a sort, and so manifestations of a universal propensity of human nature.

In those passages (including the notorious "anti-historical" passage of the *Enquiry*) where Hume is affirming (1), he is not denying (2). His point in asserting (1) is nearly always polemical and negative and must be understood by two theses he wishes to rebut. One is the extreme libertarian position that, Hume thinks, entails the absurdity that there

218

are no regularities in human action at all. His strategy is to show that no one does or could believe this and that the libertarian position is based on a verbal confusion. The other thesis is that the world, like everything else, is mortal, having "its infancy, youth, manhood, and old age" and that human nature is in its decadent stage (E, 381). If this were so, then human nature would be quite different today from what it was in its early states, roughly in the way in which an old man is different from a young man. This and kindred historical theses were quite popular in Hume's time. The question of whether the world was in a decadent stage was in the background of the seventeenth- and eighteenth-century controversy between the ancients and the moderns, and other attempts to glorify the past over the present. It bore some affinity also to that providential-prophetic view of history defended by, among other prominent thinkers, Newton and Hartley and according to which we are now living through the last days. Hartley wrote: "the latter Times are now approaching."[11]

Hume accepted the theory that the world is mortal. Experience proves "the mortality of this fabric of the world, and its passage, by corruption or dissolution, from one state or order to another," and "in all these variations, man, equally with every animal and vegetable, will partake" (E, 381). But, Hume insists, there is no evidence for the theory that the world and, in particular, human nature are in a decadent state. Contrary to what Hume urged was the widely held view that men in ancient times had a "stronger inclination and power of generation" than modern men and that, consequently, the ancient world was much more populous than the modern (E, 381). Hume grants that if the ancient world had been more populous and if no moral causes could explain the difference, then the thesis of the decadence of human nature would have received a high degree of confirmation. "Of the Populousness of Ancient Nations" was written to show that this is not true, that we cannot "presuppose any decay in human nature," and that as far "as observation reaches," the principles and powers of human nature have remained the same (E, 382). Again, to affirm this very abstract conception of the uniformity of human nature at the expense of the degeneracy thesis is not at all to deny the historical conception of human nature framed in (2).

Collingwood, like Black, viewed Hume as a typical eighteenth-century thinker caught in the grip of an antihistorical conception of human nature: "Human nature was conceived substantialistically as . . . an invarying substratum underlying the course of historical changes and all human activities."[12] But he gives the criticism a slightly different twist: "Hume never shows the slightest suspicion that the human nature he is analyzing in his philosophical work is the nature of a western European in the early eighteenth century and that the very same enterprise if undertaken at a widely different time or place might have yielded widely different results. He always assumes that *our* reasoning faculty, *our* tastes and sentiments, and so forth, are something perfectly uniform and invariable, underlying and conditioning all historical changes."[13] Black had viewed Hume's conception of human nature as historically *vacuous*, "a repeating decimal"; Collingwood views it as historically *provincial*. As I shall argue, this interpretation is profoundly mistaken; yet it contains an important half-truth, an appreciation of which will serve to illuminate an important aspect of Hume's conception of history.

We have observed two conceptions of human nature in Hume's thought: a timeless, abstract, and unchanging conception and a narrative, concrete, and changing conception. The first is not viewed as an unchanging substratum. Substance has no ontological status in Hume's philosophy, and so we can make no ontological distinction between what human nature is and what men have done. The timeless conception of human nature is merely an abstraction from the historical conception. It is necessary for Hume only in the way in which any abstract concept is necessary: without them our understanding of things would be, like that of animals, hopelessly provincial. History, however, is concerned not with man in the abstract but with man as he exists in concrete narrative orders. The difference between abstract and concrete sciences is drawn in the *Enquiry:* "Moral reasonings are either concerning particular or general facts. All deliberations in life regard the former; as also all disquisitions in history, chronology, geography, and astronomy." The sciences that treat of "general facts" and seek to establish abstract general laws are "politics, natural philosophy, physic, chemistry, etc., where the qualities, causes and effects of a whole species of objects are inquired into" (EU, 165). This is not to say, of course, that the sciences which study "particular" facts may not view them in the light of whatever general regularities are available. Indeed, this not only can be done; it must be done, for no concrete understanding of an object is possible without abstractly grasping it as one of "a whole species of objects." But granting this, what more can be said about the concrete, historical conception of human nature and its relation to the abstract, timeless conception?

The problem is taken up in "A Dialogue" where the issue of moral relativism is examined. Palamedes describes to the narrator of the dialogue the customs and morals of an imaginary country called Fourli. Although "extremely civilized and intelligent," the Fourlians have "ways of thinking. . . particularly in morals, diametrically opposite to ours" (EM, 324). A Fourlian man of merit might be such a one as with us would pass for incestuous, a parricide, an assassin, ungrateful, a perjured traitor, and a homosexual, not to mention a rustic and an ill-mannered person. Having lived in this way, he may decide to end his life by suicide. Notwithstanding this, his life may be the object of praise and admiration to his contemporaries and posterity (EM, 329). The narrator objects that such customs are not only incompatible with "a civilized, intelligent people" but are "scarcely compatible with human nature" (EM, 328). Yet it turns out that Palamedes has been describing a possible man of merit in ancient Greek culture. The reason why the Greeks were not recognized in the account is that their morals were described from an abstract, unhistorical point of view. Looked at in this way any set of customs may appear absurd. To illustrate this, Palamedes gives a parallel abstract description of modern French morals: adultery is approved; it is the highest merit to love, serve, and obey a tyrant though oppressed, disgraced, impoverished, insulted, and imprisoned by him; women, though without virtue, are objects of praise, reverence, respect, and the highest deference; friends may attempt to kill each other over the most trivial remark; the murder of friends and fellow countrymen is allowed though ordered by a stranger whose only reason is that he does not approve of their mode of worship even though he is of the same religion. To all of this the Greeks might wonder whether we were speaking of "a human society, or of some inferior, servile species" (EM, 331).

Here we should perhaps recall the famous "anti-historical" passage of the first *Enquiry:* "Would you know the sentiments, inclinations, and course of life of the Greeks and Romans? Study well the temper and actions of the French and English" (EU, 83). It is, perhaps more clear now that Hume is not saying there is parity of conduct between an ancient Greek and a modern Frenchman. He is quite clear that we cannot infer from an analysis of French love what Greek love must have been. Likewise, Greek courage is qualitatively different from French courage, as are public spirit, friendship, wit, fidelity, and, indeed, all the customs and "ways of thinking" that make up the concrete historical experience of the respective cultures. Why not say, then, that each historical period is a self-contained universe governed by its own laws and ontologically disconnected from every other period? Why not embrace absolute historicism? On the level of concrete historical experience this is, in effect, the view Hume takes. The concrete differences between the ancient Greeks and the modern French are presented as being so radically different that they do not appear to belong to the same species.

But scientific and moral understanding require that we view things abstractly, not concretely. The temporal and narrative features of things must be bracketed out to reveal whatever timeless principles may be at work. "By tracing matters . . . a little higher, and examining the first principles, which each nation establishes, of blame or censure," we discover an abstract human nature underlying and unifying the concrete diversity of historical periods. We find, for instance, that "the Greek loves," though offensive and "blameable" from the modern point of view, "arose from a very innocent cause, the frequency of the gymnastic exercises among that people; and were recommended, though absurdly, as the source of friendship, sympathy, mutual attachment, and fidelity; qualities esteemed in all nations and all ages" (EM, 334). Hume has rendered intelligible the otherwise alien and perplexing Greek loves by giving a moral causal account of them, that is, by providing us with an internal grasp of the rationale behind the practice. By entering into the Greek point of view, we can come to see why the practice existed and how they could view it as morally praiseworthy.

One reason why the morals of the modern French and the ancient Greeks appear unintelligible is that Palamedes' description of them is projected from an external point of view; all we are presented with are observable regularities, mere constant conjunctions, holding within a historical period. What is purposely excluded is any internal understanding of a practice. What Hume brilliantly shows in "A Dialogue" is that any practice in any period, if described externally, may appear unintelligible and alien: "There are no manners so innocent or reasonable, but may be rendered odious or ridiculous, if measured by a standard, unknown to the persons" (EM, 330).

What is the status of these first principles of human nature that have been abstracted out of concrete historical experience? Hume compares them to the principles of gravity (EM, 333), and this suggests that they are to be thought of as mere empirical regularities. But if that is all they are, then the principles of human nature would be as alien and unintelligible to us as the principles of gravity—a conclusion which Hume, of course, denies. The principles of human nature make sense because they have an inner rationale which the moral philosopher can rethink and reexperience in his own mind. And this process of *verstehen* is made possible by the original principle of sympathy whereby men are able to communicate to us the goods which are the objects of their actions, however strange and obscure those goods may appear. As we saw in the last chapter, it is the concept of the good as framed in that "impious maxim of the ancients" that governs moral causal explanation, not that of constant conjunction. So the unifying principle of human nature, for Hume, is not a set of regularities modeled on the principle of gravity, but the original principle of sympathy: all that is necessary is that people be able to recognize the goods that other people pursue. If there were goods pursued by some poeple which other people not only did not but could not understand, then and only then would the thesis of the unity of human nature collapse. Hume, of course, did not deny that there may be regularities undergirding the principle of sympathy itself. These would include, presumably, a minimally uniform physiology and psychology, and these deeper regularities would have to be understood on the model of the principle of gravity: a comprehensive system of brute regularities. But as a moral philosopher he does not pretend to "explain" the principle of sympathy. It functions, rather, as one of those original principles which makes moral philosophy possible.[14]

As we saw in the last chapter, Hume distinguishes between the internal and external side of a regularity in human action as well as between the internal and external side of an action whether or not that action is covered by a regularity. Always, it is the internal side of the action or regularity that explains it. This enables Hume to maintain two theses which, from the positivistic point of view, must be scandalous. (1) The thesis presented in "Of Some Remarkable Customs" is that moral philosophers have a special way of explaining actions not covered by known regularities. (2) The second thesis is Hume's frequent and apparently perverse claim that no regularities of human action can be expected to hold good beyond the period from which they are taken: "I am apt . . . to entertain a suspicion, that the world is still too young to fix many general truths in politics, which will remain true to the latest posterity. . . . It is not fully known what degree of refinement, either in virtue or vice, human nature is suceptible of, nor what may be expected of mankind from any great revolution in their education, customs or principles" (E, 89). The historical relativity of political truth is a special case of the historical relativity of all standards of human action. "Such mighty revolutions have happened in human affairs and so many events have arisen contrary to the expectation of the ancients, that they are sufficient to beget suspicion of still further changes" (E, 90). Hume never abandoned this radically contingent and historical conception of the manifestations of human nature.

But if it is possible to explain human actions independently of regularities as such, then even those holding within a historical period cease to be of primary methodological importance for moral philosophy. Of course, established regularities within a period may be used to support inductive arguments about what sort of behavior is likely to occur within the period, e.g., that feudal barons tend to act in a certain way. But what is important about such regularities is not their use in inductive arguments but that they themselves are in need of explanation. The unique task of moral philosophy is to explain why the regularity is as it is by uncovering its rationale in the thoughts and intentions of the agents.

What we appreciate is that the act was necessary, that is, reasonable or understandable, given the agent's intention and conception of the situation.

The principles of rational conduct governing such arguments may be thought of as analytic. Whether Hume thinks of them in this way is an open question. They could, perhaps, be explicated by reference to his theory of relations of ideas or distinctions of reason, although Hume does not use either theory to throw light on them. In fact, he says very little by way of theoretical clarification about the status of these principles. But from what he does say, they seem to function somewhat like the principles of virtues discussed in the *Enquiry* on morals. Both are so deeply embedded in the conventions of common life that they structure the very meanings of words and can be recognized by linguistic analysis alone; that is, they both function as analytic truths.

In a passage quoted above, Hume indicates that it is unlikely that we shall discover any "general truths in politics" that will hold good beyond the period from which they are taken. There he had in mind an external understanding of empirical regularities that would hold for all historical periods. But when it comes to appreciating the inner rationale of political regularities within a period, the matter is entirely different. We are told that "politics admit of general truths, which are invariable by the humour or education either of subject or sovereign" (E, 17). Hume mentions an observation of Machiavelli's as "one of those eternal political truths, which no time nor accident can vary" (E, 19). The "truths" Hume is concerned with here are described as "axioms" and "maxims," not as regularities (E, 17). They have to do with explicating the advantages and disadvantages that follow from various forms of government, and thus are attempts to formulate criteria for rational political action given a certain conception of things. They function more like analytical models of rational political behavior than as empirical regularities. Hume's language betrays his conception of their formal character. They are usually presented in analogy with the formal sciences: "So great is the force of laws, and of particular forms of government . . . that consequences almost as general and certain may sometimes be deduced from them, as any which the mathematical sciences afford us" (E, 14). Even forms of government quite limited in historical scope, such as the Polish and Venetian aristocracies, contain rationales which necessarily render the latter superior to the former, nor is this a matter to be determined merely by experience: "The different operations and tendencies of these two species of government might be made apparent even *a priori*" (E, 15).

Hume did not always succeed in keeping distinct the internal necessity of a model of rational behavior from the external necessity of an empirical regularity. The result was that, at times, he confused the former with the latter, thinking he had established an empirical fact when he was really just drawing out the consequences of a conceptual truth. The regularities which Hume tries to establish in "Of the Rise and Progress of the Arts and Sciences" are good examples of this confusion. The first observation is "That it is impossible for the arts and sciences to arise, at first, among any people, unless that people enjoy the blessing of a free government" (E, 116). The observation is presented as an empirical one, but the evidence Hume deploys is really conceptual, a fact that becomes obvious with the conclusion: "To expect, therefore, that the arts and sciences should take their first rise in a monarchy, is to expect a contradiction" (E, 117). Hume has, of course, repeatedly claimed that the denial of no empirical hypothesis can be contradictory.

To sum up, Collingwood's criticism that Hume was caught in the grip of a substantialistic conception of human nature and that he assumed human nature had always existed as it appeared to an eighteenth-century enlightened European is fundamentally wrong. Hume's doctrine of an unchanging human nature is historically harmless and amounts to little more than the operation of the principle of sympathy: that we are capable of recognizing intentional activity in others and the goods they pursue, however strange the content of those goods may appear. Hume stresses that history, if viewed externally (and that is how we initially view it), presents us with activity which, by the standards of our own age, appears unintelligible. The task of moral causal accounts is to show that this natural point of view is illusory by uncovering the rationale behind an activity, and this consists in showing that the activity is, from the agent's point of view, directed toward some good. The activity then appears intelligible, and our understanding of human nature is broadened and enriched. Each age, then, is governed by its own laws and principles which the historian, through the principle of sympathy and moral causal accounts, must try to empathetically understand: "The perusal of a history seems a calm entertainment; but would be no entertainment at all, did not our hearts beat with correspondent movements to those which are described by the historian" (EM, 223).

## SOCIAL WHOLES AND HISTORICAL CONTINGENCIES

Hume did not think there were any genuine empirical laws of human action that could be expected to hold for all historical periods. There are, however, regularities that hold within a period, and these constitute what Hume calls the "spirit" of an age which, in turn, is used as a background concept for explaining the actions of individuals and groups. As we have observed, the individual for Hume is an integral part of a social and historical whole. Hume is very clear on this. The question "concerning the rise and progress of the arts and sciences is not altogether a question concerning the taste, genius, and spirit of a few, but concerning those of a whole people, and may therefore be accounted for, in some measure, by general causes and principles" (E, 115). Even granting the creativity and effort of individual artists, "it is impossible but a share of the same spirit and genius must be antecedently diffused throughout the people among whom they arise, in order to produce, form, and cultivate, from their earliest infancy, the taste and judgment of those eminent writers. The mass cannot be altogether insipid from which such refined spirits are extracted" (ibid, cf. 278). The success of the obscure Oliver Cromwell was due to "the spirit of enthusiasm" which "being universally defused over the nation, disappointed all the views of human prudence and disturbed the operation of every motive which usually influences society" (H, V, lii, 64). The grotesque character of Cromwell meshed perfectly with the "gloomy enthusiasm" that permeated his time. All activities are *internally connected parts* of the spirit of an age: "*industry, knowledge,* and *humanity*, are linked together, by an indissolvable chain" (E, 278). "We cannot reasonably expect, that a piece of woollen cloth will be wrought to perfection in a nation which is ignorant of astronomy, or where ethics are neglected" (E, 277–78). Nor "Can we expect that a government will be well modelled by a people, who know not how to make a spinning wheel, or to employ a loom to advantage" (E, 280).

The spirit of an age is best grasped not through its politics but through its social life: "even trivial circumstances, which show the manners of the age, are often more instructive, as well as entertaining, than the great transactions of wars and negotiations, which are nearly similar in all periods" (H, IV, xxxviii, 41). It is perhaps not necessary now to say that Hume does not mean that politics is the same everywhere. There is an abstract similarity to man's political life just as there is to his sexual life, but the concrete content of all principles of action is determined by the spirit of the age. Thus in the sixteenth century, the "great maxims of policy" were "over-ruled, during that age, by the disputes of theology" (ibid. 52). Although *The History of England* is a political work, Hume devotes the end of some chapters and several appendices to an examination of "the state of the kingdom with regard to government, manners, finances, arms, trade, learning. Where a just notion is not formed of these particulars, history can be little instructive, and often will not be intelligible" (H, IV, appendix, 496).

But Hume does not view the individual as being wholly determined

226

by the social and historical whole of which he is a part, as Marxists and other "scientific" historians were to do: "I grant that a man, who should inquire why such a particular poet, as Homer, for instance, existed at such a place, in such a time, would throw himself headlong into chimera, and could never treat of such a subject without a multitude of false subtilties and refinements" (E, 115). The will of great men is capable of modifying an age as well as being modified by it. Competition between Francis I and Charles V "kept their whole age in movement" (H, III, xxviii, 120). Likewise, political order is not determined merely by social causes. The main cause can be a great lawgiver such as Moses or Solon, and such men deserve the highest place of honor in history: "Of all men that distinguish themselves by memorable achievements, the first place of honour seems due to Legislators and founders of states, who transmit a system of laws and institutions to secure the peace, happiness, and liberty of future generations" (E, 54).

There is, then, a contingent distance between an individual and the social whole of which he is a part. This distance is expressed by Hume's frequent reference to what might have been in history if individuals had acted otherwise and to "chance," "accident," and "fortune." Hume interpreted the rise of Parliament as due mainly to social forces, especially economic ones, but he did not view the victory of Parliament over the Crown in the civil war as the outcome of these forces. The result was due to a failure of Crown policy to deal adequately with parliamentary ambition. Similarly, the Catholic zealot James II was overthrown not by social forces inexorably moving Britain towards a Protestant constitution, but by these along with the ambition and determination of William of Orange: "While every motive, civil and religious, concurred to alienate from the king [James II] every rank and denomination of men, it might be expected that his throne would, without delay, fall to pieces by its own weight: but such is the influence of established government, so averse are men from beginning hazardous enterprises, that, had not an attack been made from abroad, affairs might long have remained in their present delicate situation, and James might at last have prevailed in his rash and ill-concerted projects" (H, VI, lxxi, 330).

Another way Hume brings out the contingency of the past is through the role of "chance" and "accident." It was not social wholes but "Fortune alone" that placed Alfred the Great in the darkest period of barbarous England (H, I, ii, 70). The occurrence of Joan of Arc was "marvellous" (H, II, xx, 389). The "accidental finding of a copy of Justinian's Pandects, about the year 1130, in the town of Amalfi in Italy" was crucial to the development of the medieval intellect. This complete code of law inherited from the ancients not only served to provide security for the arts but "by refining, and still more by bestowing solidity on the judgment, served as a model to farther improvements" (H, II, xiii, 509–10). The role of chance can be as important in determining historical events as social wholes or the most powerful individual. Consider the fate of Charles I's order limiting the emigration of Puritans to the new world: "Eight ships, lying in the Thames, and ready to sail, were detained by order of the council; and in these were embarked Sir Arthur Hazelrig, John Hambden, John Pym, and Oliver Cromwell, who had resolved forever to abandon their native country, and fly to the other extremity of the globe; where they might enjoy lectures and discourses of any length or form which pleased them. The King had afterwards full leisure to repent this exercise of his authority" (H, V, lii, 85).

The importance Hume attaches to the role of the individual and of accident in history may be easily dismissed as "the crude belief in the decisive role of the accident in history" or of the "hero in history," as a contemporary Marxist historian has put it.[15] What is the significance of Hume's reference to chance and accident in history? First of all, Hume does not grant any ontological status to chance. To talk of chance is always to talk about our ignorance of causes relative to some system of determination. "To say that any event is derived from chance, cuts short all further inquiry concerning it, and leaves the writer in the same state of ignorance with the rest of mankind" (E, 112). But chance, for Hume, is not merely a negative notion. If it were, it would have no more role to play in history than it does in natural philosophy. References to chance and accident are important parts of a historical narrative because they serve to point out an important structure of historical intelligibility. To bring this out, let us examine one of Hume's remarks on chance and causation in history.

In "Of the Rise and Progress of the Arts and Sciences," Hume lays down this methodological principle: "What depends upon a few persons is, in a great measure, to be ascribed to chance, or secret and unknown causes: what arises from a great number, may often be accounted for by determinate and known causes" (ibid.). Hume then observes: "To judge by this rule, the domestic and the gradual revolutions of a state must be a more proper subject of reasoning and observation than the foreign and the violent, which are commonly produced by single persons, and are more influenced by whim, folly, or caprice, than by general passions and interests" (ibid., 113). From this it would seem that Hume would have written a social history, but, in fact, he wrote a political history that is very much about "single persons" who "are more influenced by whim, folly, or caprice, than by general passions and interests." The conflict, however, is only apparent. When Hume says that the behavior of individuals in contrast to that of groups is due to chance or "secret and unknown causes," he has in mind the covering-law model of causation which entails the symmetry thesis of explanation and prediction. His point is that, on the whole, it is easier to predict, and therefore to explain, the behavior of groups than of individuals. Relative to the system of determination framed in the covering-law model, political history must be viewed, on the whole, as governed by accident or "secret and unknown causes." However, relative to the system of determination framed in nonpredictive moral causal accounts, the actions of individuals in political history can be fully determinate. Moral causal accounts can be given of the rationale of an individual's action whether or not that action is covered by a law having predictive power over it.

What is an "accident" relative to one system of determination may be fully determinate relative to another system of determination. The actions of individuals that are determinate from the moral point of view are often viewed as "accidents" relative to the covering-law model of explanation. Moreover, from the moral point of view, all events covered by empirical laws (and the laws themselves) are viewed as the result of chance of "secret and unknown causes"; that is, they are all brute facts in need of ultimate causal explanation which, as Hume explicates it, is something like moral causal explanation writ large.

Chance, accident, and fortune have a significance in history they do not have in natural philosophy because historical agents occupy both the moral and the natural worlds, and their actions can, accordingly, be understood either through moral causes or covering laws. This inevitably produces a conceptual tension, for whatever is determinate from one point of view must be viewed as accidental from the other. Hume's rule that what depends on social groups can be explained by causes, and that what depends on individuals is the result of chance, is simply a picturesque way of saying not only that covering laws (social or otherwise) are not available to explain the actions of historical individuals but that they are irrelevant, since moral accounts can be given. The example offered to illustrate the rule is significant. "The depression of the Lords, and rise of the Commons in England, after the statutes of alienation, and the increase of trade and industry, are more easily accounted for by general principles, than the depression of the Spanish, and rise of the French monarchy, after the death of Charles Quint. Had Harry IV., Cardinal Richelieu, and Louis XIV. been Spaniards, and Philip II., III., and IV., and Charles II. been Frenchmen, the history of these two nations had been entirely reversed" (E, 113–14). Though said to be the result of "secret and unknown causes," the actions of these historical individuals are causally efficacious and thoroughly understandable.

To talk of the actions of historical individuals as "accidents" is also a slightly eccentric way of pointing out the contingency of the historical universe and the freedom and responsibility of historical agents. This, in part, explains the strong moral atmosphere that pervades the *History*. Hume's historical agents act out of *conscious* reasons, that is, moral causes. And since to ascribe a moral cause is, at the same time, to appriase the rationality of an action, it is an easy move from making moral causal ascriptions to making judgments about the character of an agent. And this is a move Hume robustly makes (partly no doubt because his ethical theory treats character and not an individual action as the fundamental unit of moral discourse). The *History* is very much the story of the deeds of important individuals, and after each discussion Hume concludes with an appraisal of the individual's character. He considers such evaluation an extremely important part of historical inquiry, and he will go out of his way to make sure that the proper judgment of an individual's character has been made.

Such judgments have been roundly criticized as examples of Hume's "anti-historical" method. Black writes: "In virtue of his theory of uniformity he takes his stand on the existence of a normal historical man . . . every character he meets in history must be reduced to type."[16] Consider part of Hume's character of James I: "His generosity bordered on profusion; his learning, on pedantry; his pacific disposition, on pusillanimity; his wisdom, on cunning; his friendship, on light fancy and boyish fondness" (H, IV, xlix, 493). Black remarks: "How much nearer are we brought by this epigrammatic and highly-finished picture to the personality of the king?"[17] Perhaps not very far, but Hume's purpose is not to give a psychological analysis of personality. It is rather to give a normative evaluation of an individual's character by reference to the standard of qualities useful or agreeable to the individual or to others. The relevant question to ask, then, is not whether Hume's character portraits reveal a theoretically rich analysis of personality but whether his normative judgments are true.

The highly stylized portraits are not the result of an antihistorical view of human nature. As Forbes has observed, they stem in part from Hume's use of Tacitus as a literary model. But the portraits also frame moral assessments of character and, moral judgment being the application of an abstract atemporal standard, a certain timeless ordering is necessary (though this must be done, as Hume has made quite clear in full view of the historical relativity that attaches to all concrete manifestations of virtue and vice). Of course, one might hold the view that historians, qua historians, should not make value judgments. But that is simply a view of history that Hume rejects not only because he rejects the fact-value distinction but because historians necessarily employ moral accounts, and to have discovered the moral cause of an action is already to have appraised it.

Relative to covering-law determination, references to chance and accident serve to point out the freedom of historical agents who act out of conscious deliberation. Such freedom is not ontologically "accidental," since it can always be determined by moral causes. But there is another sense of "accident" which, relative to covering-reason determination, serves to point out the limits, indeed, the fated limits of conscious action. It was an accident of history that Charles prevented the nameless Cromwell from immigrating to America, an act, which looking back, he would have done almost anything to have changed. What Hume would have us appreciate is that Charles could not have changed his action not only because it was past but also, and most important, because he could not have understood the *historical significance* of any decision he could have made at the time, and so could not possibly have known what to do. Here, then, we have an absolute limit to the efficacy of moral causes. The *History* as a whole, but especially the volumes on the Stuarts, is designed to reveal this limit. Again and again Charles I learns from what Hume calls "fatal experience" how he should have dealt with the Puritans. What Hume intends to convey by this (and what we shall have occasion later on to discuss in some detail) is that Charles was dealing with a unique political crisis, one for which British constitutional experience had not prepared him. New concepts were being forged under the pressure of events. Such concepts were necessary in order to comprehend and to deal successfully with events of that sort, but the concepts had not yet entered the world. In history, especially, the paradigm that ideas follow impressions holds. Charles quite literally had no *idea* at the time of what should have been done. Hume wrote the *History* to make clear what these new ideas were and how they had come about.

## THE IDEA OF THE HISTORICAL

Twentieth-century Anglo-American philosophers have tended to explicate the idea of history through the concept of causal explanation. Covering-law theorists hold there is no such thing as specifically "historical" explanation since causal explanation has the same form in all empirical inquiry. History is, then, viewed as simply one of the social sciences. By contrast, covering-reason theorists such as Collingwood hold that there are historical explanations which are formally distinct from explanations in the natural sciences. Such explanations do not require empirical laws, but explain actions by uncovering the rationale of the act. Explanations of this sort are unique to the sciences of human action: sociology, economics, political science, and the like (the sciences that Hume would include under moral philosophy). Since Collingwood thought of covering-reason explanations as specifically historical (perhaps because of their nonpredictive character), he defined all the sciences of human action as "historical sciences." Hume holds that moral causal explanation (a form of covering-reason explanation) governs the moral sciences. But he does not equate the historical with moral causation. History is just one of the moral sciences.

Hume's conception of the historical is presided over not by a model of explanation but by a model of perception. History is a matter of seeing certain sorts of things properly, a matter of bringing things into focus. Hume's scattered comments on the historical past yield four sorts of "perceptions" about the past which I shall call covering-law perceptions, covering-reason perceptions, narrative preceptions, and historical perceptions. I shall examine these in turn.

It is one of Hume's great discoveries that rules are "able to impose on the very senses" (T, 374) and that we have no direct access to the world through either sense or memory that is not mediated by an interpretation of the imagination. The belief that there is an external world of perceivable and continuously existing objects is a result of the order-making fictions of the imagination. In the light of this belief, the imagination interprets some experiences (constant conjunctions) as being causally connected. These in turn are used to support inferences about existences that lie beyond the reach of sense or memory (T, 106–8). The historical past is what present impressions, interpreted as evidence, obliges the historian to believe. Anything that falls within the laws of nature is believable. Miracles are unbelievable because they are incompatible with laws of nature. But not every believable event is to be believed. If all we had were present impressions interpreted in a lawlike way, our knowledge of the past would be as abstract and empty as our knowledge of the future. Historians have concrete knowledge of the past only because they have records and the testimony of historical agents.

Although Hume holds that anything in the present can count as evidence about the past, he fixes on human testimony as the most important source of evidence, and he treats it metaphorically as a form of perception: "Other effects only point out their causes in an oblique manner; but the testimony of men does it directly, and is to be consider'd as an image as well as an effect" (T, 113). As a principle of method, testimony is to be accepted as true unless there are good reasons not to accept it, as there are with inconsistent testimony, testimony incompatible with contrary but equally plausible testimony, testimony incompatible with established regularities (whether natural, moral, or historical), and testimony that is clearly self-serving. Testimony that has passed these and other more refined critical tests yields knowledge of the past that is like what those at the time would have experienced (EU, 116). The goal of the critical historical imagination is to yield vicarious observations of the past: "A man acquainted with history may, in some respect, be said to have lived from the beginning of the world, and to have been making continual additions to his stock of knowledge in every century" (E, 561). The historical past is, at the very least, what the historian would have observed had he been there. I have said that these are covering-law observations because they must conform to the set of lawlike regularities available to the historian. Critical history necessarily occupies the perspective of a scientific spectator, and so Hume can write that the "chief use" of history is that of "furnishing us with materials from which we may form our observations and become acquainted with the regular springs of human action and behaviour" (EU, 83).

But the scientific perspective is an external one. History is part of moral philosophy, and the historian must interpret events in the light of their moral causes: the reasons historical agents had for doing what they did. This means that he must not only strive to understand the past as it would have appeared had he been there; he must also try to view it from the point of view of those who lived through it. We may call this the covering-reason perception of the past. And it is just this that Collingwood and other adherents to the doctrine of *verstehen* take to be the defining mark of historical inquiry. But neither covering-law nor covering-reason perceptions capture what is unique about history. Both concepts are tenseless and can, logically, be instantiated by anyone at any time. The former perception, as Hume points out, does not suffice to distinguish history from other sciences which study "particular facts"—such sciences as "chronology, geography, and astronomy" (EU, 164). The latter perception does not suffice to distinguish history from the other moral sciences. Both are necessary conditions of historical inquiry, but more is needed.

Hume supplies the deficit by bringing out the narrative features of historical observation: "In reality, what more agreeable entertainment to the mind, than to be transported into the remotest ages of the world, and to observe human society, in its infancy, making the first faint essays towards the arts and sciences; to see the policy of government, and the civility of conversation refining by degrees, and every thing which is ornamental to human life advancing towards its perfection? To remark the rise, progress, declension, and final extinction of the most flourishing empires; the virtues which contributed to their greatness, and the vices which drew on their ruin? In short, to see all the human race, from the beginning of time, pass, as it were, in review before us, appearing in their true colours, without any of those disguises which, during their lifetime, so much perplexed the judgment of the beholders" (E, 560). Here the historian is not taking a tenseless view of things; his perception is rooted in an awareness of his own unique position in tensed time. Indeed, what is interesting about his perception is that it is a privileged one: he is viewing past events not merely as he would had he been there but from the temporally later position he in fact occupies. Nor is he merely trying to gain an internal understanding of the past as it appeared to those who lived through it. On the contrary, his unique temporal perspective on the past yields a perception which the historical agents, in principle, could not have had. To perceive historical events "in their true colours" is precisely not to view them as historical agents did; nor is it to view them as a tenseless spectator would.

This conception of historical significance is a special case of the narrative associations of the imagination discussed in chapter 5. Narrative significance is read into past events by viewing them in the light of later events where both sets of events are in the spectator's past. Our primordial perception of the world is narratively structured. We may abstract tenseless concepts out of narrative concepts, but even these are embedded in some narrative context so that the world of common life remains very much a system of stories or narrative associations. A story that frames narrative significance may, as a whole, have narrative significance as part of a larger story and that, in turn, may have significance as part of an even larger story. Historical perceptions of the world are narratively structured, but Hume does not treat all narrative perceptions as historical. A historical narrative would be governed by an overarching story that orders all the other stories and so brings historical unity into common life.

As we have already observed and will have occasion to comment on more fully, Hume rejected the notion of a providential philosophy of history. God, for Hume, is thought of tenselessly and is neither the author of nor a participant in history. Historical order is mind-dependent in roughly the way moral order and aesthetic order are.[18] History is the result of temporally reflective ideas and passions ordered by the historian's "design" (EUH, 33). History, then, is not a structure in the world to be discovered by the historian, it is internal to a certain point of view of the world and would not exist at all if people did not adopt that point of view. The point of view in question is not considered by Hume to be relative to this or that historian; it is a point of view written into the very idea of history, so that a failure to adopt that point of view

is a failure to perceive the world "historically." The grand story-line
that, for Hume, critically orders all the other stories is the story of the
"improvements of the human mind" (E, 560). Hume never argues explicitly for this story line as opposed to others. He takes it for granted
that it is the received historical theme of that elite, cosmopolitan community to which all his works are addressed: "the wise and learned,"
"all reasonable people," and "the *party* of humankind" (EU, 125, 110;
EM, 275). The cosmopolitan theme is not only a point of view projected from this community, it is a constituent of the community itself.
The community would cease to be what it is if that story were no
longer told.

## BARBARIANS AND THE IDEA OF HISTORY

To appreciate more fully the structure of this universal story line, it
will be helpful to consider it against the background of Collingwood's
criticism that Hume's conception of history is antihistorical. The criticism, we may recall, is that Hume read eighteenth-century values into
the past and could not understand an age in its own terms. I have
shown that this interpretation is simply false. Hume's doctrine of moral
causes is, in fact, the earliest statement of the modern doctrine of *verstehen* or what Collingwood calls the reenactment of past thoughts.
(Here as elsewhere Hume turns out to be holding the very doctrine he
is criticized for not recognizing; but it is surely ironic that Collingwood
should fail to reenact properly Hume's own thoughts which, on this
matter, were so close to his own.) Yet there is something to Collingwood's criticism, for there are what appear to be some extremely
provincial passages in Hume's writings, the most telling of which occurs in the first volume of the *History:* "The curiosity entertained by all
civilized nations, of inquiring into the exploits and adventures of their
ancestors, commonly excites a regret that the history of remote ages
should always be so much involved in obscurity, uncertainty, and contradiction. Ingenious men, possessed of leisure, are apt to push their
researches beyond the period in which literary monuments are framed
or preserved; without reflecting, that the history of past events is immediately lost or disfigured when entrusted to memory and oral tradition,
and that the adventures of barbarous nations, even if they were recorded, could afford little or no entertainment to men born in a more
cultivated age. The convulsions of a civilized state usually compose the
most instructive and most interesting part of its history; but the sudden, violent, and unprepared revolutions incident to barbarians, are so
much guided by caprice, and terminate so often in cruelty, that they

disgust us by the uniformity of their appearance; and it is rather fortunate for letters that they are buried in silence and oblivion" (H, I, i, 1).

This is as antihistorical a statement, from Collingwood's point of view, as one could wish. But that is not all. Hume refuses to write the history of the pre-Roman Britons from their own point of view, partly because of a lack of good records but also because of the barbarous and unworthy character of the subject: "Neglecting, therefore, all traditions or rather tales, concerning the more early history of Britain, we shall only consider the state of the inhabitants as it appeared to the Romans on their invasion of this country: we shall briefly run over the events which attended the conquest made by that empire, as belonging more to Roman than British story: we shall hasten through the obscure and uninteresting period of Saxon annals; and shall reserve a more full narration for those times, when the truth is both so well ascertained and so complete, as to promise entertainment and instruction to the reader" (H, I, i, 2). And Hume, indeed, sketches out the history of the Saxons with a very broad brush: "We shall not attempt to trace any higher the origin of those princes and nations. It is evident what fruitless labour it must be to search, in those barbarous and illiterate ages, for the annals of a people, when their first leaders, known in any true history, were believed by them to be the fourth in descent from a fabulous deity, or from a man exalted by ignorance into that character" (ibid., 14). The impatience with barbarians is absolute: "It is almost impossible, and quite needless, to be more particular in relating the transactions of the East Angles. What instruction or entertainment can it give the reader, to hear a long bead-roll of barbarous names, Egric, Annas, Ethelbert, Ethelwald, Aldulf, Elfwald, Beorne, Ethelred, who successively murdered, expelled, or inherited from each other, and obscurely filled the throne of that Kingdom?" (ibid., 36).

These passages reveal a headlong flight from *verstehen*. The pre-Roman and post-Roman Britons are cast into historical outer darkness. Hume offers two reasons: there is not adequate evidence to tell their story, and the story is not worth telling. These propositions are, as we shall see, intimately connected. An exploration of them will serve to bring out important features of Hume's conception of the historical.

According to Hume's theory of historical evidence, anything in the present can, in principle, count as evidence for the past. Historians link together present existences with hypotheses about the past via lawlike regularities and moral causes. The arguments establishing these links can, in principle, be tested by anyone at any time. Given this conception of evidence, it is surprising to hear Hume complain that there is very little in the way of reliable records about British history until the sixteenth century, for by this he meant not only that the number of records is small but that the testimony of those who kept records is untrustworthy. From the sixteenth century on, "This island possesses many ancient historians of good credit, as well as many historical monuments" (H, II, xxiii, 507). This is just what Collingwood called the "scissors and paste" conception of historical method: that the task of the historian is to paste together a narrative out of the testimonies of authorities. But in Hume's theory of historical evidence, what is important about a record is not whether it is true but whether something can be inferred from it. And this is, for the most part, Hume's practice as a historian. Especially from the Tudor volumes on, the treatment of records is what we would expect of Hume: the work of a dectective forcing the records to yield up their secrets in the light of the authority, not of a veridical witness, but of his own autonomous reasoning: "though the evidence must be drawn from a source wide of the ordinary historians, it becomes only the more authentic on that account" (H, IV, app. iii, 345). To a lesser degree, this conception is practiced in the ancient medieval volumes. Thus Hume is able to extort some truth from the fables about King Arthur: poets who were "the sole historians . . . among the Britons, have commonly some foundation for their wildest exaggerations" (H, I, i, 19). Certain structures of the Saxon constitution can be known independently of ancient historians: "Though we are not informed of any of these circumstances by ancient historians, they are so much founded on the nature of things, that we may admit them as a necessary and infallible consequence of the situation of the kingdom during those ages" (H, I, app. i, 161). Structures of Saxon law can be known independently of testimony or even of records of "public statutes"; they can be inferred from "the small incidents in history, by particular customs, and sometimes by the reason and nature of things" (ibid., 165).

But despite his theory of historical evidence and his practice as a historian, there is no doubt that Hume is not entirely emancipated from the "scissors and paste" conception of history, especially in regard to pre-sixteenth-century British history. This is due not so much to Hume's conception of evidence as to his inability to sympathetically work through the moral causes behind barbarian actions. To fail to recover the moral causes of the Saxons is to fail to understand their actions, and this, in turn, makes it virtually impossible to interpret, as evidence, the documents that remain. Since history is part of moral philosophy, to interpret something as historical evidence is to interpret it as evidence for the existence of ideas and passions of reflection, i.e., as moral causes. But if the historian has logically eliminated these causes by a judgment that they are unworthy of consideration, then there is nothing that the surviving documents can be interpreted as evidence *for*, and so they cannot really be viewed as "documents" at all. This is the conceptual point behind Hume's metaphorical claim that it would be better if barbarian documents were "buried in silence and oblivion." Is Hume arbitrary in his conceptual elimination of barbarian moral cuases and hence of evidence for their past? The following considerations may serve to illuminate Hume's position.

1. The standards of historical thinking are, like all the conventions of common life, constituted by a certain point of view. The point of view of the historian is a narrative one. Narratives register the historian's passions and ideas of reflection about his location in tensed time, and so are necessarily temporally provincial. So far, then, historical relativism reigns. But Hume tries to bring order into this relativism by the cosmopolitan idea that the governing story line for all specifically historical narratives is the story of the progress of the human mind. This is the story line projected by and constitutive of that enlightened community to whom Hume's works are addressed. Hume's narrative concept of history has built into it the idea of a master story line with the authority to order and evaluate all lesser narratives: "History, also, being a collection of facts which are multiplying without end, is obliged to adopt such arts of abridgment [like other sciences], to retain the more material events, and to drop all the minute circumstances, which are only interesting during the time" (H, II, xii, 1). Given this concept, ontological selections must be made about which actions are historical and, hence, which documents are worthy to survive. Any artifact produced in the present can be used by future historians as evidence about our present (which is their past). But not all contemporary artifacts can be preserved, and the selection of those to be destroyed is made by us in the light of some story we tell of ourselves. There is no difference in principle between the destruction of contemporary artifacts (potential evidence for future historians) and Hume's conceptual elimination of pre-Roman and Saxon documents. In both cases, a narrative principle of evaluation is necessary and in both cases the documents are logically "buried in silence and oblivion." We can perhaps raise questions about Hume's choice of a master story line and about the lesser principles of selection ordered by it. What we cannot do is suppose we are free of a master story line. A selection is made, the only question being whether it is made self-consciously and with principles that are in some way defensible.

2. Hume's choice of the theme that history is the story of the progress of the human mind is not an arbitrary one. First of all, there is negative support for it in Hume's rejection of its main competitor, the providential theme: that history is the story of man's creation, fall, redemption, and judgment. In the first *Enquiry*, Hume deployed two

arguments against this view: there can be no scientific evidence from the observation of nature to believe in a providential God; and there can be no historical evidence to believe that such a being ever has acted or could act in history since any such intervention would be a miracle, an event incompatible with the lawlike conception of historical evidence. There is no evidence, then, that God is presiding over history. God does, indeed, have a relation (though a mysterious one) to the natural world as the ultimate explanation of all observable regularities. But he has no direct causal relation to the historical world. Nor does Hume view the historical world as governed by causal laws of its own, so that the whole exhibits a process directed to some final goal. He did not think there were any regularities governing human action that could be expected to hold beyond the period from which they were taken. But most important, Hume does not think of history as a *process* in the world that could be covered by laws. History is a certain point of view on things, a certain ordering of temporally reflective ideas and passions governed by the historian's "design" (EUH, 37). History is not a process that historians discover; it is something they do—the activity of telling stories about *their* past. History is presided over by Clio, not by empirical laws.

3. The historian's "design" is determined by his evaluation of his present, in the light of which significance is read into his past. Hume judged his own age to have been one of progress over the past in respect to knowledge and humanity. This implied a continuity between the present and past in human nature along with a full recognition of the uniqueness of the modern world. Since knowledge and humanity are tenseless values that, logically, can be instantiated at any time, the judgment that the present contains or fails to contain these values to some degree is not arbitrary. But the abstract, timeless standards which make such judgments possible can be used to make comparative judgments about the present and past, and these, in turn, can be used to support a story about the progress of the human mind and to explain how the present developed out of the past.

4. The reasons for accepting the story of progress as the master story line is not a decision to be made *in* history. That story, as we have observed, constitutes the Enlightenment community of "the judicious and knowing." It will be our story if we are part of that community, and the reasons for being a part of it are locked into the post-Pyrrhonian arguments of Book I of the *Treatise* and of the first *Enquiry*.

5. Relative to the theme that history is the story of progress, the British barbarians may be ruled out, as of no historical significance; as Hegel and other nineteenth-century philosophers of history were fond of saying, they were not a "historical" people. But why, exactly, is this

true? Why could not the barbarians be viewed as, at least, the initial stages or the opening chapters of the story of progress? Hume, of course, does not view them that way. *The History of England* begins and continues to Henry VIII not as the story of Britain but of Britain's relation to pagan and Christian Rome. Hume begins with what belongs "more to Roman than to British story." The post-Roman period is the dismal story of what happens after the collapse of civilization and the conversion of Britain by Christian Rome, an event important because it grafted Britain again to the roots of civilization. The candle of culture was kept alive during the Middle Ages, an "advantage we own entirely to the clergy of the church of Rome" (H, II, xxiii, 507). "The period in which the people of Christendom were the lowest sunk in ignorance, and consequently in disorders of every kind, may justly be fixed at the eleventh century, about the age of William the Conqueror; and from that era, the sun of science beginning to reascend, threw out many gleams of light, which preceded the full morning when letters were revived in the fifteenth century" (ibid., 508). It is at this period that we have "the prospect, both of greater certainty in our historical narrations, and of being able to present to the reader a spectacle more worthy of his attention." (ibid., 507). What is the standard of worth entailed in this narrative judgment?

The difference between civilized and barbarian men is that the latter are virtually unreflective. The barbarian man has not brought to the level of reflection, and therefore has not "methodized and corrected," the principles that structure the prereflective conventions of common life. Although the barbarian man is different from the savage, he lives close to the level of feeling: he does not understand the principles of causal judgment that structure his own thought about the world; he has only a dim understanding of the principles of justice and civil society, not to mention the more refined principles of economics and politics. Lacking this sort of social self-knowledge ("that science and civility which has so close a connection with virtue and humanity"), he lacks the cosmopolitan idea of himself as a human being, and thus is morally deficient as well. So conceived, the barbarian, like the savage, is capable of very little self-conscious rational activity. The barbarian falls outside the scope of history not so much because he is engaged in the wrong activity (one rejected by the historian's interests) but because what he does so little resembles activity of any kind. The Humean historian must explain the actions of historical agents by rethinking in his own mind the rational activity that is the inside or moral cause of the action. But it is impossible to rethink rational activity where there is none or where knowledge of it is impossible. Thus it is impossible to rethink for ourselves the rationale behind the natural processes God has produced in the universe (as Copernicus, Kepler, Galileo, Boyle, and Newton saw themselves as doing). For us, then, natural processes must remain an ultimate mystery. This is not true of history, which is the result of the rational (critically reflective) activity of men. Being men ourselves, we are capable of entering into the moral causes of historical activity. But there can be no history of a natural process: our understanding there is external and, therefore, is and must remain of the constant-conjunction sort.

Hume conceives of the behavior of savages and, to a lesser extent, of barbarians also as virtually a natural process. Such peoples can no more be said to have a history than can bees or moths. Parts of Hume's justification for not entering into the Saxon mind is that there was little *mind* to enter into: "Even the great learning and vigorous imagination of Milton sunk under the weight; and this author scruples not to declare, that the skirmishes of kites or crows as much merited a particular narrative, as the confused transactions and battles of the Saxon Heptarchy" (ibid., I, i, 22). The revolutions of a civilized state are usually "the most instructive and most interesting part of its history" (ibid., 1). This is because civilized revolutions involve reflections on principles which we can enter into ourselves, whereas barbarian revolutions are like cyclical animal processes and "disgust us by the uniformity of their appearance" (ibid.). The cyclical character of barbaric behavior is the background against which the medieval volumes are composed: "The ancient history of England is nothing but a catalogue of reversals: every thing is in fluctuation and movement: one faction is continually undoing what was established by another" (H, II, xvii, 304). The deposition of Richard II is unfavorably compared with that of James II: "All the circumstances of this event, compared to those which attended the late revolution in 1688, show the difference between a great and civilized nation, deliberately vindicating its established privileges, and a turbulent and barbarous aristocracy, plunging headlong from the extremes of one faction into those of another" (ibid., 313–14).

The suggestion from these passages, then, is that barbarians are excluded from history not because they are not civilized and therefore are, aesthetically, not part of the story. They are excluded because, in not being civilized, they lack fully developed rational interiors, and so it is impossible for the historian to carry out his proper task of working through, in his own mind, the rationale behind their actions. There are, of course, exceptions to this rule: Alfred the Great was a wonder in a barbarian age (ibid., I, ii, 70).

The difference between the barbarian and civilized man is (in history) an ontological one and sets up, in the nature of things, a barrier to *verstehen*. But there are also moral barriers to entering sympathetically

241

the rational interiors of other minds, whether civilized or not. The point is made in "Of the Standard of Taste." The artist no less than the historian must be capable of overcoming the provincial tastes of his own age and of entering the thoughts and sentiments that are the rational interiors of works of art from another age: "Must we throw aside the pictures of our ancestors, because of their ruffs and farthingales?" (E, 252). The easiest thoughts to rethink in our own minds are "speculative opinions of any kind," however strange they may be: "Whatever speculative errors may be found in the polite writings of any age or country. . . . There needs but a certain turn of thought or imagination to make us enter into all the opinions which then prevailed, and relish the sentiments or conclusions derived from them" (E, 253). But the "case is not the same with moral principles as with speculative opinions" (ibid.). It is extremely difficult to enter sympathetically into the norms of a contrary morality: "I cannot, nor is it proper I should, enter into such sentiments . . . and where a man is confident of the rectitude of that moral standard by which he judges, he is justly jealous of it, and will not pervert the sentiments of his heart for a moment, in complaisance to any writer whatsoever" (E, 252–53). This is not to say that the historian may not "excuse" actions because of the manners and prejudices of the age. What he cannot do is "enter into all the opinions which then prevailed, and *relish the sentiments or conclusions derived from them*" (E, 253, emphasis mine).

The loose identification of "sentiment" with "conclusion" is appropriate, given Hume's view of what it is to understand a moral cause. To understand a moral cause is to have an internal grasp of an agent's action, and this means working through a piece of practical reasoning the conclusion of which would be the idea of the action. This idea is necessarily an idea of reflection and by the principle of sympathy will be attended with the appropriate passions or sentiments of reflection. Moreover, the whole process, we recall, is governed by that "impious maxim of the ancients," according to which to understand the moral cause of an action is to see how it is directed to some good the agent had in mind. Now the good that explains may be objectively good or what an agent mistakenly thinks is good. Hume may be saying either (a) that we cannot enter into those acts of practical reasoning that are structured by what the historian's own moral principles rule out as a good but which the agent mistakenly thinks is a good; or (b) we cannot enter into those acts which are in pursuit of no good at all either from the agent's or the historian's point of view. These would be acts done not for the sake of what is thought, however confusedly, to be some good but for the sake of evil: acts of sheer malice and perversity. It is this sort of action, I think, that Hume has in mind; the kind of action described in

(a) is one that we can in principle enter into, the only barrier being emotional. But the barrier Hume has in fact erected seems much stronger than that.

Certainly there is nothing in Hume's philosophy to rule out the possibility of malicious acts. They are, of course, an impossibility under that impious maxim of the ancients. There the Platonic principle that knowledge is virtue reigns: all apparently evil actions are due to ignorance of the good, not to a failure to pursue it. But Hume is a modern philosopher: a priori, anything can cause anything. It cannot be an analytic truth for him, as it is for Plato, that there are no malicious acts. Whether there is evil in history is and must be an empirical question. But if there are any evil actions, they cannot be understood by reference to moral causes: we cannot have an internal understanding of their rationales because evil is not a rationale for something. Our understanding of evil actions must remain external, determined entirely by the constant-conjunction criterion of the moderns.

It is worth observing that Hume's discussion of the limits of sympathetic understanding is placed in the framework of the "celebrated controversy concerning ancient and modern learning; where we often find the one side excusing any seeming absurdity in the ancients from the manners of the age, and the other refusing to admit this excuse, or at least admitting it only as an apology for the author, not for the performance" (E, 252). The partisans of the ancients are able to excuse past actions by uncovering their moral causes. If *verstehen* were the only way of understanding actions, then, in the end, every action would be excusable since every action must be viewed as directed toward some good, however obscure it may be to the historian or to the agent himself. Just this view is framed in von Ranke's famous dictum that all ages are equal in the sight of God: to understand all is to forgive all. The partisans of the moderns, however, think of themselves as having standards by which past actions can be judged, as it were, from the outside. Actions rejected by such judgments are thought of as having interiors which are not *worthy* of being sympathetically entered. Hume thought there was some truth on both sides of the dispute and he, characteristically, sought to fix "the proper boundaries . . . between the contending parties" (E, 252). His own solution was to raise a moral barrier beyond which the historian's sympathetic imagination could not and should not go.

Combining this moral limit with the narrative conception of history yields Hume's position on the limits of historical understanding. The narrative perception of past actions is necessarily an external one where the significance of an action is viewed in the light of later events which the agent could not have known. This temporally provincial perspective must be modified, however, by an abstract, tenseless moral perspective. All genuinely "historical" narratives are morally structured, and so, although tensed, have a tenseless dimension; hence the importance Hume gives to evaluations of moral character. He considered the historical form of thinking to be the best for learning how to evaluate character, an exercise which itself promotes virtue. Poets, can picture virtue in a compelling way, "but as they address themselves entirely to the passions, they often become advocates for vice" (E, 561). A man of affiars is "more apt to consider the characters of men, as they have relation to his interest, than as they stand in themselves" (E, 562). Philosophers "are apt to bewilder themselves in the subtility of their speculations; and we have seen some go so far as to deny the reality of all moral distinction" (E, 561). Thus Machiavelli, as a political philosopher, justifies poisoning, assassination, and perjury as proper means of politics, but in his history of Florence, when he speaks as a historian in his particular narrations, he shows "so keen an indignation against vice, and so warm an approbation of virtue" (E, 562). The possibility of "this combination of historians in favour of virtue" is due entirely to the narrative form of thought, which combines the timeless and the temporal, the universal and the concrete. Men of affairs are blinded by the passions arising from their particular interests. The philosopher transcends this particularity but only by a "general abstract view of objects" where his interests are those of the logic of his speculative system; this "leaves the mind so cold and unmoved, that . . . he scarce feels the difference between vice and virtue" (ibid.). But, because of its narrative form, "History keeps in a just medium between these extremes, and places the objects in their true point of view. The writers of history, as well as the readers, are sufficiently interested in the characters and events, to have a lively sentiment of blame or praise: and, at the same time, have no particular interest or concern to pervert their judgment" (ibid.).

The moral structure of historical narratives is manifest also in the very language Hume uses in the *History* to describe events. Where we would expect a purely factual description of an event, Hume often gives a description having factual form but a normative content. The moral content is sometimes grounded in the historical agent's point of view (they "scattered about the sacred vases" [H, IV, xxxviii, 20]), and sometimes in the historian's point of view ("Argyle, who, by subtleties and compliances, partly led and partly was governed by this wild faction" [H, V, lx, 409]). But the peculiar style of the *History* is to unite these two aspects in a description which is formally from the agent's point of view but is artfully shaped by the historian's value judgments. Concerning Cromwell's Commonwealth, Hume writes: "All Europe stood astonished to see a nation, so turbulent and unruly, who, for some doubtful encroachments on their privileges, had dethroned and murdered an excellent prince, descended from a long line of monarchs, now at last subdued and reduced to slavery by one who, a few years before, was no better than a private gentleman, whose name was not known in the nation, and who was little regarded even in that low sphere to which he had always been confined" (ibid., 439).

Finally, the ethically laden character of historical narratives is revealed in Hume's conception of the dignity of history. Because history is the story of the progress of the human mind and the critical understanding of that progress, it is a high, solemn, and noble inquiry. The historian must approach his narrative with the respect and moral rectitude worthy of the subject. For this reason some events are excluded as falling beneath the dignity of history. Thus Hume refuses to explore in any detail James I's weakness for his favorites: "History charges herself willingly with a relation of the great crimes, and still more with that of the great virtues, of mankind; but she appears to fall from her dignity, when necessitated to dwell on such frivolous events and ignoble personages" (ibid., IV, xlvi, 428).

Actions that are part of the master story line (the story of "the improvements of the human mind") are worthy of being sympathetically understood. The actions of savages and barbarians either fall outside the scope of history proper, or, if included, are viewed externally and are significant only because of their relation to authentic historical actions; the action of the early Britons, for example, have significance only in relation to the civilizing forces of pagan and Christian Rome.

Hume's rejection of the barbarians does not show that his conception of history is antihistorical. On the contrary, the rejection follows from a well-reasoned conception of what history is. History has narrative form, and all narratives will be temporally provincial in the way the criticism finds unacceptable. The problem of historical inquiry is that of placing "objects in their true point of view" within narrative frameworks which are, themselves, shifting in time (E, 562). All that is necessary for objectivity is that the Humean narrative conception of history enable historians to criticize their own narrative judgments in the light of evidence. Hume's conception of history satisfies this condition. Only actions within a genuine historical framework are worthy of being sympathetically understood. But the only way to criticize the shape of the narrative framework is by showing that there are actions with interiors that are worthy of being included but that the framework excludes. In principle, this can always be done because moral philosophy, as such, is not tied down to narrative form: moral philosophers, through abstract, tenseless principles, can sympathetically understand any action that has a rational interior, however historically alien it may appear. This knowledge may always be used to critically modify or to reject a particular narrative framework. Using just this canon, Hume came to see that his own scissors-and-paste handling of ancient Britain was unperceptive. He wrote a lengthy review praising Robert Henry's *History of Great Britain* (1771–73), which covered in some detail that very period. Henry was able to enter the barbarian period where Hume could not: that period has "perplexed the acuteness of our most philosophical and accomplished historians" (RH, 379). Inquiries "of the antiquarian kind," Hume observes, "form four fifths of his work" (ibid., 388). But just because of these skillful labors, he has been able to shed light on "a period which has formerly been regarded as very obscure, *viz.* from the arrival of the Saxons in 449, to the landing of William Duke of Normandy in 1066. In those dark ages, this island produced few writers of history, and these few were only obscure monks of little learning and less taste. . . . It is, indeed, wonderful what an instructive, and even entertaining book, Dr. Henry has been able to compose from such unpromising materials!" (ibid., 378). Hume gained an appreciation and respect for "the science studied in England in the seventh century" (ibid., 381). But most important, he gained an internal understanding of barbarian life as a whole: "we admire the *oddness* of their manners, customs, and opinions, and are transported, as it were, into a new world" (ibid., 378).

# 9
# Correcting Narrative Judgments

New parties arose, under the appelation of *Whig* and *Tory*,
which have continued ever since to confound and distract
our government. To determine the nature of these parties
is perhaps one of the most difficult problems that can be
met with, and is a proof that history may contain
questions as uncertain as any to be found in the most
abstract sciences.

Hume's "Of the Parties of Great Britain"

## THE HISTORICITY OF PHILOSOPHY

Criticism of the *History* as antihistorical is often accompanied by the
same charge against the philosophical works. If one considers Hume as
a phenomenalist or even as the would-be Newton of the mind, this
interpretation is plausible. But it should be apparent now that Hume's
conception of philosophy is deeply historical. The theory of ideas is
built around a narrative relation between present and past existences.
The imagination has an essential narrative structure, and the moral
world that is constituted by the imagination is narratively ordered. The
moral world is a set of conventions which have developed unreflectively
over time. The task of philosophy is to bring to explicit awareness the
standards implicit in these conventions (EU 162). In this Hume agrees
with the Platonic and modern rationalistic tradition that philosophy is
to make explicit the standards implied in our judgments about reality.
But he differs in thinking of these standards as neither timeless nor
innate. They were hammered out, unreflectively, over long periods of
time as constituents of the process of common life, and cannot be
known without an understanding of their history. Here, too, the fundamental maxim that ideas follow impressions holds. The idea or rationale of the convention can be grasped only after it is established, and

247

this involves understanding both its narrative significance and its moral causes. Nor is this all. Once the standards have been brought to light, they must be "methodized and corrected" by timeless standards which are themselves abstractions from some provincial narrative context.

Since philosophers must use abstract, timeless standards, there is an inescapably ahistorical content to the critical convention of philosophy. But abstract philosophical principles can never be totally emancipated from their narrative origins. This is not only because historical understanding is required to discover a standard internal to a convention in the first place but also because abstract principles are vacuous and must be given some historical content, having independent authority, before they can be applied to the world. Otherwise the standard may apply to anything or to nothing. This is the main lesson that emerges from Hume's criticism of philosophy: the standards constituting common life have an authority that is *independent* of philosophy. Philosophers may criticize and reform these standards but only on condition that they recognize their independent authority; failure to do so yields total Pyrrhonism.

Historical understanding, then, is built into the very structure of post-Pyrrhonian philosophy. The philosopher, properly conceived, is himself a historian, firmly rooted in some narrative order and subject to its authority. But by virtue of abstraction, he is also able to transcend this order, to discover its principles, and to critically modify them, but he can never completely escape the authority of some narrative order.

In this view of philosophy, we should expect every Humean explication of a concept to contain a history which would enable us to understand how the concept came to be and the historical limits that must be placed on any critical reconstruction of it. Throughout Hume's writings this demand is apparent but is not fully satisfied. Consider the convention of making causal judgments. The possibility of such a convention is grounded in a universal disposition of human nature: experienced constant conjunctions trigger judgments about productive causal powers. So far the convention of causal judgment is a timeless structure, and, indeed, one that we share with animals. But though instinct be the causal foundation of causal judgment, the judgments themselves have a structure which is the result of ideas of reflection, and these have a rationale of their own which can be understood only by understanding their history. This history is sketched out in *The Natural History of Religion*, the first *Enquiry*, and in the *Treatise*. The convention of causal judgment is first raised from the instinctual to the reflective level by religion. The first theoretical causal judgments were polytheistic judgments about invisible divine powers. As polytheism developed into theism, the idea of many powers merged into the idea of one. Philosophy grew out of the theoretical shift from polytheism to theism, and began to view causal powers as forces independent of the Deity. Out of this perspective grew the conventions of metaphysics and eventually of modern science. With the advent of modern science, men have acquired the habit of making causal judgments independently of religion; nevertheless, owing to a propensity of our nature, we are compelled to view our isolated inductive judgments as part of an ultimate system structured in some way by "*mind* or *intelligence*" (D, 217). The idea of "philosophical theism" is mainly a development of modern times and is the possession of only those who have benefited from the Newtonian vision that the universe is a systematic whole and who have emancipated themselves from the superstitions of traditional religion and metaphysics.

As an order of instinct, the convention of causal judgment is universal, timeless, and without a history; but as an order of reflection, it has a history which begins with the superstitious judgments of polytheism and ends with the refined judgments of philosophical theism, which is the deepest and most reflective achievement of the convention of causal thinking. Throughout, Hume stresses two things: except for the very last stages, the transitions in the progressive movement are due not to rational reflection but to the grossest superstition; there is no necessary linear development—the lower, more superstitious forms are not entirely overcome but erupt, unexpectedly, in later forms (as in the case of the modern rationalistic doctrine of the "sole efficacy" of the Deity [EU, 73n]). Religion is internal to the reflective convention of making causal judgments, and there is the constant threat that superstition may, in some form or other, break out and twist the convention to its own ends or even bring it back altogether to a primitive state.

The same pattern of explication is to be found in Hume's analysis of the conventions of justice and of political order. That there are such conventions at all is due to tenselessly conceived structures: the nature of the world (scarce goods) and certain original human propensities (limited benevolence). But beyond this we cannot understand the principles of justice and politics without some grasp of the history of how men have become aware of these principles in their own experience and what they have thought about their significance. This would be the story of man's progressive self-awareness of the principles of civil society, and would be the story of civilization. The abstract story line is to be found in the *Treatise* and the second *Enquiry;* it is fleshed out somewhat in the *Essays,* and is concretely presented in the *History,* one main theme of which is the story of how the principles of civility became established in Britain. [1]

Similar remarks could be made about Hume's understanding of the arts: he refers to tenselessly conceived dispositions in human nature that ground the possibility both of the arts and of a history of the progress men have made in constituting part of the moral world by critically reflecting on their own artistic activity. Sketches of the historical part of the exercise are to be found in the *Essays* as well as in the sections entitled "Appendix" and "Miscellaneous Transactions" placed after the treatment of significant periods in the *History* where Hume pauses to discuss the historical development of law, arms, commerce, industry, finance, manners, literature, etc. Mossner has observed that if these sections were arranged in chronological order, we should have in rudimentary outline the first modern histories of many of these topics.[2] C. N. Stockton has observed that the *History* not only employs the theories of economics worked out in the *Essays* but also contains some of the earliest contributions to the idea of a history of economic theory.[3]

Hume was aware that philosophy (the convention of critically reflecting on all conventions) itself has a history, the understanding of which is necessary for understanding philosophical activity and fixing its limits. The history of philosophy is internal to the history of religion. For this reason changes in religious consciousness have brought about changes in the convention of philosophy. Hume points out, for instance, that the ancient conception of philosophy is quite different from the modern one, owing to a difference in religious consciousness (T, 272; E, 58–62). Philosophy under modern conceptual conditions poses special problems that did not exist for the ancients. What Hume thinks these problems are and how they developed historically is discussed in some detail in the remaining chapters.

We may view Hume's entire philosophy as demanding historical understanding of the conventions that constitute the concepts of causality, morality, art, religion, and the like, the concepts that are the objects of philosophical explication. This demand, however, is fulfilled only in the form of outlines, brief historical sketches, and hints. Nor is this surprising. The demand was a new one in the history of philosophy, and Hume did not have full command of it. Hegel was the first really to exploit the idea. His conception of an encyclopedia of the philosophical sciences requires historical understanding to be internal to philosophical explication, and Hegel himself made important contributions to the history of art, religion, law, logic, and philosophy.

But a historical conception of philosophy is not the armchair affair of the traditional rationalistic conception. The historically governed philosopher is not free to range with authority over the whole spectrum of human experience; or, if he does, it must be with some diffidence and skepticism about his own abstract conclusions. He cannot with Aristotle reject history as of lesser importance than philosophy and poetry merely because the latter frames abstract universal relations; nor can he accept Descartes' ideal of philosophic method which presents the true philosopher as having a mind completely purged of the past.[4] He must take narrative time seriously as a structure internal to the concepts he is out to critically understand. Ideally, this means that to do philosophy properly one must do historical work, that is, one must actually write history, a task requiring specialized knowledge and, in the nature of the case, one limited to a certain segment of time. Few philosophers have viewed philosophy and history as internally related disciplines. Vico, Hegel, Marx, Croce, and Collingwood come readily to mind. To these we must add Hume, whose *History of England* should be read as an attempt to throw light on a fundamental problem posed by his philosophy: the problem of correcting narrative judgments.

Let us see how this problem arises. Understanding, for Hume, is a matter of making reasonable judgments. The standards governing these judgments have been worked out over time in the relatively unreflective process of common life. Philosophical understanding is a matter of uncovering the standards implied in this process and of correcting and systematizing them. The judgments of common life are concrete, particular, and provincial; those of philosophy are abstract, universal, and cosmopolitan. Yet philosophical judgments are parasitic upon the authority of those very provincial judgments of common life which it seeks to correct. It is these judgments that provide content and criteria of applicability for abstract and otherwise empty philosophical judgments. Now a universal feature of the imagination is its narrative ordering of things. The original standards of common life are narratively structured, and since temporal provinciality is, as it were, the ultimate provinciality, it is precisely this narrative structure that the philosopher must overcome if he is to satisfy the legitimate demands of the ultimacy and autonomy principles and achieve a more universal and cosmopolitan perspective.

In the case of natural philosophy, the transcendence is virtually total, for the natural world is conceived as a tenseless ordering of spatial and temporal events. The natural philosopher must ignore narrative order. The moral world, however, is essentially tensed and narrative: men live, and move, and have their being within the context of narrative associations. The moral philosopher, then, cannot bracket out narrative structure without bracketing out the moral world itself. He can understand the narrative world and himself only by learning to think narratively. Consequently, there must be a standard for correcting narrative judgments. This is not to say, however, that the moral philosopher must think only in a narrative way. He must still try to achieve a tenseless and universal perspective on the moral world by reference to whatever abstract principles of morals, aesthetics, religion, politics, law, and the like are defensible. But none of these abstract principles are defensible unless they are abstractions from and are applicable to some narrative order which has been already properly understood, that is, understood through narrative judgments critically determined by the standards of correct narrative thinking.

The *History* was written backwards, beginning with the volumes on the Stuarts, which are by far the most important. The main problem of these volumes is to teach Whigs and Tories, but especially the former, how to think correctly about the nature and authority of the British constitution by working through the history of how it came to be. The British constitution was not simply an object of thought for Hume and his contemporaries, it was a set of narrative standards determining their own thought about objects. It seemed to Hume that much thinking about these standards was confused. The volumes on the Stuarts are an exercise on how to think about the nature and limits of narrative judgments. Since correcting narrative judgments is an essential part of philosophical understanding, as Hume conceives it, the Stuart volumes should be considered an integral part of Hume's philosophical work. This is not true, or at least not to the same degree, of the other volumes. The reason is that Hume thought the historical process which led to the constitutional settlement of his time began roughly with the advent of the Stuarts. Thinking through the rationale and limits of that process is an act of self-knowledge, and so has philosophical significance. The minds of the Puritans and Royalists were narratively internal to his own mind. He could not understand his own mind without understanding theirs. Hume never again so deeply penetrated the mind of a historical period as he did in the Stuart volumes. As he carries the *History* back to Roman Britain, his perception becomes increasingly external, and historical agents progressively lose their interiors until, at the very end, they reduce to a "bead role of barbarous names" and British history itself vanishes into Roman history.

What corrections, then, were needed in narrative judgments about the British constitution? The most significant error was due to the Whig party, which had dominated the political order for seventy years and had managed to make its conception of British history the conventional wisdom (MOL, 8). The elements of this ritualistic Whiggism were: a celebration of the constitution as (1) a regular "plan of liberty," (2) as the most perfect system of liberty compatible with human nature that the world has known, and (3) by comparison with which the constitutions of France and Italy are "Turkish," and the people under them "unthinking slaves." (4) The British system of liberty is not something new but is part of the national character, and can be traced back to the

Saxon forests. (5) The history of Britain has, therefore, been largely the story of defending the "ancient constitution" against usurpation by monarchs, papists, and antipatriotic factions of all kinds but especially in recent times by the Stuart monarchy. (6) With the Abdication of James II and the Glorious Revolution, a Protestant, liberty-loving constitution was restored: a modern reconstitution of the ancient constitution. But, (7) a new threat to the constitution has arisen in the form of court corruption. The king's right to appoint ministers has been carried beyond its proper bounds, resulting not only in an increase in the court magistracy but in an increase in court power, the appointments being made on the basis of favoritism.

At most Hume could participate in only steps (1) and (2) of this Whig ritual. And even here his own style of dance was awkward. As he worked through the history of the constitution, he became more and more embarassed about being in the dance at all, and sought to emancipate himself from "the plaguy Prejudices of Whiggism, with which I was too much infected when I began this work" (L, I, 379). He became less concerned to celebrate the British plan of liberty and more concerned to define its limits, to point out its dialectical relation to authority, and to chart the unhappy consequences that would follow if liberty were pushed beyond its proper bounds. But the difference between Hume and the Whigs was not due simply to a difference in historical interpretation. It was also and, for our purposes, most importantly, a difference over what is to count as an adequate historical interpretation. It was a philosophical difference about the *concept* of historical interpretation, and this is what gives the volumes on the Stuarts their transcendental character. They frame an attempt to understand certain events in the historical world, but they also are an attempt to say something about what it means to understand events in the historical world. They are both works *in* history and *about* history, and it is this conceptual character of the works, I think, that explains the strange reception Hume complained of: "I was assailed by one cry of reproach, disapprobation, and even detestation; English, Scotch, and Irish, Whig and Tory, Churchman and Sectary, Freethinker and Religionist, Patriot and Courtier united in their rage against the man who had presumed to shed a generous tear for the fate of Charles I and the Earl of Strafford" (MOL, 7). What the public found odd (and what Hume himself perhaps did not fully appreciate) was the new conceptual framework through which he interpreted historical events.

## THE FIRST WHIG ERROR

The first error made by the Whigs is to have read the present constitution into the remote past, as the modern articulation of the "ancient constitution." But, "It is ridiculous to consider the English constitution before that period [of the first two Stuarts] as a regular plan of liberty" (MOL, 8). Hume distinguished four constitutions in English history: "By the ancient constitution, is here meant that which prevailed before the settlement of our present plan of liberty. There was a more ancient constitution, where, though the people had perhaps less liberty than under the Tudors, yet the King had also less authority: the power of the barons was a great check upon him, and exercised great tyranny over them. But there was still a more ancient constitution, *viz.* that before the signing of the Charters, when neither the people nor the barons had any regular privileges; and the power of the government during the reign of an able prince was almost wholly in the King. The English constitution, like all others, has been in a state of continual fluctuation" (H, IV, app. iii, 345n). Throughout the *History,* Hume carries on a running battle with Whig constitutional historians, pointing out the qualitative difference between the seventeenth- and eighteenth-century settlement on behalf of liberty, "a new epoch in the constitution" (ibid., VI, lxxxi, 363), and the settlements of earlier periods. "Ideas of government change much in different times" (ibid., IV, n. iii, 570). The Star Chamber and the enlargement of its power in the reign of Henry VII "might have been as wise as the abolition of it in that of Charles I" (ibid., III, n. b, 453).

The Whigs were not alone in failing to appreciate the historicity of the constitution. Royalist historians treated the prerogative of the Crown "as something real and durable; like those eternal essences of the schools, which no time or force could alter" (ibid., IV, app. 499). Viewed in this way, constitutional quarrels were necessarily transformed into pseudo-historical ones, reaching back as far as Saxon times. Thus what should have been the purely historical question of the constituency of the Saxon Wittenagemot was thought of as a political one: "as our modern parties have chosen to divide on this point, the question has been disputed with the greater obstinacy; and the arguments on both sides have become, on that account, the more captious and deceitful" (ibid., I, app. i, 155). The monarchy party views the Wittenagemot as composed of wise men of the law, the popular party sees it as a body of representatives of the borough and the ancestors of the House of Commons. Hume's own conclusion is that "our knowledge of the Anglo-Saxon history and antiquities is too imperfect to afford us means of determining with certainty all the prerogatives of the crown and privileges of the people . . . of that government" (ibid., 154). But in any case, we know enough to know that there is no parity of political conduct between the Saxons and modern Englishmen: "Those who, from a pretended respect to antiquity, appeal at every turn to an original plan of the constitution, only cover their turbulent spirit and their private ambition under the appearance of venerable forms; and whatever period they pitch on for their model, they may still be carried back to a more ancient period, where they will find the measures of power entirely different, and where every circumstance, by reason of the greater barbarity of the times, will appear still less worthy of imitation" (ibid., II, xxiii, 514).

The remedy to this political error is a good dose of historical relativism: to recognize that each age is unique, with its own rationale. But such recognition requires one to step out of his own age, using tenseless causal laws and the principle of sympathy to enter into the moral causes of periods radically different from his own. Practical lessons in politics or in any other narratively structured activity cannot be learned across epochs; "a civilized nation like the English" should not regard "the maxims of uncultivated ages as certain rules for their present conduct" (ibid.). But lessons can and should be drawn from events falling *within* a historical epoch. Hume traces his own narrative order to about the time of Henry VII and the discovery of the West Indies, the rise of commerce, the flight of the scholars from Constantinople to the West, the Reformation, and the discovery of printing. These and other events brought on "a general revolution" and "men gradually attained that situation, with regard to commerce, arts, science, government, police, and cultivation, in which they have ever since persevered. Here, therefore, commences the useful, as well as the more agreeable part of modern annals . . . and as each incident has a reference to our present manners and situation, instructive lessons occur every moment during the course of the narration. Whoever carries his anxious researches into preceding periods, is moved by a curiosity, liberal indeed and commendable; not by any necessity for acquiring knowledge of public affairs, or the arts of civil government" (ibid., III, xxvi, 77).

## THE SECOND WHIG ERROR

Reading contemporary intentions into the past is the second Whig error. Just as the plan of liberty goes back to the Saxon forests, so does the intention that there be a plan of liberty. This enabled Whig writers to divide the past into a class of heroes and a class of evil men, the heroes being those who had insight into the constitution and tried to bring it to perfection, the evil men being those who knowingly sought to undermine it or to exploit it for their own advantage. All of the popular Whig errors are locked into Catharine Macaulay's *History of England*, written, in part, as a reply to Hume's *History*. It is addressed to "the friends of Liberty and the constitution" and may be taken as typical of the Whig ideology and also of the unashamedly partisan way in which history was written. She frankly confesses that "From my early youth I have read with delight those histories that exhibit Liberty in its most exalted state. . . . The effect which almost constantly attends such reading operated on my inclinations in the strongest manner, and Liberty became the object of a secondary worship in my delighted imagination."[5] One idol worshiped was the doctrine of the wickedness of the Stuart kings, whose tyranny was finally overthrown "by the toil and blood of the most exalted individuals that ever adorned humanity,"[6] that is, by the seventeenth-century Puritan party. Indeed, in comparison to her own contemporaries, they "appear more than human."[7] Hume agreed that the Puritans had brought about the plan of liberty. But he introduced a completely different concept of what it is to *bring about* something in that peculiar order known as history, a conception which after two centuries of reflection on the nature of historical knowledge and existence still bears careful attention.

We may say that Martin Luther opened up a larger sphere of civil liberty, but we cannot read that value back into his intentions: "there followed from this revolution [the Reformation] many beneficial consequences; though perhaps neither foreseen nor intended by the persons who had the chief hand in conducting it" (ibid., III, xxx, 199). A constitution of ordered liberty was the last thing the Puritans had in mind: "Never in this island was known a more severe and arbitrary government than was generally exercised by the patrons of liberty in both kingdoms" (ibid., V, lix, 365). When we examine their actual intentions, we find they were determined not by reasonable considerations of civil liberty but by theological considerations, the nature of church government, and the correct mode of worship: "they were willing to sacrifice the greatest civil interests, rather than relinquish the most minute of their theological contentions" (ibid., V, lix, 364). These theological issues were internally connected to politics. Charles was rare in perceiving "the necessary connection between trifles and important matters . . . that, when he was contending for the surplice, he was in effect fighting for his crown, and even for his head" (ibid., note n, 546). But few of the popular party could perceive this connection: "Most of them were carried headlong by fanaticism; as might be expected in the ignorant multitude. Few even of the leaders seem to have had more enlarged views" (ibid.). We cannot, therefore, "dignify this civil war and the parliamentary authors of it, by supposing it to have any other considerable foundation than theological zeal, that great and noted source of animosity among men" (ibid., n. i, 543).

Despite these unworthy motives, the Puritans jarred events into the shape of a constitution of liberty: "the precious spark of liberty had been kindled" by the Puritans "and it is to this sect, whose principles appear so frivolous, and habits so ridiculous, that the English owe the whole freedom of their constitution" (ibid., IV, xl, 141). The Whig reformer Joseph Priestley, who once had occasion to quote this passage, remarked dryly, "We shall take the compliment, and despise the reflection."[8] It was difficult to appreciate the view that events of great historical significance were not intended by anyone (neither individuals nor Providence). This thesis is not a quirk of Hume's historical thinking; it is at the center of his philosophical vision. What men consider to be rational practices are not the result of either a-priori rational structures or of rational activity; rather, they derive from the interplay of the propensities of human nature with the world. The practice of making causal judgments is a reasonable activity, but it is not the result of any rational discernment that would not presuppose the validity of the practice. The practice of making causal judgments is not established because it is reasonable, rather it is judged reasonable because it is so deeply established. Attempts of autonomous philosophy to justify the practice, independently of the practice itself, end in total skepticism. Hume's entire philosophy is an elaboration of that theme. The transition from polytheism to the more rational theism is not the result of deeper reflection but of the escalating demands of the most abject superstition (NHR, 43). Indeed Hume insists that (except for philosophical theism) the more rational theism becomes, the more absurd are its motives and popular practices (ibid., 53–54). The Reformation was an advance in rationality and "one of the greatest events in history" (H, III, xxix, 128). Yet "it owed not its success to reason and reflection" (ibid., 134). Likewise with the doctrine of religious tolerance, which grew out of the Independents, a radical Puritan faction: "It is remarkable that so reasonable a doctrine owed its origin, not to reasoning, but to the height of extravagance and fanaticism" (ibid., V, lvii, 282).

Yet in none of this did Hume commit the genetic fallacy. The nonrational origin of the causal principle, theism, the Reformation, the plan of liberty, the principle of religious tolerance, etc. does not tell against the rationality of these principles. Once they are discovered by historical reflection, they can be evaluated for their worth by whatever abstract principles are available. Moreover, these principles are treated as a kind of *gift* from the historical process of common life. By narrative associations, the value of the principle is conveyed back to those who initiated the process, and historical dignity is conferred upon them. Thus a certain piety and affection is due to the ancestors of all principles, from the Puritans to the Reformers, and even to the deep reconciling propensities of the imagination which for us are the "cement of the universe" (but to the philosophers caught by the autonomy principle are merely the "trivial" propensities of the fancy).

In the *Treatise*, Hume applies the principle of narrative associations to the question of political allegiance, and works out a narrative conception of political obligation. Not only does the present acquire legitimacy from the past, but by narrative associations the past may also acquire legitimacy from the present: "Nothing is more usual, tho' nothing may, at first sight, appear more unreasonable, than this way of thinking. Princes often *seem* to acquire a right from their successors, as well as from their ancestors. . . . Time and custom give authority to all forms of government . . . and that power, which at first was founded only on injustice and violence, becomes in time legal and obligatory. Nor does the mind rest there; but returning back upon its footsteps, transfers to their predecessors and ancestors that right, which it naturally ascribes to the posterity, as being related together, and united in the imagination. The present *king* of France makes *Hugh Capet* a more lawful prince than *Cromwell;* as the establish'd liberty of the *Dutch* is no inconsiderable apology for their obstinate resistance to *Philip* the second" (T, 566–67). This means that the *historical* past (that is, the past narratively conceived) can quite literally change. Nor is this surprising; the moral world, as we have seen, is constituted by the narrative imagination, and what the imagination gives it can take away. Thus the interpretation we give of the present form of government can "entirely change the *ancient* form of government" (T, 566; emphasis mine), and so "*Julius Caesar* is regarded as the first *Roman* emperor; while *Sylla* and *Marius*, whose titles were really [from a tenseless, abstract point of view] the same as his, are treated as tyrants and usurpers" (ibid.).

Viewed as a narrative existent, the constitution of liberty may serve as a source of illumination for remote past events. Thus Hume is prepared to grant some truth to the Whig view of an ancient Saxon origin to the constitution. The British owe the advantages of the ideal of liberty "chiefly to the seeds implanted by those generous barbarians" (H, I, app. i, 152). But he sardonically makes clear that the Saxons did not have anything in mind like the polished eighteenth-century conception of ordered liberty: "The same picture of a fierce and bold liberty, which is drawn by the masterly pencil of Tacitus, will suit those founders of the English government" (ibid., 153). To speak here of "founders" is to think of Saxon deeds behaviorally and to cover their actions with a narrative concept. The *History* abounds with narrative conceptions of this sort. A seventeenth-century Parliament places the finishing touches on "the new plan of liberty" which it could not have intended; "seeds are implanted," yielding an organism unrecognized by the parents; "sparks are kindled," leading to an unintended conflagration. The deeds of men described in this way are picked out by behavioral criteria, roughly in the way in which we might say that a person is really putting salt in his coffee, although he mistakenly thinks he is putting sugar in it.

But human actions admit also of *intentional* analysis. It is easy and perhaps natural for us to read intentions into actions when the latter are viewed under narrative conceptions. Expressions such as "plan of liberty" and Hume's own technical expression "convention" (discussed above in chapter 2) naturally give rise to an intentional interpretation and to a confusion which Hume is usually at pains to prevent. Thus he speaks of "the wisdom of the English constitution, or rather the concurrence of accidents" (ibid., V, n. e, 539). What men may be said to have done, historically, is determined not only by the unintended consequences of their actions but also by what those consequences mean to future generations, that is, how those consequences will be woven into the story they tell about themselves.

A narrative existent such as the plan of liberty, like the historical conventions of justice and language, is the work of those living, those dead, and those yet unborn. Since the narrative past is determined, in part, by what those in the future think of it and since the future is open, the nature of the British constitution has never been, and never will be, finally fixed. The same is true of the nature of the Whig and Tory political parties that began around the time of Charles II. Both are historical parties, defending not only present political proposals but, necessarily, a historical interpretation of the constitution. There is a stability and order to constitution and to party, but it is not the order of "the essences of the schools" (ibid., IV, app., 499). It is rather a narrative order to be understood in the special (and in Hume's time uncharted) way in which historians think: "To determine the nature of these parties is perhaps one of the most difficult problems that can be met with, and is a proof that history may contain questions as uncertain as any to be found in the most abstract sciences" (E, 68). After seventy years of experience with both parties in an open society where one's opinions can be freely expressed, "yet are we at a loss to tell the nature, pretensions, and principles, of the different factions" (ibid., 69).

Just as the Whigs confused the narrative dignity conferred on the Puritans by later developments in the constitution with the superhuman intention to *restore* the "ancient constitution" (in reality the post-1688 plan of liberty), so they interpreted the intentions of the Stuart kings as wicked and perverse. Hume roundly criticized the misplaced piety of Whigs and Puritans who, self-deceptively, treated their own revolutionary actions as "restorations." At the beginning of the conflict, the Puritans "though themselves the greatest innovators, employed the usual artifice of complaining against innovations, and pretended to recover the ancient and established government" (ibid., V, liv, 139). At the end of the conflict the new Great Seal proposed by Parliament betrayed the founding of a new order under the cloak of restoration. It stated: "On the first year of freedom, by God's blessing, restored, 1648" (ibid., lix, 383). And the Glorious Revolution of 1688, which finally overthrew the Stuarts, fixed the Protestant succession, and established the plan of liberty beyond all doubt, was interpreted as the restoration of what had always been really a liberty-loving Protestant country.

To Hume, all of this was the result of a profoundly disordered historical imagination. Over and over, he finds occasion to drive home the point that the intentions of James I and Charles I were worthy. They were simply maintaining as best they could the constitution they had received from the Tudors. This was, Hume shows, an authoritarian constitution, but it was firmly established and lay much lighter on the people under the Stuarts than it ever did under Henry VIII and Elizabeth. Moreover, both of these monarchs, but especially Elizabeth, had been admired as having a faithful regard for the liberties of the people. In fact, the idea of royal authority entertained and assented to by the House of Commons during Elizabeth's reign was "more worthy of a Turkish divan than of an English house of commons, according to our present idea of this assembly" (ibid., IV, xliv, 337). Indeed, "the English in that age were so thoroughly subdued, that, like Eastern slaves, they were inclined to admire those acts of violence and tyranny which were exercised over themselves, and at their own expense" (ibid., III, xxxiii, 309). Accordingly, Hume found it a great "paradox in human affairs, that Henry VIII should have been adored in his lifetime, and his memory be respected, while Charles I should, by the same people, at no greater distance than a century, have been led to a public and ignominious execution, and his name be ever after pursued by falsehood and by obloquy!" (ibid., V, n. t, 553–54).

For an understanding of the constitution, "there is not a period which deserves more to be studied than the reign of Elizabeth" (ibid., IV, app. iii, 345). There we find a firmly established authoritarian constitution with a House of Commons betraying complete ignorance of even the basic ideas of republican order. It is "curious," Hume writes, "to observe the faint dawn of the spirit of liberty among the English . . . and the ease with which it was subdued by this arbitrary princess" (ibid., xl, 133). Having demonstrated the authoritarian character of the Tudor constitution which the Stuarts inherited, Hume concludes with a challenge: "I shall only ask, whether it be not sufficiently clear from all these transactions, that in the two succeeding reigns [James I and Charles I ] it was the people who encroached upon the soveriegn, not the sovereign who attempted, as is pretended, to usurp upon the people?" (ibid., n. aa, 545).

The false narrative judgment that the Puritans were restoring the ancient constitution necessarily led to the myth of the wickedness of the

Stuart kings. Hume's remedy was to correct the narrative judgment about the external order of events and to examine the internal moral causes behind the actions of Parliament and Crown. What he discovered is that the motives that drove the Puritans "were undoubtedly not of a civil, but of a religious nature" (ibid., V, lv, 220). "[M]ingling politics with religion, they inculcated the most seditious and most turbulent principles" (ibid., IV, xlvii, 444), and thought themselves "dispensed from all the ordinary rules of morality, by which inferior mortals must allow themselves to be governed" (ibid., V, lix, 351). Their motives, consequently, were unworthy of moral respect and certainly unworthy of imitation. In a letter about changes to be made in the *History*, Hume confesses: "I own that I was so disgusted with the Licentiousness of our odious Patriots . . ." (L, II, 261).

The first two Stuarts, by contrast, were trying to maintain the established civil order. They did not understand how to deal with the Puritans because of the novel and open-ended character of their demands. Consequently, mistakes were made. But on the whole, the motives of the Stuarts were worthy because they were maintaining the established order without which liberty has no content (H, VI, lxxi, 366).

Hume is not simply offering virtuous Stuarts and wicked Puritans in an alternative to the Whig interpretation. There is a third perspective, unique to the historian, which transcends these moral categories altogether. Deep social and economic changes, with political implications, were occurring that neither the Commons nor the Crown understood: "About this period [that of James I], the minds of men throughout Europe, especially England, seem to have undergone a general, but insensible revolution" (ibid., IV, xlv, 393). The Commons did not understand, for instance, that the age of great nation-states was emerging and that the Crown had acquired new duties, especially in foreign policy, which required a larger revenue. The Crown was forced to stretch the royal prerogative to the limit and even to go beyond it to obtain revenue adequate for the needs of the nation. Nor did the Commons understand the extent of their own newly acquired wealth and, consequently, their newly acquired duties. Moreover, these changes, which were felt but not understood, were given theological and metaphysical interpretations so that what should have been a question of common life, namely, reasonably adjusting a historical constitution to changing historical conditions, hardened into a metaphysical question, placing the contending parties in implacable opposition.

And so "a secret revolution had happened in the constitution" which neither Crown nor Commons understood (ibid., V, lii, 65). To protect themselves against encroachments of the Commons, who "in those reigns were taking advantage of the necessities of the prince, and attempting every session to abolish, or circumscribe, or define, some prerogative of the crown and innovate in the usual tenor of government" (ibid., VI, lxxi, 363–64), James I and Charles I undertook to define and to defend metaphysically the royal prerogatives. The prerogatives and their ground in divine right were not "then invented; and were only found by the court to be more necessary at that period, by reason of the opposite doctrines, which *began* to be promulgated by the Puritanical party" (ibid., IV, app. 499). The Stuarts made the fatal mistake of thinking of the constitution as a timeless substance sanctioned by God. That they really did believe this is evident from the fact that James I "possessed not so much as a single regiment of guards to maintain his extensive claims," and Charles I had little better, "a strong presumption that [the claims] were at least built on what were then deemed plausible arguments" (ibid., 512). Having failed to appreciate the historicity of their own authority and the fact that constitutions are fragile narrative structures depending on nothing more than what people think about their past, present, and future, the Stuarts could not understand the authority behind some of the new demands being made by the Commons. Looking back, we can excuse Charles I's defense of the prerogative, but at the same time, having experienced a constitution of liberty, we must also appreciate "that public liberty must be so precarious under this exorbitant prerogative, as to render an opposition not only excusable, but laudable in the people" (ibid., V, lii, 80). The point, though, is that Charles could not look back; he was forced to perceive events through a narrative framework which distorted everything: "It was the fate of the house of Stuart to govern England at a period when the former source of authority was already much diminished, and before the latter began to flow in any tolerable abundance" (ibid., n. e, 540). The constitution of England was at the time of James I an "inconsistent fabric, whose jarring and discordant parts must soon destroy each other, and from the dissolution of the old, beget some new form of civil government more uniform and consistent" (ibid., IV, xlvii, 434). It was impossible to think rationally about what should be done because the concrete standards of political thought were themselves changing: "The fluctuating nature of the constitution, the impatient humour of the people, and the variety of events . . . produced exceptions and contradictions" (ibid., V, lii, 80). Nor was this a problem only for Charles I. When the narrative standards that inform a social and political order change, historical existence becomes a surd, and it is impossible for anyone, even with hindsight, to know what should be done: "even after the event, when it is commonly easy to correct all errors, one is at a loss to determine what conduct, in his circumstances, could have maintained the authority of the crown, and preserved the peace of the nation" (ibid., 380). Throughout, Hume stresses that Crown and Commons were locked into a historical situation which limited the range of what could count as rational action. Steps that appeared reasonable at the time served only to entangle the disputants in dialectical knots which they could not untie. The inconveniences people suffered under the reign of the first two Stuarts proceeded neither from wicked intentions nor from misguided policy but "in a great measure from the unavoidable situation of affairs; and scarcely anything could have prevented those events" (ibid., VI, lxxi, 363). Looking back at the consequences, we may be "inclined to throw the blame equally on both parties," but "whoever enlarges his view, and reflects on the situations, will remark the necessary progress of human affairs, and the operation of those principles which are inherent in human nature" (ibid., IV, xxxviii, 16).

The Humean historian views the English Civil War dialectically in much the same way that the Humean philosopher understood the conflict between sense, imagination, and reason in book I, part IV of the *Treatise*, namely, as embodying "principles, which are contrary to each other, which are both at once embrac'd by the mind, and which are unable mutually to destroy each other" (T, 215). But it is the nature of the imagination to reconcile contradictions. Post-Pyrrhonian philosophy is the reconciliation of autonomous reason with philosophically unreflective common life, but the two are held together in uneasy tension. Similarly, faced with the chaos brought on by a breakdown of narrative standards (this is what the Civil War was, for Hume), the reconciling imagination of the historian begins to weave a new narrative order which binds Puritan "patriots" to the present plan of liberty by virtue of the *objective significance* of their actions (as determined by the judgments of later generations) and which includes also the first two Stuart kings by virtue of the *moral worth* of their intentions in defending the established constitution. The action of the Stuarts is universalizable since established authority is necessary for the very existence of government; whereas liberty is a perfection or ornament of government, and so of secondary importance. Although the ancestors of the Whig party may have been "More noble perhaps in their ends, and highly beneficial to mankind, they must also be allowed to have often been less justifiable in the means, and in many of their enterprises to have paid more regard to political than to moral considerations" (ibid., VI, lxxi, 365). This is the meaning of Hume's remark about the *History* that "My views of *things* are more conformable to Whig principles; my representations of *persons* to Tory prejudices" (L, I, 237; Humes's emphasis). The Puritans enjoy external narrative dignity, the Stuarts internal moral dignity.

Many Whig writers could not accept Hume's dialectical reconciliation of the nation with itself. Catharine Macaulay, for whom liberty was an "object of secondary worship," confesses that she could never view the conflict between Crown and Commons "through the medium held up by party writers; or incline to that extreme candour [a barb aimed at Hume] which, by colouring the enormous vices, and magnifying the petty virtues, of wicked men, confound together in one undistinguished groupe, the exalted patriots that have illustriously figured in this country, with those time-serving placemen who have sacrificed the most essential interests of the public to the benefits of their private affections."[9] The vision of a new national unity which included the Stuarts and the Puritans, "in one undistinguished groupe," was unthinkable.

It was unthinkable also to Thomas Jefferson, who viewed Hume's *History* as a threat to the survival of liberty in the new republic: "it is this book which has undermined free principles of the English government, has persuaded readers of all classes that there were usurpations on the legitimate and salutary rights of the crown, and has spread universal toryism over the land."[10] Jefferson replaced Hume's *History* at the University of Virginia with John Baxter's *A New and Impartial History of England* (1796), which was a paraphrase of Hume's work from an unbending republican point of view. Of it Jefferson wrote: "Baxter has performed a good operation on [Hume's *History*]. He has taken the text . . . as his ground work, abridging it by the omission of some details of little interest, and wherever he has found him endeavoring to mislead, by either the suppression of a truth, or by giving it a false coloring, he has changed the text to what it should be, so that we may properly call it Hume's history republicanized."[11]

Baxter followed the usual Whig story line of showing how the liberties framed in the "ancient constitution" were invaded by usurping tyrants and enriched the account with radical republican interpretations gained from the French Revolution. Hume's insight into the historicity of the constitution, that it was something new in human affairs and if it was "not the best system of government" was "at least the most entire system of liberty that ever was known amongst mankind" (H, VI, lxxi, 363), that the new plan of liberty revealed dimensions and possibilities of human nature which could not have been imagined by previous generations, that properly to celebrate and preserve this new system, we must clearly understand its fragile historical character and its dark, unintended origins—all of this was overrun by Baxter's misplaced Whig piety: "Neither can we agree with those who say, the constitution, as it exists at present, is the height of human perfection, improved by time, and sanctioned by experience; for we have pointed out a time when it existed in much greater perfection, and had the universal suffrage of the people."[12] It is ironic that Jefferson, a champion of liberty and especially of freedom of thought, should seek to suppress the *History*. But to Hume the matter would have come as no surprise. He appears to have been the first to really appreciate that concepts such as "liberty," "reason," "justice," and the like are vacuous unless given a historical (narrative) content without which they may easily be twisted into their opposites. There "Never in this island was known a more severe and arbitrary government than was generally exercised by the patrons of liberty" (ibid., V, lix, 365). Just as the rationalist alienated from the usual maxims of common life by the autonomy principle of false philosophy is not reasonable, so the man of liberty caught in the grip of the same philosophical error may not be liberal: "Even that party amongst us, which boasts of the highest regard to liberty, has not possessed sufficient liberty of thought to decide impartially of their own merit, compared with that of their antagonists" (ibid., VI, lxxi, 365).

## The Third Whig Error

We come now to the final Whig error. In failing to understand the narrative past, one fails to understand the present. The Manichean idea of English history as the story of how the ancient constitution has been maintained despite unceasing attempts to overthrow it includes a paranoid view of the present constitutional order.[13] Catharine Macaulay saw, in her own time, the same dark forces at work, forces which would "remove the limitations necessary to render monarchy consistent with liberty . . . such a faction has ever existed in this state, from the earliest period of our present constitution."[14] These are "rebels in the worst sense; rebels to the laws of their country, the law of nature, the law of reason, and the law of God."[15] The constitution is treated here as a legal substance, an object of thought which one could accept or reject; whereas Hume treats it as a narrative existent internal to a way of life. The plan of liberty is not established because we or our ancestors desired it; rather, it is desired by us because it is established. The plan of liberty is woven throughout the historical fabric of common life. The advantages of it are enjoyed by all. It is not so much an object of thought to be judged as it is a *form* of thought through which judgments are made. Throughout the political *Essays* and in the *History* Hume tries to liberate Whigs and Tories from thinking of the constitution as an abstract legal structure and to force them to recognize it as a historical structure internal to their own thought and existence.

The contrast between this kind of historical analysis and the prevail-

ing legalistic way of thinking of both Whigs and Tories comes out clearly in Hume's treatment of the problem of court corruption. The power
of the Crown to fill offices in government had led, in the minds of many
Whigs, to a corrupt system of government by patronage that had grown
so large and powerful as to threaten the balance between Crown and
Commons towards an absolute monarchy. Hume pointed out that both
Whigs and Tories believed in a balanced constitution: Tories were not
about to abandon the liberties of the Commons that they themselves
enjoyed, and Whigs recognized the importance of a central executive
independent of Parliament. But Parliament had over the years acquired
more power than is compatible with a balanced constitution. So legally
the Crown did not have sufficient power to maintain the independent
authority required by the legal fiction of a balanced constitution. Yet
the balance is maintained as a matter of fact by the very patronage
system which the Whigs find a threat to the moral virtue necessary to
maintain the constitution. Nor is this arrangement peculiar to the present constitution: "the wisdom of the English constitution, or rather the
concurrence of accidents, has provided, in different periods, certain
irregular checks to this privilege of parliament, and thereby maintained, in some tolerable measure, the dignity and authority of the
crown" (ibid., V, n. e, 539–40). Again there is the familiar Humean
point, first made in the *Treatise*, that so-called "rational" structures such
as the "balanced constitution" or the causal principle are determined by
nonrational structures (court corruption or the trivial propensities of
the fancy). The lesson is that abstract principles such as that of a balanced constitution are empty unless given a narrative historical interpretation. Unless disciplined by historical understanding, they can
be used to justify virtually any action.

The errors in narrative judgments made by Whigs were not, for
Hume, of mere academic interest; they led to serious moral and political consequences. Hume viewed Britain as a country on the verge of
being torn apart by these errors. It was not a tragic but a pathetic
spectacle. The historical plan of liberty was in fact established in the
minds and actions of both parties and opened up unthought of possibilities for human nature; yet these parties were alienated from the
very constitution they enjoyed in common life by mistakes in narrative
judgments made about the relations between their past and present.
British politics suffered from historical hallucinations, and the *History*
was presented as therapy.

Whig defense of the ancient constitution had led to a siege mentality
which perceived enemies everywhere, at home and abroad, and which
extolled only those activities (mainly political, moral, and religious)
which served to maintain and justify the system of liberty. Develop-

ment of literature and the fine arts was considered by some as corrupting threats to republican virtue. Authoritarian ("Turkish") countries in which the arts flourished, such as France and Italy, were seen as corrupting influences on British youth. Catharine Macaulay complains that British education is mainly a matter of studying Greek and Latin literature and is finished off with "what is called the tour of Europe, that is a residence for two or three years in the countries of France and Italy. This is the finishing stroke that renders them useless to all the good purposes of preserving the birth-right of an Englishman [the ancient constitution of liberty]." Being uneducated about the principles of a free government, they "are caught with the gaudy tinsel of a superb court, the frolic levity of unreflecting slaves, and thus deceived by appearances, are rivited in a taste for servitude."[16]

Hume had no sympathy with this sort of English chauvinism. He was a Scotsman whose kinsmen had century-old political and family ties with France. All of this tended to give him a cosmopolitan view of the Continent. Nor could he at all identify with the Whig "birthright of an Englishman." Scottish law was Roman and continental. English common law was virtually a foreign system. As a philosopher with a keen sense of the historicity of political order, he had no particular prejudice against absolute monarchy or republics. Abstractions such as liberty and authority have to be given historical interpretations before we can evaluate governments which instantiate them, and no one knows what future arrangements, under radically different historical conditions, might be workable (E, 89). Hume agreed that the British had the most perfect system of liberty known to man, but historical studies showed that the plan of liberty was not unique to England; it was, in large part, the result of a civilizing process which had occurred throughout Europe and had liberalized all governments to some degree. Although he granted that some forms of government under certain historical circumstances were more suited to human nature than others (ibid., 13–28), British history and his own experience of British politics convinced him that the best form of government could be torn apart by factions having historically and philosophically disordered minds.

It is against this background that we must understand the harsh things Hume has to say about the English in letters from around 1768 on. He wrote in 1769: "It has been my Misfortune to write in the Language of the most stupid and factious Barbarians in the World" (L, II, 209). The English are barbarians because they have neglected the cultivation of literature which, for Hume, is the deepest of all human activities: it is nothing less than the perfecting and understanding of the human mind. But the English for over a century have thrown their energies into ideological disputes about their rights and their constitution to the neglect of literature.[17] This is a constant theme throughout Hume's writings and letters.

Mossner has observed that the *History* contains within it a rudimentary history of English literature, and Hume uses the cultivation of literature, not the establishment of justice, government, or civil liberty, as the ultimate standard of progress: "a total degeneracy of style and language prepares the way for barbarism and ignorance" (H, IV, app. 522).[18] With this idea in mind, Hume cannot forebear pointing out the superiority of James I and Charles I in relation to their Puritan opponents in the mastery of language: "the harangue of his majesty [James] will always be found superior to that of the speaker, in every parliament during this reign" (ibid., 527). "Such superiority do the pursuits of literature possess above every other occupation, that even he who attains but a mediocrity in them, merits the preeminence above those that excel the most in the common and vulgar professions" (ibid.). And Hume includes in the latter all political activity. Of Charles I's *Icon Basiliké*, published immediately after his execution, Hume remarks that "it must be acknowledged the best prose composition which, at the time of its publication, was to be found in the English language" (H, V, lix, 385). The impression is left that Cromwell, whose style of speech and writing was full of "obscurity, confusion, embarrassment, and absurdity," had murdered Britain's best prose writer (ibid., lxi, 441n).

Although not without literary monuments, for example, Shakespeare and Milton, the English have given themselves over to theological and political quarrels and have shown little interest in cultivating literature for its own sake. Throughout his career, Hume complained of the "indifference of [state] ministers towards literature, which has been long, and indeed always, the case in England" (L, II, 186). James I was able to establish a theological school for the purpose of refuting Puritans and papists, but "All the efforts of the Great Bacon could not procure an establishment for the cultivation of natural philosophy: even to this day, no society has been instituted for the polishing and fixing of our language" (H, IV, app. 503). In a letter of 1773, he thought that "the great Decline, if we ought not rather to say, the total Extinction of Literature in England, prognosticates a very short Duration of all our other Improvements, and threatens a new and sudden Inroad of Ignorance, Superstition and Barbarism" (NHL, 199). Three years later, in a letter to Gibbon praising *The Decline and Fall of the Roman Empire*, he expresses surprise that such a fine production could come from England: "but as it seems to me that your Countrymen, for almost a whole Generation, have given themselves up to barbarous and absurd Faction, and have totally neglected all polite Letters, I no longer expected any valuable Production ever to come from them." Hume warned Gibbon that "among many other marks of Decline, the Prevalence of Superstition in England, prognosticates the Fall of Philosophy and Decay of Taste; and though no body be more capable than you to revive them, you will probably find a Struggle in your first Advances" (L, II, 310). Within three years Gibbon was forced to publish a *Vindication* of his treatment of Christianity against the attack of religious pamphleteers.

## WILKES AND ABSTRACT LIBERTY

In the late 1760s and throughout the remainder of his life, Hume thought he perceived a "sudden Inroad of Ignorance, Superstition and Barbarism." The usual Whig paranoia about liberty had taken a quantum jump in the "Wilkes and Liberty" affair in London. As Hume saw it, the demands of "the Wilkites and the Bill of Rights-men" (ibid., 235) were "founded on nothing, and had no connexion with any higher order of the state" (ibid., 178). The affair was "without a Cause" (ibid., 210), and yet the government, instead of exercising its authority and punishing the "insolent Rascals, the Mayor and Sheriffs," had done nothing and so had lent a certain legitimacy to the demands. Hume thought that "this is a new Experiment to reconcile such extreme Licence with Government" (ibid., 221). And the experiment, he thought, was doomed to failure: "if in a case, where popular Complaints had not the smallest Shadow of Pretence, the King and Parliament have prevail'd after a long Struggle and with much Difficulty, what must it be, where there is some plausible Appearance, and perhaps some real Ground of Complaint, such as it is natural to expect in all Governments?" (ibid.). The Wilkes affair and the consequent riots in London were perplexing to Hume (and not only to Hume) because they were completely out of proportion to the grievance: the refusal of Parliament to seat the obscure, scandalous, and disobedient representative from Middlesex.[19] Looking back, historians today can perhaps see what Hume could not, that the Wilkes affair left to England a new conception of liberty, the constitution, the objectivity of law, and the meaning of representation.[20] Viewed in this way, many have taken Hume's reaction to the Wilkes' affair as a typical case of the petulant conservatism that comes with age. Because of this ungenerous reactionary disposition, Hume was blinded to the new conception of liberty that was emerging; more generous spirits, however, could discern it.

But to interpret Hume in this way is to make just that "Whig" error in narrative judgment that Hume had labored in the Stuart and Tudor volumes to expose. To read narrative dignity into the Wilkes affair through the lens of a later conception of liberty has no logical bearing on the question of whether Hume's interpretation of events is worthy of consideration. To appreciate Hume's interpretation, we must do what he did in trying to understand the actions of Charles I: bracket out the narrative perspective and examine the moral causes of the action.

First of all, whatever we may say of Hume's interpretation, it was not reactionary. The conceptual framework he employed to understand the conflict between the London "Mob and the Constitution" (ibid., 218) was, in essentials, the same used to understand the seventeenth-century conflict between the Puritan Parliament and the Crown and extends back even to the time of the *Treatise* (T, 563–67). The Puritans were driven by theological fanaticism, not by any grievance that could be understood or dealt with within the historical framework of the common life they shared with their countrymen. Their metaphysical commitments "dissolved every moral and civil obligation" (H, V, lv, 220). The "sacred boundaries of the laws being once violated, nothing remained to confine the wild projects of zeal and ambition: and every successive revolution became a precedent for that which followed it" (ibid., lix, 330). The revolution followed the classical pattern of antiquity, devoured its own children, and issued in a one-man military dictatorship. And so the nation fell into "slavery . . . from the too eager pursuit of liberty" (ibid., 339).

Hume thought he saw the same sort of metaphysical tempest brewing in the Wilkes and Liberty riots, which, like the Puritan challenge, could not be articulated within the established constitutional framework. But there was a difference; the Puritans acted under theological concepts; the Wilkites acted under the secular concept of liberty. This change had already begun to take place during the reign of Charles II when, as Hume observed, the opposition ceased calling themselves the "*godly*" party and took up the name of the "*good* and *honest* party" (ibid., VI, lxviii, 215). Moreover, the word "liberty" was beginning to lose some of its old Whig historical connotations as the birthright of an Englishman in favor of the coming metaphysical notion of the "rights of man." But Hume died before the idea of the rights of man came down to earth in the form of the French Revolution. What to us might appear as a transition from the provincial Whig notion of the rights of an Englishman to the abstract metaphysical notion of the rights of man was to Hume a move towards greater hallucination—a move of which only the English, because of their peculiar historical circumstances, were capable: it demonstrated "those foolish English Prejudices, which all Nations and all Ages disavow" (L, II, 216), that is, the treatment of liberty not as a perfection of government but as a condition for its legitimacy.

For nearly seventy years the Whigs had been in possession of "bestowing all places, both in the state and in literature" (MOL, 8). From this powerful rostrum, the historically misplaced Whig conception of liberty had been drummed into the national consciousness. Alienated by false narrative judgments from the liberty they actually enjoyed and from a due regard for authority, the Whigs had spawned in their own minds, independent of common life, an increasingly abstract conception of liberty, one that was losing the sanction of even a confused historical authority and was in danger of being cut loose from authority altogether: "Our Government has become a Chimera; and is too perfect in point of Liberty, for so vile a Beast as an Englishman, who is a Man . . . corrupted by above a Century of Licentiousness. The Misfortune is, that this Liberty can scarcely be retrench'd without Danger of being entirely lost" (L, II, 216). Hume did not think of the "London mob" that was rioting and burning buildings as the rabble of classical theory, but as English middle-class merchants, craftsmen, and professional men, men who should know better but who were caught in the grip of an idea: "The Madness and Wickedness of the English (for do not say, the Scum of London) appear astonishing, even after all the Experience we have had [the Civil War and its aftermath]" (ibid., 226). It seemed to Hume that the Hampdens, the Pyms, the Hollises, and the Cromwells had appeared in secular form but with the same sort of implacable metaphysical demands which no authentic political reasoning from common life could slake.

It appeared that "those foolish English Prejudices" about liberty had moved from the level of historical judgment to that of metaphysical judgment, as they had in the seventeenth century. And this brings us to a deeper theme of the *History*. We have observed that political order for Hume is an order of moral causes located in a narrative structure. To think correctly about political matters is, at the very least, to avoid making errors in narrative judgment: these distort not only the order of events but also our perception of the moral causes motivating historical agents. One theme of the *History* exposes the errors in narrative judgment made by the Whig literary and political establishment. These are errors made within the narrative framework of English constitutional history. But there is a philosophically deeper theme in the *History* which works to expose the errors of philosophers who seek a source of political authority independent of *all* narrative frameworks. This is an error that arises not from making narrative judgments but from denying the authority of all narrative judgments. In the next three chapters we shall examine in some detail Hume's reflections on the structure of this error. These reflections begin with the *Treatise* and continue throughout his writings; they constitute the guiding theme which unites Hume's historical and philosophical work into a coherent whole.

# 10
# *Metaphysical Rebellion*

There is a set of men lately sprung up amongst us, who
endeavour to distinguish themselves by ridiculing every
thing, that has hitherto appeared sacred and venerable in
the eyes of mankind. Reason, sobriety, honour,
friendship, marriage, are the perpetual subjects of their
insipid raillery; and even public spirit, and a regard to our
country, are treated as chimerical and romantic.

Hume's "Of Moral Prejudices"

## THE POLITICAL MEANING OF HUME'S PHILOSOPHY

Hume did not accept the radical distinction between facts and values
which has been so important in all forms of positivism and in most
forms of empiricism. For Hume, facts are grasped through perceptions,
and all perceptions (ideas as well as impressions) are emotionally
charged (T, 373–75). Passion is built into the very structure of facts and
also of reason, which is thought of as a "calm passion." This gives
theoretical backing to Hume's view, common in his time but somewhat
out of joint with our own, that the task of philosophy is to entertain and
instruct. In this and the next chapters we shall see how Hume's philosophical and historical works are unified by a moral or, more precisely,
a political purpose.

A main task of book I of the *Treatise* is to settle the normative question of the nature and limits of philosophical inquiry. Philosophy first
appears on the scene informed by the autonomy principle: philosophical inquiry has an authority all its own which is logically independent
of the unreflective maxims and standards that make up the order of
common life; thus, philosophy has the authority to criticize that order
as a whole. The dialectic between philosophy and common life is designed to show that the autonomy principle is incoherent. The attempt

to throw into question the whole unreflective order of common life and to replace it with an alternative, philosophically certified system logically ends in total skepticism (T, 267–68). Philosophers are in fact never reduced to skepticism because they do not consistently apply the autonomy principle. It is this failure to really press home the principle that makes it appear plausible and obscures its fundamental impossibility. Philosophers do not consistently apply the autonomy principle because they cannot. Psycologically, they cannot avoid having such unreflectively received opinions as that there is an external world containing other minds and causal connections (not to mention that vast range of beliefs that are virtually as well-established: that there are moral and aesthetic distinctions, that there is an intelligent author of the universe, etc.), though logically and empirically such opinions are not justified. Logically, philosophers cannot avoid having those beliefs because the beliefs are presupposed in any attempt to criticize them philosophically.

Philosophy, as traditionally conceived, pompously displays the autonomy principle as the ground for a total emancipation from the unreflective maxims of common life. Hume calls this "false philosophy." It is not only incoherent but also deeply self-deceptive. The lesson is that we must abandon the autonomy principle in favor of "true philosophy," which recognizes the order of common life as a category of philosophical thought. Philosophical criticism can apply to structures *within* the order of common life, but the order itself cannot be criticized on pain of logical and psychological absurdity. True philosophy is limited to the task of systematizing and rendering mutually coherent the established beliefs and principles of common life. A main task of book I is to purge common life of false philosophy. The task of books II and III is to uncover and systematize the abstract standards and the historical standards that constitute the moral and political conventions of common life.

The attempt of the alienated philosopher to deny the authority of common life as a whole and to impose an alternative scheme upon it is, as an affair of the closet, merely ridiculous, but when carried out in political form it is destructive of society. Hume thought the beliefs of false philosophy were woven throughout the political conventions of common life, bringing to politics the alienation and self-deception which properly belong in the closet. In the *Treatise*, false philosophy in politics is thought of mainly as "superstition." Hume had in mind the religious-political wars that had racked the political order of Europe during the last two centuries, but especially the war between Crown and Parliament. The moral mission of the *Treatise* is to purge the concepts of false philosophy from common life, but it is officially presented as a theoretical work, and its moral mission is played down.

The case is otherwise with the *Enquiry* on understanding. From the beginning on through to the famous book-burning passage at the end, Hume is out to eliminate "the false and adulterate" conceptions of philosophy from common life and to establish his own reformed conception. Hume thought that the development of true philosophy and the stability of modern government were mutually reinforcing and were the greatest achievements of the modern age: "The stability of modern governments above the ancient and the accuracy of modern philosophy have improved, and probably will still improve, by similar gradations" (EU, 10). Hume's language in the *Enquiry* is political and militant. False philosophy, guided by the autonomy principle, arises either "from the fruitless efforts of human vanity, which would penetrate into subjects utterly inaccessible to the understanding, or from the craft of popular superstitions, which, being unable to defend themselves on fair ground, raise these entangling brambles to cover and protect their weakness. Chased from the open country, these robbers fly into the forest, and lie in wait to break in upon every unguarded avenue of the mind, and overwhelm it with religious fears and prejudices . . . . and many, through cowardice and folly, open the gates to the enemies, and willingly receive them with reverence and submission as their legal sovereigns" (EU, 10–11).

False philosophy in politics is a special sort of sedition and subversion, and so it is rhetorically fitting that the *Enquiry* should appear as a counterrevolutionary work and that in the last paragraph Hume should sum the whole project up with the metaphor of a new political inquisition where we are instructed to make "havoc" in our libraries and to cast into the flames all books of metaphysics that contain neither abstract reasonings concerning quantity or number nor experimental reasoning concerning matters of fact. Here, as elsewhere, the rhetorical devices Hume uses are important for understanding his philosophy. The message of the *Enquiry* is that false philosophy in common life is a serious threat to social and political order and not merely an amusing error of closet philosophers. If it were only the latter, the image would more properly be pity for the deluded than the image of the Inquisition. The *Treatise*, which is mainly concerned to expose the illusions of the closet, does employ a pathetic image: the punishment of *"Sisyphus* and *Tantalus"* (T, 223). But in later works, Hume's criticism is focused more clearly on the deleterious practical effects of "extravagant philosophy" and "philosophical enthusiasm" (EM, 343).

The criticism of metaphysics in common life is the unifying theme of Hume's philosophical and historical writings. The practical point of that criticism is the elimination of false metaphysics from politics: "nor have the political interests of society any connexion with the philosophical disputes concerning metaphysics and religion" (EU, 147). Within the general criticism, one can distinguish two philosophical errors that Hume is concerned to purge from the politics of common life. The first is based on a false conception of reason in politics. The second is based on a false conception of narrative order which I shall call the providential conception of politics. I turn now to an examination of the first error; the second occupies the whole of the next chapter.

## CARTESIANISM IN POLITICS

The Cartesian conception of reason contains a methodological principle and an ontological principle. Both are spawned by the autonomy principle, and both are the special objects of Hume's thorough critique of false philosophy in book I of the *Treatise*. Descartes laid it down as a principle of method for thinking rationally about the world that all former opinions are to be treated as false unless they can be made to "conform to the uniformity of a rational scheme," by which Descartes meant a deductive system based on propositions about which we cannot be mistaken.

The ontological principle entailed in Descartes' conception of reason is that reality is that to which the rational scheme refers. As Hegel was to put it: the rational is the real and the real is the rational. Since the world of common life is a narrative order, held together by the passions internal to traditions, customs, and prejudices, all of its maxims are dubitable. Reason liberated from this narrative order can never go home again, but must seek out a "world of its own," populated with "beings, and objects, which are altogether new" (T, 271). This yields what Hume dryly calls the doctrine of "double existence" that he considered characteristic of "the modern philosophy" (T, 215, 225–31).[1] This doctrine can best be introduced by considering Descartes' analysis of how knowledge of the physical world is possible. Like Galileo, Descartes believed that nature is a book "written in the language of mathematics." Parallel to the theoretical language of physics is the ordinary language of common life, with which the former language is often confused. To say of a piece of wax that it has the sensory properties of yellowness and sweetness is a mistake, since sensory objects are private mental entities. Wax as it really is has only the properties specified by autonomous reason, and these are and must be logically unobservable. Since in common life we invariably predicate sensory properties of material things, the sensory judgments of common life are illusory *as a whole*. The doctrine of double existence has continued down to our own

275

time. In a famous passage, Sir Arthur Eddington explains that he is sitting down to two tables; one is the colored, solid, and textured table of common life; the other is the table of theoretical physics which is devoid of sensory properties. But only the latter table is real, the table of common life being a "strange compound of external nature, mental imagery and inherited prejudice."[2]

The doctrine of double existence is not merely a result of Descartes' analysis of physics; it is implied in his general conception of reason: to understand anything, we must give two prima facie incompatible descriptions of it—an ordinary description from the language of common life and a theoretical description certified by autonomous reason. Of Sir Arthur Eddington's table we shall have to say both that it has a color and that it has no color. The contradiction is avoided by ontologizing the theoretical description and declaring the ordinary description to be an illusory identification.

This conception of reason causes a profound alienation in the philosopher's consciousness. By the demands of philosophical autonomy, he must liberate himself totally from the order of common life; but he is also, inescapably, a participant in the standards and opinions of that very order. The solution of Berkeley and others was to think with the learned and talk with the vulgar. But a main point of book I is to show that philosophers *think* as well as talk with the vulgar. Logically and psychologically, philosophy governed by the autonomy principle "has no original authority of its own" but "must derive all its authority from the vulgar system" (T, 213). The attempt to talk with the vulgar and think with the learned, then, is merely a case of bad faith, fed by the vanity of the autonomy principle and serving only to conceal philosophical incoherence and the logical dependence of philosophy on the norms of common life: "Do you come to a philosopher as to a *cunning man*, to learn something by magic or witchcraft, beyond what can be known by common prudence and discretion?" (E, 163).

For Hume, beliefs in natural objects, causal connections, and philosophical theism are determined in various ways by custom, and, as in the Augustinian maxim *credo ut intelligam*, these are beliefs through which our understanding of the world is increased. Likewise, custom determines a vast range of conventions, traditions, prejudices, and fashions of varying degrees of stability and utility, and these are not only ways of understanding the moral world, they constitute that very order. Thus, custom has, for Hume, an epistemological significance and, in the case of the moral world, an ontological significance as well. But for Descartes, custom, in all its forms, is a positive barrier to understanding. Instead of viewing custom and tradition as cognitive instruments to be "methodized and corrected," Descartes views them as structures to be totally overturned. Porphyry relates that Plotinus was embarrassed that he had a body. Similarly, Descartes is methodologically embarrassed that his own mind was formed by the customs and traditions of human society: "it is almost impossible that our judgments should be so excellent or solid as they should have been had we had complete use of our reason since our birth, and had we been guided by its means alone."[3] The true thinker is governed only by the autonomy principle and must think of himself as one who has lived all his life in a "desert and never received more than the light of nature to illumine him."[4] Whereas Hume could celebrate the "precious relics of antiquity" and the recovery of classical literature as containing the most important kind of self-knowledge, Descartes was persuaded "that it is no more the duty of an ordinary well-disposed man to know Greek or Latin than it is to know the languages of Switzerland or Brittany; or that the history of the Empire should be known any more than that of the smallest state in Europe."[5] The passions are not understood through a tradition of interpretation but through direct inspection of one's own mind: "since every one has experience of the passions within himself, there is no necessity to borrow one's observations from elsewhere in order to discover their nature."[6]

The Cartesian conception of reason, with its method of doubt and its doctrine of double existence, can lead to a profound alienation not only from the tables and chairs of common life but from the social and political order as well. In that conception, we must treat the standards of the existing order as false until they can be made to conform to timeless, universal, and self-evident principles. But the standards that constitute the existing political order are narrative existences and, as such, are tensed and contingent. Consequently, they cannot be the objects of self-evident and timelessly true propositions and so must be thought of not only as possibly false but as in fact false. The conceptual effect of Cartesianism in politics would be to deny the rational authority and, hence, the *reality* of existing social and political orders. By the rationale of the evil-demon hypothesis, the whole historical order is thought of as a grand hoax. True social and political order is viewed as an order of *nature:* a timeless object of reason existing independently of the historical process.

This yields the modern doctrine of double existence in politics. Instead of two tables, there are two societies: the existing historical society (an interconnecting web of illusion and contingency) which is conceptually confused with the timeless and rationally ordered society of nature.

The purported confusion here is roughly the same as that of mistaking the sensory order (secondary qualities) with the physical order (primary qualities). But whereas emancipation from sensory illusion can be achieved by philosophical reflection alone, emancipation from historical social and political illusions may be thought to require more sanguinary measures. Cartesianism in politics leads to a frame of mind that I shall call that of "metaphysical rebellion." It is metaphysical because it does not merely reject this or that standard in a political order, it rejects the authority of the whole order and with it the possibility of making distinctions of good and evil within that order. Reform is impossible: "I know no better remedy than absolutely to raze it to the ground, in order to raise a new one in its stead."[7] It is metaphysical also in that the historical order is viewed not so much through the moral categories of good and evil as through the metaphysical categories of *reality* and *illusion*.

## REVOLUTION AS RESTORATION

Descartes applied his revolutionary conception of reason to metaphysics, physics, and mathematics, but he was not unaware of its possible application to politics. The Cartesian conception of reason would appear to entail that the only way "to reform a state" is "by altering everything, and by overturning it throughout, in order to set it right again."[8] But Descartes is quick to quarantine this dangerous conception or reason from politics: "I cannot in any way approve of those turbulent and unrestful spirits who . . . never fail to have always in their minds some new reforms. . . . And if I thought that in this treatise there was contained the smallest justification for this folly, I should be very sorry to allow it to be published."[9] Although this was Descartes' own opinion, it does not follow from his revolutionary conception of reason. And it was not long before that very conception was applied to politics in France, resulting in a movement of left-wing Cartesianism which included such thinkers as Jean Meslier, Morelley, the Abbé de Mably, and Rousseau. This pattern of thought later took on practical shape in the French Revolution and especially in Gracchus Babeuf's Conspiracy of the Equals.[10]

The doctrine of double existence is behind Morelley's yearning for total change in the *Code de La Nature:* "since I hold that vulgar morality [historical morality] has been established on the ruins of the laws of nature, one must totally overturn the former in order to reestablish the latter."[11] Here the historical order is not viewed merely as an illusion, as Descartes had viewed the sensory order, but as a *usurpation* of the order of nature. By the time of the French Revolution such remarks were so common that Richard Price could describe the Revolution as "the recovery of their rights by the people."[12]

Applied to politics, the doctrine of double existence yields paradoxical claims such as Proudhon's statement that "property is robbery" and Rousseau's famous remarks that "man is born free but everywhere he is in chains" and that man must be "forced to be free." These are metaphysically exhilarating statements and are, perhaps, splendid examples of Hume's complaint in the *Treatise* that "Whatever has the air of paradox, and is contrary to the first and most unprejudic'd notions of mankind is often greedily embrac'd by philosophers, as shewing the superiority of their science, which cou'd discover opinions so remote from vulgar conception" (T, 26). The special rhetorical effect of such paradoxical remarks is due entirely to the modern doctrine of double existence. To bring this out, it will be helpful to distinguish this doctrine from an idealistic criticism with which it can easily be confused.

We may form an abstract ideal of a just society and use it to rank-order actual societies. We should then be conceiving of society in two ways: the existing society and the ideal of a just society. It would be easy to suppose that Rousseau's reference to nature is just a way of talking about an ideal of freedom and that Proudhon is simply appealing to an ideal system of property relations. But this would be fundamentally mistaken. Ideals and similar transcendent entities such as natural law or Kant's categorical imperative are not, ontologically, part of the world of facts they judge. Although a historical society is a fact in the world, the ideal of the just society is not another fact in the world but is rather a standard for measuring the success or failure with respect to justice of any existing society. Transcendent standards of this sort do not imply that the existing political order is illusory as a whole. Indeed, the idealist criticism necessarily views the existing order as an order of *goods* (in this case an order of justice), the only question being about the degree of goodness realized. The transcendent standards of traditional idealism, then, enable one both to affirm the authority of existing institutions and to criticize them.

But the modern doctrine of double existence implies that the standard of judgment and the thing judged are *both* facts in the world. Consider Eddington's two tables. The theoretically conceived table is simply a fact in the world, and the colored table of common life is also a fact in the world. But the theoretical facts are alone judged to be real. Likewise, Rousseau's claim is not that it is an ideal that man should be born free, that we should try to arrange things so that men are born free. He is claiming that man is, in fact, born free but is artificially and perversely enslaved by historical society. It is as if someone were to say that you are in fact heir to a great fortune, a fact which is being kept hidden from you by the corrupt aldermen at city hall. The rhetorical effect of such claims is a feeling of outrage and resentment that one's own has been taken away. The feeling of outrage attendant upon Cartesianism in politics is that of metaphysical rebellion and is directed not against this or that act or institution but against the whole of historical society: *everywhere* man is in chains.

The state of mind I have called metaphysical rebellion may or may not lead to revolutionary action. Some, like Babeuf and Lenin, have been led to form revolutionary conspiracies as the Archimedean point from which to overturn the existing order. Others, like Rousseau, have lived out a melancholy on-again, off-again affair with the world of men in chains. Hume characterized the frame of mind very well in the Conclusion to book I when he retraced the steps that led him to the Pyrrhonian illumination. He is "affrighted and confounded with that forlorn solitude, in which I am plac'd in my philosophy" (T, 264). The alienated philosopher views the historical order in which he exists as illusory and unreal: "All the world conspires to oppose and contradict me" (ibid.). At times he would return to the historical world "for shelter and warmth." But in the black mood of metaphysical rebellion, he is not able "to mingle and unite in society." He cannot prevail "to mix with such deformity" (ibid.).

We have examined in chapter 1 Hume's way out of this "philosophical melancholy and delirium." I wish to stress here only that it is a state of mind following upon the Cartesian conception of reason. But it is not a way of thinking unique to Descartes. It was a pattern of thinking in the air. Hume identified it with what he called "the modern philosophy," and in one form or another it is very much alive today, which is why Hume's criticism is worth working through.

What is essential to Cartesianism is the method of doubt: the presumption that all historical standards are to be thought of as false until brought to conformity with "the uniformity of a rational scheme."[13] The nature of the rational scheme can vary. Descartes conceived it as a set of infallible intuitions. But that is not necessary. Bentham, for instance, proposed a utilitarian conception of reason, but he is still in the grip of the Cartesian method: "Rude establishments" must be brought "to the test of polished reason." According to Mill, it was Bentham's ahistorical method more than any particular conviction that was the driving force behind his work: "He begins all his inquiries by supposing nothing to be known on the subject, and reconstructs all philosophy *ab initio*, without reference to his predecessors."[14] (Compare this with Descartes' conviction that he is "obliged to write as though I were treating of a matter which no one had ever touched on before me.")[15] A similar method informs the thought of Proudhon: "If your will is untrammelled, if your conscience is free, if your mind can unite two propositions and deduce a third therefrom, my ideas will inevitably become yours."[16] Even Marx, who took very seriously the historical content of political standards, is not emanicpated from the heroic Cartesian conception of reason. In a letter to Ruge, he writes that what must be accomplished is "the *ruthless criticism of all that exists*, ruthless also in the sense that criticism does not fear its results and even less so a struggle with the existing powers" (Marx's emphasis).[17]

To these examples we may add that ahistorical model of reason running through the thought of Hobbes, Locke, Rousseau, Kant, and Rawls which seeks to determine what our moral and political obligations are by reference to standards we would have chosen by contract in an original, timeless position of equality. The conception of equality can vary. For Hobbes, it is a state of nature of all against all. For Kant it is a state of rational reflection where all are equal under the universalizing demands of abstract reason. For Rawls it is the "veil of ignorance" behind which timeless autonomous agents, stripped of all historical properties and guided only by self-interest and prudence, decide what principles of justice they will live under.[18] But whatever the favored notion of equality, there is always the Cartesian demand for a timeless Archimedean point independent of the actual historical order, which is thought of as having no authority in its own right to command judgment at all.

Cartesianism in politics is also implied in the recent revival of various forms of anarchism. Two are worth mentioning. One derives from Kant and is succinctly stated in Robert Wolff's *In Defense of Anarchism*: our moral autonomy is absolute and, consequently, a moral agent cannot submit to the will of political authority just because it is political authority. Laws are binding only if they can be made to conform to one's moral autonomy.[19] Robert Nozick in *State, Anarchy, and Utopia* reaches a similar result with a ahistorical doctrine of natural right. The only legitimate government is the "nightwatchman state" constituted by free consent and for the purpose of ensuring the protection of one's natural rights.[20] Since no existing government satisfies these conditions, no existing government is legitimate.

To be sure, such thinkers typically do not advocate that illegitimate states be overthrown. There is always some ad-hoc acceptance on pragmatic or other grounds of the prevailing illegitimacy, similar to Descartes' arbitrary refusal to apply his conception of reason to politics. But such ad-hoc manuevers must be viewed as straight-out moral compromises with, and violations of, self-professed moral imperatives. Again we have the alienated modern philosopher plagued by guilt as he, in violation of his own integrity as a thinker, is forced by common life itself to embrace the authority of the historical world (T, 264). It is precisely at this point of moral compromise with the world that Hume proposes we reflect on the possibility of an entirely different way of thinking about the legitimacy of social and political order.[21]

## HUME'S CRITICISM OF CARTESIANISM IN POLITICS

Cartesianism in politics and the metaphysical alienation that follows from it was well established in Hume's time and not merely as an error of the closet. Hume was the first to identify it with the conceptual structure of modern political parties. These parties are driven by metaphysical ideas, not interests or affection. They are "known only to modern times" and are "the most extraordinary and unaccountable *phenomenon* that has yet appeared in human affairs" (E, 58). The metaphysical political parties that Hume had to deal with were conceptually structured by some form of the social contract theory or the theory of natural law. Both are based on timeless principles known through reason: natural law is grounded on an eternal fit between natural situations and acts; the social contract, made outside of historical time, is based on a timeless obligation to keep promises. But neither theory explains how historical institutions as such can have authority. They simply assert that historical institutions have authority only insofar as they conform to the natural law or to the social contract. Although antedating Descartes, both theories contain the fundamental principles of Cartesianism in politics: the methodological presumption that all historical institutions are illusory unless certified by atemporal principles independent of the historical order, and the doctrine of double existence. The natural law and the social contract traditions could be given a historical interpretation, and Hume does reconstruct them in just that way, but that is not how seventeenth- and eighteenth-century philosophers typically thought of them. Natural law theorists, of course, did hold that the utilities framed in long-established institutions confirmed the natural law. But historical institutions themselves were thought of as having no *original* authority. So conceived, natural law could be used as a ruthless measuring rod to which all historical institutions must conform under pain of illusion. Likewise with the social contract theory. Locke had argued that absolute monarchy is "*inconsistent with Civil Society*, and so can be no Form of Civil Government at all."[22] Likewise Sidney writes: "Whatever . . . proceeds not from the consent of the people, must be 'de facto' only, that is, void of all right."[23] Again the Cartesian twist: it is not just that absolute monarchy is not a good form of government, as might follow on an idealist criticism; it is no form of government at all. Conceptually, then, if Locke and Sidney are right, the subjects of an absolute monarchy are in a state of metaphysical rebellion. Hume drove home the point that, if the social contract were taken seriously, not only absolute monarchy but any actual government could be denied to be legitimate (E, 456).

Hume's rejection of natural law and of the social contract follows from his rejection of reason as the ground of moral distinctions. The ancients, he thought, based morality on sentiment. It was left to the moderns to suppose "all right to be founded on certain *rapports* or relations." Hume traces the origin of this modern way of thinking about rights and duties close to its Cartesian roots in "Father Malebranche," who "as far as I can learn, was the first that started this abstract theory of morals, which was afterwards adopted by Cudworth, Clarke, and others" (EM, 197n). It is a theory well suited to flatter the vanity of the moderns, who pride themselves on their rationality: "as it excludes all sentiment, and pretends to found everything on reason, it has not wanted followers in this philosophic age" (ibid).

By building sentiment and narrative time into the nature of moral, social, and political standards, Hume erected a formal barrier to all forms of Cartesianism in politics. The standards of judgment that constitute the moral world are narrative existences, held together by the narrative associations of the temporally reflective imagination. Narrative standards have authority within a historical order independently of any temporally neutral evaluation of them. Corrections of particular judgments within the order are made by reference to other particular judgments, and so reform is possible, but the order as a whole is affirmed. As in the case of the sensory order, one sensory judgment, with the help of abstract ideas, may be used to correct another. But if, by the autonomy principle, the whole order, whether sensory, political, or whatever, is thrown into question, then distinctions of true and false, good and evil within the order are impossible, and reform is impossible. If property is theft, as Proudhon says, then reform of the existing order of property relations is a conceptual impossibility. There would then be no alternative but to "raze it to the ground, in order to raise a new one in its stead."[24]

Suppose one accepts the imperative for total change that the autonomy principle must always carry with it, and one really tries, not only conceptually but physically, to establish a new order, and suppose that, somehow, this attempt is successful. What will be established is a social and political order in conformity to timeless universal principles, that is, a society completely purged of temporally provincial narrative thinking. B. F. Skinner, in his Cartesian tract *Walden Two*, has the founder of the utopian community put it this way: "We don't teach history. . . . What we give our young people in Walden Two is a grasp of the current forces which a culture must deal with. None of your myths, none of your heroes—no history, no destiny—simply the

283

Now!"[25] In such a society, people would and must think of themselves in a tenseless way. Ideally, only tenseless predicates would apply, such as "is a man," "is a woman," "is a person." It is possible for a society to think of itself in only a tenseless way; theoretical science, mathematics, logic, aesthetics, morals, and religion (when not based on historical revelation) are forms of thinking that are tenseless. So it is conceivable that we could be emancipated from narrative thought and existence.

But Hume's point is that this is only an abstract possibility because the imagination itself is essentially tensed and narrative. His past-entailing theory of meaning treats conceptualization itself as having narrative form. From simple narrative ideas we can, by ignoring their tensed features, form abstract, tenseless ideas and these can be used to criticize the present. But such ideas always have a narrative content that constitutes part of their meaning and is a limit on their applicability. We *do* think of the natural world as an alien existence and so think of it in an abstract and tenseless way. But the moral world is a world of interiors ordered by sympathy and narrative existences: products of narrative associations. But it is just this temporally provincial world of custom, tradition, and prejudice that the Cartesian, standing at the Archimedean point of the autonomy principle, finds rationally repugnant; he cannot prevail with himself "to mix with such deformity" (T, 264). The overthrow of this order is a demand of reason itself.

But if Hume is right, any Cartesian-type tenseless order that replaces the historical one will immediately become the object of the narrative imagination. Soon there will be a new set of narrative associations of ideas and from these a new order of unique narrative existences and duties. And when this occurs, Catesianism in politics and the metaphysical rebellion attendant upon it will, senselessly, once again appear as a demand of reason itself against habit, custom, tradition, and prejudice. Liberation comes from recognizing the impossibility and bad faith of this "philosophical enthusiasm," returning to the historical norms of common life, and applying to them the modest critical tools of post-Pyrrhonian philosophy.

# 11

# *Politics and Providential History*

I ask; who carried them into the celestial regions, who
admitted them into the councils of the gods, who opened
to them the book of fate, that they thus rashly affirm, that
their deities have executed, or will execute, any purpose
beyond what has actually appeared?
Hume's *Enquiry Concerning Human Understanding*

## SACRED PROVIDENTIAL HISTORY

We have now to examine a form of metaphysical rebellion in politics
different from Cartesianism. It follows upon what I shall call the providential theory of politics. This theory, like Hume's theory of political
order, locates social and political authority not in some timeless order of
nature known by reason but in the historical order. Yet it, too, is in
total alienation from the standards that constitute the present social and
political order. This order is viewed as an illusion not because it has a
historical character which alienates it from the timeless order of nature
(as with Cartesianism) but because it has the wrong sort of historical
character. For Hume, the original authority of all political order is explicated as a narrative relation between *past* and *present* existences, timeless principles being merely abstractions from and corrections of some
narrative context. The providential theory, however, views the authority of political order as a narrative relation between present and future
existences where the authority for judging the present lies in the *future*,
not the past. There is a sacred and a secular form of the theory. I shall
devote a section to each, ending with a discussion of Hume's criticism
of both.

The sacred version of the providential theory is deeply rooted in the
Hebrew-Christian tradition. Its main theses are that, on the basis of
God's revelation in history or through natural theology or both, one can

know that God has certain properties such that the existence of a future state of perfection in the world can be inferred and in the light of which the present can be judged to be a passing, inadequate stage of existence. The Hebrew-Christian tradition has always taken time seriously and has patterned its thought openly around temporal standards grounded in what are thought to be narratively significant acts of God in history. Events interpreted as divine actions are sacred and are thought of as rallying points for understanding the meaning of one's existence in time.

This eschatological way of thinking is in conflict with the tradition of rationalism which derives from Greek philosophy and of which the Cartesian conception of reason is a development. Aristotle considered history to be inferior to poetry as a rational endeavor because poetry is about the universal whereas history is about the particular.[1] Similarly, Descartes, in the *Discourse*, rejected history as incapable of rational reform; he favored, instead, mathematics, physics, and metaphysics, all of which are tenseless, universalizing inquiries. But a Hebrew reflecting on the meaning of the Exodus from Egypt or a Christian reflecting on the meaning of the Resurrection must veiw history, not metaphysics, as the most profound inquiry of all.

The providential view of the world was firmly established in Hume's time not only in the popular consciousness but in the metaphysical framework in which most of the advanced scientific thinkers of the age worked. And the conception of Providence was distinctly prophetic. God's activity was viewed as grounded in a future in the light of which the historical meaning of the present and past is revealed. Isaac Newton spent much of the prime of his life studying and writing on biblical prophecy to determine the historical significance of his present.[2] David Hartley firmly believed that biblical prophecy could be scientifically established and used it to understand the historical significance of his own age: "the latter times are now approaching," times that call for a "more full Discovery of the true Meaning of the prophetic Writings, and of the Aptness to signify the Events predicted."[2]

Joseph Priestley also believed in prophecy, but he stressed the possibility of a scientific understanding of the providential plan being unfolded in history. History is, as yet, an imperfect science, but it promises to provide the most important source of insight into the divine activity and plan. Priestley's *Lectures on History* is an attempt to show how the methods of history as well as the methods of natural philosophy can be used to provide scientific knowledge of God: "Both methods are equally attempts to trace out the perfections and providence of God, by means of different footsteps which he has left us of them."[3] Because of advances in scientific history, what is providentially valuable in the history of past ages "is every day cleared from more and more of the obscurity in which it has been involved . . . the series and connexion of events may be more strictly traced, so that we may say, the plan of this divine drama is opening more and more, and the grand catastrophe growing nearer and nearer perpetually."[4]

Modern science began as an attempt to understand the handiwork of the Creator in nature. This is why Kepler could describe science as "sacred madness." Descartes especially realized that, in this view, scientific knowledge is not possible unless we can know a priori that the Creator has produced a rational universe. His ontological argument that God exists and is not a deceiver was brought forth to secure the foundations of science. By Hume's time, science had become sufficiently secularized so that it was no longer thought of as an inquiry presupposing a rational creator known a priori. Rather, it was conceived as a purely secular inquiry on the basis of which one could have empirical knowledge of the Creator. The design argument replaced the ontological argument. Natural theology was carried out through the ahistorical natural sciences, ahistorical in the sense that their essential task was establishing tenseless laws of nature such as Newton's laws of gravity.

It is this picture of natural theology that Hume is supposed to have upset by showing that natural science cannot provide the sort of conclusion demanded by natural theology. What is not widely appreciated is that, in Hume's time, natural science was not the only avenue to empirical knowledge of God. History was also considered a ground for an empirical theology, and, indeed, a more important one than natural science because of history's congruence with the Hebrew-Christian tradition, which had always claimed to know God not through the inferences of a Greek type of natural science but through revelations in narrative time. By Priestley's day, it could be said confidently that "true history," history as scientifically considered, is "an exhibition of the conduct of divine Providence . . . an inexhaustible mine of the most valuable knowledge."[5]

It was history, then, and not natural science that provided eighteenth-century thinkers with what they considered to be the most important sort of empirical knowledge of God. The seventeenth century was, philosophically, the age of physics and mathematics. Epistemology and ontology were modeled on paradigms taken from reflection on these tenseless disciplines. But the eighteenth century was the age of history and the moral sciences: ethics, aesthetics, politics, economics, law, social theory. Hume called it "the historical age," and it was very much the age of Voltaire, Vico, Gibbon, Robertson, and Turgot. Despite all the talk about following Newton's method and of the perfection of natural science, attention was being directed away from physics and mathematics as the paradigms of knowledge to history and the moral sciences. We have seen that Hume's epistemology treats historical understanding as the paradigm of knowledge and is an attempt to account for its possibility. We have also discussed Hume's view that moral philosophy is more intelligible in certain important respects than natural philosophy. A similar thesis was reached, independently, by Vico, who argued (against Descartes) that history is a form of knowledge superior to natural philosophy. To genuinely know something, to understand it as opposed to merely perceiving it, is to have made it: *verum et factum convertuntur.* Since God made nature, the principles of nature are fully intelligible only to him. Man, however, has made history, and history can be fully known to men.

The providential veiw of history provides an a-priori framework for interpreting historical events, according to which we see all things as "being in a progress towards a state of greater perfection." The master statement of the method was laid down by Priestley: "Let an historian, therefore, attend to every instance of improvement, and a better state of things being brought about, by the events which are presented to him in history, and let him ascribe those events to an *intention* in the Divine Being to bring about that better state of things by means of those events; and if he cannot see the same benevolent tendency in all other appearances let him remain in suspense with regard to them."[6] So although the providential theory can be confirmed by history, it is impossible to ever disconfirm it; all purported counterexamples are treated a priori as cases of possible confirmation by historians yet unborn who will have a unique narrative perspective on events in our present and past unavailable to us now. The thesis that the whole of history is moving inexorably to a state of perfection is not a thesis in history but an a-priori condition of history. The grounds for viewing history this way are the evidence of revelation in Scripture and the knowledge of God's nature as revealed to empirical reason in natural theology. As Priestley says, the evidence is to be gathered "from his works and from his word."[7] Given this evidence, the thesis that history is moving to a state of perfection is a "fair presumption." The strongest sort of confirming evidence for this presumption "are great events being brought about contrary to the intention of the persons who were the chief instruments of them and by the very means which were intended to produce a contrary event."[8] The attempt, for instance, to eliminate Christianity by persecution served only to establish it.

The providential theory of history is at the same time a theory of politics. Priestley's view was the common one: "The great instrument in the hand of divine providence, of this progress of the species towards perfection, is *society*, and consequently *government*."[9] The providential outlook was also defended by Kant, who argued that "philosophy may also have its millennial view."[10] In "Idea of a Universal History from a Cosmopolitan Point of View" (1784), he wrote: "The history of the human race, viewed as a whole, may be regarded as the realization of a hidden plan of nature to bring about a political constitution internally, and for this purpose, also externally perfect, as the only state in which all the capacities implanted by her in mankind can be fully developed."[11] We are to view present political institutions as transitory stages in the light of the future endstate of history.

This way of thinking must affect our conception of the norms of present political institutions. If humanity is progressing to its future state of perfection, then we must view the present state of politics as an inadequate and improper, although necessary, stage in the drama. If we have no knowledge of the exact date of the future perfect society (and this is typically assumed by the providential theories we are considering), then we may either fatalistically accept the status quo, with the satisfying conviction that it is a passing stage, or we may be led to hasten the coming of the future state which alone is truly real and legitimate. Hartley, though he firmly believed in "the latter happy Times predicted by the Prophecies,"[12] took a fatalistic and contemplative attitude towards present political institutions: "How near the Dissolution of the present Governments . . . may be, would be great rashness to affirm. Christ will come in this sense also *as a Thief in the Night*. Our Duty is therefore to watch and to pray . . . and to endeavour by these and all other lawful means, to preserve the Government, under whose protection we live."[13] Kant clearly reveals the second attitude. He has a millennial view of history, whereby our past and present is evaluated in terms of "a great future political body, such as the world has never yet seen."[14] This view is presented as a regulative idea justified by two reasons: there is empirical support for it (the history of the past does appear to be the story of the progressive unfolding of human perfections and, in a teleological view of nature, the future must have locked into it the continuing perfection of human nature); the future perfection of human nature is a desirable goal which, if firmly believed in, would make men dissatisfied with their present state and give them both the motive and the hope to hasten the coming of the goal of history. "Human nature . . . cannot be indifferent even in regard to the most distant epoch that may affect our race, if only it can be expected with certainty. And such indifference is the less possible in the case before us when it appears that we might by our own rational arrangements hasten the coming of this joyous period for our descendents."[15]

Using this progressive conceptual framework, we are to judge our present political institutions in the light of a perfect social and political order in the future. Our duty is to keep our minds fixed on this future order of perfection and in veiw of it to watch solicitously for and to celebrate any providential crack in the existing order and, indeed, to make such cracks ourselves as are practically possible. In this way, present political events such as the struggle between the American colonies and the British government, and, after Hume, the French Revolution were eagerly celebrated by radical reformers of the time not so much because of the good these events were actually achieving as because of the narrative form imposed upon them which required that they be interpreted as phases in the a-priori providential narrative. Consider Richard Price's remarks during the early days of the French Revolution, an event which he interpreted as part of the same narrative unity that included the American Revolution and the war between Crown and Parliament which ended in the Glorious Revolution of 1688: "What an eventful period is this! I am thankful that I have lived to it; and I could almost say, *Lord, now* lettest thou thy servant depart in peace, for mine eyes have seen thy salvation. . . . I have lived to see the rights of men better understood than ever; and nations panting for liberty, which seemed to have lost the idea of it. . . . After sharing in the benefits of one Revolution, I have been spared to be a witness to two other Revolutions, both glorious."[16] It was about this time that the term "revolution" began to be used in a vaguely value-laden sense. During Hume's lifetime and earlier "revolution" framed a value-neutral concept so that one had to qualify a revolution as being either good or bad, roughly in the way that one must specify whether an act of killing is murder or self-defense. This is why the Revolution of 1688 had to be qualified as "Glorious" in distinction from some other quality. For Price, revolution is a narrative concept (he has lived through one, two, three revolutions) having a positive value specified by the a-priori providential framework. Price is convinced that the French Revolution is a good-making event not because of any empirical analysis of what is actually going on at the time or of what is likely to be the outcome but because of the providential framework through which the event is interpreted. As we have learned from Kant and Priestley, the framework can be confirmed by historical events, but it cannot be disconfirmed by them. Any recalcitrant narrative unity can and must be viewed as part of some larger narrative context which historians in the future will be able to perceive: "if he cannot see the same benevolent tendency in all other appearances let him remain in suspense with regard to them."[17]

The same providential interpretation of the present is expressed in a pamphlet written by Catharine Macaulay against Burke's *Reflection on the Revolution in France:* "the events of human life, when *properly* consid-

POLITICS AND PROVIDENTIAL HISTORY

ered, are but a series of *benevolent providences:* many of them, though very important in their consequences, are too much confounded with the common transactions of men to be observed; but whenever the believer thinks he perceives the *omnipotent will* more immediately declaring itself in favour of the future *perfection* and happiness of the moral world, he is naturally led into the same ecstasies of hope and *gratitude,* with which Simeon was transported by the view of the infant messiah."[18] She goes out of her way to stress that this providential manner of looking at things is not visionary but is based on rational and scientific authority: "Has Mr. Burke never heard of any millennium, but that fanciful one which is supposed to exist in the Kingdom of Saints? If this should be the case, I would recommend to him to read *Newton* on *the prophecies.*"[19]

One who thinks in this providential way about the narrative standards that constitute the present is necessarily alienated from them. Narrative standards are internal to an order of passion, and they cannot inform our thought if we are alienated from that order. The historical standards in the light of which one judges the present are grounded in the future, not the past, and just as Simeon rejoiced in seeing the infant messiah, so, prior to seeing him, he languished in melancholy alienation from the present historical order. The temporal standards that inform the customs, traditions, and prescriptions of the present must logically be viewed as illegitimate but burdensome necessities. One can no longer consistently think in terms of them, and judgments of good and evil within the present order are blurred. One may and, in fact, will, for reasons of convenience, adopt some part of the order and thus speak with the vulgar and think with the learned. But one's final loyalty must lie not with the present order but with that of the future. Against the background of this bad-faith grip on the present, we must constantly survey present events, relative to the providential framework, to determine which are pregnant with the future and which are not and, therefore, which are marks of our duty to change things and which are not. Such a frame of mind cannot find itself at home in any kind of present.

## SECULAR PROVIDENTIAL HISTORY

The sacred providential theory of history we have been examining began as a scientific doctrine about history which was taken to lend support to theological beliefs. But just as skepticism began to arise in the eighteenth century about the soundness of theological conclusions derived from natural science, so, near the end of the century, doubt began to arise as to whether history could really support the sacred providential view of things. The result was a secular providential theo-ry, so called because it contains the same destiny-laden modality of the sacred version, the only difference being that the historical process it-self takes the place of God's acts in history. The first secular counter-part to the sacred providential theory appears to have been Turgot's two addresses given in 1750 when he was Prior of the Sorbonne: "Dis-course on the Advantages Which the Establishment of Christianity Has Procured for Mankind" and "Philosophical Tableau on the Successive Advancements of the Human Mind." In these addresses, Turgot in-terpreted history as a natural causal mechanism moving toward the "inevitable" future perfection of human capacities without the benefit of either divine or conscious human guidance. Turgot does talk of the progress of history as providential, but this appears to be simply a ref-erence of courtesy. The driving forces of history are the private and conflicting passions of men which unwittingly and, with occasional lapses, relentlessly produce higher and high states of perfection.

Each age is seen as locked into its succeeding age, and the meaning of each age is not in itself but in the age to which it gives birth. The past is viewed with a certain amount of impatience; after a brief account of the significance of the Reformation, Turgot cannot forbear to exclaim: "Time spread your swift wings! Century of Louis, century of great men, century of reason, hasten!"[20] Logically, the same impatience must also apply to our own time, which is equally alienated from the sort of perfection Turgot has in mind.

Even Kant, the critic of speculative metaphysics, took very seriously the providential view of history and offered his own sort of "transcen-dental deduction" for it. Although Kant refers to God's governance of history, just as Turgot does, the logical core of his theory is secular. Kant grants that we have as yet no scientific laws which could afford knowledge of the future and so we cannot know at present whether history may not be "preparing for us, even in this civilized state of society, a hell of evils at the end; nay, that it is not perhaps advancing even now to annihilate again by barbaric devastation this actual state of society and all the progress hitherto made in civilization."[21] The chiliastic picture of history as a whole leading to an inevitable state of perfection is justified as a regulative idea of reason and falls under Kant's general argument for viewing nature teleologically. The main postulates are that the capacities of the human species are destined to reach their perfection in the course of time. The goal of this progress is the establishment of a "perfect civil union."[22] As with Turgot, perfec-tion is the end-state of a natural causal process where the self-centered passions of men, as a matter of causal fact, fall into an unintended pattern of political perfection.

Although there are no conclusive empirical grounds for this thesis, Kant argues that there is some evidence for it. History up to the present does reveal a steady, unintended progress, and within that general story line there are any number of cases where evils have turned into goods and have contributed to the general course of progress. Viewing history in terms of this a-priori chiliastic framework enables us to perceive what empirical evidence there is for it and also provides us with a deeper knowledge of progress and of its causal conditions. Kant did not claim to have discovered the causes that would give one knowledge of future history, but he hoped that upon establishment of the framework nature might bring forth "a Newton" of history to explain the laws of the historical process as a whole. Such laws would support what Kant called "the art of political prophecy."[23]

Most important, Kant also thought that imposing the chiliastic framework was justified on practical grounds. It yields hope for the future and a special ethic which imposes on us a peculiar *historical* duty to hasten the coming of nature's highest good, the perfect political order locked into the unfolding of human nature.[24] The establishment of the framework in the minds of men might lead not only to a discovery of the laws of political prophecy but also to a self-fulfilling political prophecy. Indeed, Kant hoped that the chiliastic framework would attract the mind of some ambitious absolute ruler who could begin the task of dismantling the present order with the end in view of hastening the coming of history's goal.[25]

Condorcet published his *Sketch of a Historical Picture of the Progress of the Human Mind* in 1785, a work which owed much to his friend and mentor Turgot. In it he claimed to have discovered ten stages through which the historical process as a whole must pass. But Condorcet, like Turgot and Kant, did not pretend to have discovered the laws governing the process. It was Charles Fourier who first claimed to be Kant's hoped-for Newton of history. In 1808, he published the *Theory of the Four Movements* in which the whole of history was thrown into a narrative form having four movements. Since Fourier thought he had discovered the laws governing the movements, he could temporally locate his own age in the process and could view it in the light of the final and happy stages to come. Such future-historical perceptions of the present alienate the thinker from the standards of the present, and Fourier is led to a morbid, revolutionary rejection of them. Piecemeal reform is rejected because it requires acceptance of the present order as a whole: "The vice of our so-called reformers is to indict this or that defect, instead of indicting civilization as a whole, inasmuch as it is nothing but a vicious circle of evil in all its parts; one must get out of this hell."[26]

By the time of Comte and Marx the purely secular idea of a science of

293

the whole of history, as an inevitably progressive movement, was well established among intellectuals and was finding its way into popular political thinking. Mill observed in *A System of Logic* (1843) that the idea "has been familiar for generations to the scientific thinkers of the Continent, and has for the last quarter of a century passed out of their peculiar domain, into that of newspapers and ordinary political discussion."[27] And he complains that England, in this respect as in others, is "usually the last to enter into the general movement of the European mind."[28]

## HUME'S CRITICISM OF PROVIDENTIAL HISTORY

Hume's criticism of the providential theory of politics is part and parcel of his criticism of the "religious hypothesis" in the first *Enquiry*, sections X and XI. In that theory, the historical standards for judging the present order are built not out of narrative relations between past and present events but out of narrative relations between the present and a set of future events known to be inevitable either through revelation or through empirical knowledge of God's properties. In section XI, entitled "Of a Particular Providence and of a Future State," Hume argues that experience cannot afford an inference to the properties of God on the basis of which we can claim to know that there is a set of future events toward which history is moving: "No new fact can ever be inferred from the religious hypothesis; no event foreseen or foretold" (EU, 146). The principle guiding the argument is that where a cause is inferred from its effect we cannot infer from the cause new properties in the effect except in those cases where the cause and effect are connected to other regularities we know. But the Deity "is a single being in the universe, not comprehended under any species or genus, from whose experienced attributes or qualities we can, by analogy, infer any attribute or quality in him" (EU, 144). Hume grants that we can infer from observable effects that God is their cause, but the unobservable properties we ascribe to God must be precisely proportioned to their observable effects. So as "the universe shows wisdom and goodness, we infer wisdom and goodness. As it shows a particular degree of these perfections, we infer a particular degree of them, precisely adapted to the effect which we examine" (EU, 144). We may infer a benevolent Providence as cause of the progress in benevolence that history demonstrates has occurred up to the present. But there we must stop. We cannot infer from the progress of benevolence in history that the benevolent will of the Deity has been exerted only in part and that there is "a more finished scheme or plan which will receive its completion in some distant point of space or time" (EU, 143, 145n). But this is precisely how radical whigs such as Priestley, Price, and Macaulay interpreted events. The French Revolution was celebrated in its early stage not because of any good achieved at the time but because it was viewed as a "benevolent providence," as Catharine Macaulay put it, a case of "the omnipotent will more immediately declaring itself in favour of the future perfection and happiness of the moral world."[29] Hume allows that we can, if we like, read benevolent providences into relations between past and present events. What we cannot do is project these narrative relations into the future so as to read the significance of *present* events in the light of future events. God's providence, for Hume, most emphatically ends with the present, "only so far as you see it, *at present*, exert itself" (EU, 142, Hume's emphasis). The historical significance of our present is unknown to us and must remain so.

We cannot, either by the empirical study of nature or history, discover any evidence that we are living through the unfolding of a divine plan. Nor can revelation, conceived as the story of God's miraculous acts in history, provide us with such knowledge. The other prong of Hume's attack on the providential theory of history is section X, "Of Miracles," where he argues that historical testimony could never provide evidence that a miracle has occurred which could support "a system of religion." The elimination of miracles as a source of revelation entails the elimination of prophecy: "What we have said of miracles may be applied without any variation to prophecies; and, indeed, all prophecies are real miracles and as such only can be admitted as proofs of any revelation. If it did not exceed the capacity of human nature to foretell future events, it would be absurd to employ any prophecy as an argument for a divine mission or authority from heaven" (EU, 130–31). The conclusions to be drawn from sections X and XI are that empirical canons in natural science and in history rule out any possible evidence for a providential interpretation of history that would make a claim to knowledge of the future.

Hume, of course, was not familiar with nineteenth-century secular versions of the providential theory which replaced knowledge of God's plan for knowledge of scientific laws governing the process of history as a whole. But he was familiar with the prototype of all such later views in Turgot's theory of inevitable progress through natural causation. Hume did not think there were any empirical regularities governing human action that could hold beyond the historical period from which they were taken, and so he did not think it possible to know *now* whether history is in a state of progress or decline. Nor does he offer any hope, so prominent in the thought of Turgot, Kant, and Condorcet, that such laws will ever be forthcoming. Aside from this theoretical objection, Hume offered empirical arguments against Turgot's theory, one of which made reference to the Wilkes' riots: "I know you are one of those, who entertain the agreeable and laudable, if not too sanguine hope, that human Society is capable of perpetual Progress towards Perfection, that the Encrease of Knowledge will still prove favorable to good Government, and that since the Discovery of Printing we need no longer Dread the usual Returns of Barbarism and Ignorance. Pray, do not the late Events in this Country appear a little contrary to your System? Here is a People thrown into Disorders . . . merely from the Abuse of Liberty, chiefly the Liberty of the Press; without any Grievance, I do not only say, real, but even imaginary; and without any of them being able to tell one Circumstance of Government which they wish to have corrected: They roar Liberty, tho' they have apparently more Liberty than any People in the World; a great deal more than they deserve; and perhaps more than any men ought to have." Hume goes on to list other evils in British society and government attendant upon the establishment of liberty (one of Turgot's perfections of history). To the possible reply that such disorders "proceed from the still imperfect State of our Knowledge," Hume asks why we should think that men will "ever reach a much more perfect State," when without wealth there is no leisure to pursue knowledge and with wealth there are "so many more alluring appetites to gratify than that for Knowledge." And then there are "foreign Wars, an incurable Evil, which often springs from the greatest and most unexpected Absurdity, and discourages every Project for serving or improving human Society" (L, II, 180–81).

One reason why the idea that history is inevitably moving to a state of perfection was so readily received is that it seemed to be a noble and happy one, belief in which would serve to regulate social action in its image and render the idea self-fulfilling. Hume's rejection of the idea on mere theoretical and empirical grounds may appear as the mark of a small and ungenerous mind. There is a parallel with belief in God. Hume did not think that empirical canons could support belief in an intelligent author of the universe, but he did allow that the belief admits of a post-Pyrrhonian justification analogous to that which can be given for belief in external objects and causal connections. No one can approach the universe in a scientific spirit and not arrive at a strong belief in an intelligent author of the universe, a belief which is not only causally consequent upon scientific inquiry but, logically, is an ultimate belief guiding it. Belief in philosophical theism is a *virtue* and is socially reinforced by the scientific as well as by the religious community. It is for this reason that Hume thought there really are no "speculative atheist[s]," (EU, 149). One could reject this or that form of popular theism, but Hume thought it extremely unlikely that anyone could, upon reflection, fail to have the beliefs of "philosophical theism." Consequently, anyone who would reject theism merely because there are no good empirical reasons for it would betray a disingenuous mind. Similarly, the idea that history is moving inevitably to perfection may be taken as a virtue because of its self-fulfilling character. Anyone who would reject the idea merely because it does not have empirical support would reveal a petty and even misanthropic spirit.

Hume's complete rejection of the idea of Providence in sacred or secular form is remarkable among the major thinkers of his time. He does not consider the idea of historical perfectibility a natural propensity like philosophical theism; nor is it an idea that guides historical inquiry (as Priestley and Kant thought) in the way that philosophical theism guides scientific inquiry; nor does Hume show the slightest respect for the supposed nobility or self-fulfilling character of the idea. Indeed, he appears to think that, in addition to being without rational support, the idea is perverse and dangerous. Against all providential conceptions of history, whether sacred or secular, Hume rhetorically asks: "But what must a philosopher think of those vain reasoners who, instead of regarding the present scene of things as the sole object of their contemplation; so far reverse the whole course of nature, as to render this life merely a passage to something further—a porch which leads to a greater and vastly different building, a prologue, which serves only to introduce the piece, and give it more grace and propriety?" (EU, 141)

Kant found a sublime joy in viewing the present world as an instrument in the service of bringing about the perfect political order. Priestley had the same attitude toward the present: "whatever was the beginning of this world, the end will be glorious and paradisiacal, beyond what our imaginations can now conceive." Nor is this merely a utopian vision; it arises from a scientific understanding of "the natural course of human affairs" which he confesses is an object "the contemplation of which always makes me happy."[30] But such a thought did not make Hume happy, and the reason is that one who thinks in the providential way cannot view the present order as a place in which to dwell. Hume taught that the good life is to be lived now, in its entirety, and not as a prologue to some greater work. The providential philosopher is alienated from the social and political standards that constitute the present, and so we have again the frame of mind that I have called metaphysical rebellion. But in this case, the Archimedean point for alienation from the present is not conceptual location in some timeless order of nature, but location in some future, perfect society viewed as the standard of legitimacy and relative to which the present order must seem unreal and without authority.

Again, the choice is between (1) accepting the present not as a going concern, as others do in common life, but merely for pragmatic reasons and in bad faith, or (2) beginning the process of destroying the unreal present to hasten the coming of the future society. Such a frame of mind is constantly scanning the present for "signs" of the next stage of history. Kant saw (2) as a special "historical duty" (and seemed completely unaware that any such purported duty must be ruled out by the categorical imperative). Like Simeon he looked for a historically enlightened "ambitious ruler" who might be able to undo the present and to bring about the future more quickly. It was just this a-priori providential conceptual framework that enabled Kant to be infatuated by the French Revolution. Likewise, radical reformers such as Price, Macaulay, and Priestley were disposed to receive favorably any revolution on its first appearance as long as it was done in the name of liberty and could be interpreted as a sign of the future order, so lightly did the legitimacy of the present order sit in their imagination.

The providential framework disposes one to criticize the present in terms of total revolution rather than of reform: "it is nothing but a vicious circle of evil in all its parts; one must get out of this hell,"[31] wrote Fourier, who wanted to get on to the next stage of history. The belief that there is a higher stage on the way enables one to launch into radical destruction of the present with confidence; any excesses or mistakes will be, as it were, self-corrected in the next stage. It is only some such belief that can render intelligible, for instance, Herbert Marcuse's completely vacuous conception of "the power of negative thinking," that is, the total negation of Western industrial society: "this society is irrational as a whole."[32] The standard for *totally* rejecting the present social and political order is not a set of timeless principles locked into an "order of nature," as was the case with the Cartesian critique of society. Rather, the standards are internal to the historical process itself: "Ethical standards by virtue of their imperative claim transcend any given state of affairs, and they transcend it, not to any metaphysical entities but to the historical continuum in which every given state of affairs has emerged . . . and in which every given state of affairs will be altered and surpassed by other states."[33] This sounds very much like Hume, but there is a fundamental difference: Hume explicates historical standards as narrative relations between past and present existences, whereas Marcuse (and the providential view generally) thinks of them as narrative relations between present and future existences: "For the true positive is the society of the future and therefore beyond definition and determination, while the existing positive is that which must be surmounted."[34] The providential moralist has a freedom and sweep of thought and action which mere reformers in common life cannot conceive.

Priestley observes that Providence uses "the most disastrous events which disfigure the face of history, upon our first looking at it, to bring about the most happy and desirable state of things."[35] The more we understand the work of Providence "the more desirous shall we be to promote, by our conduct, and by methods of operation of which we are able to judge, that end, which we perceive the Divine Being is pursuing."[36] But having imposed upon us this "historical" duty, Priestley withdraws the means for carrying it out. Those would be the sanguinary methods of Providence itself, "of which we are not always competent judges, and which, therefore, we ought not to attempt to imitate." Generally, our rule of life should be "the plain duties of morality."[37] But these are abstract tenseless duties which presuppose the legitimacy of the present order. If, as Priestley maintains, we can discern the hand of Providence at work and can discern also our historical duty to assist in this work, then it is difficult to see how we could use any methods other than those that Providence itself employs, and this would mean that we too may have to "disfigure the face of history" somewhat to help bring about the purpose toward which history is working. Our "historical" duties must be in conflict with our "plain" duties. The latter operates within the legitimacy of the present order; but the former must view the present as a dying and illegitimate stage to be destroyed in favor of a higher order. And any such dismantling would indeed, from the point of view of "plain" morality, "at first alarm our narrow apprehensions, on account of their seeming to have a contrary tendency."[38]

Despite Priestley's qualms, if we can discern the work of Providence in the present we are obliged to assist it with whatever means the historical situation demands. And these must offend against the established order. Marcuse is more consistent than Priestley. Marcuse poses the question of whether a revolution conceived as the total overthrow of "a legally established" social and political order can be morally justified, and he imagines this as a conflict between "two historical rights . . . the right of that which is, the established commonwealth on which the life and perhaps even the happiness of the individuals depend; and on the other side, the right of that which can be because it may reduce toil, misery, and injustice."[39] One decides between these "two historical rights" using what Marcuse calls a "historical calculus." This calculus considers, on the one hand, the number of victims required to maintain the existing society and also the resources of the society and whether they are used to capacity to satisfy vital needs and pacify the struggle for existence; on the other hand, it considers the number of victims required by the revolutionary society and the probability of that society improving the prevailing conditions. If it is probable that conditions will be improved and if the number of victims exacted by the revolutionary society is less than that exacted by the existing society, the decision to make a revolution is justified. Of this historical calculus Marcuse writes: "Even prior to the question as to the possibility of such a calculus . . . its inhuman quantifying character is evident. But its inhumanity is that of history itself, token of its empirical, rational foundation. No hypocrisy should from the beginning distort the examination. Nor is this brutal calculus an empty intellectual abstraction; in fact, at its decisive turns, history became such a calculated experiment."[40] So for Marcuse we may, indeed, abandon the plain morality of the established order for the imperatives of the historical process itself.

It should be observed that Marcuse's historical calculus is not in the same order of discourse as Bentham's hedonistic calculus, with which it may easily be confused. The utilitarian principle is tenseless and is one of the family of Cartesian critiques of society. The transcendence of the standards in Marcuse's historical calculus is not vertical: a tenseless order, which he considers a "meaningless abstraction." Rather, it is horizontal: a future society locked into the "historical continuum" itself and in the light of which the present must necessarily be judged inadequate.

Belief in providential history is not only dangerous, it is perverse because it requires that we "reverse the whole course of nature, as to render this life merely a passage to something farther." What Hume means by "reversing the whole course of nature" is that the providential perception of the present is, logically, a form of fatalism: "who opened to them the book of fate, that they thus rashly affirm that their deities have executed, or will execute, any purpose beyond what has actually appeared?" (EU, 138). We cannot view our present as a "prologue" unless we have knowledge of future events relative to which the present can be a prologue. We can view the struggles prior to the firing on Fort Sumter as the fated prologue to the Civil War but only because we know there *was* a war and its outcome. In the light of this knowledge, we can, by association of ideas, form a narrative unity and view successive events as passing through a story having a beginning, middle, and end. We have observed that, for Hume, the moral world is understood through and constituted by narrative unities. But there are categorical limits beyond which narrative unities cannot be projected onto the world. The story-mode of thought is always cast in the past tense. Even if the story were about events in our future, it would have to be in the past tense, and we would have to view events as if they had already happened: "In the year 3009, on a planet in the galaxy Nubecula Major, there *lived* a people who. . . ." We may view our present as narratively significant in the light of past events. And we may view a past event as narratively significant in the light of earlier events and in the light of later events up to and including our present. What we cannot do is view our present as narratively significant in the light of future events. This would be to have a fated perception of the present. For us to perceive now the narrative significance of our present would be to treat the future as having already happened. And this would, indeed, be "to reverse the whole course of nature," giving the future a status that, ontologically, it cannot have.

There is another sense in which fated perceptions of the present reverse the order of nature. According to Hume we may think of the present in two ways: as abstract and tenseless, as we do in natural philosophy, or as tensed and narrative, as in moral philosophy. The tenseless present is covered by tenseless predicates, "is a man," "is a woman," "is a person," "is a house," "is a tree," and so on. These predicates logically can be applied to the present independently of the past or of any other tensed structure. The narrative present is covered by past-entailing predicates, "is a senator," "is a policeman," "is a Rembrandt," "is a priest," and so on. These predicates logically cannot apply to the present unless some past-tense statement is true. Past-entailing ideas are woven by the narrative imagination and constitute the conceptual framework of the moral world. Ontologically, they pick out a class of narrative existences which are the entities that populate the moral world. These entities have the past ontologically built into their present existence. They also have a normative structure which is determined, in part, by the narrative relation which unites the past and present.[41] To truly describe something as a priest, a senator, or a Rembrandt is also to refer to a system of values, standards, rights, and duties. Social and political legitimacy, in the broadest sense, is constituted by narrative relations holding between past and present existences where the past is viewed as a standard conferring legitimacy on the present and, as Hume paradoxically observes, where the present may also be taken as a standard for conferring legitimacy on the past (T, 566). Thus the ratification of the U.S. Constitution was an event in 1789 which by narrative association of ideas (along with later interpretations of it) serves as a standard conveying legitimacy to present political and legal actions. Similarly, the establishment of the plan of liberty in the Glorious Revolution of 1688 confers a special "historical" (not moral) legitimacy on the Puritan rebellion against Charles I. The same holds for all social and political norms however serious or trivial. But the providential theory reverses this order. The standards for social and political reality are not determined by an order of past or present events but by an order of future events, and these confer not legitimacy but, necessarily, illegitimacy on the present society.

Priestley wrote that "History . . . may be called . . . anticipated experience," by which he meant that the significance of the past and present is constituted by the future.[42] Because Mill, Kant, Marcuse and many others have tried to hold onto something like the providential view of history, they have had to view the future as having a narrative relation to the present that can be satisfied only by the past. Mill greatly admired Comte's central principle: "the axiom of Leibnitz—*the present is big with the future.*"[43] Similar maxims have been popular with twentieth-century process philosophers such as Whitehead, who once remarked that, if the future is cut away, "the present collapses, emptied of its proper content."[44] We examined Hume's views on narrative time in chapter 4. Here we may recall that he conceives of the future as an order of hope and fear and as the possibility of an "advance" in our existence. But there is no sense in which Hume thinks the present is "big" with the future or that the future is the "proper" content of the present. If anything, Hume's maxim would be that the present is big with the past and that the past is the proper content of the present: "Hence we imagine our ancestors to be, in a manner, mounted above us, and our posterity to lie below us" (T, 437).

In order to appreciate the important role the past has in our understanding of the present, Hume invites us to consider how empty a world would be that had no past (A, 13–16). God could create a world out of nothing, without a past, complete with newly made adults such as Adam and all the other objects of tenseless predicates. This would be the world of Humean impressions prior to any narrative interpretation of them—in fact the world as it is now, populated with women, persons, typewriters, trees, and the like. But it would not be the present of common life because no past-entailing ideas would apply, and so there would be no past-entailing existences in the present: no fathers, presidents, queens, harlots, civil rights, or Olivetti typewriters. If the past were somehow cut away, the present would lose its normative structure; every concrete standard of value would vanish, and we should be left with tenseless existences governed only by abstract tenseless standards which, without a historical context, could not be applied in a nonarbitrary way. The present without the past would not be at all what we consider the present in common life to be.

But if only the future were cut away—if, for instance, the world should end in one hour—the past-entailing existences of the normative present would remain just as they are. Our hopes and anticipations would be without ontological foundation, but our understanding of what exists in the present would be unchanged. Presidents, Rembrandts, and friends would be, logically, just as they are now. Even future-referring ideas such as "is the heir apparent," and "is a mother to be" can be applied to the present independently of the future. There is no contradiction in saying that someone *is* the heir apparent but will never become king. But there would be a contradiction in saying that someone is *now* a senator and that he has no past. He could be a man without a past, but not a senator. So, however important it might be, the future, unlike the past, contains no entities or values that structure the normative present of common life.[45]

We may, of course, view someone's present as being big with the future when *their* present and future are in our past. Thus Hume could and did view the dim outlines of the constitutional settlement of 1688 in the struggle between Charles I and Parliament. What we cannot do, on pain of fatalism, is view *our* present as big with the future. Hume was entirely emancipated from any form of providential thought because he did not ontologize narrative relations. For him there is no "historical process" in nature. Narrative relations are constituted by narrative associations of ideas and these are entirely mind-dependent. There are, indeed, narrative existences in the moral world, but their being is dependent upon opinion. We may say that the being of narrative existences is that their story is told. As new events occur, the story is necessarily reinterpreted and the nature of narrative existences change. So for Hume there is, ontologically, no historical process in which God could act, or about which "historical" laws could be discovered. History is not a process that goes anywhere. It is a relation of ideas spawned by the temporally provincial imagination. History is made by the stories historians tell about the significance of their existence in time.

If Hume is correct, then, providential morality of any sort is impossible. The "benevolent providences" which radical Whigs read into the early stages of revolutionary events, Turgot's impatience with the past and present, Kant's "historical duty," Hegel's "world historical individuals" who can read the signs of the time and act in accord with them heedless of "conventional" morality, Fourier's total alienation from the present, Marx's "scientific" vision of history as the story of class struggle, and his special duty to advance the coming of the classless society, Marcuse's "historical calculus," all are based on grotesque confusions about the status of narrative thought. They are dangerous as well because they license usurpations of the "plain" morality that binds together and disciplines the narrative existences that populate the present of common life.

There is another way to unpack Hume's intuition that it is perverse to think of the present as a prologue to something else. I have argued that the providential criticism of the present makes sense only on condition that some form of fatalism is true. Hume did not undertake a refutation of fatalism, though he observes that fatalism and predestination tend to accompany religious groups that are tainted with "enthusiasm" and whose members imagine themselves the elect of God (H, IV, app., 503). He also believed that any form of foreknowledge is incompatible with freedom and moral responsibility: "To reconcile the indifference and contingency of human actions with prescience or to defend absolute decrees, and yet free the Deity from being the author of sin, has been found hitherto to exceed all the power of philosophy" (EU, 103). And there is some hint in "The Stoic" and "The Sceptic" that Hume thought of Stoic fatalism as one of those philosophical extravagances which can neither be logically nor psychologically maintained in common life. But there is no doubt that Hume himself rejected fatalism, and little doubt, I think, that he would have found congenial Aristotle's argument against it. Like Hume, Aristotle thought fatalism incompatible with freedom and responsibility. Fatalism, he thought, could be avoided by holding that future-tense statements have an indeterminate truth value. If so, then, nothing we could say *now* about the future could be true, and fatalism would be impossible. Similarly, since knowledge presupposes truth, "prescience" would be impossible. This solution introduces a certain inelegance into logic, for it means that all propositions have determinate truth-values except future-tense propositions. But it accords well with our ordinary notion that the future *is* contingent, and Aristotle, like Hume, tended to take seriously our common ways of thinking about reality.[46]

Let us now apply this Aristotelian solution to the problem of fatalism to the providential criticism of the present social and political order. We may treat the propositions framed in a Humean narrative association of ideas as a complex truth-functional conjunction where the conjuncts have different tenses. To describe a past event in the light of a present event is to say something about the past that is not true unless past-tense and present-tense propositions are true. Now in Aristotle's account past-tense and present-tense propositions have definite truth values. So any Humean narrative association of ideas uniting ideas of past and present events could express a true proposition about either the present or past. But any narrative association of ideas uniting ideas of the present with those of the future could not express a true proposition *about the present* because the future-tense conjunct does not have a definite truth value, and a truth functional conjunction cannot be true unless both conjuncts are true. Criticisms of the present in the light of standards rooted in the past can be true. Thus to say of a present law that it is unconstitutional could be true since that is to utter a statement about the present in the light of statements about past events (the constitutional settlement of 1789 along with certain interpretations of it), and both sets of statements could be true. All Humean criticism of the present will have at the very least this narrative form and could be a criticism that is true. But any providential criticism of the present in the light of a future order taken as a standard, however vaguely it might be conceived, could not be true of the present since future-tense statements cannot be true. What is wrong, then, with the providential criticism of the present social and political order is not that it is too radical. Rather, it is not a *criticism* of the present at all because nothing that is said could be true. Having cut himself off from the past and present as the source of norms in favor of the future, it is logically impossible for the providential thinker to discern the good and evil that exists within the normative present. He can neither celebrate the good nor work to correct the evil. Nothing he says about the present can be true. Any new order he may attempt to impose on the world is derived not from a searching criticism of the present but from his "own conceit and imagination" (EU, 141).

# 12
# Conservatism

The gloomy enthusiasm which prevailed among the
parliamentary party, is surely the most curious spectacle
presented by any history; and the most instructive, as well
as entertaining, to a philosophical mind.
                                    Hume's *History of England*

## HUME AND THE CONSERVATIVE TRADITION

Hume's political philosophy and, indeed, his philosophy generally has
been recognized as a form of conservatism. Leslie Stephen described it
as a "cynical conservatism," by which he meant that Hume's thought
was so grounded in the dried clay of the past and in the status quo that
he had no feeling for the philosophical and religious ideas that have led
men to rebel on behalf of a broader extension of liberty and democratic
sovereignty.[1] This is also how it appeared to the Whigs of Hume's
time. Catharine Macaulay was not unusual in viewing the whole outlook of Hume's philosophy as one of almost amoral complacency: "It is
allowed by that famous sceptic, Mr. Hume, that the felicities of a good
constitution, a gay and volatile temper, with the advantages of temporal
prosperity, will secure an impunity from those stings of conscience,
and that keen remorse which commonly follows the blacker acts of
turpitude."[2] The Whigs were outraged by Hume's *History* because they
found it to be written on the principles of just such moral complacency.
His account of the constitution was considered to be not only factually
mistaken but deeply perverse, a celebration of "those time-serving
placemen who have sacrificed the most essential interests of the public
to the benefits of their private affections."[3] Sheldon Wolin has argued
that Hume's conservatism, as a defense of the status quo, was overriden
by events: "Hume, appropriately enough, died in 1776, and from this
point on revolutionary events worked to make a mockery of Hume's

comfortable conclusions. The realm of fact provided cold comfort for conservatives; it was now controlled by the revolutionaries."[4]

In order to evaluate these criticisms, we must examine the nature of Hume's conservatism. The main barrier to doing this is the term "conservatism" itself. The term first entered political discourse some time after the French Revolution. Chateaubriand (1768–1848) published a journal entitled *Le Conservateur* which sought to restore the prerevolutionary order. By 1830 the American National Republicans could call themselves "conservatives," and in 1832 the "Conservative Party" became the official name of the British Tory party.[5] No one prior to the French Revolution could have recognized himself as a conservative any more than Constable and Turner could have recognized that they were introducing elements of impressionism into their paintings, although that is, in fact, what, among other things, they were doing. The characterization of Hume as a conservative, "cynical" or otherwise, cannot be made without careful qualifications which take account of the narrative framework in which the term has meaning. There is, of course, a tenseless concept of conservatism which is often used to characterize conservatives: a conservative is one who is disposed to defend the status quo and to look with suspicion on any proposal for a fundamental change in the established order. But this cannot be an adequate conception of the political outlook of those who have called themselves conservatives. For one thing, it is a conception satisfied by any ideology whatsoever. Marxists, Liberals, and Socialists in power have a disposition to defend the status quo and to look with dark suspicion on any proposal for a fundamental change in the established order. Moreover, as the history of conservatism shows, thinkers such as Burke, De Maistre, Metternich, De Bonald, Coleridge, Eliot and Solzhenitsyn have been quite capable of reformist and even radical action. Hume himself gloried in the revolutionary character of his philosophy, making it clear that acceptance of his principles would bring about extensive conceptual changes, if not a total revolution, in the concept of what philosophy is.

To understand the conservative mind and Hume's relation to it, we should begin with what self-professed conservatives have said about their position. Erik von Kuehnelt-Leddihn, a contemporary Austrian conservative, views his own thinking as a criticism of various forms of what J. L. Talmon has called "totalitarian democracy," a way of thinking that Kuehnelt-Leddihn traces to the French Revolution: "the roots of the evil are historically-genetically the same all over the Western World. The fatal year is 1789, and the symbol of iniquity is the Jacobin Cap. Its heresy is the denial of personality and of personal liberty. Its concrete manifestations are Jacobin mass democracy, all forms of national collectivism and statism, Marxism producing socialism and communism, fascism, and national socialism, leftism in all its modern guises and manifestations to which in America the good term 'liberalism,' perversely enough, is being applied."[6] Although shaped by twentieth-century conditions, this manifestation of the conservative mind is, in all essentials, that contained in Edmund Burke's *Reflections on the Revolution in France* (1790), which is usually taken as the founding document of conservatism.

So understood, conservatism is a narrative conception based on a doctrine of catastrophe, the fatal event being the French Revolution and later political movements conceptually connected to it. Conservatism, then, is not a timeless disposition to defend the status quo but a historically limited movement that appears on the scene only to defend a certain sort of value and to combat a certain sort of enemy. Although differing widely on many things, conservatives have agreed about the enemy: the violent intrusion of rationalistic metaphysics into politics. Burke attacked the "adulterated metaphysics" of the Enlightenment which he thought gave the French Revolution its unique shape. Hegel, likewise, rejected the "alienated reason" and "absolute freedom" of the French Revolution, and Metternich condemned "presumptuous man" who by reason alone seeks to understand and to reconstruct the foundations of social and political order. Thus in the process of trying to defend the ancien régime, conservatives succeeded in exposing a certain sort of intellectual and practical error which they considered to be a threat to *any* legitimate social and political order. Conservatism, then, should not be viewed as a mindless disposition to preserve the established regime but as a substantial intellectual tradition. In its broadest outlines, this tradition is a doctrine of limits, in particular a doctrine of the limits beyond which philosophical criticism of social and political order cannot go.

The question we must now ask is whether Hume can be considered part of the conservative tradition. Conventional historiography marks the reaction to the French Revolution and particularly Burke's *Reflections* as the beginning of the conservative tradition. Since Hume died thirteen years prior to the French Revolution, it may appear anachronistic to view him as part of this tradition. There are, however, good reasons to revise this particular story line in the history of modern political ideology. What is peculiar about conservative thought is its criticism of philosophy in politics. Burke was a Whig and one of the great reformers of his age (he had worked courageously for reform in the administration of the American colonies, Ireland, and India). But when asked to support the Revolution in France, he was forced out of his ritualistic liberty-loving Whig stance to consider more carefully the foundations of political authority. He saw the French Revolution not as an understandable outrage at oppression but as an attempt to totally restructure society according to a metaphysical theory. The Glorious Revolution of 1688 and the American Revolution, he interpreted, in Whig fashion, as "restorations" of historical rights against usurpation. But the French Revolution was not an ordinary case of rebellion, understandable in terms of the historical goods and evils of common life. It was a metaphysical rebellion, and to Burke's mind a unique event the nature of which few understood. He devoted the rest of his life to instructing his countrymen (especially radical Whigs such as Macaulay, Priestley, and Price) on the difference between Whig reform and the metaphysical nature of the French Revolution.

Conservatism, then, is a criticism of a certain pattern of thought. Insofar as Hume identified this pattern of ideas and criticized them in a characteristically conservative way, he should be considered part of the conservative intellectual tradition. That Burke first became aware of these ideas through the shock of the Terror and that others learned of them through Burke's *Reflections* should not lead us to think that the ideas did not exist prior to 1790. They did exist, and Hume more than anyone else must be considered the first to have identified them and to have offered a philosophical criticism of them. Moreover, Hume was not brought to reflection on the limits of philosophy in politics by events like the Terror, but by the conceptual and psychological pressures of the autonomy principle internal to the nature of philosophy itself. However, something like the conceptual reform of philosophy (post-Pyrrhonian philosophy) which Hume worked out in the closet was hammered out, inelegantly, on the anvil of events by the reaction to the French Revolution.

In 1783 General George Washington, in a circular letter to the state governors, urging the union of the states, observed that "The foundation of our Empire was not laid in the gloomy age of Ignorance and Superstition" but that "the researches of the human mind after social happiness, have been carried to a great extent, the treasures of knowledge, acquired by the labours of Philosophers, Sages, and Legislators, through a long succession of years, are laid open for our use, and their collected wisdom may be happily applied in the Establishment of our forms of Government. . . . At this auspicious period, the United States came into existence as a Nation, and if their Citizens should not be completely free and happy, the fault will be entirely their own."[7] This was written at the high tide of the Enlightenment when one could with innocence and hopefulness speak, in a public forum, of the philosopher as a sage and legislator who could preside over the founding of a state. But after the French Revolution the term "philosopher" began to take on unfavorable connotations, and for some time thereafter, especially in the Anglo-American world, it would denote an alienated social theorist whose attempt to totally restructure society on a rational plan had led to the Terror and to what has come to be known as totalitarianism.

British conservatives following Burke have thought of conservatism not as a philosophy or ideology but as an inarticulate state of mind. Professor Viereck observes: "According to this British approach, the logical deductive reasoning of Latin conservatives like De Maistre is too doctrinaire, too eighteenth-century. It may even be generalized that the conservative mind does not like to generalize. Conservative theory is anti-theoretical. The liberal and rationalist mind consciously articulates abstract blueprints; the conservative mind unconsciously incarnates concrete traditions."[8] There is something to be said for this view not only of British conservatives but of the conservative movement generally. It is remarkable that most of the great conservative thinkers have been literary men such as Johnson, Coleridge, Dostoyevsky, and Eliot, or statesmen-philosophers such as Burke, Metternich, Tocqueville, Disraeli, and Churchill. Except by Hegel (whose work can and has been put to revolutionary ends), there has been no deep philosophic articulation of the conservative view.

In Hume's philosophy, however, we find a conceptual structure designed to rebut revolutionary thought and capable of explaining in broad outline the conservative view of legitimate social and political order. This was recognized by the first conservatives in France after the Revolution who, as Professor Bongie has shown, took not Burke's *Reflections* but Hume's *History of England* and Hume's political essays as founding documents of the Counter-Revolution.[9] Burke's *Reflections* were written for the British, to persuade radical Whigs not to imitate the Revolution and to explain the conceptual differences between the Whig tradition of evolutionary reform and the peculiar metaphysical rebellion of the Revolution. There is a certain strident British chauvinism running through the work, along with Gothic elements which foreshadow the coming romantic age and nostalgia for medieval unity. Hume's historical and philosophical works, however, are framed from a cosmopolitan point of view and ordered around a system of philosophy. They were not hastily constructed as a reaction to events but were deliberately worked out in the very mid-day of the Enlightenment. His work was, therefore, more congenial to those more theoretically inclined "Latin conservatives." They could appeal to Hume as one who had achieved almost superhuman objectivity in history and who as a skeptic used the very tools of reason to limit the range of reason in politics.[10]

In the sections that follow I want to explore the reasons why Hume should be thought of as the first conservative philosopher. Such a thesis, if correct, can serve to expand and to enrich our conception of the conservative intellectual tradition, a tradition of thought that has yet to be appreciated by Anglo-American philosophers. But most important, reading Hume through the conceptual framework of the conservative tradition will enable us to discern structures of his thought which would otherwise not appear.

## RELIGION AS A PHILOSOPHICAL ERROR

I have characterized the conservative tradition as, at the very least, a reaction, thoughtful or otherwise, to the attempt to determine the social and political affairs of common life by metaphysical thinking. Conservatism is much more than this, but it is at least this. Some conservatives have retreated to the nonreflective regions of art, tradition, or feeling. Few have attempted philosophically to criticize philosophy itself, and to distinguish true from false philosophy, using the former to combat the latter. Hume is a conservative of this sort. We saw in chapter 1 that his philosophy begins as a dialectical criticism of philosophy itself where philosophy is forced to abandon the autonomy principle and to absorb common life as a category of its own critical activity. In chapters 10 and 11 we saw how Hume uses this reformed conception of philosophy to argue against two forms of alienation in politics: Cartesianism and the providential theory of history. But given the close connection between religion and politics in Hume's time and the fact that much of his criticism of politics involves a criticism of religious beliefs and institutions, it may appear that the real focus of his criticism of politics is religion, not philosophy. If so, then Hume could not be considered part of the conservative tradition as I have defined it. And it is, indeed, easy to view his extensive attack on religious institutions as of a piece with the attack of the philosophes: an assault by Enlightenment and philosophy against tradition, prejudice, and superstition. But this Manichean picture of the relation between philosophy and religion, however true it may be of the philosophes, is not true of Hume. As we shall see, for Hume philosophy and religion are not separate activities but are internally connected in such a way that the criticism of religion turns out to be philosophical self-criticism. Consequently, criticism of religion in politics is criticism of philosophy in politics.

In a famous passage of the *Treatise*, Hume remarks: "Generally speaking, the errors of religion are dangerous; those in philosophy only ridiculous." This suggests that philosophy and religion are independent activities, the former being a threat to society, the latter not. But as the context makes clear, this is not Hume's intention, for he acknowledges that the errors of philosophy can be as dangerous as those of religion:

"The Cynics are an extraordinary instance of philosophers, who from reasonings purely philosophical ran into as great extravagancies of conduct as any *Monk* or *Dervise* that ever was in the world" (T, 272). Whether the errors of philosophy can be a threat to society is a factual, not a conceptual, question.

In the *Treatise*, Hume wrote: "There is only one occasion, when philosophy will think it necessary and even honourable to justify herself, and that is, when religion may seem to be in the least offended; whose rights are as dear to her as her own, and are indeed the same" (T, 250). Presumably, the rights are the same because philosophy and religion are forms of the same activity, a point which is made explicit in the first *Enquiry:* "religion . . . is nothing but a species of philosophy" (EU, 146). The *Enquiry* also makes clearer that it is not religion as such but religion conceived as a species of philosophy that poses a threat to society: "nor have the political interests of society any connection with the philosophical disputes concerning metaphysics and religion" (ibid.). As a species of philosophy, religion is a threat to society because of its philosophic errors. This is why "true philosophy" is a sovereign antidote to superstition (EU, 12; T, 271).

Hume's conception of the relation between philosophy and religion is this. True philosophy (post-Pyrrhonian philosophy) is distinguished from false philosophy (philosophy governed by the autonomy principle). Falling under these, respectively, is true religion (philosophical theism) and false religion (superstition and enthusiasm). The "craft of popular superstition" presided over by the priests was a common enemy for Hume and the Enlightenment generally. But Hume differed in thinking of religious superstition as continuous with autonomous philosophical thinking and of a piece with the errors of ancient and modern metaphysics, none of which recognize the independent authority of unreflective common life.

False philosophy can take on a religious or secular form in the individual or in society, and so Hume can speak indifferently of "sects of philosophy and religion" (E, 51). Hume discusses Diogenes as an ancient example and Pascal as a modern one of how from purely philosophical arguments one can be led to an "artificial life" in total alienation from the usual maxims of common life. Such an existence is lived not "in the air" of common life but "in a vacuum" and is the result of "the illusions" of "extravagant philosophy" and of "philosophical enthusiasm" (EM, 341–43). The deleterious influence of false philosophy on the individual is again taken up in the light essay "Of Moral Prejudices," where Hume takes on an early feminist of Cartesian mold and defends not departing "too far from the received maxims of conduct and behaviour" against "that grave philosophic endeavour after perfection" (E, 576, 573).

Because Hume thought of the errors of religion as essentially philosophic, he was able to identify a rising threat to the politics of common life which was lost on his contemporaries: the emergence of secular metaphysical political parties. I turn now to Hume's original and prophetic discussion of this new sort of political party.

## METAPHYSICAL POLITICAL PARTIES

Philosophy and religion have histories and, according to Hume, their relation to politics has not always been the same. In "Of Parties in General," he distinguishes between parties that operate properly within the confines of common life and those that do not. The former are parties of interest and affection, the latter are parties of metaphysical principle. Parties of interest such as the division between "the *landed* and *trading* part of the nation" are the most "reasonable, and the most excusable" (E, 58). Parties of affection such as an attachment to a particular ruling family, though not as reasonable, are, nonetheless, a quite common and understandable phenomenon. But parties based on metaphysical principles are conceptually absurd and, moreover, are unique to modern times: "Parties from *principle*, especially abstract speculative principle, are known only to modern times, and are, perhaps, the most extraordinary and unaccountable *phenomenon* that has yet appeared in human affairs" (ibid.). They are absurd because, unlike parties of interest and affection, they foment violent opposition with principles that do not lead to contrary patterns of conduct: "Where different principles beget a contrariety of conduct, which is the case with all different political principles, the matter may be more easily explained. . . . But where the difference of principle is attended with no contrariety of action . . . what madness, what fury, can beget such an unhappy and such fatal divisions?" (ibid., 58–59). The point urged here against metaphysics in politics is just part of Hume's general attack on metaphysics in common life, namely, that metaphysical principles determined by the autonomy principle tell us nothing either factually or normatively about the world of experience, because they cannot, except arbitrarily, be applied to the world.

The metaphysical political parties that Hume has in mind are not merely religious parties, though, in his view, these too are informed by metaphysical principles—"the speculative doctrines, or the metaphysics of religion" (H, III, xxxv, 370). His point applies, and was intended to apply, to the secular philosophical parties that were beginning to appear in his day. He accepted but lamented the fact that "no party, in the present age, can well support itself without a philosophical or speculative system of principles annexed to its political or practical one" (E, 452). The fact that political parties require metaphysical principles as rationalizations indicates that there is a tendency, even among the vulgar, to govern their actions by metaphysical principles and to respond to parties that invoke the authority not merely of interest or affection but of philosophical legitimacy. Though, of course, "The people being commonly very rude builders, especially in this speculative way . . . their workmanship must be a little unshapely, and discover evident marks of that violence and hurry in which it was raised" (ibid.). There is, then, a quite definite philosophical consciousness among the masses. How did men achieve this philosophical consciousness? The rise of a commercial and industrial society that encouraged personal liberty and therefore personal judgment was an important contributing factor, and so was the emergence of republican institutions. But the main cause was the historic union of philosophy and religion in Christianity that occurred at the close of the ancient world and that, he thinks, "contributed to render Christendom the scene of religious wars and divisions" (E, 61).

In barbarous times, before the appearance of philosophy as a special sort of inquiry, religious sects consisted mostly of "traditional tales and fictions, which may be different in every sect, without being contrary to each other; and even when they are contrary, every one adheres to the tradition of his own sect, without much reasoning or disputation. But as philosophy was widely spread over the world at the time when Christianity arose, the teachers of the new sect were obliged to form a system of speculative opinions. . . . Hence naturally arose keenness in dispute, when the Christian religion came to be split into new divisions and heresies: and this keenness assisted the priests in their policy of begetting a mutual hatred and antipathy among their deluded followers" (ibid.). Another reason why Christianity took on philosophic shape is that it was a theistic religion: "where theism forms the fundamental principle of any popular religion, that tenet is so conformable to sound reason, that philosophy is apt to incorporate itself with such a system of theology" (NHR, 53).

In the ancient world, "Sects of philosophy . . . were more zealous than parties of religion; but, in modern times, parties of religion are more furious and enraged than the most cruel factions that ever arose from interest and ambition" (E, 61). The union of philosophy and religion in Christian civilization, along with the union of ecclesiastical and civil power, has accustomed men to think of political issues in a metaphysical way. But the full-fledged and self-conscious introduction of metaphysics into politics and on a popular level is unique to modern times and has been, Hume thinks, an unmitigated disaster. It has spread "the greatest misery and devastation" and "has ever since been the poison of human society, and the source of the most inveterate factions in every government" (ibid., 60–61).

The greatest enemies of political order are those who work to found political parties, particularly parties of metaphysical principle. Just "as much as legislators and founders of states ought to be honoured and respected among men, as much ought the founders of sects and factions to be detested and hated. . . . Factions subvert government, render laws impotent, and beget the fiercest animosities among men of the same nation, who ought to give mutual assistance and protection to each other" (ibid., 55). Hume continues with imagery reminiscent of the book-burning passage at the end of the *Enquiry:* "And what should render the founders of parties more odious, is the difficulty of extirpating these weeds, when once they have taken root in any state" (ibid.). Moreover, they grow more easily and propagate themselves faster "in free governments" (ibid.). Though sympathetic with republican ideals, Hume always considered this susceptibility to factions, especially (under modern intellectual conditions) factions of metaphysical principle, a major defect of free government and one that, unless remedied, would lead to its dissolution. This is why he drew the bonds of authority very tight and always viewed absolute monarchy as being, if not the ideal form of government, at least the best working arrangement for the modern age: "I should rather wish to see an absolute monarch than a republic in this Island. . . . Absolute monarchy . . . is the easiest death, the true *Euthanasia* of the British constitution" (E, 52–53; L, I, 194).

Hume's most extensive examination of the modern phenomenon of metaphysical political parties is in the volumes of the *History* dealing with the revolutionary events that occurred during the reign of the Stuarts. He considered the war between Parliament and Crown to be a uniquely modern and metaphysical war, roughly in the way that Burke thought of the French Revolution. The metaphysical character of the war was due in part to the nature of Protestantism and especially Puritanism, which "being chiefly spiritual, resembles more a system of metaphysics" (H, IV, xxxviii, 12). The Protestants were somewhat like "the Stoics," who "join a philosophical enthusiasm to a religious superstition" (NHR, 63). On the other hand, "the Catholic religion, adapting itself to the senses, and enjoining observances which enter into the common train of life," is a less metaphysical sort of religion, and to Hume is, for that reason, more reasonable though not more rational.

Generally, Hume is more approving in the *History* of the Catholic-Anglican tradition than he is of the Protestant-Puritan tradition. The former is often described as "superstition," the latter as "enthusiasm," a concept which he also uses to characterize the futile and destructive

315

efforts of the alienated philosopher to impose his abstractions upon the world. Protestantism is viewed as a metaphysical system, the origin of which was part of "that spirit of innovation with which the age was generally seized" (H, III, xxxi, 204). The Protestants were a revolutionary force alienated from common life and willing to die for "their speculative and abstract principles" (ibid., IV, xxxviii, 12). Until Protestantism became established, Catholicism is described in the *History*, as the "ancient and deep-founded" religion of the British. Hume is amused at the radical and *impious* character of the Protestant rebellion: "a little humanity . . . was due by the nation to the religion of their ancestors" (ibid., V, 1, 10). He criticizes "protestant historians" for ridiculing the veneration of relics (ibid., III, xxxi, 242), and those of a "philosophical mind" who ridicule "pious ceremonies" (ibid., V, lvii, 298). Hume appreciated the beauty and humanizing character of high liturgy, observing that "during a very religous age, no institutions can be more advantageous to the rude multitude, and tend more to mollify that fierce and gloomy spirit of devotion to which they are subject" (ibid.). Hume was sympathetic with the "humane and inoffensive liturgy" defended by Charles I against the Puritans. And he had respect for Charles's Anglicanism which, unlike Puritan Protestantism, "contained nothing fierce or gloomy, nothing which enraged him against his adversaries, or terrified him with the dismal prospect of futurity" (ibid., V, lix, 355). Hume also believed in an established church, not because of the beneficent influence religion could have on the state but because of the beneficent influence the civil authority and the morality of common life could have on the alienated and always threatening metaphysical institution of religion (ibid., III, xxix, 128–29).

It was, in part, sentiments such as the above which motivated the letters of encouragement in the face of the apparent failure of the first volume on the Stuarts from two high churchmen, Dr. Herring, primate of England, and Dr. Stone, primate of Ireland, "two odd exceptions" which Hume gratefully acknowledged in his autobiography (MOL, 7). He would have found it odder still to have learned that these and other sentiments, under the conceptually shattering conditions of the French Revolution, would earn him the title of the "Scottish Bossuet" among the Catholic right in France.

The central theme of the Stuart volumes is that the war was a metaphysical one worthy of philosophical analysis and pregnant with lessons about the elimination of false philosophy from politics: "The gloomy enthusiasm which prevailed among the parliamentary party, is surely the most curious spectacle presented by any history; and the most instructive, as well as entertaining, to a philosophical mind" (H, V, lxii, 519). Perhaps the first to understand this theme was Louis

XVI. Hume was presented to him at court in 1763 when the king was just ten years old (but old enough to confess himself an admirer of Hume's works!). He was a careful student of the *History* throughout his life, and as events began to take on revolutionary shape, he sought guidance by finding parallels between his own situation and that of Charles I. Bongie has shown that "as the time of his trial approached . . . his preoccupation with the events of Charles I's reign, Hume's account of which he seems finally to have preferred above all others, had become a veritable obsession." And his valet records that, upon having just learned that the Convention had voted for the death sentence: "Le roi m'ordonna de chercher dans la bibliothèque, le volume de l'Histoire d'Angleterre où se trouve la mort de Charles Ier: il en fit la lecture les jours suivants."[11]

The metaphysical conflict between Charles and Parliament involved not only conflicts over church doctrine and government but also philosophical disputes concerning the foundations of political authority. The "general humour of the time was . . . intent on plans of imaginary republics" (H, V, Lix, 334). Practical issues of state were transformed into grotesque metaphysical shapes: "The inquiries and debates concerning tonnage and poundage went hand in hand with these theological or metaphysical controversies" (ibid., li, 58). The philosophic conflict extended to the masses through the medium of the pulpit, each of which housed a "ghostly practitioner" whose thought and mode of being, like that of Diogenes and Pascal, were contrived in the vacuum of the autonomy principle (ibid., III, xxix, 129). These "wretched composers of metaphysical polemics" worked tirelessly to instill their "speculative and abstract principles" into the unguarded minds of the credulous multitude (ibid., xxxi, 214). Over this din, the king and Parliament fought not only for the hearts but also for the *minds* of men: "The war of the pen preceded that of the sword, and daily sharpened the humours of the opposite parties. . . . the king and parliament themselves carried on the controversy by messages, remonstrances, and declarations; where the nation was really the party to whom all arguments were addressed" (ibid., V, lv, 221).

The special philosophical character of the conflict was determined in part by the union of philosophy and Christianity, the rise of the more self-reflective and philosophically inclined Puritanism, and a general "spirit of innovation." But the specific cause is traced to James I, who had "established within his own mind a speculative system of absolute government" which he was zealous to defend before the Parliament (ibid., IV, xlv, 393). The theory was purely philosophic and showed no understanding at all of the historical forces in common life which mold political authority. Moreover, such theorizing could not have come at a worse time. Social, cultural, and economic changes had vested in Parliament unprecedented authority and responsibility, which were felt but not understood. These same changes meant a loss of authority in the Crown which James did not understand but which he felt as a threat. The metaphysical defense of his authority merely provided a conceptual framework whereby an otherwise unreflective Parliament could begin to understand dimly its own de facto authority and to seek metaphysical principles that could justify it and render it ultimate. And so "The King having . . . torn off that sacred veil which had hitherto covered the English constitution, and which threw an obscurity upon it so advantageous to royal prerogative, every man began to indulge himself in political reasonings and inquiries; and the same factions which commenced in parliament, were propagated throughout the nation" (ibid., xlviii, 466).

Marx once said that his criticism of society was not against any "wrong in particular" but against "wrong in general"; his criticism was not an attempt to reform society but to change it totally. Likewise, as Hume understood them, the Puritan revolutionaries were driven by metaphysical rebellion and not by a passion to correct this or that wrong. They viewed the political order of common life not as a form through which to think but as an object of theoretical reflection, a complete system to be totally and all pervasively replaced by an alternative system. "Every man had framed the model of a republic; and, however new it was, or fantastical, he was eager in recommending it to his fellow citizens, or even imposing it by force upon them" (ibid., V, lx, 386). The Crown could do nothing to placate "the endless demands of certain insatiable and turbulent spirits, whom nothing less will content than a total subversion of the ancient constitution" (ibid., liv, 163). And again, the intention of the Commons was "to subvert the whole system of the constitution" (ibid., lv, 196). As the conflict progressed, "The bands of society were everywhere loosened, and the irregular passions of men were encouraged by speculative principles, still more unsocial and irregular" (ibid., lx, 387). Once men are conceptually emancipated from the existing social and political order, the usual judgments of right and wrong no longer apply. And so the Puritan revolutionaries thought themselves "dispensed from all the ordinary rules of morality, by which inferior mortals must allow themselves to be governed" (ibid., lix, 351). Because of their transcendent metaphysical character, the revolutionary principles were considered "superior to the *beggarly elements* of justice and humanity" (ibid., lx, 386).

Hume proposes a theme that has since become a familiar one, that revolutions devour their children: "The sacred boundaries of the laws being once violated, nothing remained to confine the wild projects of zeal and ambition: and every successive revolution became a precedent for that which followed it" (ibid., lix, 330). The result was, in the end, a Puritan Republic under the military dictatorship of Cromwell which sought to impose not only a different political constitution but a different *social and moral* order as well. The Puritan revolutionaries were "sanctified robbers . . . who, under pretence of superior illuminations, would soon extirpate, if possible, all private morality, as they had already done all public law and justice, from the British dominions" (ibid., lxii, 499). There was to be a total change in the social order, seen now as a grand illusion. A Quaker woman walks into Cromwell's presence naked because, among the elect, there is no rational necessity for clothing. Some thought that Christ had fully descended into the heart of his saints and that ministers, magistrates, and the Bible itself were abolished (ibid., n. u, 554). One faction "inveighed against the law and its professors; and, on pretence of rendering more simple the distribution of justice, were desirous of abolishing the whole system of English jurisprudence, which seemed interwoven with monarchical government" (ibid., lx, 386–87). Hume observes that "It became pretty common doctrine at that time, that it was unworthy of a Christian man to pay rent to his fellow creatures; and landlords were obliged to use all the penalties of law against their tenants, whose conscience was scrupulous" (ibid., n. u, 554). Mirth itself was to be regulated by metaphysical principle: "parliament appointed the second Tuesday of every month for play and recreation," but, as Hume dryly remarks, "the people were resolved to be merry when they themselves pleased, not when the parliament should prescribe it to them" (ibid., lvii, 291n). Hume would have clearly understood the rationale behind twentieth-century totalitarian regimes: total control is necessary to instantiate a new social and political order, a project that is intelligible only if, through the autonomy principle of false philosophy, one has conceptually eliminated the social and political world of common life.

The theme of total control is also taken up in the *Enquiry* on morals. Hume observes that in ancient time religion had "very little influence on common life," and that after men had performed their duties in the temple, "the gods left the rest of their conduct to themselves, and were little pleased or offended with those virtues or vices, which only affected the peace and happiness of human society." It "was the business of philosophy alone to regulate men's ordinary behaviour and deportment; and . . . this being the sole principle, by which a man could elevate himself above his fellows, it acquired a mighty ascendent over many, and produced great singularities of maxims and of conduct." But at present "philosophy has lost the allurement of novelty" and "has no such extensive influence; but seems to confine itself mostly to speculations in the closet; in the same manner, as the ancient religion was limited to sacrifices in the temple. Its place is now supplied by *the modern religion*, which inspects our whole conduct, and prescribes an universal rule to our actions, to our words, to our very thoughts and inclinations" (EM, 341–42, emphasis added).

The contrast here between philosophy and religion, as we have observed, is not between two logically independent activities. Hume has not forgotten his claim that "religion . . . is nothing but a species of philosophy" (EU, 146), nor that modern political parties must seek not only practical but also philosophical legitimacy among the multitude (E, 452). The contrast is between religion governed by the concept of the *sacred* and philosophy governed by *reason* (the autonomy principle). Philosophy does not require the concept of the sacred; religion does. But every religious conception of the sacred presupposes some philosophical system, however inchoate it may be, which can afford the mind "some satisfaction" (NHR, 29). Hume's point is that it is the sacred, not autonomous reason, that publicly regulates "men's ordinary behaviour and deportment." Yet what is oppressive about modern religion is not the sacred, as such, but the metaphysical system internal to it which is alienating and all-pervasive (E, 61). It is a contigent question whether false philosophy works unseen beneath the mantle of the sacred ("religious superstition") or whether, discarding the sacred, it appears before the public as reason itself ("philosophical enthusiasm"), "prescribing laws, and imposing maxims, with an absolute sway and authority" (EM, 343; T, 186). In Hume's time, the former way was still paramount; in our time, the latter has come to dominate. Marx wrote that "philosophy has become secularized, and the striking proof thereof is that the philosophical consciousness itself has been pulled into the torment of struggle not only externally but also internally."[12] Political life today is very much governed by philosophical systems: Marxism, communism, socialism, capitalism, liberalism, conservatism. The peculiar conceptual struggles and absurdities of the closet have moved openly into the public arena and have become incarnate in policy.

There were signs of this transition in Hume's time, and being a lifelong and profound student of the nature of philosophic error, he had a special eye for its appearance in public affairs. This explains his outrage at the Wilkes and Liberty affair, spawned, he thought, entirely by ideas and not by any real grievance. It also explains his blistering attack on the policy proposals of the Physiocrats, who held that all economic value is determined by the use of land. Land is true money, and productive land true production. Trade and industrial production create no independent value. To Hume, their ahistorical rationalistic system made it conceptually impossible for them to observe and to cultivate the new and powerful productive forces of trade and industry that had emerged before their very eyes. He hoped in 1769 that Abbé Morellet would deal adequately with them: "I hope that in your work you will thunder them, and crush them, and pound them, and reduce them to dust and ashes! They are, indeed, the set of men the most chimerical and most arrogant that now exist. . . . I wonder what could engage our friend, M. Turgot, to herd among them" (L, II, 205).

The main lesson of the Stuart volumes is that, ideally, parties of metaphysical principle should be barred from the state; or, since that is impossible, under modern conditions, they should be purged of the autonomy principle and accepted in full recognition of their limits, namely, that they can operate critically within the confines of common life but cannot legitimately criticize the order as a whole. Our political actions, then, are never to be guided by autonomous metaphysical principles. When the principles are of that sort, "it may safely be averred, that the more sincere and the more disinterested they are, they only become the more ridiculous and the more odious" (H, V, lix, 364). The lesson can be put in what might be called Hume's law: "the more principle any person possesses, the more apt is he, on such occasions, to neglect and abandon his domestic duties" (ibid., VI, lxxi, 346).

Hume argued that political parties of metaphysical principle had led to more evil than had ever been caused by parties of interest, ambition, and affection (E, 61). He had in mind mainly religious metaphysical parties, but his point logically applies to secular parties and, in fact, was intended to apply to the secular metaphysical parties beginning to emerge in his time (E, 452) and which have since come to replace the religious ones, imposing laws and moving men and armies under such secular concepts as the rights of man, the class struggle, equality, and social justice. Something very like Hume's position of purging politics of metaphysics is stated by Albert Camus in *The Rebel*, a work profoundly critical of the tradition of the French Revolution and one which seeks to determine a logical and moral limit beyond which rebellion cannot go. Camus remarks: "There are crimes of passion and crimes of logic. . . . We are living in the era of . . . the perfect crime. Our criminals are no longer helpless children who could plead love as their excuse. On the contrary, they are adults, and they have a perfect alibi: philosophy, which can be used for any purpose—even for transforming murderers into judges. . . . In more ingenuous times, when the tyrant razed cities for his own greater glory, when the slave chained to the conqueror's chariot was dragged through the rejoicing streets . . . the mind did not reel before such unabashed crimes, and judgment remained unclouded. But slave camps under the flag of freedom, massacres justified by philanthropy . . . in one sense cripple judgment. On the day when crime dons the apparel of innocence through a curious transposition peculiar to our times—it is innocence that is called upon to justify itself."[13]

Camus's "crimes of logic" is parallel to Hume's characterization of false philosophers in politics as "common robbers" and to Orwell's "newspeak." But the curious transposition of concepts to which Camus refers, although more widespread in the twentieth century, is not peculiar to it. Hume was the first to point it out: in the *Treatise* it appears as the doctrine of "double existence," and in the second *Enquiry* as "philosophical chymistry," whereby ordinary concepts of common life such as justice and benevolence are twisted by the autonomy principle into their opposites: benevolence is really self-love, property is really theft, and so on (T, 215; EM, 297).

Expressions such as "reason," "justice," "liberty," "equality," and "humanity" express goods which are recognized by all men in common life and which form part of the order of virtue. These are virtue-laden expressions because it is necessarily the case that whatever promotes justice, liberty, etc, is good. But for this to be the case, the meanings of such expressions must be tied to some actual historical context (EM, 173–74). However, when the autonomy principle of false philosophy appears on the scene, it "bends every branch of knowledge to its own purpose, without much regard to the phenomena of nature, or to the unbiased sentiments of the mind, hence reasoning, and even language, have been warped from their natural course" (EM, 322). When this occurs, the meanings of value-laden expressions are thrown into confusion. The favorable connotations of common life are still there, but they are bent by the autonomy principle to serve entirely different ends.

This "crime of logic," in turn, makes possible Hume's paradoxical and thankless project of throwing into question what appears to be analytically true. Much of his career as a writer can be viewed as an attempt to bring order into two concepts that had been rendered incoherent by the autonomy principle of modern philosophy: reason and liberty. Hume was the first to undertake this sort of critique, a conceptual reflection of which is to be found in Wittgenstein's *Philosophical Investigations*. In the nature of the case, language itself is a problem, and the ordinary use of words breaks down. When communication is a problem, a systematic method in philosophy can no longer be used. Hume, like Wittgenstein, employs a dialectical method in which the shock of skeptical paradox and the Pyrrhonian illumination are used both to expose conceptual error and to bring about conceptual revision. A maxim such as "reason is and ought to be the slave of the passions" was designed to shock the conceptual framework of the Age of Reason, and to throw into question not reason but a philosophical theory of reason. Owing to the novelty of the enterprise and to a failure of language, Hume's critique of "reason" appeared not only paradoxical but also perverse; hence, the long interpretation of Hume as an irrational and negative thinker. Similarly, Hume's criticism, in the *Essays* and in the *History*, of the Whig conception of liberty was interpreted by Whigs as an attack on liberty itself and Hume was viewed as a defender of tyranny. The Whig literary and political establishment, for nearly a century, had been drumming the Whig-Lockean conception of liberty into the national consciousness so that the public conception of liberty had become progressively inapplicable to common life. The peculiar philosophical confusions of the closet were entering public policy, making communication about liberty and authority virtually impossible. As a result, Hume could wish "that People do not take a Disgust at Liberty; a word, that has been so much profaned by these polluted Mouths, that men of Sense are sick at the very mention of it. I hope a new term will be invented to express so valuable and good a thing" (NHL, 196).

## WILKES AND LIBERTY AS PHILOSOPHICAL ERROR

The Wilkes and Liberty riots of 1768–71 and the popular sovereignty movement of which they were a part drew forth from Hume a surprising and violent stream of political invective that flows through much of his correspondence from 1768 to his death. Forbes has observed that Hume's tone in these letters is "so urgent and despondent that in retrospect it appears exaggerated and pessimistic to the point of absurdity."[14] Hume himself remarked in 1770 that "As I had renounced the World, I did not think it had been possible for any public Business to have interested me so much as I am against the Success of those Banditti" (NHL, 189). There is no anticipation of this outburst in Hume's remarks on politics in earlier letters, and it has been easy to view it as due to the reactionary conservatism of old age. The violence of Hume's outburst, sustained over eight years, bears resemblance to Burke's unexpected invective against the French Revolution, an attack that ceased only with his death in 1797. Neither men were reactionaries. Both believed in the historicity of social and political order and in evolutionary reform. Burke has a reputation as one of the great Whig reformers of his time. Hume supported total independence for the colonies long before it occurred to Burke to do so, and, indeed, before it occurred to most Americans to do so. "I am an American in my Principles," he could write in 1775, "and wish we woud let them alone to govern or misgovern themselves as they think proper" (L, II, 303).[15] Burke saw the French Revolution as a violent intrusion of metaphysics into politics.

Hume saw the same thing in the Wilkes and Liberty affair. But the events they perceived were shaped by different historical contexts, and so were the conceptual frameworks through which they perceived them. Consequently, their concrete perceptions and reactions were different. These differences serve to point out the different places Burke and Hume occupy in the conservative tradition.

Burke's tone is that of prophetic alarm. Something new and dangerous had entered the world. Rationalistic metaphysics had taken on political and military shape, becoming an "armed doctrine." Tradition, custom, prescription are not only illusions without authority, they are to be purged by force and a new, rationally certified order established. The evil cannot be contained within France but must spread throughout Europe and to England. The Whig establishment must recognize the conceptual difference between its own tradition of reform and the new metaphysical project of total revolution. This difference was lost on many of Burke's contemporaries. The *Reflections* created a scandal on its first appearance, and not only among Lockean-inspired radical Whigs who hailed the Revolution as a liberating event. Burke estimated that two-thirds of the clergy of the Church of England initially supported the Revolution.

Hume's reaction to Wilkes and Liberty is, by contrast, not alarm that something new has entered the world but grinding despair over the repetition of an evil not yet understood. For Hume, the intrusion of the autonomy principle of false philosophy in common life was nothing new. It was thoroughly dealt with, and on the most general conceptual level, in the *Treatise*. What he considered to be the unique modern phenomenon of metaphysical political parties was examined in the *Essays*. The historical possibility of these parties and their acceptance on a popular level was traced to the union of philosophy and religion in the emergence of Christianity. The English Civil War is presented in the *History* as a unique modern occurrence, a pure case of metaphysical rebellion. Hume was drawn to the subject not only out of the political motive to understand the origins of the present constitution and to correct Whig historical and constitutional errors. As a philosopher, he was conceptually fascinated with the ideological motives that moved men and affairs. These made up "the most curious spectacle presented by any history" and "the most instructive, as well as entertaining, to a philosophical mind" (H, V, lx, 519). The metaphysical character of the war was not clearly perceived by Hume's contemporaries because they did not understand the Pyrrhonian illumination, and there was no alternative conceptual framework available through which that special aspect of the war could be discerned.

When Hume referred to the "Barbarians on the Thames," "the London mob," and "the scum of London" as being at the center of the Wilkes affair, he had in mind not the classical rabble but middle-class leaders, including the earl of Chatham (L, II, 300–301). In the frenzied chants of "Wilkes and liberty!" Hume could hear the rantings of the Hampdens, the Pyms, and the Cromwells. The cry for liberty was not for redress of any concrete grievance; it was "without any Grievance" "founded on nothing" and was "without a Cause" (L, II, 178, 210). To Turgot he wrote: "They roar Liberty, tho' they have apparently more Liberty than any People in the world; a great deal more than they deserve; and perhaps more than any men ought to have" (L, II, 180). The demand was ritualistic and destructive, with no regard for the proper balance of liberty and authority which historical circumstances demanded. But unlike the Puritan mutiny, it was a purely secular, not a religious, affair. It was not the will of Christ that presided over Wilkes and Liberty but the arguments of John Locke and the Whig historians. The philosophic was replacing the sacred as the ground of political order and change. Hume observed that this intellectual shift began during the reign of Charles II, when the Puritan opposition ceased calling themselves the *"godly"* party and took on the name of the *"good* and *honest* party" (H, VI, lxviii, 215). In "Of Parties in General" (1741), he explained the special nature of metaphysical political parties and gave a historical account of their origins. In "Of the Original Contract" (1748), he stated explicitly that "no party, in the present age, can well support itself without a philosophical or speculative system of principles annexed to its political or practical one" (E, 452).

Nearly a century later, in 1843, Marx could say that "the philosophical consciousness itself has been pulled into the torment of struggle." The autonomous philosopher is now completely out of the closet and sets for himself the project of "the *ruthless criticism of all that exists,* ruthless also in the sense that criticism does not fear its results and even less so a struggle with the existing powers." The union of philosophy and religion in Christianity which, in Hume's view, had made the politics of modern Christendom a scene of war and devastation was breaking down. Modern philosophy was freeing itself from its sacred roots. Henceforth, "philosophical enthusiasm" rather than "religious enthusiasm" would pose a threat to the politics of common life. Wilkes and Liberty "exceeds the Absurdity of Titus Oates and the popish Plot; and is so much more disgraceful to the Nation, as the former Folly, being derived from Religion, flow'd from a Source, which has, from uniform Prescription, acquird a Right to impose Nonsense on all Nations & all Ages" (L, II, 197). Philosophers, in Hume's time, had not yet fully acquired this right.

The Wilkes affair was "a sudden Inroad of Ignorance, Superstition

and Barbarism," and Hume imagined that it foreshadowed a great conflict like the ideological war between Crown and Parliament but one
which would be modified by contemporary circumstances and which,
consequently, could not be kept within the bounds of Britain but
would spread throughout the empire and to the Continent. From this
apprehension, Hume could fantasize: "O! how I long to see America
and the East Indies revolted totally & finally, the Revenue reduc'd to
half, public Credit fully discredited by Bankruptcy, the third of London in Ruins, and the rascally Mob subdu'd. I think I am not too old to
despair of being Witness to all these Blessings" (ibid., II, 184). Hume
was not alone in seeing a parallel between the Wilkes affair and the
Civil War. Walpole wrote to Mann in October, 1769 that England "approaches by fast strides to some great crisis, and to me never wore so
serious an air, except in the Rebellion."[16]

Hume could not forbear viewing the crisis in narrative categories. The
"true ingredients for making a fine Narrative in History" were emerging, and he envied "the lot of that Historian, who is to transmit to
Posterity an account of these mad abandon'd times" (ibid., 208; NHL,
189). But the events demanded a philosophical historian who could
understand the peculiar philosophical and historical errors of the Whigs
and of English national prejudices that were bringing on the crisis: "the
present Extravagance is peculiar to Ourselves, and quite risible" (L, II,
197). "I dare not," Hume wrote, "venture to play the Prophet" (ibid.,
210). But his philosophical system provided him with the concepts
through which he could see that something deep was happening; yet,
with frustration, he realized that its historical significance was shut up in
the darkness of the future: "I fancy we shall have curious Scenes coming,
worthy the Pen of the greatest Historian. I am tird and disgusted with
Conjecture" (ibid., 214). Hume could not see that it would not be radical
English Whigs, "corrupted by above a Century of Licentiousness"
(ibid., 216), who would throw Europe into convulsion but rather their
French counterparts in the second generation of philosophes. And it
would not be Hume's philosophical and historical analysis that would
teach the English to purge their politics of false philosophy but the glare
of the Terror and the rhetoric of the great Whig orator.

Yet Burke's legacy has not been an entirely happy one. He gave a
rhetorical, Gothic, and romantic tone to Anglo-American conservatism
at the expense of philosophy. The result has been a deep prejudice in
the Anglo-American polity against "philosophers" and "intellectuals."
Hume, as much as Burke, appreciated the role of sentiment and passion
in thinking, and he too was a critic of what he scornfully described as
"this philosophic age" (EM, 197n). But Hume was a philosopher's philosopher who threw into question the nature and limits of philosophy

itself. He taught in the *Treatise* that the mind demands philosophy in some form or other and that the only remedy for false philosophy is the cultivation of the true. So the deepest and most satisfying criticism of misplaced philosophy in politics is and must be a philosophical criticism. The conceptual foundations of the modern revolutionary mystique were laid out in Descartes' *Discourse*. The conceptual foundations for the corresponding counterrevolution were worked out not in Burke's *Reflections* but in the meandering criticism of philosophy running throughout book I of the *Treatise*.

Burke did not share Hume's outrage over Wilkes and Liberty. In fact, Burke was sympathetic to Wilkes and saw in the affair a need to liberalize the concept of representation. But then Burke was part of the Whig establishment; he, too, was caught in the grip of those "plaguy Prejudices of Whiggism" (L, I, 379) against which Hume himself struggled: the tendency to view English political history as the restoration of the ancient constitution, to view reforms generally as "restorations," and to view the legitimacy of government as grounded in the consent of the governed. Hume did not have the classical aristocrat's disdain for the masses: "It has also been found, as the experience of mankind increases, that the *people* are no such dangerous monsters as they have been represented" (E, 12n). Yet he opposed the popular sovereignty movement which surrounded the Wilkes affair and was presided over by radical Whigs such as Price and Priestley and by political leaders such as the earl of Chatham, that "wicked Madman Pitt" (ibid., II, 301), who held power by appealing to nationalistic passions and the vanity of democratic sovereignty. The former meant imperial wars, the latter an extension of liberty which the British constitution could not bear. One reason Hume hoped Britain would lose its eastern and western colonies was that because of the "Frenzy of Liberty that has taken possession of us" the government had lost authority; as the Wilkes riots demonstrated, it could not make itself respected at home, much less in its far-flung dominions. The attempt to gain such respect must result in foreign wars, an increase in the national debt, and an extension of authority that must extinguish the very constitutional order of liberty which is the glory of British history. In "Of the Balance of Power," Hume had gone so far as to describe Britain's historical role as that of "the guardian of the general liberties of Europe, and patron of mankind."

The struggle between Crown and Parliament in the seventeenth century ended in a military dictatorship and the loss of liberty from the "too eager pursuit of liberty"; a similar thing was about to happen again. The problem was that the excessive liberty had been gained at the cost of government authority and, as Hume wrote to Eliot in February 1770, could "scarcely be retrench'd without Danger of being entirely lost"; the alternative was a republic which, given Britain's historical circumstances, would mean anarchy and despotism (L, II, 306; cf. E, 52–53). To Hume, the Wilkes and Liberty affair was nothing less than a confrontation "between the Mob and the Constitution," where "the Mob" was understood to include not only those chanting "Wilkes and Liberty" but the entire Whig literary and political establishment that made such chants possible. Hume advocated the strongest measures and despaired that the government seemed too weak to carry them out (L, II, 218).

Another point of frustration which touched Hume the philosopher was that, this time around, the pursuit of liberty was guided not by philosophical-religious ideas (as in the seventeenth century) but by philosophical-secular ideas. The Enlightenment hope that the cultivation of philosophy would promote stable government (EU, 10) depended on the establishment in society of true, not false, philosophy. Hume now wondered if this really could be done. It had not been done in Britain. What of France where, despite the lack of liberty, letters were better cultivated? Hume was friends with the philosophes; together they were laborers in the vineyard of reason against a common enemy: clerical superstition. For that project, mutual uncritical praise was sufficient. But it is doubtful that the philosophes really understood Hume's distinction between true and false philosophy and the skeptical conservative implications of it. The unhappy Rousseau affair[17] caused Hume to look more critically at Rousseau's philosophical writings, which, in a letter to Turgot in September 1766, he judged to be "full of Extravagance and of Sophystry" and "whose general Tendency is surely to do hurt than Service to Mankind" (L, II, 91). Turgot strongly disagreed with Hume's assessment of the value of Rousseau's philosophical writings and during the next two years carried on a frank correspondence with Hume which revealed, perhaps to the surprise of both, the vast gulf that separated Hume's philosophy of limits from Turgot's philosophy of perpetual progress. In June 1768, Hume presented Wilkes and Liberty as a counterinstance to the theory of "perpetual Progress towards Perfection" and to the thesis "that the Encrease of Knowledge will still prove favourable to good Government" (L, II, 180), the very thesis he had affirmed in the first *Enquiry* (EU, 10). Turgot, along with d'Alembert, was one of Hume's closest friends on the Continent. The exchange with Turgot must have given him pause to wonder how well (ritualistic anticlericalism aside) he and the philosophes had understood each other. If Hume had these reflections, they were no doubt sharpened by the letter from d'Alembert recommending his friend Abbé de Vauxcelles: "il va en Angleterre," d'Alembert writes enthusiastically, "pour avoir le plaisir de crier avec vous 'Wilkes and Liberty!'"[18]

Leslie Stephen observed that the popular leader Chatham "was inclined towards the absolute dogmas of the revolutionary school" and that given proper circumstances he "might have developed into a Mirabeau."[19] Neither Burke nor Hume could, at the time, have viewed the popular sovereignty movement of Pitt and of Wilkes and Liberty as foreshadowing the ideology of the French Revolution. Hume died in August of 1776, but he had a deeper understanding of the special ideological content informing the events of 1768–71 than did Burke. After 1789, Burke severed his connections with the radical Whigs and was forced to rethink the meaning of his past efforts at reform and his understanding of the British constitution. Faced with what he considered to be an unprecedented event, the intrusion of metaphysics into politics, Burke hastily began putting into theoretical-rhetorical shape the sorts of insights already scattered throughout Hume's cranky letters. The insights were there because the letters observing Wilkes and Liberty were written by the man who composed book I of the *Treatise* and the *History* of the Stuart kings.

## TRUE RELIGION

Most conservatives have rejected misplaced philosophy in politics not by a searching philosophical criticism but by an appeal to a sacred ordering of things. The revolutionary is in rebellion not only against the established order of things but against God. Samuel Johnson could say that "the Devil was the first Whig."[20] De Maistre interpreted the entrance of philosophic reason into politics as an instance of the "fierce and rebellious pride" of the "intellectuals" whose "insolent doctrines . . . unceremoniously judge God."[21] Burke believed in a providential order and interpreted the norms of historical society (especially the British constitution) as the work of a "mysterious wisdom." Coleridge viewed the Bible as a statesman's manual and held that the first duty of the state is to make men "soberly and steadily religious."[22] That established social and political order is, in some way, grounded in a divine ordering of things has been vigorously taught by twentieth-century conservatives such as T. S. Eliot, Jacques Maritain, Leo Strauss, and Eric Voegelin. We may call these thinkers metaphysical conservatives because they seek to rebut metaphysical rebellion by appealing to an alternative metaphysical theory.

Metaphysical conservatives and metaphysical revolutionaries operate on the same logical level; their positions are logical contraries. Consider Marx's description of his own revolutionary thinking: "Thus the criticism of heaven is transformed into the criticism of earth, the *criticism of religion* into the *criticism of law*, and the *criticism of theology* into the *criticism of politics*."[23] Marx's metaphysical total criticism of the established order is logically tied to the falsity of certain theological propositions. Should those propositions be true, the criticism would be unjustified. Because their criticism is of the same logical type, metaphysical conservatives may become as totally alienated from the historical norms of common life as any revolutionary, depending on what the divine ordering is supposed to be and whether or not historical society conforms to it. But since the principle of correct order is a metaphysical thesis structured by the autonomy principle, there will always be, as we have repeatedly observed, a logical gap between the metaphysical principle and the historical norms it is supposed to certify or reject. Failing an original, unprincipled affirmation of these norms, no nonarbitrary criticism of them is possible. Thus a metaphysical conservative may, if he likes, remain in total alienation from the established order no matter what changes are made.

Again, the familiar Humean point is that the proper way to criticize the goings-on in the world is to affirm the legitimacy of the world as a whole, abstract out the norms implicit in it, render them as coherent as possible, and then critically apply them to the practice. Always the movement is from the concrete to the abstract. Ideas follow impressions. We cannot begin with a theistic vision of the world (as metaphysical conservatives do) or an atheistic vision (as metaphysical rebels such as Marx do) and use these as standards to criticize the world. We could justify a choice between these metaphysical alternatives, but, even if one of them were preferable, criticism of the world would still be impossible since anything could appear to satisfy the alternative or not to satisfy it. The actual goods and evils which are lived out in common life cannot be distinguished by such standards. Whatever legitimate content theism, atheism, or any other metaphysical theory may have as a ground for criticizing the doings of common life must be determined by an original affirmation and involvement in the order of common life itself.

Although we may not class Hume among the metaphysical conservatives, he does, in his own way, share with them the conviction that established order has a sacred character and that this sacred character constitutes part of the authority of that order. To appreciate this, we must examine more closely Hume's conception of the relation between religion and philosophy.

In an earlier section, we observed that Hume's attack on religion is not against religion per se but against the modern notion of religion which, since the emergence of Christianity, has had philosophy, analytically, built into it. Hume is not opposed to those pre-Christian civic religions consisting of "traditional tales and fictions" where "every one adheres to the tradition of his own sect without much reasoning or disputation" (E, 61). Likewise, the Epicurean (who may be taken to speak for Hume) in the first *Enquiry*, defending himself before the Athenians, attacks "The religious philosophers," not "the tradition of your forefathers and doctrine of your priests (in which I willingly acquiesce)" (EU, 135). Nor would Hume have any objection to Christianity purged, if it could be purged, of its philosophic structure.

What would religion be like for Hume if purged of philosophy? Pre-Christian religion would, of course, be one example, but Hume did not think it possible in the modern world to return to a completely non-philosophic practice of religion. He viewed his own age as one determined to establish science, morals, politics, and religion on the basis of something called *reason*, that is, on principles determined by autonomous philosophy. He called it, sarcastically, "this philosophic age," by which he meant an age governed by false philosophy (EM, 197n). In such an age, any reformed conception of religion must have a critical philosophic base. So we can only consider religion purged of false philosophy, not of philosophy as such. The result is what Hume calls "true religion," a concept mentioned often in his works but not systematically discussed. Piecing together his scattered remarks, we can discern the main features of this concept.

True religion, epistemologically, presupposes the critical work of "true philosophy" (post-Pyrrhonian philosophy) and is what Hume calls "philosophical theism." Theistic belief under this conception is neither caused nor justified by inductive or a-priori arguments, and so is not supported by reason as traditionally understood. Its justification, rather, follows the line of Hume's justification of the popular system in the *Treatise:* there is a psychological and a logical justification. Once we have consciously formed a policy of guiding our thought and action by empirical regularities, we are led by virtue of a propensity of our nature to veiw these regularities as a system produced by a single intelligence. This propensity to philosophical theism, though more variable by custom than the propensity to believe that our perceptions are of continuously and independently existing objects, is, nevertheless, a universal propensity of human nature. The logical justification consists in the fact that the convention of scientific inquiry presupposes the belief: "astronomers often, *without thinking of it*, lay this strong foundation of piety and religion" and "all the sciences almost lead us *insensibly* to acknowledge a first intelligent Author; and their authority is often so much the greater, as they do not directly profess that intention" (D, 214–15, emphasis mine).

God as conceived by "true religion" is "*mind* or *intelligence*" but is not a person and therefore has no moral relations to the world: the supreme being issues no commands, imposes no sanctions, and responds to no invocations. The moral world is no more than a set of social relations framed by men for men. Yet morality, for Hume, is not entirely independent of true religion: "The proper office of religion is to regulate the heart of men, humanize their conduct, infuse the spirit of temperance, order, and obedience; and as its operation is silent, and only enforces the motives of morality and justice, it is in danger of being overlooked, and confounded with these other motives. When it distinguishes itself, and acts as a separate principle over men, it has departed from its proper sphere, and has become only a cover to faction and ambition" (D,220). True religion is perverted when it becomes "a separate principle over men." But this is precisely the error of false philosophy structured by the autonomy principle, which leads to the alienated philosopher caught within and without the world of common life and for whom "no one can answer for what will please or displease [him]" (EM, 343). Again, the "errors of religion" are just those of philosophy, and true religion, like true philosophy, must abandon the autonomy principle. Both must accept common life not as an object of critical reflection but as a category of their own activity. Just as the task of true philosophy is to methodize and correct the historically established maxims of common life, so true religion works within the order of common life to "humanize" conduct by giving men a pious regard for the sacredness of their common order.[24]

In this way, true philosophy and true religion are internally connected. True religion is of "the philosophical and rational kind" and presupposes the critical work of true philosophy as a condition (D,220). But the permanent temptation of philosophy is to slip back into the impious arrogance of the autonomy principle. To this, true religion sets up a barrier of *passion*, in the form of a feeling of the sacredness of common life which provides a motive for keeping philosophy within its proper sphere. Since, for Hume, false philosophy in politics is the greatest threat to morality under modern conditions, true religion and the reverence for common life that it inspires may be viewed as an essential support for morality. The "profound adoration" which Philo has for the "divine Being" issues in a total acceptance of and reverence for the order of common life as it is. The effect of philosophical theism is to endorse a deeply traditionalistic and conservative view of social and political order. But it is conservative only in the sense of protecting the order against the revolutionary intrusion of the autonomy principle which always has the conceptual effect of transforming the world of common life as a whole into an order of illusion, having no authority.

I would now like to sketch briefly how Hume understands the content of the sacredness of common life which is an essential part of true religion. One of his most original discoveries is that of the performative use of language. Language used in ritual acts constitutes essential realities of common life such as property, contracts, courtesy, marriage, political authority, and the entire hierarchy of status and rank among men, the whole of which, for Hume, is the moral world. So conceived, the moral world is an order of nonnatural relations held together by the ritualistic use of language, which is, Hume says, "one of the most mysterious and incomprehensible operations that can possibly be imagin'd, and may even be compar'd to *transubstantiation*, or *holy orders*, where a certain form of words, along with a certain intention, changes entirely the nature of an external object" (T, 524). Hume's criticism of popular religious ritual is not that it is merely "ritualistic"; it is, rather, that it purports to be cognitive and causal: a power is invoked by a sacred use of words to transform a natural object.[25] For Hume, the power of the ritual lies not in supernaturally changing the natural order but in constituting some part of the moral order: "Had I worn this apparel an hour ago, I had merited the severest punishment; but a man, by pronouncing a few magical syllables, has now rendered it fit for my use and service" (EM, 199). True religion, unlike popular religion, has no special set of sacred rituals for which reverence is due, precisely because the whole of the moral order is the set of rituals to which reverence is due.

The rationale behind the word-magic that constitutes the moral world is social utility. That is why the system of ritual acts in common life is more flexible, less systematic, and less consistent than that of popular religion which acts as "a separate principle over men" and is not guided by social utility (T, 524–25). But though utility is the origin of the ritualistic order of common life, its reality is not directly experienced or appreciated as utilitarian. It is a world of its own whose symbolic acts and the status they generate have intrinsic value; indeed, it is the distinctively human world. But it is not possible at all without an established social and political order, which is why Hume had to rework the concepts of philosophy and reason to include a broadly conservative view of common life as a category of philosophical thinking. It is against the background of this ritualistic conception of the moral world that we are to appreciate Hume's lifelong effort to promote literature, manners, and eloquence, and his dismay that philosophical and religious fanaticism were threatening to tear apart the constitutional system of liberty and the emerging commercial and industrial society in Britain that would enable the cultivation of letters (and all that that meant) to flourish.

The moral world emerges as a delicate structure held together by the narrative imagination and by the ritualistic use of language. It is especially vulnerable to the autonomy principle of false philosophy which under modern intellectual conditions informs both religion and philosophy. When false philosophy takes on ritualistic form, it spawns a world of *its* own. This is the world of superstition and of metaphysical politics which is logically and psychologically parasitic upon, yet destructive of, the world of common life. In Hume's own special way, it is conceived as a desecration of the sacredness of the secular order.

## THE ETHICS OF TIME

Does the sacredness of common life mean that change or reform is impossible? Not at all. Reforms of all sort are possible. As Hume observes, the sacred character of common life is based on social utility and is not absolute and systematic as in philosophy and religion. What cannot be done is to use the autonomy principle to critically reject the authority of common life as a whole and to attempt to replace it, even in concept, with a different order. Hume's conservatism is aimed at only that new "set of men lately sprung up amongst us, who endeavour to distinguish themselves by ridiculing every thing, that has hitherto appeared sacred and venerable in the eyes of mankind" (E, 573). He, significantly, characterizes this new group of men as "anti-reformers," suggesting that the pattern of thought at work is that of the autonomy principle, for which practical concepts like "correction" and "reform" are logically inadmissible. The concept of reform is internal to the concept of an established order having authority. We can reform sensory judgments only if we accept the authority of sensory judgments as a whole, and the same holds for the order of property relations or any other order of common life. We know what the principles are that determine the various orders of common life by "our experience of their reality" (T, xviii), where "experience" is understood broadly to include scientific, historical, and a-priori analysis.

The conservative character of Hume's philosophy is often thought of as an appeal to moderation, but that would be a fundamental mistake. Moderation implies an activity that is acceptable: eating is acceptable and even necessary, it is just that one should not go too far with it. But that is not the model for thinking about Hume's conservatism. Philosophical criticism of common life structured by the autonomy principle is not an acceptable activity. It is logically incoherent and self-deceptive, and one cannot speak of a proper degree of that activity. There is a radical criticism of philosophy at the core of Hume's conservatism. And one must stress that it is not merely a criticism of seventeenth- and eighteenth-century rationalistic metaphysics. Hume's criticism is aimed at the activity of philosophy as such. Philosophers have always allowed, and still do, the autonomy principle to have free play in their thought whether they are rationalists, idealists, empiricists, pragmatists, or whatever. The autonomy principle is dialectically internal to the activity and can never be totally eliminated, but it can be kept at bay by the constraints of post-Pyrrhonian philosophy.

Revolutionary activity, then, informed by the autonomy principle, is not something about which one can be moderate; it is simply something one ought not to do.[26] From what we have discovered in previous chapters, a Humean demonstration against the possibility of total revolution can be constructed. Any change in the present order can be made if it is justified. But justification requires standards. The standards must be either abstract tenseless standards or concrete narrative standards. Narrative standards are the result of narrative associations of ideas where one temporally disposed event is taken as a standard for judging other temporally disposed events in some narrative context. Thus the constitutional events surrounding the ratification of the U.S. Constitution in 1789 (the intention of the framers, etc.) are taken as standards of varying degrees of authority for judging later events, and later events are used as standards for interpreting the original document (though it is the founding past events that have primordial authority). Now if the standards for judging the present are narrative, then the events constituting the original standard must be either present, past, or future. If they are present, then criticism of the present order is impossible since that order is the standard for criticism. If the original standards are grounded in past events, then criticism of the present must take the form of conservative dissent and reform (a present law is judged oppressive because it violates the Constitution of 1789) or some other deeply established tradition or custom of which the Constitution is a part. If the original standards are grounded in the future (as in the providential view of history), then no criticism at all about the present is justified since no narrative statement about the present can be true on condition that some future-tense statement is true.[27]

If the standards are tenseless and universal, they may apply to the present or, indeed, to any period of time; but we are narrative existences, and for this very reason the standards are vacuous unless interpreted by the standards of some actual historical order having independent authority. And, as we have seen, this must be a narrative unity holding between present and past existences.

So the concept of revolution as a project for totally changing an established social and political order with the view in mind of replacing it, is an incoherent concept, requiring conditions that logically cannot be satisfied. This is the deep lesson of Hume's conservatism and of his philosophy generally: that total criticisms (made possible by the autonomy principle) of any order of common life are incoherent. The lesson may seem trivial until one reflects on intellectual and political developments since 1789 and the mass destruction that has been wrought in the name of revolution and the justifications that have been presented in the name of philosophy. The great political conflicts in the world today are rationalized by philosophical theories: socialism, communism, fascism, liberalism, conservatism, and a host of lesser "isms," and "movements" which permeate every aspect of culture and on a popular level. In all of these, the autonomy principle may move about unfettered. Nor can this attempt to understand *philosophically* our social and political existence be avoided. But just for that reason there is need to apply the lessons implied in Hume's distinction between true and false philosophy to social and political discourse.

F. L. Lucas appears to be the only commentator to have remarked on the need to apply these Humean lessons to an understanding of twentieth-century political life: "Had men taken him to heart, there would have been no French Terror, no Paris commune, no Marxism and no Nazism, no World Wars. Our own century, more fanatical than any of its predecessors since the seventeenth, has certainly no less need to learn from his 'mitigated' scepticism; unlikely as it may be that it ever will. The family motto of the Humes was 'True to the end'. . . . His philosophy may not have been true: *he* was."[28] I have tried to show, however, that the heart of Hume's philosophy (his analysis of the nature and limits of philosophy) is essentially correct.

Hume's strictures against false philosophy in politics apply not only to virtuous fire-eaters such as Cromwell, Robespierre, Lenin, Mao, and Pol Pot, but also to closet philosophers such as Locke, Kant, and Rawls. As we have seen, the autonomy principle is conceptually at work in the theories of the latter as much as in the activities of the former, the only difference being a lack of will in taking the theories seriously and in applying them to the world. Locke, as if to outrage common sense, stressed that, in his theory of government by consent, absolute monarchy is "no Form of Civil Government at all." Hume went further and argued that, if Locke's theory were taken seriously, then no government has been legitimate. Such theories are taken seriously by philosophical outriders who popularize them and attempt to apply them in practical politics. It seldom ever occurs to closet philosophers to clothe the mere conceptual destruction of established authority with an actual physical destruction and remaking of society. But they have often been able to look with a certain philosophic pride on the work of those who have done so. Kant admired the French Revolution as a move away from external political authority (which is not grounded in self-imposed rules of reason) to moral autonomy: to "the authority, not of governments, but of conscience within us." Kant conceptually eliminated established authority on behalf of moral autonomy. Robespierre, we may say, simply took this view seriously and actually tried to carve out an order of perfect freedom and justice in the world by eliminating the established authority, which was based on the rejected tradition, custom, and prejudice that Hume celebrated. Robespierre's Reign of terror, then, may be viewed as a reign of virtue on behalf of moral autonomy. When confronted with the degrading results of the Terror, Kant lightly reflected in the *Critique of Judgment* that one should expect "the first attempts [at moral autonomy] will be brutal, and will bring about a more painful, more dangerous state than when one was under orders, but also under the protection of a third party."[29] A few eggs must be cracked to make an omelette. One should, perhaps, recall here Hume's maxim that "the more principle" a man has, the more he can be expected "to neglect and abandon his domestic duties" (H, VI, lxxi, 346).

One of Hume's great discoveries is his perception that most modern political philosophy is not emancipated from the free play of the autonomy principle and logically contains at its center a justification for total revolution. It places him logically outside the liberal democratic tradition of Locke, Rousseau, Kant, and Mill. This tradition has no adequate theory of how established authority *as such* is legitimate. The whole order of established authority can be rejected not because it has been embraced, lived through, and found wanting, but because it fails to conform to some philosophically autonomous principle: in the liberal democratic tradition, the principle that no political authority is legitimate unless it is, in some way, self-imposed (Locke's consent of the governed, Rousseau's general will, Kant's doctrine of moral autonomy). The fact that philosophers in this tradition seldom ever take seriously the claims to illegitimacy entailed in their doctrines and are not willing, as revolutionaries are, to push them through consistently simply confirms Hume's view that philosophy undisciplined by post-Pyrrhonian constraints is either theoretically frivolous or, if taken seriously, dangerous. "Of all mankind, there are none so pernicious as political projectors, if they have power, nor so ridiculous, if they want it: as, on the other hand, a wise politician is the most beneficial character in nature, if accompanied with authority, and the most innocent, and not altogether useless, even if deprived of it" (E, 499n).

Liberal democratic theorists have recently tended to discuss the legitimacy of social and political order by reference to the concept of distributive justice. Attempts to bring Hume into this contemporary debate have proved disappointing, yielding the interpretation that Hume has no theory of social justice at all, and that what he does say about justice appears to ratify whatever distribution of goods is locked into the status quo no matter how bad it might be. As one commentator has observed: "for admirers of Hume interested in theories of social (or distributive) justice, his failure to state a preference among these various 'principles of distribution' is downright depressing."[30] The rationale of justice, for Hume, is social utility, but, as is well known, he does not accept the utilitarian standard of maximizing the greatest happiness as a measure either of personal morality or of the justness of actions. Utility is satisfied merely by those practices which hold society together and without which it would go to rack and ruin. "The rules of natural justice" which satisfy the conditions of social utility are "the stability of possession," "its transference by consent," and "the performance of promises" (T, 526; EM, 196). Treated as the principles of a theory of distributive justice, these "laws of nature" yield, as David Miller has put it, "an unusually narrow version of conservative justice."[31]

But this is to misunderstand the logical status of Hume's laws. They are, indeed, "conservative" laws, but they do not function as grim measuring rods to be used in a project to reform society. They function rather as a-priori categories of the institution of justice. How are they to be interpreted? What is meant by "stability of possession," "transference," "consent"? As always, the Humean answer is that the rules we use to interpret abstract principles are the narrative standards framed in the customs, traditions, and prejudices that constitute common life (EM, 196–97). Narrative time is a value internal to Hume's conception of social utility. To employ these standards (and if we do not employ them, the laws of justice remain empty abstractions), we must think in a narrative way; that is, we must occupy or sympathetically enter into some actual narrative order (EM, 330). And to do this, we must abandon the abstract, tenseless, and universal perspective of philosophy. Hume goes out of his way to stress that if, by the autonomy principle (a "too abstracted reflection"), we bracket out the tradition-laden and ritualistic character of social utility, there will be no way to distinguish justice from superstition. And this is just the error that false philosophers make: they view the rules of present possession as superstition. In both cases, it is the ritualistic use of language grounded in the authority of a received tradition that constitutes order and provides philosophers with rules for interpreting their abstractions (EM, 198–211).

The laws of nature serve a purpose other than that of illuminating the formal structure of the institution of justice. They serve categorically to

rule out certain classes of philosophical theories: "Any one, who finding the impossibility of accounting for the right of the present possessor, by any receiv'd system of ethics, shou'd resolve to deny
absolutely that right, and assert, that it is not authoriz'd by morality,
wou'd be justly thought to maintain a very extravagant paradox, and to
shock the common sense and judgment of mankind" (T, 558). This
formally excludes any theory of social justice determined by autonomous philosophy. The only theories acceptable are post-Pyrrhonian
theories which recognize the independent authority of common life (in
this case the independent authority of present possession). And this
would exclude most all contemporary theories of distributive justice.
The point of a theory of distributive justice is to determine who ought
to have what, but if this question is taken seriously, then all norms
determining present possession are illegitimate unless they can be made
to rationally conform to some principle of distributive justice. But this
can never happen, for having rejected the rules establishing present
possession, we are without any rules (except arbitrary ones) for applying the abstract principle to the world. Virtually any arrangement may
appear to be included or excluded from the principle. So the whole
class of theories of distributive justice from Aristotle to Rawls which
seek to determine the content of some such principle as "From each
according to his x, to each according to his y" is formally excluded from
the post-Pyrrhonian reform in philosophy.

A theory of social justice will either not be taken seriously (the rules
of present possession are not really thrown into question), in which case
it is "ridiculous" because pompously displayed as having authority to
criticize what it cannot criticize (T, 272); or it will be taken seriously, in
which case it is dangerous, not so much because the rights of the present possessor will be violated by a determined attempt to enforce the
principle but because, in the nature of the case, an antinomic way of
thinking will be let loose which cannot make distinctions of good and
evil within the narrative order it seeks to criticize. Trying to apply a
principle of distributive justice to the historical world without recognizing the independent authority of the rules determining the present possessor would be like trying to apply a principle of theoretical physics or
geometry to the world without recognizing the independent authority
of sensory judgment. It is for this conceptual reason that, having rejected merit and need as principles of distributive justice, Hume takes
on once again (as he did in the famous book-burning passage at the end
of the first *Enquiry*) the tone of the Inquisition: "the civil magistrate
very justly puts these sublime theorists on the same footing with common robbers, and teaches them by the severest discipline, that a rule,
which, in speculation, may seem the most advantageous to society,

may yet be found, in practice, totally pernicious and destructive" (EM, 193).

But suppose we accept the legitimacy of the present possessor. What reforms can be made? No answer can be given to this question a priori. Whatever changes are made will occur in some actual narrative context and will be a case of correcting a particular narrative judgment (see chapter 9 above) by reference to some other narrative judgment. Conflict over particular claims to property or over established property rules are settled by reference to other established property rules. Grievances are settled by the established rules, and by virtue of retrospective narrative associations the settlement changes the interpretation of the rules. Such changes may lead to a gradual evolution of new rules and eventually to an entirely different narrative order. Evolutionary reform, then, is not only possible in Hume's system, it is internal to the narrative imagination and, consequently, to the moral world which the imagination weaves into existence.

The principle for justifying reforms is social utility, and, for Hume, narrative time is a value internal to the social utility that constitutes established institutions: "There is no abuse so great in civil society, as not to be attended with a variety of beneficial consequences; and in the beginnings of reformation, the loss of these advantages is always felt very sensibly, while the benefit . . . is the slow effect of time, and is seldom perceived by the bulk of a nation" (H, III, xxxv, 354). There is a presumption on behalf of established institutions, and the more firmly established the firmer the presumption. Hume, then, would reject the maxim of autonomous philosophy (whether of utilitarian, rationalistic, or whatever form) that the mere fact that a practice is established is, in itself, no reason to continue it. Hume's narrative conception of social utility yields the contrary maxim: the mere fact that a practice is established *is* a reason to continue it, the standard of reason being social utility and narrative time being a value constitutive of social utility. Again, one must make a special effort to distinguish the utilitarian conception of reform from Hume's. Utilitarian reformers conceive of society as a tenseless object which can be experimented upon to satisfy the demands of the abstract imperative to maximize the greatest happiness. By contrast, Hume's conception of society is not tenseless but structured by narrative time with the concept of the sacred built into it. Because society is a sacred order, the utilitarian conception of "experiment" logically has no place: "To tamper, therefore, in this affair, or try experiments merely upon the credit of supposed argument and philosophy, can never be the part of a wise magistrate, who will bear a reverence to what carries the marks of age; and though he may attempt some improvements for the public good, yet will he adjust his innovations as much as possible to the ancient fabric, and preserve entire the chief pillars and supports of the constitution" (E, 499).

This conservative theory of reform is squarely in the classical skeptical tradition: we should worship the gods whether or not we know they exist, and should attempt only those reforms that are pleasing to them, i.e., that are in accord with "the chief pillars and supports of the constitution." And so, despite the temptation to invoke the autonomy principle, post-Pyrrhonian philosophers will hold that "the common botched and inaccurate governments . . . serve the purposes of society" well enough (ibid. 500). But there is a deeper skepticism entailed in Hume's conception of reform, one that derives from his reflection on the historicity of society and which gives his skepticism a distinctively modern shape.

If we could think of society in a tenseless way, as we do of generations of silkworms and of the flies of a summer, perhaps a contract or utilitarian model of reform would be appropriate, but we are narrative existences with the past built into the meaning of our present: "Did one generation of men go off the stage at once, and another succeed, as is the case with silk-worms and butterflies, the new race, if they had sense enough to choose their government, which surely is never the case with men, might voluntarily, and by general consent, establish their own form of civil polity, without any regard to the laws or precedents, which prevailed among their ancestors. But as human society is in perpetual flux, one man every hour going out of the world, another coming into it, it is necessary, in order to preserve stability in government, that the new brood should conform themselves to the established constitution" (E, 463). It goes without saying that "Some innovations must necessarily have place in every human institution . . . but violent innovations no individual is entitled to make: they are even dangerous to be attempted by the legislature: more ill than good is ever to be expected from them: and if history affords examples to the contrary, they are not to be drawn into precedent, and are only to be regarded as proofs, that the science of politics affords few rules, which will not admit of some exception" (ibid., 463–64).

One exception which Hume thoroughly examined was the Puritan rebellion during the reign of Charles I which led to the happy constitution of ordered liberty of 1688. But the Puritans were driven by "faction and fanaticism," and if "the measures of allegiance were to be taken from [them], a total anarchy must have place in human society, and a final period at once be put to every government" (ibid., 464). The standard of allegiance is to be taken from Charles I, who defended the constitution but who was also willing to reform. Yet of what value is this conservative rule? Charles did not succeed in preserving the constitution, and Hume made clear that no one could have prevented its collapse (H, V, lix, 380). Parliament and Crown had worked themselves into a dialectical knot which no one could untie. Looking back, we can see that the constitution itself was changing, and so the rules for rational reform were not available. Both sides were acting in the dark, and neither side could understand what they were doing because the significance of their actions lay in the narrative perceptions of future generations.

The moral world is a narrative unity of ancestors, contemporaries, and posterity. For reform to be rational it must be possible that we know what we are doing, and for this we need standards. But the standards of thought for the moral world are structured by narrative associations and are vulnerable to the future. In such a world we can be said to know what we are doing only if we can understand the future significance of our acts, and this we cannot do: "It affords a violent prejudice against almost every science, that no prudent man, however sure of his principles, dares prophesy concerning any event, or foretell the remote consequences of things" (E, 48). The future is open and constantly threatens to break through the narrative cords that hold the moral world together and to upset the most established institutions: "It is not fully known what degree of refinement, either in virtue or vice, human nature is susceptible of, nor what may be expected of mankind from any great revolution in their education, customs, or principles" (E, 89). And even if we knew what was to happen, we could not know *now* what narrative associations either we or generations yet unborn would place on those events after having lived through them. Given this ignorance of the temporal world and of ourselves, any standards structured by narrative associations, such as the British constitution, must be radically obscure, and any debate about reform, employing such standards, must be equally obscure. In this historical darkness, post-Pyrrhonian philosophy offers only this light: keep the autonomy principle at bay; discover through historical research the deep narrative order of which one is a part; work for the stability and improvement of this order, but be skeptical and diffident about the significance of one's efforts at reform or preservation.

# Notes

## INTRODUCTION

1. Nicholas Capaldi, *David Hume: The Newtonian Philosopher* (Boston: Twayne, 1975), p. 9.

2. Harold A. Prichard, *Knowledge and Perception* (Oxford: Clarendon Press, 1950), p. 174.

3. L. A. Selby-Bigge, Introduction to *David Hume's Enquiries Concerning Human Understanding and Concerning the Principles of Morals* 3d ed. with text revised and notes by P. H. Nidditch (Oxford: Clarendon Press, 1975), p. vii.

4. The question was first explored in David Norton and Richard Popkin, eds., *David Hume: Philosophical Historian* (New York: Bobbs-Merrill, 1965). Duncan Forbes relates Hume's political thought to Hume's *The History of England* in *Hume's Philosophical Politics* (Cambridge: Cambridge University Press, 1975).

5. Tom Beauchamp and Alexander Rosenberg, *Hume and the Problem of Causation* (New York: Oxford University Press, 1981).

## CHAPTER ONE

1. A. J. Ayer, ed., *Logical Positivism* (Glencoe: The Free Press, 1959), p. 4.

2. William Knight, *Hume* (Edinburgh: William Blackwood, 1886), p. 124.

3. Antony Flew, *Hume's Philosophy of Belief* (London: Routledge and Kegan Paul, 1961), p. 19.

4. I shall not explore the answers in any depth in this study. The term "perception" in Hume has been captured by phenomenalistic connotations both because of phenomenalistic preconceptions brought to his work and because of the language he inherited. These must be cleared away before there can be any fruitful discussion of Hume's thought on how perceptions are related to physical objects. In chapter 2 I suggest that a phenomenological reading of "perception" might be more appropriate. In this study, I am concerned mainly with Hume's theory of what philosophy is, and that theory can be considered independently of his analysis of perceptions.

5. Talk here of the a-priori structure of common life and other references in this chapter to internal relations and transcendental perspectives may appear

perverse in a discussion of Hume's thought. It might be if Hume's conception of the a priori were the formal notion of an analytic truth. But Hume has a richer and more concrete notion of the a priori than that of analyticity, and one, moreover, which justifies the language I have used here to interpret his thought. The richer notion is discussed in chapter 2.

6. William Warburton, *A Selection from Unpublished Works*, ed. Francis Kilvert (London, 1841), pp. 309–10.

7. James Beattie, *Essay on Truth*, 8th ed. (London, 1812), pp. 448, 213.

8. John Stuart Mill, review of Brodie, *History of the British Empire*, in *The Westminster Review*, 2 (1824), p. 34.

9. John Randall, Jr., "David Hume: Radical Empiricist and Pragmatist," in *Freedom and Experience: Essays Presented to Horace W. Kallen*, ed. Sidney Hook and Milton R. Konnitz (Ithaca and New York, 1947), p. 296.

10. Prichard, *Knowledge and Perception*, p. 174.

11. D. C. Stove, "Hume, the Causal Principle, and Kemp Smith," *Hume Studies* 1, no. 1 (1975): 21.

12. See Norman Kemp Smith, *The Philosophy of David Hume* (New York: Macmillan, 1964), pp. 447, 543. Barry Stroud follows Kemp Smith here in *Hume* (London: Routledge and Kegan Paul, 1978), p. 14. Both exemplify what David Norton calls the "subordination thesis," that Hume thoroughly subordinates reason to instinct and feeling. Norton, it seems to me, has decisively refuted this interpretation. See David Norton, *David Hume: Common-Sense Moralist, Sceptical Metaphysician* (Princeton: Princeton University Press, 1982), chapter 5.

13. Richard Popkin, "David Hume: His Pyrrhonism and His Critique of Pyrrhonism," in *The High Road to Pyrrhonism*, ed. by Richard Watson and James Force (San Diego: Austin Hill Press, 1980), pp. 103–32.

14. For an interesting discussion of the psychological possibilities of Pyrrhonian doubt, see Terence Penelhum, "Hume's Skepticism and the Dialogues," in *McGill Hume Studies*, ed. David Norton et al. (San Diego: Austin Hill Press, 1976), pp. 253–78.

15. For a discussion of how reason, for Hume, can shape, modify, and, in some cases, even overturn natural belief, see Norton, *Hume* chapter 5, especially pp. 229–38.

16. *Popkin*, "David Hume," p. 130.

17. See Norton, *Hume*, pp. 192–208. This book also contains an important discussion of how Hume's thought is related to that of his Scottish contemporaries: Hutcheson, Turnbull, Kames, and Reid.

## Chapter Two

1. John Passmore, *Hume's Intentions* (Cambridge: The University Press, 1952), p. 93.

2. Flew, *Hume's Philosophy of Belief*, p. 47.

3. J. A. Robinson, "Hume's Two Definitions of 'Cause'," in *Hume*, ed. V. C. Chappell (New York: Anchor Books, 1966), p. 129, and Passmore, *Hume's Intentions*, p. 94.

4. Ludwig Wittgenstein, *Tractatus Logico-Philosophicus*, trans. D. F. Pears and B. F. McGuiness (New York: The Humanities Press, 1961), p. 151.

5. See the discussion of Hume's concept of contrariety and the a priori in the next section of this chapter.

6. For an interesting discussion of how passion is related to reason, see Páll Árdal, "Some Implications of the Virtue of Reasonableness in Hume's *Treatise*," in *Hume, A Re-Evaluation*, ed. Donald Livingston and James King (New York: Fordham University Press, 1976), pp. 91–106.

7. Páll Árdal, "Convention and Value" in *David Hume, Bicentenary Papers*, ed. G. P. Morice (Edinburgh: Edinburgh University Press, 1977), pp. 51–67.

8. See E. C. Mossner, "An Apology for David Hume Historian," *PMLA* 56 (1941): 686–88, and Michael Morrisroe, "Linguistic Analysis as Rhetorical Pattern in David Hume," in *Hume and the Enlightenment*, ed. W. B. Todd (Austin: University of Texas Press, 1974), pp. 72–82; Donald Henze, "The Linguistic Aspect of Hume's Method," *Journal of the History of Ideas* (1969): 116–26.

9. See Nicholas Capaldi, *David Hume*, pp. 82–83, 88; R. J. Butler, "Hume's Impressions," *Royal Institute of Philosophy Lectures, 1974–75*, vol. 9 (London: Macmillan, 1976), pp. 122–36; Páll Árdal, "Convention and Value," pp. 51–67; J. C. A. Gaskin, *Hume's Philosophy of Religion* (London: Macmillan, 1978), pp. 74–79.

10. See Farhang Zabeeh, *Hume: Precursor of Modern Empiricism* (The Hague: Martinus Nijhoff, 1973).

11. Adolf Reinach, "Kant's Interpretation of Hume's Problem," in *David Hume, Many-Sided Genius*, ed. Kenneth Merrill and Robert Shahan (Norman: University of Oklahoma Press, 1976), pp. 161–88.

12. There is an obvious affinity here with the phenomenologists' "material *a priori*." See Richard T. Murphy, *Hume and Husserl* (The Hague: Martinus Nijhoff, 1980), chapter 2.

13. On the Hume-Husserl connection, see George Davie, "Edmund Husserl and 'the as yet, in its most important respect, unrecognized greatness of Hume,'" in Morice, *Bicentenary Papers*, pp. 69–76. I am indebted in this discussion to a number of Professor Davie's unpublished papers on Hume and the phenomenological movement. Also Murphy, *Hume and Husserl*, and R. A. Mall, *Experience and Reason, The Phenomenology of Husserl and Its Relation to Hume's Philosophy* (The Hague: Martinus Nijhoff, 1973).

14. The discussion of Hume's distinctions-of-reason method of examining the a-priori structure of perceptions in the remaining part of this chapter is due to R. J. Butler's article, "Hume's Impressions," pp. 122–36. Butler brilliantly exploits this doctrine which had lain dormant in the text almost from the beginning. There is need for an in-depth study of Hume's concept of the a priori both in respect to its historical background and its application in his work. The latter is especially important. Hume not only states a theory of the a priori (relations of ideas and distinctions of reason), he actually applies it. The theory, then, is to be evaluated not only for its epistemic worth, it is to be used as a hermeneutical principle for reading Hume's works. Hume's *Essays*, for instance, are filled with intriguing remarks about necessary connections in the moral world. The "different operations and tendencies" of "these two species of government might be made apparent even *a priori*" (E, 15); Hume discovers "one of those eternal political truths, which no time nor accident can vary" (E, 19); "sound understanding and delicate affections" are "characters, it is to be

presumed, we shall always find inseparable" (E, 570). The "experiments" in *Treatise*, book II, part II, section ii, which are examples of Hume's "experimental method" in moral subjects are as much a priori as empirical. The a-priori truths Hume "discovers" there are not analytic in the sense that their denials are self-contradictory but are internal to acts of consciousness. See, for instance, the *Treatise*, p. 334.

15. I am indebted to George Davie for this observation.

16. In a letter to A. Metzger, Husserl recognizes a debt to Hume but not to Kant: "I possessed the deepest antipathy against Kant and he (Kant) has not, if I judge rightly, influenced me at all." Quoted in R. A. Mall, *Experience and Reason*, p. 6.

17. Butler, "Hume's Impressions."

18. Hume admired Cicero's union of philosophy and rhetoric. For Cicero's influence on Hume, see Peter Jones, *Hume's Sentiments, Their Ciceronian and French Context* (Edinburgh: Edinburgh University Press, 1982), pp. 29–40.

## CHAPTER THREE

1. Ralph W. Church, *Hume's Theory of the Understanding* (Ithaca: Cornell University Press, 1935), p. 27.

2. C. D. Broad, "Hume's Doctrine of Space," Dawes Hicks Lecture on Philosophy, *Proceedings of the British Academy*, 47 (1961): 165.

3. Flew, *Hume's Philosophy of Belief*, p. 22.

4. Jonathan Bennett, *Locke, Berkeley, Hume* (Oxford: Clarendon Press, 1971), p. 234.

5. Flew, *Hume's Philosophy of Belief*, p. 37.

6. Ibid.

7. Bennett, *Locke, Berkeley, Hume* p. 222.

8. John Locke, *An Essay Concerning Human Understanding*, 2 vols, ed. Alexander Campbell Fraser (New York: Dover, 1959), 1:11–12.

9. Flew, *Hume's Philosophy of Belief*, p. 51.

10. Ibid., p. 37.

11. Ibid., p. 50.

12. Locke, *Essay*, p. 38.

13. *The Philosophical Works of Descartes*, 2 vols., trans. and ed. Elizabeth S. Haldane and G. R. T. Ross (Cambridge: Cambridge University Press, 1969), 1:331.

14. Páll Árdal, "Convention and Value," p. 64.

15. In Morice, *Bicentenary Papers*, p. 64.

16. Antony Flew, "Was Berkeley a Precursor of Wittgenstein?" in *Hume and the Enlightenment: Essays Presented to Ernest Campbell Mossner*, ed. W. B. Todd (Austin: University of Texas Press, 1974), pp. 153–163.

17. Peter Jones explores Hume's actual knowledge of Newton and cautions us not to exaggerate Hume's "Newtonianism." Humanistic writers such as Bayle and Cicero had a much greater influence in molding Hume's conception of what the problems of philosophy are and what methods can be forged to deal

with them. Hume emerges from this study as an up-to-date Ciceronian humanist. See *Hume's Sentiments*, expecially chapters 1 and 5.

18. Flew, *Hume's Philosophy of Belief*, p. 45.

19. Ibid.

20. See James Farr's important essay on Hume's principle of sympathy, "Hume, Hermeneutics, and History: A Sympathetic Account" *History and Theory*, 17 (1978): 285–310.

21. One reason the missing shade of blue appears to be a problem is that the opening pages of the *Treatise* are not read narratively. When read in the light of doctrines introduced later in the *Treatise*, the purported counterexample falls into place. Daniel Flage has shown how Hume's doctrine of *relative ideas* can account for the missing shade, and Ronald Butler has shown how Hume's doctrine of *distinctions of reason* can be used to account for it. Butler observes that the idea of the missing shade of blue is presented by Hume as the first of many ideas that the mind can construct for itself even though it is still constrained in certain ways by experience. See Daniel Flage, "Hume's Relative Ideas," *Hume Studies* 7 (April 1981): 68, and R. J. Butler, "Hume's Impressions" pp. 130–31.

22. Flew, *Hume's Philosophy of Belief*, p. 26.

23. Ludwig Wittgenstein, *On Certainty*, ed. G. E. M. Anscombe and G. H. von Wright (Oxford: Clarendon Press, 1969), par. 167; see also pars. 98, 321.

24. A. H. Basson, *David Hume* (Harmondsworth: Penguin, 1958), p. 37.

25. Bennett, *Locke, Berkeley, Hume*, p. 229.

## CHAPTER FOUR

1. Bertrand Russell, *The Analysis of Mind* (London: Allen and Unwin, 1924), p. 159.

2. Church, "Hume's Doctrine of Space," p. 27.

3. John Laird, *Hume's Philosophy of Human Nature* (New York: Dutton, 1931), p. 32.

4. H. H. Price, *Hume's Theory of the External World* (Oxford: Clarendon Press, 1948), p. 5.

5. Zabeeh, *Hume*, p. 57.

6. Passmore, *Hume's Intentions*, p. 94.

7. A. J. Ayer, *Language, Truth, and Logic* (London: Gollancz, 1946), p. 19.

8. C. I. Lewis, *Mind and the World Order* (New York: Dover, 1956), p. 140.

9. Ibid., p. 142.

10. Rudolf Carnap, *Philosophy and Logical Syntax* (New York: AMS, 1976), p. 15.

11. A. J. Ayer, *The Problem of Knowledge* (New York: St. Martins, 1956), p. 160.

12. Bertrand Russell, *Our Knowledge of the External World* (London: Allen and Unwin, 1929), p. 171.

13. Bernard Bosanquet, *The Principle of Individuality and Value* (London: Macmillan, 1912), pp. 146–147.

14. Michael Oakeshott, *Experience and Its Modes* (Cambridge: Cambridge University Press, 1933), pp. 146–47.

15. Jack Meiland, *Scepticism and Historical Knowledge* (New York: Random House, 1965), p. 192.

16. D. G. C. McNabb, *David Hume* (Hamden: Archon Books, 1966), p. 42.

17. Ibid.

18. Russell, *Our Knowledge of the External World*, p. 159.

19. Price, *Hume's Theory*, p. 5.

20. Bennett, *Locke, Berkeley, Hume*, pp. 229–30.

21. Ibid., p. 228.

22. The idea of a past-entailing concept is based on Arthur Danto's profound discussion of temporal language in *Analytical Philosophy of History* (Cambridge: Cambridge University Press, 1965), chapter 4.

23. Descartes, *Works*, 1: 85.

24. G. W. F. Hegel, *Philosophy of Right and Law*, trans. J. M. Sterret and C. J. Friedrich, in *The Philosophy of Hegel*, ed. Carl J. Friedrich (New York: Modern Library, 1954), p. 227.

25. Bennett, *Locke, Berkeley, Hume*, p. 228.

26. Basson, *Hume*, p. 37.

27. Zabeeh, *Hume*, p. 55.

28. Gottlob Frege, *The Foundations of Arithmetic* (Oxford: Clarendon Press, 1950), p. viii.


## CHAPTER FIVE

1. Laird, *Hume's Philosophy*, p. 77; Smith, *Philosophy of Hume*, p. 310.

2. For what more might be involved, see J. P. Monteiro "Hume, Induction, and Natural Selection," in *McGill Hume Studies*, ed. David Norton et al. (San Diego: Austin Hill Press, 1976), pp. 291–308.

3. A perfect history, then, would be a fated history where past and present events are viewed in the light of knowledge about the outcome of that great causal "chain of events which compose the history of mankind" (EUH, 34). Although this is the idea of a perfect historical narrative, Hume does not think such a history is possible because the required knowledge of the future is impossible. (See the last section of this chapter and chapter 11.) Yet the future-referring propensity of the fancy internal to the imagination constitutes a permanent temptation to write history in a fated mode, secretly viewing past and present events in the light of some vision of the future (the last judgment, the classless society, progress, and the like).

4. During the period from 1745 to 1749, Hume produced four large manuscripts of notes chronologically arranged and an abridgement of English history from the Roman invasion through the reign of Henry II. (See Mossner, "An Apology for David Hume Historian.") These are no doubt part of the "historical projects" Hume was contemplating in a letter of 1747 and for the composition of which he thought a military expedition with St. Clair would benefit him (L, I, 99). They also throw light on Hume's confession in a letter of 1748 that he "had long had an intention, in . . . my riper years, of composing some History" for which he "had treasured up stores of study & plans of thinking for many years" (ibid., 109). If we may count "many years" as ten years, then

348

Hume was seriously turning over in his mind the idea of writing a history of England by 1738, two years before publication of book III of the *Treatise*.

5. See chapters 9 and 12 below.

6. Hume's implicit views on the limits of narrative thought and its application to history and philosophy are discussed in detail in chapters 9, 11, and 12 below.

7. See chapters 11 and 12 below.

8. The truth functional analysis of narrative judgments presented here and in chapters 9 and 11 is due to Arthur Danto's theory of narrative sentences in *Analytical Philosophy of History*, chapters 8 and 9.

9. See EU, 27 and A, 13–15. See also EU, 164n, and D, 145–46.

## CHAPTER SIX

1. See Fred Wilson's important article on the two definitions and on Hume's conception of how to correct natural judgments about causality, "Hume's Theory of Mental Activity," in *McGill Hume Studies*, pp. 101–20.

2. Francis Bacon, *Aphorisms*, book I, no. 48.

3. Isaac Newton, *Opticks* (New York: McGraw-Hill, 1931), p. 404.

4. Ibid., p. 376.

5. Ibid., p. 369–70.

6. One might object that it is not Hume but Philo who is attempting to say something about ultimate causation. There is, of course, always a problem with taking Philo to speak for Hume. But the point made here is the obviously Humean one that we cannot help wondering about the ultimate principle of order in things, and, as with all beliefs, whether purely natural or arrived at through the medium of a convention, we should methodize and correct them as best we can. The cosmology presupposed by modern science is materialist. Philo is suggesting that if we take physics (Hume's: "the most intelligible philosophy" [NHR, 29]) as the paradigm of knowledge, then materialism is the cosmology that seems most natural. Hume, as I shall show shortly, did not accept materialism, but he took it seriously as a thought that naturally occurs to philosophical consciousness as it moves on to the higher but more obscure stage of philosophical theism. R. F. Anderson has presented a well-documented case for thinking that materialism *is* Hume's ultimate metaphysical framework. See his *Hume's First Principles* (Lincoln: University of Nebraska Press, 1966).

7. Further support for the thesis that Hume accepted some form of theism is in George J. Nathan's "The Existence and Nature of God in Hume's Theism," in *Hume: A Re-Evaluation*, ed. Donald Livingston and James King (New York: Fordham University Press, 1976), pp. 126–49, and in Keith E. Yandell, "Hume on Religious Belief" *Hume: A Re-Evaluation*, pp. 109–25.

8. See chapter 11 below.

9. See Richard Popkin's study of the widespread belief in providential and prophetic history in Hume's time, "Hume: Philosophical Versus Prophetic Historian," pp. 83–95, and James Force "Hume in the 'Dialogues,' the Dictates of Convention and the Millennial Future State of Biblical Prophecy," *Southwestern Journal of Philosophy*, 8, no. 1 (1977): 131–44.

10. See Norton, *Hume: Common-Sense Moralist*, p. 290. Discussions of

whether Hume is a skeptic about this or that are often carried on without regard to the actual tradition of skepticism in which Hume thought, with the result that Hume is often described as being or not being a skeptic in a sense that is inappropriate. Chapter 6 of Norton's work contains a valuable discussion of traditional skepticisms and their relation to Hume's thought.

## CHAPTER SEVEN

1. Carl G. Hempel, "Explanation in Science and in History," in *Philosophical Analysis and History*, ed. William Dray (New York: Harper and Row, 1966), p. 117.

2. The best defense of the thesis that Hume does have an adequate conception of lawlikeness is to be found in Tom Beauchamp and Alexander Rosenberg's thorough and deep discussion of Hume's conception of causality, *Hume and the Problem of Causation*, chapter 4.

3. The central insight of this essay was discovered during the time Hume was working on the *Treatise* and is recorded in the Memoranda he kept from 1729 to 1740 (HEM, 516).

4. Alan Donagan, *The Later Philosophy of R. G. Collingwood* (Oxford: Clarendon Press, 1962), p. 171.

5. G. W. Leibniz, "On the Ultimate Origins of Things," in *Leibniz Selections*, ed. Philip P. Weiner (New York: Scribner's, 1951), p. 347.

6. Fred Wilson has argued that Hume's second definition of cause contains implicitly the notion that causal (lawlike) regularities must be capable of supporting subjunctive conditional statements. See "Hume's Theory of Mental Activity," pp. 106–7. Wilson makes clear in this essay that the Humean scientist is not a passive spectator of regularities but is actively engaged in distinguishing accidental regularities from lawlike ones using the eight "Rules by which to judge of causes and effects" (T, 173–75). These rules are derived in accord with the principles of true philosophy, that is, they are abstractions from the deeply established practice in common life of making causal judgments. For a detailed discussion and defense of Hume's conception of lawlikeness, see Beauchamp and Rosenberg, *Hume and the Problem of Causation*, Chapter 4.

7. For a discussion of how Newtonianism functioned as a paradigm in Hume's thought, see Nicholas Capaldi, *David Hume: The Newtonian Philosopher*.

8. *Phaedo* in *The Collected Dialogues of Plato*, ed. Edith Hamilton and Huntington Cairns (Princeton: Princeton University Press, 1963), p. 79.

9. Ibid., p. 80.

## CHAPTER EIGHT

1. Norton and Popkin, *David Hume: Philosophical Historian*, pp. 413–17. This volume contains selections from Hume's historical and philosophical writings which yield a picture of Hume as a philosopher of history. There are also essays by David Norton and Richard Popkin on the relation of history and philosophy in Hume's thinking. I owe a special debt to this volume, for it was through it that I first began to see a unity in Hume's historical and philosophical work.

2. R. G. Collingwood, *The Idea of History* (Oxford: Clarendon Press, 1962), p. 73.

3. Laird, *Hume's Philosophy*, p. 266.

4. John B. Stewart, *The Moral and Political Philosophy of David Hume* (New York: Columbia University Press, 1963), p. 289.

5. Haskell Fain, *Between Philosophy and History* (Princeton: Princeton University Press, 1970), p. 9.

6. Mossner, "An Apology for David Hume Historian," pp. 675–76.

7. J. B. Black, *The Art of History* (London: Methuen, 1926), p. 85.

8. Ibid., p. 87.

9. Ibid., p. 86.

10. Ibid., p. 98.

11. David Hartley, *Observations on Man, His Frame, His Duty, and His Expectations*, 2 vols. (London, 1769), 2: 159. The providential-prophetic view of history is discussed at some length in chapter 11 below.

12. Collingwood, *The Idea of History*, p. 82.

13. Ibid., p. 83.

14. See Farr's penetrating essay "Hume, Hermeneutics, And History," pp. 285–310. Farr argues that "sympathy or communication" between researchers and agents functions in Hume's thought as a hermeneutic and a-priori principle which applies uniquely to history. As such, it is a nonpositivistic and nonempathetic prototype of the later doctrine of *verstehen*. See also Nicholas Capaldi, "Hume as Social Scientist," *The Review of Metaphysics* 32 (1978): 99–123.

15. Isaac Deutscher, "The Future of Russian Society," *Dissent* 1 (1954): 227.

16. Black, *The Art of History*, pp. 98–99.

17. Ibid., p. 102.

18. See the discussion of the status of narrative time in chapter 5 above, especially the last two sections.

## CHAPTER NINE

1. Book III, part II, sketches out an abstract history of the principles of civil society, that is, the principles of justice and government. The same story line underlies the account of justice and government in the second *Enquiry*, sections III and IV, along with a frank recognition in the last section, entitled "A Dialogue," that the concrete principles ordered by the abstract story line are relative to historical periods and cannot be understood without a sympathetic examination of the special mind that produced them. Almost all of the *Essays*, but especially those dealing with economic, political, and cultural issues, are so many attempts to explain the story of man's progressive self-awareness of the principles of civil society (justice and government) and to show how the arts and sciences are connected to these principles.

2. Mossner, "An Apology for David Hume Historian," p. 679.

3. Constant Noble Stockton, "Economics and the Mechanism of Historical Progress in Hume's *History*," in *Hume, A Re-Evaluation*, pp. 296–320.

4. Aristotle wrote that poetry is "something more philosophical and of graver import than history, because its statements are of the nature rather of univer-

sals, whereas those of history are particulars" (*Poetics*, 1451b, 5). Descartes' method was "to write just as though I were treating of a matter which no one had ever touched on before me" (Descartes, 1: 331).

5. Catharine Macaulay, *The History of England* (London, 1763), pp. vii–viii.

6. Ibid., p. xi.

7. Ibid., ix.

8. Priestley, *Lectures on History and General Policy* (Dublin 1778), p. 369.

9. Macaulay, *History of England*, pp. vii–viii.

10. Quoted in Craig Walton, "Hume and Jefferson on History," in *Hume: A Re-Evaluation*, p. 393.

11. Ibid., p. 390.

12. Ibid., p. 391.

13. We must keep in mind that eighteenth-century British politics contained within it the hostility and suspicion of over a century of civil war and violent political strife. Professor J. H. Plumb observes that by the constitutional settlement of 1689 "conspiracy and rebellion, treason and plot, were part of the history and experience of at least three generations of Englishmen" (J. H. Plumb, *The Growth of Political Stability in England, 1675–1725* [London, Macmillan, 1967], p. 1). Sir Robert Walpole's administration lasted from 1721 to 1742, but Walpole lived in constant fear of a Jacobite uprising: "Just beyond his grasp the conspirators were at work. Jacobite agents lurked in the most unlikely places. Every suspicion, every hint needed to be tracked down. . . . Year after year Walpole built up a vast web of counterespionage with his own spies in all the capitals and ports of Europe" (J. H. Plumb, *Sir Robert Walpole*, 2 vols. (London: Cresset, 1956), 2: 41.) Walpole was not paranoid. A Jacobite uprising had occurred six years before his administration and the largest one was to occur three years after. But if Walpole feared a conspiracy by malcontents in the opposition party, the opposition feared a conspiracy on the part of the ministry to seize the whole power of government. Bernard Bailyn has argued in a number of works that conspiratorial thinking was built into the very conception of eighteenth-century British constitutional politics. See especially his *The Origins of American Politics* (New York: Knopf, 1968), chapter 1, and *The Ideological Origins of the American Revolution* (Cambridge: Harvard University Press, 1967), chapter 4. It is remarkable that something like the logic of conspiracy that Bailyn perceives in British politics was recognized by Hume. A main task of Hume's historical thinking is to emancipate the English from the view that the constitution is an order of *intentions* (to be evaluated by moral and legal categories) by pointing out that the constitution is, for the most part, the *unintended* result of historical conditions. Where intentions do not exist, there can be no conspiracy. But such a sophisticated interpretation of the constitution requires being able to correct bad narrative judgments, a critical activity not clearly understood in Hume's time and one in which he was a pioneer.

14. Macaulay, *History of England* p. xi.

15. Ibid.

16. Ibid., pp. xv–xvi.

17. Bernard Bailyn observes: "It would be difficult to exaggerate the keenness of eighteenth-century Britain's sense of their . . . world eminence and their distinctiveness in the achievement of liberty. From the end of the war in 1713 until the crisis over America a half-century later the triumph of Britain in

warfare, in commerce, and in statecraft was the constant theme not only of formal state pronouncements and of political essays, tracts, and orations but of belles-lettres as well. . . . No writer, however famous or obscure, could afford to neglect the theme of British liberty and power" (*The Origins of American Politics*, pp. 17–18). It was this attitude that Hume complained about in his autobiography: "I had been taught, by experience, that the Whig party were in possession of bestowing all places, both in the state and in literature" (MOL, 8).

18. Mossner, "An Apology for David Hume Historian," p. 679; see also Mossner's remarks about Hume's views that style is essential to conceptualization and not a mere ornament (pp. 686–88); also Morrisroe "Linguistic Analysis in David Hume," pp. 72–82.

19. John Wilkes had written a scandalous article on George III's government and on the Scottish influence in the ministry. His trial for libel and repeated efforts of the House of Commons to unseat him led to popular demonstrations in support of Wilkes which lasted for days and were often violent. Wilkes's trouble with the government became a symbol which enabled a number of inchoate popular grievances to emerge: the demand for a free press, the legitimacy of extraparliamentary political activity, and the rights of electors to send representatives to Parliament. For an account of the political meaning of the affair, see G. F. E. Rudé, *Wilkes and Liberty* (Oxford: Clarendon Press, 1962). For a detailed account of the influence of the affair on Hume's political thought, see Duncan Forbes, *Hume's Philosophical Politics* chapter 5.

20. Rudé, *Wilkes and Liberty*, pp. 191–98.

## CHAPTER TEN

1. As we saw in chapter 1, the doctrine of double existence is a philosophic error that applies to the ancients as much as to the moderns, but it is the moderns more than the ancients that have introduced the dogma into morals. On the whole, Hume considered the ancients to be superior to the moderns in respect to moral philosophy because the former grounded morality in sentiment (the good) whereas the latter, who pretend "to found everything on reason," ground morality in "certain *rapports* or relations," a position that, in Hume's opinion, "never will be reconciled with true philosophy" (EM, 197n).

2. Arthur Eddington, *The Nature of the Physical World* (Ann Arbor: University of Michigan Press, 1968), p. xiv.

3. Descartes, 1: 88.

4. Ibid., p. 311.

5. Ibid., p. 309.

6. Ibid., p. 331.

7. Ibid., p. 313.

8. Ibid., p. 89.

9. Ibid., p. 90.

10. Gerhardt Niemeyer, *Between Nothingness and Paradise* (Baton Rouge: Louisiana State University Press, 1971), chapter 1.

11. Morelly, *Code de la Nature*, ed. G. Chinard (Paris, 1950), p. 180, my translation.

12. Letter to Thomas Jefferson, October 26, 1788, in *The Papers of Thomas*

*Jefferson*, ed. Julian P. Boyd (Princeton: Princeton University Press, 1950–), 14: 38–40.

13. Descartes, I, p. 89.

14. *Mill on Bentham and Coleridge*, ed., F. R. Leavis (New York: G. W. Stewart, 1950), p. 57.

15. Descartes, I, p. 331.

16. P. J. Proudhon, *What is Property?* (New York: Humbolt, 1893), p. 13.

17. *Karl Marx on Revolution*, 13 vols., ed. and trans. Saul K. Padover (New York: McGraw-Hill, 1971), I, p. 516.

18. John Rawls, *A Theory of Justice* (Cambridge: Belknap Press, 1971), pp. 136–142.

19. Robert Paul Wolff, *In Defense of Anarchism* (New York: Harper and Row, 1970), p. 19.

20. Robert Nozick, *Anarchy, State*, and *Utopia* (New York: Basic Books, 1974), p. ix.

21. The common error is the confusion of the ideal order with the legitimate order. The confusion is especially difficult to avoid if the ideal is thought of as a set of *rights* rather than as a good. States that are not the best can still be good and so legitimate. Again it is the moderns who ground legitimacy on *natural rights* known through autonomous reason ("certain *rapports* or relations") a position that cannot be "reconciled with true philosophy" (EM, 197n).

22. John Locke, *Two Treatises of Government* (New York: Mentor Books, 1963), p. 369.

23. Algernon Sidney, "Discourses Concerning Government," in *The Works of Algernon Sidney* (London, 1772), p. 446.

24. Descartes, I, p. 313.

25. B. F. Skinner, *Walden Two* (New York: Macmillan, 1967), p. 239.

## CHAPTER ELEVEN

1. Aristotle, *Poetics*, 145b, 5.

2. Hartley, *Observations*, 2: 159.

3. Joseph Priestley, *Lectures*, p. 453.

4. Ibid., p. 452.

5. Ibid., p. 4–5.

6. Ibid., p. 454.

7. Ibid., p. 453.

8. Ibid., pp. 24–25.

9. Joseph Priestley, *An Essay on the First Principles of Government*, 2d e. (London, 1961), pp. 2–3.

10. Immanuel Kant, "Idea for a Universal History from a Cosmopolitan Point of View," trans. W. Hastie, in *Theories of History*, ed. Patrick Gardiner (Glencoe: The Free Press, 1959), p. 30.

11. Ibid.

12. Hartley, *Observations*, 2: 316.

13. Ibid., p. 368.

14. Kant, "Idea for a Universal History," p. 32.

15. Ibid., p. 31.

16. Richard Price, *A Discourse on the Laws of our Country* (London, 1789), pp. 49–51.

17. Priestley, *Lectures*, p. 454.

18. Catharine Macaulay, *Observations on the Reflections of the Right Hon. Edmund Burke, On the Revolution in France in a Letter to the Right Hon. The Earl of Stanhope* (London, 1790), pp. 20–21.

19. Ibid., p. 21.

20. A. R. J. Turgot, "A Philosophical Review of the Successive Advances of the Human Mind," in *Turgot on Progress, Sociology and Economics*, trans. and ed. Ronald L. Meek (Cambridge: Cambridge University Press, 1973), p. 57.

21. Kant, "Idea for a Universal History," p. 29.

22. Ibid., p. 32.

23. Ibid., p. 23, 33.

24. Ibid., pp. 31–34.

25. Ibid.

26. Charles Fourier, *Oeuvres complètes*, 6 vols. (Paris, 1846–48), 6: xv.

27. John Stuart Mill, *A System of Logic*, in *Collected Works*, 19 vols. (Toronto: University of Toronto Press, 1974), 8: 931.

28. Ibid., p. 930.

29. Macaulay, *Observations*, p. 20–21.

30. Joseph Priestley, *An Essay on the First Principles of Government*, p. 5.

31. Fourier, *Oeuvres complètes*, 6: xv.

32. Herbert Marcuse, *One-Dimensional Man* (Boston: Beacon Press, 1966), p. ix.

33. Herbert Marcuse, "Ethics and Revolution," in *Ethics and Society*, ed. Richard T. De George (New York: Anchor Books, 1966), pp. 142–43.

34. Herbert Marcuse, "Repressive Tolerance," in *A Critique of Pure Tolerance* (Boston: Beacon Press, 1965), p. 19.

35. Priestley, *Lectures on History*, p. 470.

36. Ibid., p. 471.

37. Ibid.

38. Ibid.

39. Marcuse, "Ethics and Revolution," p. 139.

40. Ibid., p. 140.

41. How the imagination constitutes narrative existences is discussed in the last two sections of chapter 5.

42. Priestley, *Lectures on History*, p. 6.

43. August Comte, *The Positive Philosophy*, 2 vols., trans. Harriet Martineau (London: Kegan Paul, 1893), 2: 69.

44. Alfred North Whitehead, *Adventures of Ideas* (New York: Macmillan, 1933), p. 246.

45. This is not to say that the future is irrelevant to the present of common life. Hume observed in the *Treatise* that our idea of the future is the idea of an

increase in our existence (T, 432). The idea of the future is the idea of an order of hope and possibility and is associated by the imagination with the present so as to convey these values to the present. In this sense the present is big with the future: it opens out into the future. A present without a future would be a present without hope or possibility. But it is still true that the future cannot constitute any narrative existent in the present. If we were to know that the world is to end a week from now, the Rembrandts in the present would still be Rembrandts, the president would still be the president. No one might care any more, but this could not affect the reality of any narrative existent in the present. Narrative existences are constituted by narrative associations of ideas of present and past existences. See chapter Five, last section.

46. See Steven Cahn's interpretation and defense of Aristotle's thesis that future-tense propositions must have indeterminate truth values on pain of fatalism, in *Fate, Logic, and Time* (New Haven: Yale University Press, 1967), especially chapter 8, and also Danto, *Analytical Philosophy of History*, chapters 8 and 9.

## CHAPTER TWELVE

1. Leslie Stephen, *History of English Thought in the Eighteenth Century*, 2 vols. (New York: Harcourt, 1962), 1: 157.

2. Catharine Macaulay, *Letters on Education* (London, 1790), pp. 391–392.

3. Macaulay, *History of England*, pp. vii–viii.

4. Sheldon Wolin, "Hume and Conservatism," in *Hume, A Re-Evaluation*, p. 253.

5. N. K. O'Sullivan, *Conservatism* (New York: St. Martin's Press, 1976), pp. 9–10.

6. Erik von Kuehnelt-Leddihn, *Leftism* (New Rochelle: Arlington House, 1974), pp. 11–12.

7. Quoted in Douglas Adair, "David Hume, James Madison, and the *Tenth Federalist*," in *Hume, A Re-Evaluation*, p. 404.

8. Peter Viereck, *Conservatism* (New York: Anvil Books, 1959), p. 16.

9. Laurence L. Bongie, *David Hume, Prophet of the Counter-Revolution* (Oxford: Clarendon Press, 1965), see especially chapter 3.

10. Ibid., p. 45.

11. J. B. A. Clèry, *Journal de ce qui s'est passè a la tour du Temple pendant la captivitè de Louis XVI, Roi de France* (London, 1798), p. 203.

12. *Karl Marx on Revolution*, I, p. 516.

13. Albert Camus, *The Rebel* (New York: Vintage Books, 1956), p. 23.

14. Duncan Forbes, *Hume's Philosophical Politics* (Cambridge: Cambridge University Press, 1975), p. 188.

15. For a discussion of how Hume's support for an independent American republic is compatible with his rejection of a republican Britain, see my "Hume and America," forthcoming in the *Kentucky Review*.

16. Quoted by J. Y. T. Greig, *Letters of David Hume*, 2: 209.

17. The personal conflict between Hume and Rousseau is discussed by Ernest Campbell Mossner, *The Life of David Hume*, 2d ed. (Oxford: Clarendon Press, 1980), chapter 35.

18. Quoted in Laurence Bongie, *David Hume, Prophet of the Counter-Revolution*, p. 30. Bongie explores in some depth the failure of the *philosophes* to understand the conservative character of Hume's moral and political philosophy. See pp. 30–52.

19. Leslie Stephen, *History of English Thought*, 1: 174.

20. James Boswell, *Boswell's Life of Johnson*, ed. George Birkbeck Hill, 2d ed., 6 vols. (Oxford: Clarendon Press, 1964), 3: 326.

21. Joseph de Maistre, *The Saint Petersburg Dialogues*, in *The Works of Joseph de Maistre*, trans. Jack Lively (New York: Macmillan, 1965).

22. Samuel T. Coleridge, *On the Constitution of the Church and State* (London: J. M. Dent, 1972), p. 53.

23. Karl Marx, *Marx and Engels, Basic Writings on Politics and Philosophy*, ed. Lewis S. Feuer (Garden City: Anchor, 1959), p. 263.

24. David Norton has discussed in some depth Hume's view that philosophy, if done properly, "softens and humanizes the temper" and "insensibly refines the temper," pointing out "those dispositions which we should endeavour to attain, by a constant *bent* of mind, and by repeated *habit*." Quoted in Norton's *David Hume, Common-Sense Moralist*, p. 219. See also chapter 5 above. That the reflections of true philosophy have ethical implications provides additional support for the thesis advanced here that true philosophy and true religion are internally connected, as are false philosophy and false religion. Consider also Hume's remark in "Of Essay Writing" that "sound understanding and delicate affections" are "characters, it is to be presumed, we shall always find *inseparable*" (E, 570, emphasis mine), and Pàll Àrdal's thesis that Hume treats reason (the reason of true philosophy) as a virtue, "The Virtue of Reasonableness in Hume's *Treatise*," pp. 91–106.

25. For a brief but interesting discussion of the role of ritual in Hume's thought, see Karl Britton, "Hume on some Non-Natural Distinctions," in *David Hume, Bicentenary Papers*, ed. by G. P. Morice (Edinburgh University Press, 1977), pp. 205–09.

26. By revolutionary activity, I mean a form of action governed by the autonomy principle: the project of totally replacing an established social and political order with a different one. This would, of course, exclude rebellions of all sorts which occur *within* the authority of an established social and political order and are aimed only at correcting a limited wrong, a wrong that is conceived as limited precisely because the remaining part of the order is viewed as legitimate. Such rebellions are justified depending on the historical context. Under certain conditions, however, the question of justification is undecidable. How this can be is explained later in this chapter.

27. See above, chapter 5, last section, and Arthur Danto's discussion of the truth conditions for narrative judgments in *Analytical Philosophy of History*, chapters 7–9.

28. F. L. Lucas, *The Art of Living, Four Eighteenth-Century Minds* (London: Cassell, 1959). p. 78.

29. I am indebted here to N. K. O'Sullivan's insightful discussion of the metaphysical rebellion implicit in Kant's ideal of moral autonomy, *Conservatism*, pp. 20–21. This book brings out clearly, as few studies do, that the conservative tradition is ordered around a set of ideas that are philosophically interesting and that the tradition is not simply an ungenerous, if not mean-

spirited, reaction to "progressive" events. For a comparison of Hume and Burke as conservative thinkers, see David Miller's *Philosophy and Ideology in Hume's Political Thought* (Oxford: Oxford University Press, 1982), chapter 8 and conclusion. This is also the first comprehensive study of Hume's political philosophy.

30. Richard Hiskes, "Does Hume Have a Theory of Social Justice?" *Hume Studies* 3, no. 2, (November 1977): 72.

31. David Miller, "The Ideological Backgrounds to Conceptions of Social Justice," *Political Studies* 22, no. 4 (December, 1974), p. 391.

# Bibliography

The following is a list of works cited in the course of this study. The editions of Hume's works that have been used can be found in the Abbreviations of Hume's Works, p. vii. For a more comprehensive bibliography, see T. E. Jessop, *A Bibliography of David Hume and of Scottish Philosophy, from Francis Hutcheson to Lord Balfour* (New York: Russell and Russell, 1966), and Roland Hall, *Fifty Years of Hume Scholarship: A Bibliographical Guide* (Edinburgh: Edinburgh University Press, 1978). This bibliography has been kept up to date in *Hume Studies*, where in volumes 3–8 Professor Hall has published an annual supplementary bibliography of contemporary Hume scholarship for the years 1976–81. *Hume Studies* intends to keep the bibliography up-to-date.

Adair, Douglas. "David Hume, James Madison, and the *Tenth Federalist.*" In *Hume: A Re-Evaluation.* Edited by Donald Livingston and James King. New York: Fordham University Press, 1976.

Anderson, Robert F. *Hume's First Principles.* Lincoln: University of Nebraska Press, 1966.

Àrdal, Pàll. "Convention and Value." In *David Hume: Bicentenary Papers.* Edited by G. P. Morice. Edinburgh: Edinburgh University Press, 1977.

———. "Some Implications of the Virtue of Reasonableness in Hume's *Treatise.*" In *Hume: A Re-Evaluation.* Edited by Donald Livingston and James King. New York: Fordham University Press, 1976.

Aristotle. *Poetics.* In *Introduction to Aristotle.* Edited by Richard McKeon. Chicago: The University of Chicago Press, 1973.

Ayer, A. J. *Language, Truth, and Logic.* London: Gollancz, 1946.

———. *The Problem of Knowledge.* New York: St. Martins, 1956.

———, editor. *Logical Positivism.* Glencoe: The Free Press, 1959.

Bacon, Francis. *Novum Organum. Essays, Advancement of Learning, New Atlantis and Other Pieces.* Edited by Richard F. Jones. New York: Odyssey Press, 1937.

Bailyn, Bernard. *The Ideological Origins of the American Revolution.* Cambridge: Harvard University Press, 1967.

———. *The Origins of American Politics.* New York: Knopf, 1968.

Basson, A. H. *David Hume.* Harmondsworth: Penguin, 1958.

Beattie, James. *Essay on Truth*. 8th edition. London, 1812.

Beauchamp, Tom and Alexander Rosenberg. *Hume and the Problem of Causation*. Oxford: Oxford University Press, 1981.

Bennett, Jonathan. *Locke, Berkeley, Hume*. Oxford: Clarendon Press, 1971.

Black, J. B. *The Art of History*. London: Methuen, 1926.

Bongie, Laurence L. *David Hume, Prophet of the Counter-Revolution*. Oxford: Clarendon Press, 1965.

Bosanquet, Bernard. *The Principle of Individuality and Value*, London: Macmillan, 1912.

Boswell, James. *Boswell's Life of Johnson*. 6 vols. 2d edition. Edited by George Birbeck Hill. Oxford: Clarendon Press, 1964.

Britton, Karl. "Hume on Some Non-Natural Distinctions." In *David Hume: Bicentenary Papers*. Edited by G. P. Morice. Edinburgh: Edinburgh University Press, 1977.

Broad, C. D. "Hume's Doctrine of Space." *Proceedings of the British Academy* 47 (1961).

Burton, J. H., ed. *Letters of Eminent Persons Addressed to David Hume*. Edinburgh, 1849.

Butler, R. J. "Hume's Impressions." *Royal Institute of Philosophy Lectures, 1974–1975*. Vol. 9. London: Macmillan, 1976.

Cahn, Steven. *Fate, Logic, and Time*. New Haven: Yale University Press, 1967.

Camus, Albert. *The Rebel*. New York: Vintage Books, 1956.

Capaldi, Nicholas. *David Hume: The Newtonian Philosopher*. Boston: Twayne, 1975.

———. "Hume as Social Scientist." *The Review of Metaphysics* 32 (1978).

Carnap, Rudolf. *Philosophy and Logical Syntax*. New York: AMS, 1976.

Church, Ralph W. *Hume's Theory of the Understanding*. Ithaca: Cornell University Press, 1935.

Clèry, J. B. A. *Journal de ce qui s'est passè a la tour du Temple pendant la captivitè de Louis XVI, Roi de France*. London, 1798.

Coleridge, Samuel T. *On the Constitution of the Church and State*. London: J. M. Dent, 1972.

Collingwood, R. G. *The Idea of History*. Oxford: Clarendon Press, 1962.

Comte, August. *The Positive Philosophy*. 2 vols. Translated by Harriet Martineau. London: Kegan Paul, 1893.

Danto, Arthur. *Analytical Philosophy of History*. Cambridge: Cambridge University Press, 1965.

Davie, George. "Edumund Husserl and 'the as yet, in its most important respect, unrecognized greatness of Hume.'" In *David Hume: Bicentenary Papers*. Edited by G. P. Morice. Edinburgh: At the University Press, 1977.

De Maistre, Joseph. *The Saint Petersburg Dialogues*. In *The Works of Joseph de Maistre*. Translated by Jack Lively. New York: Macmillan, 1965.

Descartes, René. *The Philosophical Works of Descartes*. 2 vols. Translated and edited by Elizabeth S. Haldane and G. R. T. Ross. Cambridge: Cambridge University Press, 1969.

Deutscher, Issac. "The Future of Russian Society." *Dissent* 1 (1954).

Donagan, Alan. *The Later Philosophy of R. G. Collingwood.* Oxford: Clarendon Press, 1962.

Eddington, Arthur. *The Nature of the Physical World.* Ann Arbor: University of Michigan Press, 1968.

Fain, Haskell. *Between Philosophy and History.* Princeton: Princeton University Press, 1970.

Farr, James. "Hume, Hermeneutics, and History: A Sympathetic Account." *History and Theory* 17 (1978).

Flage, Daniel. "Hume's Relative Ideas." *Hume Studies* 7 (1981).

Flew, Antony. *Hume's Philosophy of Belief.* London: Routledge and Kegan Paul, 1961.

————. "Was Berkeley a Precursor of Wittgenstein?" In *Hume and the Enlightenment.* Edited by W. B. Todd. Austin: University of Texas Press, 1974.

Forbes, Duncan. *Hume's Philosophical Politics.* Cambridge: Cambridge University Press, 1975.

Force, James. "Hume in the 'Dialogues', the Dictates of Convention and the Millennial Future State of Biblical Prophecy." *Southwestern Journal of Philosophy* 8 (1977).

Fourier, Charles. *Oeuvres complètes.* 6 vols. Paris, 1846–48.

Frege, Gottlob. *The Foundations of Arithmetic.* Oxford: Clarendon Press, 1950.

Gaskin, J. C. A. *Hume's Philosophy of Religion.* London: Macmillan, 1978.

Hartley, David. *Observations on Man, His Frame, His Duty, and His Expectations.* 2 vols. London, 1769.

Hegel, G. W. F. *Philosophy of Right and Law.* Translated by J. M. Sterret and C. J. Friedrich. In *The Philosophy of Hegel.* Edited by Carl J. Friedrich. New York: Modern Library, 1954.

Hempel, Carl G. "Explanation in Science and in History." In *Philosophical Analysis and History.* Edited by William Dray. New York: Harper and Row, 1966.

Henze, Donald. "The Linguistic Aspect of Hume's Method." *Journal of the History of Ideas* 30 (1969).

Hiskes, Richard. "Does Hume Have a Theory of Social Justice?" *Hume Studies* 3 (1977).

Jones, Peter. *Hume's Sentiments, Their Ciceronian and French Context.* Edinburgh: Edinburgh University Press, 1982.

Kant, Immanuel. "Idea for a Universal History from a Cosmopolitan Point of View." Translated by W. Hastie. In *Theories of History.* Edited by Patrick Gardiner. Glencoe: The Free Press, 1959.

Knight, William. *Hume.* Edinburgh: William Blackwood, 1886.

Laird, John. *Hume's Philosophy of Human Nature.* New York: Dutton, 1931.

Leibniz, G. W. "On the Ultimate Origins of Things." In *Leibniz Selections.* Edited by Philip P. Wiener. New York: Scribner's, 1951.

Lewis, C. I. *Mind and the World Order.* New York: Dover, 1956.

Livingston, D. W. "Hume's Historical Theory of Meaning." In *Hume: A Re-Evaluation.* Edited by D. W. Livingston and James King. New York: Fordham University Press, 1976.

───────. "Hume on the Problem of Historical and Scientific Explanation." *The New Scholasticism* 37 (1973).

───────. "Hume and America." *Kentucky Review*. Forthcoming.

───────. "Time and Value in Hume's Social and Political Philosophy." In *McGill Hume Studies*. Edited by D. F. Norton, N. Capaldi, and W. Robison. San Diego: Austin Hill Press, 1979.

Locke, John. *An Essay Concerning Human Understanding*. 2 vols. Edited by Alexander Campbell Fraser. New York: Dover, 1959.

───────. *Two Treatises of Government*. New York: Mentor Books, 1963.

Lucas, F. L. *The Art of Living, Four Eighteenth Century Minds*. London: Cassell. 1959.

Macaulay, Catharine. *Letters on Education*. London, 1790.

───────. *Observations on the Reflections of the Right Hon. Edmund Burke, On the Revolution in France, in a Letter to the Right Hon. The Earl of Stanhope*. London, 1790.

───────. *The History of England*. London, 1763.

Mall, R. A. *Experience and Reason, The Phenomenology of Husserl and Its Relation to Hume's Philosophy*. The Hague: Martinus Nijhoff, 1973.

Marcuse, Harbert. "Ethics and Revolution." In *Ethics and Society*. Edited by Richard T. De George. New York: Anchor Books, 1966.

───────. *One-Dimensional Man*. Boston: Beacon Press, 1966.

───────. "Repressive Tolerance." In *A Critique of Pure Tolerance*. Boston: Beacon Press, 1965.

Marx, Karl. *Marx and Engels Basic Writings on Politics and Philosophy*. Edited by Lewis S. Feuer. Garden City: Anchor, 1959.

───────. *Karl Marx on Revolution*. 13 vols. Edited and translated by Saul K. Padover. New York: McGraw-Hill, 1971.

McNabb, D. G. C. *David Hume*. Hampton: Archon Books, 1966.

Meiland, Jack. *Scepticism and Historical Knowledge*. New York: Random House, 1965.

Mill, John Stuart. *A System of Logic. Collected Works*. 19 vols. Toronto: Toronto University Press, 1974.

───────. *Mill on Bentham and Coleridge*. Edited by F. R. Leavis. New York: G. W. Stewart, 1950.

───────. Review of Brodie, *History of the British Empire*. *The Westminster Review* 2 (1824).

Miller, David. *Philosophy and Ideology in Hume's Political Thought*. Oxford: Oxford University Press, 1982.

───────. "The Ideological Backgrounds to Conceptions of Social Justice." *Political Studies* 22 (1974).

Monteiro, J. P. "Hume, Induction, and Natural Selection." In *McGill Hume Studies*. Edited by David Norton, Nicholas Capaldi, and Wade Robison. San Diego: Austin Hill Press, 1976.

Morelly. *Code de la Nature*. Edited by G. Chinard. Paris, 1950.

Morice, G. P., ed. *David Hume: Bicentenary Papers*. Edinburgh: Edinburgh University Press, 1977.

Morrisroe, Michael. "Linguistic Analysis as Rhetorical Pattern in David Hume." *Hume and the Enlightenment.* Edited by W. B. Todd. Austin: University of Texas Press, 1974.

Mossner, E. C. "An Apology for David Hume Historian." *PMLA* 56 (1941).

_____. *The Life of David Hume.* 2d ed. Oxford: Clarendon Press, 1980.

Murphy, Richard T. *Hume and Husserl.* The Hague: Martinus Nijhoff, 1980.

Nathan, George J. "The Existence and Nature of God in Hume's Theism." In *Hume: A Re-Evaluation.* Edited by Donald Livingston and James King. New York: Fordham University Press, 1976.

Newton, Issac. *Opticks.* New York: McGraw-Hill, 1931.

Niemeyer, Gerhardt, *Between Nothingness and Paradise.* Baton Rouge: Louisiana State University Press, 1971.

Norton, David Fate. *David Hume: Common-Sense Moralist, Sceptical Metaphysician.* Princeton: Princeton University Press, 1982.

Norton, David and Richard Popkin. *David Hume: Philosophical Historian.* New York: Bobbs-Merrill, 1965.

Nozick, Robert. *Anarchy, State, and Utopia.* New York: Basic Books, 1974.

Oakeshott, Michael. *Experience and Its Modes.* Cambridge: Cambridge University Press, 1933.

O'Sullivan, N. K. *Conservatism.* New York: St. Martin's Press, 1976.

Passmore, John. *Hume's Intentions.* Cambridge: Cambridge University Press, 1952.

Penelhum, Terence. "Hume's Skepticism and the Dialogues." In *McGill Hume Studies.* Edited by David Norton, Nicholas Capaldi, and Wade Robison. San Diego: Austin Hill Press, 1976.

Plato. *Phaedo.* In *The Collected Dialogues of Plato.* Edited by Edith Hamilton and Huntington Cairns. Princeton: Princeton University Press, 1963.

Plumb, J. H. *Sir Robert Walpole.* 2 vols. London: The Cresset Press, 1956.

_____. *The Growth of Political Stability in England, 1675–1725.* London: Macmillan, 1967.

Popkin, Richard. "Hume: Philosophical Versus Prophetic Historian." In *David Hume, Many-Sided Genius.* Norman: University of Oklahoma Press, 1976. Edited by Kenneth R. Merrill and Robert W. Shahan.

_____. "David Hume: His Pyrrhonism and His Critique of Pyrrhonism." In *The High Road to Pyrrhonism.* Edited by Richard Watson and James Force. San Diego: Austin Hill Press, 1980.

Price, H. H. *Hume's Theory of the External World.* Oxford: Clarendon Press, 1948.

Price, Richard. *A Discourse on the Laws of Our Country.* London, 1789.

_____. Letter to Thomas Jefferson, October 26, 1788. *The Papers of Thomas Jefferson.* 60 vols. Edited by Julian P. Boyd. Vol. 14. Princeton: Princeton University Press, 1950.

Prichard, Harold A. *Knowledge and Perception.* Oxford: Clarendon Press, 1950.

Priestley, Joseph. *An Essay on the First Principles of Government.* 2d. ed. London, 1961.

_____. *Lectures on History and General Policy.* Dublin, 1778.

Proudhon, P. J. *What Is Property?* New York: Humbolt, 1893.

Randall, John, Jr. "David Hume: Radical Empiricist and Pragmatist." In *Freedom and Experience: Essays Presented to Horace W. Kallen.* Edited by Sidney Hook and Milton R. Konnitz. Ithaca and New York: Cornell University Press, 1947.

Rawls, John. *A Theory of Justice.* Cambridge: The Belknap Press, Harvard University Press, 1971.

Reinach, Adolf. "Kant's Interpretation of Hume's Problem." In *David Hume, Many-Sided Genius.* Norman: University of Oklahoma Press, 1976. Edited by Kenneth R. Merrill and Robert W. Shahan.

Robinson, J. A. "Hume's Two Definitions of 'Cause'." In *Hume.* Edited by V. C. Chappell. New York: Anchor Books, 1966.

Rudé, G. F. E. *Wilkes and Liberty.* Oxford: Clarendon Press, 1962.

Russell, Bertrand. *Our Knowledge of the External World.* London: Allen and Unwin, 1929.

———. *The Analysis of Mind.* London: Allen and Unwin, 1924.

Sidney, Algernon. *Discourses Concerning Government.* In *The Works of Algernon Sidney.* London, 1772.

Skinner, B. F. *Walden Two.* New York: Macmillan, 1967.

Smith, Norman Kemp. *The Philosophy of David Hume.* New York: Macmillan, 1964.

Stephen, Leslie. *History of English Thought in the Eighteenth Century.* 2 vols. New York: Harcourt, 1962.

Stewart, John B. *The Moral and Political Philosophy of David Hume.* New York: Columbia University Press, 1963.

Stockton, Constant Noble. "Economics and the Mechanism of Historical Progress in Hume's *History*." In *Hume: A Re-Evaluation.* Edited by Donald Livingston and James King. New York: Fordham University Press, 1976.

Stove, D. C. "Hume, the Causal Principle, and Kemp Smith." *Hume Studies* 1 (1975).

Stroud, Barry. *Hume.* London: Routledge and Kegan Paul, 1978.

Turgot, A. R. J. "A Philosophical Review of the Successive Advances of the Human Mind." In *Turgot on Progress, Sociology and Economics.* Translated and edited by Ronald L. Meek. Cambridge: Cambridge University Press, 1973.

Viereck, Peter. *Conservatism.* New York: Anvil Books, 1959.

Von Kuehnelt-Leddihn, Erik. *Leftism.* New Rochelle: Arlington House, 1974.

Walton, Craig. "Hume and Jefferson on History." In *Hume: A Re-Evaluation.* Edited by Donald Livington and James King. New York: Fordham University Press, 1976.

Warburton, William. *A Selection from Unpublished Works.* Edited by Francis Kilvert. London, 1841.

Whitehead, Alfred North. *Adventures of Ideas.* New York: Macmillan, 1933.

Wilson, Fred. "Hume's Theory of Mental Activity." In *McGill Hume Studies.* Edited by David Norton, Nicholas Capaldi, and Wade Robison. San Diego: Austin Hill Press, 1976.

Wittgenstein, Ludwig. *On Certainty.* Edited by G. E. M. Anscombe and G. H. von Wright. Oxford: Clarendon Press, 1969.

———. *Tractatus Logico-Philosophicus*. Translated by D. F. Pears and B. F. McGuiness. New York: The Humanities Press, 1961.

Wolff, Robert Paul. *In Defense of Anarchism*. New York: Harper and Row, 1970.

Wolin, Sheldon. "Hume and Conservatism." In *Hume: A Re-Evaluation*. Edited by Donald Livingston and James King. New York: Fordham University Press, 1976.

Yandell, Keith E. "Hume on Religious Belief." In *Hume: A Re-Evaluation*. Edited by Donald Livingston and James King. New York: Fordham University Press, 1976.

Zabeeh, Farhang. *Hume: Precursor of Modern Empiricism*. The Hague: Martinus Nijhoff, 1973.

# Index

America: independence of, supported by Hume, 326; political principles of, Hume's, 323
Anderson, R. F., 349
Árdal, Páll, x, 39, 345, 357
Aristotle, 35, 250, 286, 304, 339, 351
Ayer, A. J., 9, 46, 94, 95, 110

Babeuf, Gracchus, 278, 280
Bacon, Francis, 161, 162
Bailyn, Bernard, 352–53
Basson, A. H., 106
Baxter, John, 264
Beattie, James, 25
Beauchamp, Tom, 5, 350
Bennett, Jonathan, 98, 101, 106
Bentham, Jeremy, 280, 300
Berkeley, George, 11, 45, 46, 49
Black, J. B., 214, 219, 220, 230
Bongie, Laurence, 310, 357
Bosanquet, Bernard, 95
Boyle, Robert, 170, 171, 178, 241
Brentano, F., 54
Burke, Edmund, 7, 290–91, 307–10, 315, 323–24, 326, 329
Butler, Ronald, 54, 345, 347

Camus, Albert, 321
Capaldi, Nicholas, x
Carnap, Rudolf, 46, 95
Cartesianism in politics, 277–80, 282–85, 298, 300, 311
Casuality: history of concept, 5, 179–86, 202–3, 208–9, 248–49; Hume's view

of, 150–60; moral, 193–200, 205–9 (see also *Verstehen;* causal explanation, moral); positivist interpretation of, 150–55; theism and ultimate, 172–80, 207–9; ultimate, 160–67, 193–96, 207–9
Causal explanation: and existence thesis, 188, 190, 196, 201–2, 205–9; and law-likeness, 189, 202–5; moral, 187, 190–92, 195–96, 205–8, 213; moral more intelligible than natural, 189, 192–99, 209, 222, 225, 288; moral and ultimate, 193–209; in natural science, 150–60, 187–89, 200–209; and symmetry thesis of explanation and prediction, 188, 190, 196, 209; and unity of science thesis, 187, 190, 196, 209
Charles I, 228, 231, 253, 256, 260, 262, 268, 301, 303, 316, 341
Chateaubriand, F. A. R., 307
Chatham, earl of, 325, 327, 329
Church, R. W., 92
Churchill, Winston, 310
Clarke, Samuel, 181, 283
Coleridge, Samuel Taylor, 307, 310, 329
Collingwood, R. G., 6, 211–12, 219, 220, 225, 231, 232, 235–37, 251
Common life: alienation from, 23, 24, 32–33, 273 (*see also* Philosophy [false]); dialectical relation between philosophy and, 3, 32–33, 38, 58–59, 88, 272; different from Scottish common sense, 30; internal-external aspects of, 17, 34, 64, 81; narrative order of, 234, 275 (*see also* Narrative existence); philosophy presupposes, 24, 35, 45, 273, 276, 311, 332, 333; public and private world of,